Date Due

10/18/0

J

HUMAN RESOURCE STRATEGIES

The Open Business School

The Open Business School offers a three-tier ladder of opportunity for managers at different stages of their careers: the Professional Certificate in Management; the Professional Diploma in Management; and the MBA. If you would like to receive information on these open learning programmes, please write to the Open Business School, The Open University, Milton Keynes MK7 6AA, England.

This volume is a Course Reader for Open University Course B884 *Human Resource Strategies*.

HUMAN RESOURCE STRATEGIES

edited by
Graeme Salaman
Sheila Cameron
Heather Hamblin
Paul Iles
Christopher Mabey
Kenneth Thompson

The Open
University

Published in association
with The Open University

SAGE Publications
London • Newbury Park • New Delhi

Selection and editorial matter © The Open University
1992

First published 1992

 SAGE Publications Ltd
6 Bonhill Street
London EC2A 4PU

SAGE Publications Inc
2455 Teller Road
Newbury Park, California 91320

SAGE Publications India Pvt Ltd
32, M-Block Market
Greater Kailash – I
New Delhi 110 048

British Library Cataloguing in Publication Data

Salaman, Graeme
  Human resource strategies.
  I. Title
  658.3

  ISBN 0-8039-8626-2
  ISBN 0-8039-8627-0 pbk

Library of Congress catalog card number 91-050657

Typeset by Mayhew Typesetting, Rhayader, Powys
Printed in Great Britain by Billings and Sons Ltd,
Worcester

Contents

Acknowledgements

The editors and publishers wish to thank the following for permission to use copyright material: Basil Blackwell Ltd for John Storey, 'Human Resource Management in the Public Sector', *Public Money and Management*, Vol. 9, No. 3, Autumn 1989; Business and Economics Review and the author for Chris Argyris, 'A Leadership Dilemma: Skilled Incompetence', *Business and Economics Review*, No. 1, Summer 1987; Harvard Business Review for Peter F. Drucker, 'The Coming of the New Organization', Jan/Feb. 1988. Copyright © 1988 by the President and Fellows of Harvard College; and Peter F. Drucker, 'What Business Can Learn from Nonprofits', *Harvard Business Review*, July/Aug. 1989. Copyright © 1989 by the President and Fellows of Harvard College; Organization Studies for Paul Bate, 'The Impact of Organizational Culture on Approaches to Organizational Problem-Solving', *Organization Studies*, Vol. 5, No. 1, 1984; Alan McKinley and Ken Starkey, 'Competitive Strategies and Organizational Change', *Organization Studies*, Vol. 9, No. 4, 1988; and Lynn V. Meek, 'Organizational Culture: Origins and Weaknesses', *Organization Studies*, Vol. 9, No. 4, 1988; Routledge for material from Ewart Keep, 'Corporate training strategies: the vital component?' and John Purcell, 'The impact of corporate strategy on human resource management' in *New Perspectives on Human Resource Management*, ed. John Storey, 1989; Sage Publications Ltd for Stuart Clegg, 'Modernist and Postmodernist Organization' in *Modern Organizations*, 1990; Sloan Management Review for Edgar H. Schein, 'Coming to a New Awareness of Organizational Culture', *Sloan Management Review*, Winter 1984. Copyright © 1984 by the Sloan Management Review Association; University Associates, Inc. for R. Beckhard, 'A Model for the Executive Management of Transformational Change' in *The 1989 Annual: Developing Human Resources*, ed. J. William Pfeiffer, 1989; John Wiley and Sons, Ltd for David A. Buchanan, 'High Performance: New Boundaries of Acceptability in Worker Control' in *Job Control and Worker Health*, eds Steven L. Sauter, Joseph J. Hurrell Jnr and Cary L. Cooper, 1989; and Jeroen J.J.L. Seegers, 'Assessment Centres for Identifying Long-term Potential and for Self-development' in *Assessment and Selection in Organizations*, ed. P. Herriot, 1989; John Wiley and Sons, Inc. for Jeffrey A. Sonnenfeld, Maury A. Peiperl and John P. Kotter, 'Strategic Determinants of Managerial Labour Markets: A Career Systems View', *Human Resource Management*, Vol. 27, No. 4, Winter 1988; Thomas A. Mahoney, 'Multiple Pay Contingencies: Strategic Design of Compensation', *Human Resource Management*, Vol. 28, No. 3, Fall 1989; and material from *The Competent Manager: A Model for Effective Performance* by Richard E. Boyatzis, 1982. Every effort has been made to trace all the copyright holders, but if any have been inadvertently overlooked the publishers will be pleased to make the necessary arrangement at the first opportunity.

Introduction

Graeme Salaman

In this volume we present a selection of what we regard as the best and most interesting contributions to the growing area of research and activity that is known as human resource strategies (HRS). This encompasses the attempt to identify, and where necessary change, organizational structure, work design, organizational culture, and personnel systems so as to generate the behaviours and attitudes necessary to achieve whatever it is that senior managers intend the organizations to achieve. This approach assumes (with reason) that organizational systems and structures vary; that to some degree they can be changed, and that the forms they take can have a significant influence on organizational effectiveness. The HRS approach assumes that it is possible and fruitful to coordinate organizational structures and organizational strategies.

It is therefore important to assess the current contribution – positive and negative – of all aspects of those organizational systems and structures which impact on employees' behaviours and attitudes, and when appropriate to change them in the necessary direction. This seems like obvious good sense and in principle the articles in this volume support this project. But it is also likely to be a difficult and even contradictory project. We would be doing you no favours if we minimized or disregarded the difficulties. This volume seeks to present both the advantages and the difficulties of the human resource strategies approach. It assumes that enthusiasm is not enough: managers are best served by being clear-headed, dispassionate and well-informed.

However, it is far from easy to identify the changes to structures and systems that will expedite the fulfilment of an organization's objectives. There are those who, from messianic zeal, short-sightedness or personal interest, will push a particular package of solutions. Paradoxically, they thus merely replace one set of sacred nostrums with another, by insisting again that there is only *one* best way. Our approach rejects any universalistic solution, whether it be the old-fashioned virtues of (much maligned) bureaucracy or the currently fashionable mix of flatter structures, deregulation and devolution. Bureaucracy, with its distinctive features – clear job descriptions, clear lines of responsibility and authority, selection based on merit, career structures, precise rules and procedures, etc. – has more in its favour than is currently acknowledged. These bureaucratic principles make trains run to schedule, keep aeroplanes properly maintained and enable the Open University to function. They also

444444444

have obvious limitations. Quite possibly current fashions in organizational change and restructuring (largely derived from the work of Peters, which is addressed in this volume) will also be revealed to have contradictions and limitations.

In drawing together this collection we have been guided by a number of principles. First, we have tried to avoid articles that already occur in other collections. In this we have not always been successful, partly because of our second principle: that we also wished to offer a collection of really first-rate pieces, and in some cases this meant using articles that other editors had already used. A third principle was that we wished the collection to offer pieces which covered the key dimensions of HRS: structures (both organizational and work), culture and personnel systems (including payment, training). These three main components of any human resource strategy constitute the three major sections of the volume. The first section establishes the background to HRS and addresses some of the most important issues raised by this approach.

PART ONE
HUMAN RESOURCE STRATEGIES

Introduction

Graeme Salaman and Christopher Mabey

The approach to organizational structuring and change with which this book deals involves the attempt to support chosen organizational strategies with appropriate human resource strategies. These strategies address three key aspects of organizational structuring, all of which have an impact on employees' behaviour and attitudes: organizational and work structures, organizational cultures, and personnel systems and practices.

The idea that these three discrete human resource elements should be integrated with each other *and* integrated with the organizational strategies so that they produce the behaviours necessary for strategic achievement makes evident good sense, in principle (but it also raises major questions and difficulties). Hence the current popularity of the approach at a time when environmental pressures make the achievement of increased efficiency – usually through programmes of systematic organizational change – ever more important.

This reader and the Open University Business School MBA course – *Human Resource Strategies* – of which it is a component, support the value of the HRS approach. But it is essential to address the questions, some of them fundamental to our understanding of how modern work organizations work, which the HRS approach raises. The first section of the reader addresses these questions. It does so in a broadly critical manner, not demolishing ideas in a negative way, but appraising them positively in order to build a reasoned, analytical and thorough-going evaluation of the HRS approach.

Such detachment and analytical rigour are highly important at a time when managers are increasingly surrounded by consultants and theorists all peddling solutions. These often sound fine, because as David Guest argues in Chapter 1, their analyses and prescriptions chime well with current thinking and values. But this makes it all the more important to adopt a searching and questioning approach to these prescriptions. The fact that they seem so sensible, so obvious, in itself means nothing. The recent history of theories and prescriptions in the area of management is

littered with the abandoned shrines of yesterday's false gods, all of which
had their devotees at some time. Yet now, with the wisdom of hindsight,
we wonder how yesterday's managers were so naive as to accept as
obvious and necessary the precepts and practices of Taylorism, the rules
and regulations of bureaucracy, the management principles of Urwick,
MBO, mechanistic appraisal schemes, and so on. But how can we be sure
that today's managers will not, ten years hence, also seem naive for their
enthusiastic support of culture change and 'flat' organization structures
for their opposition to bureaucracy and central control? Why should
today's prescriptions and assumptions be superior to yesterday's? How
do we know that this time they – those who take it upon themselves to
prescribe the necessary forms and directions of change – have got it
right?

Because the HRS approach is important in influencing the speed, direction and content of organizational change it is crucial that we give this
approach considered and critical assessment. That is the object of the first
section of the reader. The articles offered in this first section have been
selected to cover a number of different debates and to address a wide
range of aspects of the HRS approach. The common theme is that they
all eschew glib prescriptions and easy answers, and all offer a detached
assessment of key aspects of the HRS approach – where it comes from,
what it consists of, whether it's actually occurring, and if it is, whether
it is beneficial.

The first chapter is concerned with some of the main ideas of the HRS
approach – their origin and their appeal. David Guest addresses a type of
literature which is hugely influential within the HRS movement – the
'excellence literature'. In a refreshing manner the chapter does not simply
accept the ideas of this approach at face value and treat them as hallowed
truths, as common sense. On the contrary, Guest takes as his point of
departure the evaluation of these ideas and an explanation of their strange
powers – why are they so attractive to managers?

The second chapter, by Phil Beaumont, also addresses the origins of
HRS, through a consideration of the American HRS literature. This
material has been very influential in defining the scope and content of
HRS in general – an influence that this chapter and the reader as a whole
seek to question and to place in perspective. The chapter focuses on the
literature which analyses the relationship between human resource
strategies and stages in the development of product market or business
development. Of particular interest is the consideration of key themes
within American writings, and particularly approaches to and assumptions about industrial relations. An important implication of the
American HRS writing is that it is founded upon largely implicit and
unquestioned approaches to organized labour. It therefore encapsulates a
particular form of management thinking, and advocates a view of
organizational structure and functioning which reflects this thinking. This
conception of human resource strategies is itself strategic, part of an

effort to impose a particular conception of how organizations *should* work and of the *proper* role of trade unions.

The American HRS literature reflects an emphasis on the role of market forces. This ideological emphasis on 'the market' assumes that commercial pressures are better and stronger spurs to change and adjustment than any other. This in itself is highly questionable. The third chapter, by Peter Drucker, argues that many of the most exciting changes now apparent within American business are occurring within non-profit organizations.

The fourth chapter, by John Storey, also addresses this issue of the specificity of HRS developments to those organizations exposed to the demands of the market. His article considers how far HRS changes evident within the private sector have been – and could – be transferred to public sector organizations.

The chapter by John Purcell takes our assessment one stage further. Purcell seeks to explore the relationship between corporate and human resource strategies. He does this via a classification of three different levels of strategic decision-making: the first describes business or organizational strategies, the second refers to the chosen relationships between parts of the firm, and the third to its human resource strategies.

His conclusions are by his own admission pessimistic. Purcell argues that decisions taken at the first level will have significant implications for the possibility of developing the sorts of human resource strategies necessary for long-term success. That is, fundamental, strategic decisions may limit room for manoeuvre at the human resource level. Organizational success seems to be determined by firms' ability and willingness to develop long-term, integrated human resource strategies. Yet the increasingly pervasive emphasis on performance control systems oriented around portfolio planning principles makes it hard to develop integrated and meaningful institutional strategies or management style. Also, to the degree that short-run rates of return on investment, emphasis on margin improvement, and tight financial controls are imposed on unit managers, it is hard at the unit level to develop and maintain long-run human resource policies.

The sixth chapter in this section, by Chris Argyris, takes us to a different level of difficulty: the ability of senior managers to think and analyse clearly and radically when addressing high-level issues of strategy formulation. Argyris points out that if this sort of thinking and analysis – which is fundamental to the development of appropriate strategies – is to be of value, it must be prepared to confront issues that are delicate, political, even threatening. When senior managers discuss strategy and performance they are dealing with issues which are significant at a personal level to themselves and to their colleagues. Argyris argues that because such discussions are seen by management to be potentially threatening and embarrassing, they assume that people will react to them in a defensive way. They therefore try to circumvent this defensiveness, but by acknowledging its existence they in fact encourage it. A self-fulfilling prophecy is thus established. He argues that this pattern is endemic within organizations and is a critical factor limiting the capacity of most senior managers to think clearly and radically about their organization's direction and their performance. One of the exciting things about Argyris' article is that he moves beyond the analytical and descriptive and begins to chart the sort of approach and to describe the skills which he sees as offering a way out of the cycle of defensiveness.

The seventh chapter, by Richard Beckhard, also focuses on practical aspects of what the author describes as transformational change – i.e. radical change in an organization of the sort that could well be associated with HRS developments. Like the other authors in this section Beckhard focuses less on the elements of HRS and more on the conditions under which HRS changes – if they are radical – can be implemented.

The final article offers us an up-beat ending to this section. Written by McKinlay and Starkey, it analyses three processes of organizational change and assesses their impact on performance. The authors offer a classic HRS argument, although in this case one based not on speculation or prescription, but on analysis of three actual cases of organizational change. Their conclusions are most significant. Despite the difficulties described in the case studies, the achievement of improved performance is significantly influenced by human resource strategies when these strategies are conceived and implemented as elements of the competitive strategy. Despite the difficulties of designing and implementing human resource strategies – many of which are documented in this volume – these authors at least are persuaded, on the basis of their evidence, that such HRS can work!

1

Right enough to be dangerously wrong: an analysis of the *In Search of Excellence* phenomenon

David Guest

Peters and Waterman's (1982) book *In Search of Excellence* has had a profound impact upon management thinking and upon the behavioural science of organizations. Those outside the field of organizational behaviour may be forgiven for wondering what all the fuss is about and why an apparently rather poorly researched book by two consultants should create so much interest, not only among managers but also among academics. This chapter attempts to analyse and explain the phenomenon and to consider how far and in what respects the book should be treated as serious social science.

A feature of the 1980s was the success of a number of books directed mainly at management readers, which were based largely on social science ideas and methodology. Indeed, in 1982 three of the four bestselling non-fiction books in the United States fell into this category. At number four was *The One Minute Manager* (Blanchard and Johnson, 1982), at number two, *Megatrends* (Naisbitt, 1982) and at number one, Peters and Waterman's *In Search of Excellence*. It is this book that has attracted most attention, spawning a number of other books as well as research, consultancy and even a new managerial vocabulary.

There is a tendency for social scientists to be suspicious of books in their own field that are commercially successful. The suspicion, particularly if management is the main readership, is that the writing must either reflect a particular set of values or that it is over-simplistic and over-prescriptive. This tendency to look down on success is not just a British phenomenon; for example Freeman, an American behavioural scientist, noted that his reactions to *In Search of Excellence* 'include (in proportions I choose not to reveal) curiosity, envy, and self-righteous disdain for commercial pandering' (1985: 346). Although it is invariably easy to comment critically on a book like *In Search of Excellence*, there are strong reasons for treating it seriously. If it is one of the very few business books that managers read, then it may exert a considerable influence on their thinking. Furthermore, since it is critical of certain well-respected ideas from within the social sciences and more especially those typically associated with leading business schools and their advocacy of rational strategic management, it may well colour their reaction to other work within the social sciences. Another issue which should be of interest to social scientists is the analysis of why certain books and articles seem to strike a chord with a non-specialist readership, and the lessons this holds for the communication of research and ideas at a time when the social sciences are under pressure to justify themselves.

The *In Search of Excellence* argument

At the time when the book was written, Peters and Waterman were employed by McKinsey, the leading firm of management consultants with a long established reputation for structural reorganization of major companies. The book describes the business practices of a number of leading American companies and in particular identifies eight attributes common to most of these excellent companies. Briefly summarized, these attributes are:

1 *A Bias for Action*   This is a preference for getting on with it and doing something rather than engaging in excessive analysis of a problem or allowing committees and other bureaucratic manifestations of large organizations to cause delays.
2 *Close to the Customer*   These companies show considerable concern for, and interest in, the wishes of their customers. The emphasis is on customer service.
3 *Autonomy and Entrepreneurship*   The company is broken down into small units within each of which initiative is encouraged. Innovative behaviour is highly valued.
4 *Productivity Through People*   Employees are seen as the key resources of the organization and this is emphasized in involvement programmes and through activities designed to reinforce in employees the importance of their contribution to the success of the organization and therefore to their own rewards.
5 *Hands-On, Value-Driven*   Senior executives promote a strong corporate culture and obtain feedback by keeping in close touch with core business activities.
6 *Stick to the Knitting*   Successful companies stay close to the business they know best and avoid the temptation to become conglomerates.
7 *Simple Form, Lean Staff*   These companies maintain a simple organization structure, avoiding the complexities of matrix organization, and employ relatively few senior head office staff.
8 *Simultaneous Loose–Tight Properties*   Core company values are strongly emphasized but those who adhere to them are given considerable freedom and errors are tolerated.

In addition to identifying, and by implication advocating, practice of the attributes of the excellent companies, Peters and Waterman were critical of what they call the rational model of management. This model, which they particularly associate with the business schools, places weight upon the importance of centralized strategic planning, on centralized control systems and on complex formal organization. It is also associated with an advocacy of sophisticated analytic methods of decision-making, often involving a high degree of numeracy. Peters and Waterman are at pains to point out that they are not opposed to analytical techniques *per se*; rather, they are against over-complex, spuriously precise quantitative analysis, particularly where it squeezes out the more difficult, qualitative human dimension. Despite the superficial attractions of these quantitative techniques, they believe that they do not in themselves bring about success and that by overemphasizing the rational side of management they are 'right enough to be dangerously wrong . . . [they have] . . . arguably led us seriously astray' (1982: 29).

In summary, Peters and Waterman argued against the conventional propositions, found in much of the teaching in business schools, that a concern for strategy and structure combined with rational decision-making based on the use of sophisticated techniques are the main ingredients necessary for the financial success of organizations. Instead they identified eight attributes associated with success and offer the implicit theoretical assertion that organizations seeking financial success should concentrate more on the development of these attributes than on management technique.

The dimensions of excellence were derived from an investigation of the practices of successful American companies. The investigation started with an internal McKinsey review of such practices combined with an analysis of their more successful clients. This was followed by a series of interviews and discussions with academics and business leaders. On the basis of these discussions, more detailed interviews were conducted in 'about half' of 75 'highly regarded' companies. In fact this meant structured interviews in 33 companies in selected sectors of the economy. Thirteen European companies which had appeared in the original list of 75 were omitted 'because they do not represent a fair cross-section of European companies' (1982: 19). These interviews were conducted during 1979 and 1980. To ensure that only the best companies were included, a within-industry rating of innovativeness was obtained and a set of financial indicators was applied. These were compounded asset growth, compounded equity growth, average ratio of market to book value, average return on total capital, average return on equity and average return on sales. To qualify for inclusion, companies had to be in the top half of their industry over a period of twenty years (1960–80) on a minimum of four out of the six financial criteria. On this basis, 36 companies qualified; by giving some weighting to innovativeness this number rose to 43 of the original 62.

Interview programmes were conducted in 21 of these organizations, although it is never entirely clear who was interviewed, and also in a further 12 organizations which had been classed as 'near misses' on the criteria for inclusion. The remaining 22 companies were examined in considerably less depth. Throughout the book there are many references to companies which do not appear in the list of successful companies. As the authors explain,

these are included because 'our inquiry into corporate innovation and
excellence is a continuing effort and much work has been done since 1979'
(1982: 25).

Criticisms of *In Search of Excellence*

Criticisms of the book fall into two major categories: those concerned with
methodological aspects of the study, including the research design, and
those concerned with the analysis and argument.

Methodological criticisms

The starting point for criticism of the methodology is the nature of the
sample. General claims about success in American industry are made on the
basis of companies selected from the high technology, consumer goods,
general industrial, service, project management and resource-based sectors
of the economy. The assumption is that if common themes can be identified
across the successful companies in these sectors, they can be generalized to
the rest of industry. However, as noted earlier, even this claim can only
partly be supported because the book reports findings from only some of
the successful companies and includes sometimes quite extensive information from companies which failed to qualify on the criteria of financial
performance and innovativeness. Furthermore, the original sampling frame
of 75 companies was based on an unsystematic intelligence-gathering exercise which might possibly have omitted from consideration a number of
financially successful companies which had failed to establish a high profile
for their management style. Some of the companies which were included
failed to meet the financial criteria but appear to have attracted the attention of the researchers precisely because they displayed many of the eight
desirable attributes. As Peters and Waterman note, they are 'a group of
exemplars which without benefit of specific selection criteria, do seem to
represent especially well both sound performance and the eight traits we
have identified' (1982: 24). In so far as this is the case, it casts doubts on
the independence of the criteria of excellence and raises the possibility that
the research was an exercise in self-fulfilling prophecy.

A second methodological concern is the lack of information about how
data from within the companies were collected. There appear to have been
interviews with chief executives and some group discussions but it is not
clear whether data were collected systematically from a specified range of
individuals at different levels and across different functions within each
organization. The often sketchy and impressionistic presentation of information implies that this was not the case. Indeed, the general quality of the
evidence used to argue for the eight attributes is often very weak, compris-
ing quotes from chief executives or the observations of a range of
individuals who, on sometimes dubious grounds, are classed as relevant
experts. Carroll (1983) cites several examples of these individuals, who

range from journalists to retired politicians such as Jacques Servan-Schreiber. Carroll also questions the implicit assumption made by Peters and Waterman that the chief executives of organizations are in a good position to know what really goes on inside their organization. The poor quality of the information about the methods of data collection and the lack of any clear presentation of that data leave the reader uncertain about the basis on which the eight attributes were identified and measured.

Turning to the research design, the approach adopted by Peters and Waterman can be criticized because they concentrated only on successful companies. By failing to collect information about less successful companies, they are not in a position to claim that the eight attributes are peculiar to the successful companies. It is conceivable that many unsuccessful companies also possess these attributes and that the factors differentiating the more and less successful have not been considered in the research. These might, for example, include aspects of the external environment such as market share or government intervention, or internal factors such as technology.

It is possible from two rather different perspectives to challenge the whole basis of the criteria of success. Johnson et al. (1985) note that Peters and Waterman measured financial performance based on accounting indices rather than economic performance based on share price. They argue that their measure of economic performance is the more appropriate criterion of success. Their analysis of share prices shows that the companies cited as excellent by Peters and Waterman did not show consistently superior performance compared with all the companies listed on the New York Stock Exchange. Hitt and Ireland (1987) take this a stage further by comparing some of the companies on Peters and Waterman's list with a sample of Fortune 1000 companies, with each group broken down by strategy, industry and pattern of diversification. Analysis revealed no significant differences on a five-year measure of stock market returns. Nor did they find any evidence that the 'excellent' companies were any more likely to display any of the attributes of excellence than the control group from the Fortune 1000 list. They conclude

> the excellent firms identified by Peters and Waterman may not have been excellent performers, and they may not have applied the excellence principles to any greater extent than did the general population of firms. Additionally, the data call into question whether these excellence principles are, in fact, related to performance. (Hitt and Ireland, 1987: 95)

The second challenge to the criteria of success is based on the view that if the aim is to identify the characteristics of good management, then arguably greater demands are placed upon those who have to turn around ailing companies than on those who are building on a long-term record of success. Certainly there may be more lessons for those who wish to lead their company to success in the type of analysis presented by Kanter (1983) in her book *The Change Masters*, which examines how companies such as General Motors escaped from crisis.

Conceptual criticisms

One of the implications of the eight attributes of excellent companies is that success can be explained largely in terms of factors internal to the organization. As Carroll and others have noted, this fails to take account of the external environment including various forms of protective legislation, market dominance, access to supplies and possibly an advantageous geographical location. Even within the organization little attention is paid to technology. At the start of the book, Peters and Waterman explain the necessity for a shift in emphasis from the traditional focus on the 'hard s's' of strategy and structure to the 'soft s's' of style, systems, staff, skills and shared values. In the event they seem to have focused almost exclusively on these soft s's and on the general issue of culture to the exclusion of any concern for technology and its implications for structure. The failure to take sufficient account of the variety of external and internal circumstances flies in the face of contingency theory, which provides a general basis for much organizational analysis. This disregard for variations in context is reflected in the advocacy of the universalistic application of the eight attributes of excellence in all organizations.

A rather different danger in the advocacy of the eight attributes lies in the assumptions made by Peters and Waterman about the degree of sophistication of organizations. It is reasonable to assume that in the excellent companies there was a considerable use of advanced management techniques resulting in a range of effective control systems. The emphasis on the eight attributes in these organizations provides a plausible way of going beyond technique and putting it in perspective. However, for organizations which have not yet sufficiently developed these control systems there is a danger that pursuit of the eight attributes may encourage them to run before they can walk. The result may be chaos and possible disaster.

Since the empirical basis for the eight attributes is not very clearly articulated, one of the best tests of the implicit theory which they represent is to monitor over time the progress of the excellent companies. A *Business Week* (1984) analysis showed that even by 1984 at least 14 of the 43 had gone into decline since the study, to the point where several could no longer justify inclusion on the basis of the six financial criteria. The analysis suggests that in many cases this decline can be explained in terms of external factors and had often occurred despite the persistent pursuit of the attributes of excellence. This implies that on a rigorous test of this sort the 'theory' does not stand up impressively.

Doubts about the quality of the evidence on which conclusions about the eight attributes are reached have already been noted. These are compounded by a lack of conceptual clarity. For example, are all the attributes equally important? Are they all necessary for business success or will, say, six out of eight suffice – and if so, which six? There appears to be some overlap between the attributes since more than one deal with values and more than one deal with structure.

Perhaps a more telling albeit unintended criticism can be found in the subsequent work of the authors. In 1985 Peters co-authored a follow-up book, *A Passion for Excellence* (Peters and Austin, 1985). This addresses the question of how to put the principles of *In Search of Excellence* into practice. Without denying the validity of the eight attributes, emphasis is placed on the four elements which are considered to be the most important: concern for customers, innovation, attention to the people in the organization and, above all, leadership. The emphasis on leadership is new; Peters acknowledges this but at the same time claims that it is embedded in the original book. This claim is plausible; most of the interviews and certainly most of the more telling quotes focus on leaders of organizations. Their role, and especially that of founding fathers, is considered crucial in shaping the culture of an organization. From an attributional perspective this is not too surprising since leaders of successful organizations are more likely than most in the process of an interview to explain that success at least partly in terms of their own contribution and their own beliefs about how to run a successful organization.

Peters' third book, *Thriving on Chaos* (1988) appears to depart even further from the approach of *In Search of Excellence*. The opening sentence provocatively asserts 'There are no excellent companies'. The message now emphasizes the need for constant, rapid change to survive in a rapidly changing world. Although some of the themes from *In Search of Excellence* remain, the ever more frenetic message is much closer to that of quality gurus such as Deming with their emphasis on constant improvement and ever more rapid responsiveness to the customer. Waterman's follow-up book, *The Renewal Factor* (1988) is a more measured analysis of a similar theme: in a rapidly changing world the key factor in sustained excellence is constant renewal. His research, similar in many ways to that which informed the original book, results once again in eight attributes of renewing organizations. Although these are very different from the original list, there is a conscious attempt to integrate the approaches.

Mitchell (1985) has highlighted a comparison between *In Search of Excellence* and *The Hundred Best Companies to Work For in America* (Levering et al., 1984) Although the second book is in many ways even weaker methodologically than the first, the main point of interest is the rather limited overlap between the companies described in the two books. Apparently, by judging companies from the perspective of those who work in them, only some of the excellent companies are deemed to be good places to work. Superficially there is a similarity in the emphasis placed on concern for the individual and the importance of values in providing meaning, but as Mitchell notes, *In Search of Excellence* emphasizes

> the underlying notion throughout that management's job is to shape the person and his or her values so that they conform with the values of effort, productivity, teamwork, and striving for excellence . . . it is done not through factor or conviction but through myths, fables, and fairy tales. That is, management not only manipulates people to believe in certain values; management constructs the values without any real adherence or belief in them. (Mitchell, 1985: 352–3)

The message is reinforced in the linked book, also written by McKinsey employees, on corporate cultures (Deal and Kennedy, 1982).

It is perhaps not surprising to discover that the excellent companies place a great deal of emphasis on selection and socialization of new recruits and on means of constantly communicating and reinforcing the central values of the organization. Nor is it surprising to find that notions of pluralism and of collective representation of sectional interests, perhaps through a trade union, are almost absent from Peters and Waterman's book. It reflects what has been described as 'the deep-seated opposition to unions embedded in the ideology of American management and the culture of many firms' (Kochan et al., 1986: 56). It appears to be primarily concerned with those sectors of the American economy where unions are absent or at best very marginal. As such it would appear to have much less to offer to managers working in highly unionized settings and in the public sector.

The criticisms which have been discussed cover aspects of methodology, interpretation of the findings of the study, a variety of conceptual issues and questions of values. Given the force of these criticisms, why has the book been so successful? The next section addresses this question.

Explaining the success of *In Search of Excellence*

The success of *In Search of Excellence* can be explained in a variety of ways. In exploring these much can be learned about both management and the social sciences and the often uneasy relationship between them.

The message is valid

An initial possibility that must be considered is that Peters and Waterman are right; in other words those organizations that manifest the eight attributes, irrespective of what else they do, will be conspicuously successful. Some support for this contention can be found in the attempts to replicate the original study in a number of different countries. For example, a British attempt to repeat the Peters and Waterman study, reported in *The Winning Streak* (Goldsmith and Clutterbuck, 1984), while striving to identify different characteristics, nevertheless produced a list of eight attributes that overlap considerably with the Peters and Waterman list. Unfortunately their list is based on even flimsier evidence and analysis than Peters and Waterman were able to provide.

A British study by Grinyer et al. (1988) adopted a rather different criterion. They examined the characteristics of a set of companies they termed 'sharpbenders' because of the sudden improvement in their performance, and compared them with a smaller sample of companies from the same sectors which had failed to show any change. They found differences between the two groups on a number of dimensions including perceptions of the market, cost cutting and business strategy. However, they note that these dimensions fail to capture critical qualitative differences between sharpbenders and controls.

In sharpbender after sharpbender we were impressed by the sense of commitment, excitement, shared vision and hungry search for improvements in all aspects of the business. The chief executive, or in some cases a small group of senior executives operating together, seem to us to be the key ingredient in producing this heady potion. (Grinyer et al., 1988: 14)

At another point they note that 'Peters and Waterman . . . proved to be a useful source of widely recurring characteristics' (ibid.: 12). Even Edwards (1987), in a study of factory managers, claimed that his data on the link between forms of central control and productivity was supported by the Peters and Waterman characteristic of 'simultaneous loose–tight properties'.

What these various studies hint at is that Peters and Waterman might have been right despite their poor methodology, their weak presentation of results and their vague categories. They might be right more generally in so far as they give weight to the importance of informal qualitative factors such as leadership and culture in shaping the performance of organizations. What is more difficult to accept is the disproportionate weight given to them at the expense of other variables, and more particularly to external factors. This flies in the face of much of our knowledge about organizations. Since the subsequent performance of several of the companies in the original study has raised serious questions about their long-term financial excellence and since that performance can be best explained by reference to external factors such as changes in market conditions (*Business Week*, 1984), it would be unwise to give too much credence to the most simply expressed 'theory' about the impact of the attributes.

The message is perceived as valid

A second explanation for the success of the book is that whatever its academic validity, managers and other readers believe the message to be correct. In one sense the medium is the message. *In Search of Excellence* is about values and feelings, issues central to the behavioural sciences. But because it also taps values and feelings, it has a greater impact than a sounder, more dispassionate academic analysis of the same issues. The emphasis, highlighted by Mitchell (1985), on values and on the manipulation of symbols is put into practice by the authors. The book is written with panache and conviction. It has many references to authoritative sources as well as references to other sources which we are assured are authoritative. Most convincing of all are the comments and quotes from those working in the excellent companies and especially the chief executives. At various points the chapters are laced with quotes from, and references to, literature and the arts. What may be an illusion of validity gains sufficient impetus and has sufficient appeal to subdue and deflect attention from what might be more critical questions about the real quality of the evidence and therefore of the argument.

In Search of Excellence is essentially about the 'soft' s's. It is telling managers that their intuitive judgements and more especially their judgements about people are crucially important for organizational success.

In making this claim the authors appear to be distilling the wisdom and experience of successful managers rather than deriving their conclusions from the more academic perspective of the business schools with their emphasis on management techniques. As these techniques have become ever more sophisticated, they have become more difficult for a manager fully to understand unless that manager is a narrow, quantitative specialist or a recent graduate of one of the business schools. In a sense therefore managers have lost control of the process of management. Part of the success of Peters and Waterman seems to lie in giving management back to the managers. They reinforce this message by devoting a chapter to the failure of rational management techniques to produce business success.

It is an easy read

Another element in the appeal of the book to managers is that it is easy for busy managers to read while it avoids being patronizing or unduly simplistic. Not only does it have a high level of readability, it can be tackled at several levels. It is possible to distil the essence of the book in no more than ten minutes with the introductory chapter. On the other hand a chapter is devoted to each of the attributes and any one of them can be explored in more depth. It may be no coincidence that one of the other management bestsellers alongside *In Search of Excellence* was *The One Minute Manager*, a short parable which very simply and effectively communicates three central ideas about how to manage subordinates. In important respects, therefore, Drucker's dismissive criticism of *In Search of Excellence* as 'a book for juveniles' (*Business Week*, 1984) may miss the point.

Conrad, in reviewing *A Passion for Excellence*, takes this a step further.

> As literary critic Kenneth Burke noted more than fifty years ago, the appeal of a book like *A Passion for Excellence* lies in its mythos, its capacity to transport readers symbolically from a world of everyday experience to a mythical realm. 'The reading of a book on the attaining of success is in itself the symbolic attaining of that success . . . I'll wager that, in by far the majority of cases, such readers make no serious attempt to apply the book's recipes. The lure of the book resides in the fact that the reader, while reading it, is then living in the aura of success.' (Conrad, 1985)

This analysis would appear to apply at least as well to *In Search of Excellence* although it may be a little harsh to claim that so few readers have taken it seriously.

Good timing

Another factor in the success of *In Search of Excellence* was undoubtedly its timing. The book appeared in the early years of the Reagan era when the United States was beginning to rebuild its self-confidence after several years of introspective self-doubt. In industry this had been reflected in uncertainty about how to cope with the increasing threat of Japanese competition. The success of Japan had kindled an interest in Japanese management, and several bestselling business books had appeared either extolling the virtues of Japanese compared with American management (e.g. Pascale and Athos, 1981) or extracting elements of Japanese management for the American market. The most successful illustration of this was Ouchi's (1981) *Theory Z*. The message from *In Search of Excellence* was rather different and fitted in well with Reaganite America. It was that to find the lessons for success in American industry you need to look no further than in your own back yard. The lessons were to be found by exploring the practices of the best American companies and not by looking overseas. Furthermore, what one found by looking at these companies was a return to a number of traditional American beliefs based on keeping things simple, building on what you know best and reinforcing essential values. There is also a careful blend of rugged individualism and reinforcement of the family based on the concept of the organizational family. It is understandable that this optimistic message should strike a chord in American industry (Guest, 1990).

At the same time, Peters and Waterman were able both to reflect a growing academic research interest in, and to stimulate a greater interest for, ideas about symbolic management, human resource management, culture in organizations and, above all, leadership. Each of these topics has become a major focus of research. There has also been a wider application of the methodology used by Peters and Waterman of identifying successes along some dimension and then seeking common themes across organizations or even sub-units, departments or individuals which manifest success. One example of the many books in this genre is Bennis and Nanus's (1985) *Leaders*. This is based on interviews with, and analyses of, 90 successful leaders from a variety of walks of life, on the basis of which it offers certain observations about effective leadership and about paths to effective leadership.

Its marketing and practicality

The success of *In Search of Excellence* has been attributed by some writers to its perceived practicality and common sense (see, for example, Hitt and Ireland, 1987). This is more a function of successful marketing than a reflection of its content, since it is not a particularly practical book. It promises a new approach and points to the dimensions on which managers ought to focus their attention. But there is no direct guidance about what managers should do to achieve excellence. The authors themselves implicitly acknowledge this and Peters in particular uses it as one justification for the much more practical orientation of his subsequent books.

Less overtly, the book has also been a careful marketing of McKinsey, the consulting firm by whom both Peters and Waterman were employed when they wrote the book. Many of the attributes can be traced back to the idea of the 'seven s's' developed within the consultancy with the aid of Pascale and Athos, who subsequently presented them in their own highly influential *The Art of Japanese Management* (1981) which helped to pave the way for *In Search of Excellence*; and the 'seven s's' certainly appear to

provide an important part of the conceptual framework for their thinking
and research. The association with McKinsey also helps to change the image
of McKinsey. The most trenchant comments on this come in a review of the
book by Berry, a one-time McKinsey colleague of Peters and Waterman. He
claims that 'the book is more than a book. It's an advertisement: unquestionably the most successful one a consulting firm has ever sponsored . . . .
The strategy of the book is to revitalise the image of the sponsoring firm'
(Berry, 1983: 329). He also notes an inherent dishonesty in this in that
Peters and Waterman seem to blame everyone except the consultants for the
problems of American industry: 'the conclusions show that the best companies of the 1980s pointedly do *not* do what the top consulting firms were
telling their clients to do in the 1960s and 1970s' (1983: 330). Taking this
a step further he notes that the authors

> laud 'small, competitive bands of pragmatic bureaucracy-beaters, the source of
> much innovation' whereas the consultants have fought on the side of bureaucracy
> for decades. They cheer for the 'unshackling of the average man', whereas the
> control processes the consultants invented shackled the average employee to
> forms that had recorded the use of 15 minute periods of time. (ibid.)

The implication of all this is that the promotion of *In Search of Excellence*
was a promotion of McKinsey. Furthermore, the support of McKinsey,
recognized as one of the top consultants of the 'old school' of strategy and
structure, was a signal to the industrial community both that McKinsey was
in the vanguard of innovation and that the book and what it stood for
should be taken seriously.

In this context it is worth emphasizing again that *In Search of Excellence*
was not the only product to signal a change in McKinsey thinking. 1982 also
saw the publication of *Corporate Cultures* by Deal and Kennedy (1982),
both McKinsey employees who, in their Introduction effusively ackowledge
their debt to their colleagues Peters and Waterman. This book, with its
emphasis on the softer side of organization, could easily have been
subsumed within *In Search of Excellence*. It is a somewhat down-beat
version of the same message, a message which is in stark contrast to that
presented by McKinsey in previous years.

Implications for the social sciences

To those interested in the behavioural sciences and more especially the
field of organizational behaviour, much of what has been written about
In Search of Excellence may have a familiar ring. During the 1960s and
1970s the writers on management who most influenced managers, in
America at least, include Maslow, McGregor and Herzberg. Whereas
Peters and Waterman wrote about culture and leadership, they were
concerned with the equally nebulous and yet equally important and, to
many managers, equally intriguing subject of motivation. Like Peters and
Waterman their theoretical claims are highly susceptible to critical

scrutiny and the empirical evidence cited in support of their theories is either hinted at rather than clearly presented or, in the case of Herzberg, so weak as to open the floodgates of academic criticism.

Despite the dismissive criticism from academics, managers found these writers useful. (One indication of this is the recent reprinting in the *Harvard Business Review* of one of Herzberg's articles which, by a clear margin, has been the most requested offprint of all time: Herzberg, 1987.) What these writers share with Peters and Waterman, in addition to fortunate timing, is a capacity to present a coherent, positive and optimistic philosophy about management. For them this was built around the possibility of achieving personal growth and fulfilment through experiences in an integrated, humane organization. Crucially, they saw no conflict between personal growth and organizational growth: indeed, where appropriately managed, they should be mutually reinforcing. A further attraction of the assumptions, perhaps best captured in McGregor's (1960) notion of Theory Y, is that they correspond closely to the values of managerial and professional employees. Apparently, faced with an appealing and well-communicated message of this sort, which both prescribes and justifies the management role, the more considered, complex and sometimes essentially negative reaction of academics can be disregarded.

In a sense the academic response reflects the rational, techniques-oriented approach of which Peters and Waterman are so dismissive. Furthermore, it is reflective and cautious whereas the approaches to which managers are attracted display a bias for action and a capacity to simplify rather than complicate. Peters and Waterman recognized that 'people issues' in organizations are generally tackled in a subjective and intuitive manner, so that evidence becomes relatively unimportant. If a message rings true, if it appeals to values and to emotion and if it appears to have some practical implications, then all the social science evidence that can be assembled against it becomes relatively unimportant.

Where does this leave the social sciences? If one aim of the social sciences is to demonstrate their relevance and usefulness (and to many this may understandably be a contentious aim or at best a low priority), then we would do well to learn the lessons of *In Search of Excellence*. These can be considered in terms of the traditional paradigm for social communication which focuses on the communicator, the receiver and the message. Clearly in UK industry the image of social science is not good; leaving aside any perceptions of ideological bias, one predominant impression of social scientists is likely to be that of outsiders looking in and making unhelpful observations within conceptual frameworks which appear to have little relevance to the concerns of policy-makers. The message is consequently not seen as relevant. The receivers of any messages, the managers in industry, may be ill equipped to understand the significance of social science ideas because of their own limited training.

The pursuit of a dialogue between the social sciences and industry, on the basis of sound social science research, is possible, as several books well received in both academic and business circles in the USA attest. Within the same broad field as *In Search of Excellence*, Kochan et al. (1986) have produced a careful and thoughtful analysis of trends in industrial relations and human resource management in their book, *The Transformation of American Industrial Relations*. Foulkes (1980), using a similar methodology in some respects to Peters and Waterman, produced a more detailed and convincing analysis of *Personnel Policies in Large Non-Union Firms*. Kanter (1983) in *The Change Masters* uses detailed and insightful case studies to point to a number of practical lessons. As a result her book has been particularly well received in both academic and industrial circles.

In the UK the research traditions are rather different. While consultants may try to capitalize on *In Search of Excellence*, academics have preferred either the single case, such as Burns' (1977) book on the BBC or Pettigrew's (1985) book on ICI, or have conducted research on more representative samples, such as the *Workplace Industrial Relations Survey* (Millward and Stevens, 1986). There is no research tradition of the analysis and explanation of success in British industry. Stimulated by the success of *In Search of Excellence*, this is now changing (see, for example, Grinyer et al., 1988).

The more limited success of management books in the UK can be attributed, at least in part, to the lower level of education among managers and their failure to develop habits of reading and of keeping up to date with new ideas about management (NEDO, 1987). The problem of management training in the UK has been widely recognized. Social scientists in the UK and elsewhere may have to consider whether they too need training in the skills of communicating their ideas to management if they are to demonstrate the relevance of their ideas and thereby defend and promote the role of the social sciences in the community. The need for this is pressing since by default it is the wrong or the oversimplified messages that are received.

Social scientists in America are learning these lessons as the range of better-quality books on successful organizations and their practices demonstrates. As Freeman's review of bestselling management books over the years in America shows American social scientists have a long-established and more receptive audience. In the UK both managers in industry and social scientists still have a long way to go.

References

Bennis, W. and Nanus, G. (1985) *Leaders*. New York: Harper & Row.
Berry, J. (1983) Review of *In Search of Excellence, Human Resource Management*, 22 (3): 329–33.
Blanchard, K. and Johnson, S. (1982) *The One Minute Manager*. London: Collins.

Burns, T. (1977) *The BBC*. London: Macmillan.

Business Week (1984) 'Who's excellent now?', *Business Week*, 5 November: 46–55.

Carroll, D. (1983) 'A disappointing search for excellence', *Harvard Business Review*, Nov.–Dec.: 78–88.

Conrad, C. (1985) Review of *A Passion for Excellence*, *Administrative Science Quarterly*, 30 (3): 426–8.

Deal, T. and Kennedy, A. (1982) *Corporate Cultures*. Reading, Mass.: Addison-Wesley.

Edwards, P. (1987) *Managing the Factory*. Oxford: Blackwell.

Foulkes, F. (1980) *Personnel Policies in Large Non-Union Companies*. Englewood Cliffs, NJ: Prentice-Hall.

Goldsmith, W. and Clutterbuck, D. (1984) *The Winning Streak*. London: Weidenfeld & Nicolson.

Grinyer, P., Mayes, D. and McKiernan, P. (1988) *Sharpbenders*. Oxford: Blackwell.

Guest, D. (1990) 'Human resource management and the American Dream', *Journal of Management Studies*, 27 (4): 377–97.

Herzberg, F. (1987) 'One more time, how do you motivate employees?', *Harvard Business Review*, Sept.–Oct.: 109–20.

Hitt, M. and Ireland, D. (1987) 'Peters and Waterman revisited: the unending quest for excellence', *Academy of Management Executive*, 1 (2): 91–8.

Johnson, B., Natarajan, A. and Rappaport, A. (1985) 'Shareholder returns and corporate excellence', *Journal of Business Strategy*, Fall: 52–62.

Kanter, R. (1983) *The Change Masters*. New York: Simon & Schuster.

Kochan, T., Katz, H. and McKersie, R. (1986) *The Transformation of American Industrial Relations*. New York: Basic Books.

Levering, R., Moskowitz, M. and Katz, M. (1984) *The 100 Best Companies to Work for in America*. Reading, Mass.: Addison-Wesley.

McGregor, D. (1960) *The Human Side of Enterprise*. New York: McGraw-Hill.

Millward, N. and Stevens, M. (1986) *British Workplace Industrial Relations: 1980–1984*. Aldershot: Gower.

Mitchell, T. (1985) '*In Search of Excellence* versus *The 100 Best Companies to Work for in America*: a question of perspectives and value', *Academy of Management Review*, 10 (2): 350–5.

Naisbitt, J. (1982) *Megatrends*. New York: Warner.

Ouchi, W. (1981) *Theory Z*. Reading, Mass.: Addison-Wesley.

Pascale, R. and Athos, A. (1981) *The Art of Japanese Management*. New York: Simon & Schuster.

Peters, T. (1988) *Thriving on Chaos*. London: Macmillan.

Peters, T. and Austin, N. (1985) *A Passion for Excellence*. New York: Random House.

Peters, T. and Waterman, R. (1982) *In Search of Excellence*. New York: Harper & Row.

Pettigrew, A. (1985) *The Awakening Giant*. Oxford: Blackwell.

Waterman, R. (1988) *The Renewal Factor*. London: Bantam.

2

The US human resource management literature: a review

Phil B. Beaumont

The term 'human resource management' (HRM) is one that came to be increasingly used in organizations and business schools in the US in the 1980s; it essentially replaced the terms 'personnel management' or 'personnel administration' which had been used previously. The American origins of the term inevitably mean (for good or bad) that the definitions, scope, coverage and themes of the relevant body of US literature will play a major role in setting the parameters and agendas of both teaching courses and research on human resource management in Britain. For this reason alone it is clearly important for students, teachers and researchers in Britain interested in the human resource management area to have at least some degree of familiarity with the relevant US literature.

This being said, it is important to recognize that the US human resource management literature is overwhelmingly of a highly descriptive and prescriptive nature, with many of its leading assumptions, values and orientations being subject to a great deal of critical comment both in and outside of the US. For example, the following important questions have frequently been raised about human resource management: how extensive are actual developments along these lines? Do they derive from a coherent, long-run management strategy in individual organizations? Are they anything more than personnel management with a new name? Do they contribute to organizational effectiveness, *ceteris paribus*? Are they anti-union? Are they essentially limited to the operation of new plants or greenfield sites? There are, as yet, few definite answers to such questions, but the very fact that they have been raised means that a review, such as this one, needs to identify and highlight some of the existing weaknesses in the current body of US literature. Accordingly, in this chapter an attempt will be made to identify the origins of human resource management in the US, indicate the basic scope or coverage of the literature, highlight some of the leading, individual themes emphasized or pursued in it and point to some of its existing weaknesses. The implications of the rise of human resource management for the research and practice of industrial relations will also be highlighted, and finally we raise some questions about the future of human resource management in the US.

The origins of HRM

In the US the concept and practice of HRM is widely held to have evolved out of the area of personnel administration (Mahoney and Deckop, 1986). The essence of this evolutionary process is that employees (broadly defined) are now viewed as a valuable resource (rather than a cost to be minimized) which if effectively managed, rather than administered, from the strategic point of view will contribute significantly to organizational effectiveness, and thus will be a source of competitive advantage to the organization concerned. This broad, general (not to say rather idealized) perspective is viewed as embodying a number of important, *specific* departures from the previous practice of personnel administration. The specific changes identified by Mahoney and Deckop (1986: 229–34) in this regard are essentially as follows:

1 the practice of employment planning (e.g. succession planning) has moved beyond its early, relatively narrow, technical focus and concern with forecasting work to a concern with establishing linkages between human resource planning and the larger organizational strategy and business planning of the organization;
2 the traditional concern of the personnel function with negotiating and administering a collective agreement (in a unionized organization) has broadened to a concern with a larger notion of 'workforce governance' in which non-collective bargaining mechanisms (e.g. quality circles) are all-important in permitting employee involvement and participation in work-related decisions;
3 the early concern of personnel administration with the job satisfaction of individual employees (a notion of 'morale') developed into an interest in the notion of 'organizational climate' which has further evolved into a focus on the notion of 'organizational culture';
4 the idea of selection, training, performance appraisal and compensation decisions being heavily centred on the role of individual employees (with their detailed individual job descriptions) has given way to the belief that effective team or group working is the all-important route through which effective performance is achieved;
5 the basic concern of personnel administration to reduce costs through minimizing employee turnover and absence rates has given way to the view that HRM can make a distinctive, positive contribution to organizational effectiveness (a 'bottom line' contribution);
6 the relatively narrow focus of training on the teaching and learning of individual job skills has been broadened into a concern with developing (via both training and non-training means) the full, longer-term employment potential of employees.

As is obvious from the terminology of the above summary, the leading, single theme which is held to differentiate HRM from its predecessor, personnel administration, is a broadening or widening notion; the leading advocates of HRM, who are typically behavioural scientists in the US, see it essentially as an organization-wide 'philosophy' which is much broader, more long-run orientated and less problem-centred than personnel administration (Schein, 1987). As to why such a move away or development from personnel administration has come about in the 1980s, the following influences are frequently highlighted:

1 the increasingly competitive, integrated characteristics of the product market environment;
2 the 'positive lessons' of the Japanese system and the high performance of individual US companies which accord human resource management a relatively high priority;
3 the declining levels of workforce unionization, particularly in the private sector, in the US;
4 the relative growth of the service, white-collar sector of employment;
5 the relatively limited power and status of the personnel management function in individual organizations due to its inability to demonstrate a distinctive contribution to individual, organizational performance. (Guest, 1987: 504)

In short, it is viewed as a change or development driven by fundamental environmental changes (particularly in product market conditions) which were not capable of being adequately responded to by the traditional concerns, orientations and 'power' of the personnel management function.

It is also useful at this stage to view HRM as the latest in a series of stages of a line of management research and practice which began with the human relations movement of the 1940s and 1950s. In a paper entitled 'Human relations – 1968 style', Strauss compared the messages of the original human relations literature with that of the 1960s and 1970s organization development and change models (Strauss: 1986). He noted some differences between them, such as the movement from a concentration of blue-collar workers to a concentration on management personnel, a movement from an interest in the social needs of workers to one emphasizing the achievement of 'self-actualization' and a change from seeking to eliminate conflict to that of seeking to make conflict more joint problem-solving in nature. At the same time, however, he argued that both bodies of literature were subject to essentially the same sorts of criticisms, namely that they ignored external, economic variables, were anti-union or ignored unions, were potentially manipulative approaches, and sought to have the organization operate as a harmonious, co-operative system which would act virtually as a community surrogate. As we shall see, the strategic HRM literature, at the latest stage of writing in this tradition, no longer ignores external, economic variables, although the other three sets of criticisms continue to be made of it.

The strategic perspective and the product market environment

The US literature contains a great deal of discussion of the need for a *strategic* focus on HRM, which follows from a distinction being drawn between: (1) the *strategic* level (of managerial work), which deals with policy formulation and overall goal setting; (2) the *managerial* level, which focuses on the processes by which the organization obtains and allocates resources to achieve its strategic objectives; and (3) the *operational* level, which is concerned with the day-to-day management of the organization (Fombrun et al., 1984: 42). Such discussions of the need for a strategic perspective on HRM typically identify the broad substantive areas where this should occur (for example, selection, appraisal, compensation and development) and then emphasize the need for an appropriate linkage with the external, competitive strategy of the individual organization. For example, Beer and Spector (1985: 5–6) comment as follows:

> a business enterprise has an external strategy: a chosen way of competing in the market place. It also needs an internal strategy: a strategy for how its internal resources are to be developed, deployed, motivated and controlled. There are several implications to the strategic perspective. One is that the external and internal strategies must be linked. Each strategy provides goals and constraints for the other. A competitive strategy based on becoming the low-cost producer may indicate different approaches to compensation and employment security than a competitive strategy that depends on product innovation. The very idea of an internal strategy implies there is consistency among all the specific tactics or activities that affect human resources. Hence the need for practices to be guided by conscious policy choices to increase the likelihood that practices will reinforce each other and will be consistent over time.

This widely held view that there needs to be an explicit, complementary relationship between the internal HRM strategy of individual organizations and their external product market or larger business strategy has led to the formulation of a number of typologies of product market strategies and their (desirably) associated HRM strategies and practices. For example, one recent paper (Schuler and Jackson, 1987) identified:

1 an innovation strategy designed to gain competitive advantage (i.e. develop products or services different from those of competitors);
2 a quality enhancement strategy (i.e. enhance product and/or service quality);
3 a cost-reduction strategy (i.e. be a low-cost producer).

The patterns of employee role behaviour and human resource management policies held to be associated with these particular business strategies are set out in Table 1. The article from which this table is drawn went on to argue that whichever competitive strategy is adopted is essentially a contingency-based decision, being determined by factors such as the demands of customers and the nature of competition, and that individual

Table 1 *Employee role behaviour and HRM policies associated with particular business strategies*

Strategy	Employee role behaviour	HRM policies
1 Innovation	a high degree of creative behaviour	jobs that require close interaction and co-ordination among groups of individuals
	longer-term focus	performance appraisals that are more likely to reflect longer-term and group-based achievements
	a relatively high level of co-operative, interdependent behaviour	jobs that allow employees to develop skills that can be used in other positions in the firm
		compensation systems that emphasize internal equity rather than external or market-based equity
	a moderate degree of concern for quality	pay rates that tend to be low, but that allow employees to be stockholders and have more freedom to choose the mix of components that make up their pay package
	a moderate concern for quantity	
	an equal degree of concern for process and results	broad career paths to reinforce the development of a broad range of skills
	a greater degree of risk taking	
	a high tolerance of ambiguity and unpredictability	
2 Quality enhancement	relatively repetitive and predictable behaviours	relatively fixed and explicit job descriptions
	a more long-term or intermediate focus	high levels of employee participation in decisions relevant to immediate work conditions and the job itself
	a moderate amount of co-operative, interdependent behaviour	a mix of individual and group criteria for performance appraisal that is mostly short term and results orientated
	a high concern for quality	a relatively egalitarian treatment of employees and some guarantees of employment security
	a modest concern for quantity of output	extensive and continuous training and development of employees

continued

Table 1 *contd*

Strategy	Employee role behaviour	HRM policies
	high concern for process	
	low risk-taking activity	
	commitment to the goals of the organization	
3 Cost reduction	relatively repetitive and predictable behaviour	relatively fixed and explicit job descriptions that allow little room for ambiguity
	a rather short-term focus	narrowly designed jobs and narrowly defined career paths that encourage specialization expertise and efficiency
	primarily autonomous or individual activity	short-term results-orientated performance appraisals
	moderate concern for quality	close monitoring of market pay levels for use in making compensation decisions
	high concern for quantity of output	minimal levels of employee training and development
	primary concern for results	
	low risk-taking activity	
	relatively high degree of comfort with stability	

Source: Schuler and Jackson (1987)

organizations may pursue multiple strategies (in different business units or functional areas) at any one point in time, and may have to change strategies over the course of time. The reference to changing product market strategies over the course of time is all-important because of the perceived need for HRM priorities, strategies and practices to change accordingly. This perspective suggests the importance of incorporating the notion of product or organizational life-cycles, which are typically held to involve the four stages of start-up, growth, maturity and decline, in HRM strategy formulation. Table 2 shows one view of how HRM priorities and strategies may change over the course of these four stages. The contents of this table, and the previous one, suggest that the interest in strategic HRM has largely arisen out of product market developments, although there is 'no one best way' to manage in the HRM area in that the priorities, desired employee role behaviours, policy mix and so on in an individual organization will be highly contingent upon the related phenomena of larger business strategy and the particular stage of the product life cycle of the organization concerned.

This said, one recent report in the US has argued that the 'best practice'

Table 2 *Critical human resource activities at different organizational or business unit stages*

Human resource functions	Introduction	Growth	Life cycle stages Maturity	Decline
Recruitment, selection and staffing	Attract best technical/professional talent	Recruit adequate numbers and mix of qualified workers. Management succession planning. Manage rapid internal labour market movements	Encourage sufficient turnover to minimize lay-offs and provide new openings. Encourage mobility as reorganizations shift jobs around	Plan and implement workforce reductions and reallocation
Compensation and benefits	Meet or exceed labour market rates to attract needed talent	Meet external market but consider internal equity effects. Establish formal compensation structures	Control compensation	Tighter cost control
Employee training and development	Define future skill requirements and begin establishing career ladders	Mould effective management team through management development and organizational development	Maintain flexibility and skills of an ageing workforce	Implement retraining and career consulting services
Labour/employee relations	Set basic employee relations philosophy and organization	Maintain labour peace and employee motivation and morale	Control labour costs and maintain labour peace. Improve productivity	Improve productivity and achieve flexibility in work rules. Negotiate job security and employment adjustment policies

Source: Kochan and Barocci (1985: 104)

firms which are adapting most successfully to the new product market environment tend to be characterized by:

1 a focus on simultaneous improvement in cost, quality, and delivery;
2 closer links with customers;
3 closer relationships with suppliers;
4 the effective use of technology for strategic advantage;
5 less hierarchical and less compartmentalized organizations for greater flexibility;
6 human resource policies that promote continuous learning, teamwork, participation and flexibility. (Dertouzos et al., 1989: 118)

The presence of item (6) above raises the obvious question of just what are the individual elements or components of a relatively sophisticated, cohesive and integrated HRM package; such a package approach is generally viewed as most likely to be associated with organizations that have adopted an innovation or quality enhancement product market strategy (or at least not solely a cost reduction one). The major, individual items typically mentioned in the US literature are

1 relatively well-developed internal labour market arrangements (in matters of promotion, training and individual career development);
2 flexible work organization systems;
3 contingent compensation practices and/or skills – or knowledge-based pay structures;
4 high levels of individual employee and work group participation in task-related decisions;
5 extensive internal communications arrangements.

It is, however, widely conceded that this is an *idealized* HRM system that will in practice be approached by relatively few organizations. The particular organizations which are typically held to come closest to such arrangements are new plants or greenfield site operations. This is because of the *inherent* advantages such organizations have in ability to introduce such arrangements; such advantages include the lack of vested interest in the maintenance of the status quo, the ability to use the selection process to hire people who wish to work in this type of organization, and the ability to introduce a consistent, mutually reinforcing organization-wide set of arrangements and practices (Lawler, 1982: 307). This issue of the potentially limited applicability of full, as opposed to partial, human resource management systems will be returned to later.

The leading themes in the HRM literature

According to Kochan and Barocci, the two leading, individual themes which have dominated the US HRM literature are those of corporate culture and the linking of business planning and competitive strategy with that of HRM planning (1985: 95). The interest in the subject of corporate culture, which as noted earlier has evolved out of the prior notions of employee morale and organizational climate, was particularly stimulated by the 'companies of excellence' literature (Peters and Waterman, 1982), in which a positive relationship was identified between 'strong cultures' and the performance of individual organizations; it must, of course, be acknowledged that this particular body of literature has not been without its critics (Mitroff et al., 1987). The essence of the corporate culture notion is that employees' patterns of behaviour should be g iided by and consistent with the values and philosophies of the top executives in the organization, with the latter being heavily shaped by the particular business or competitive strategy adopted (see Table 1). The individual companies with strong corporate cultures which are invariably cited and discussed in the literature are those, such as IBM and Hewlett-Packard, which Ouchi (1981) has labelled Theory Z organizations, and which combine the best features of both Japanese and American companies. For illustrative purposes Table 3 lists the individual objectives that make up the Hewlett-Packard corporate culture. A recent review of the organizational culture of Hewlett-Packard (Harris, 1984: 229) has suggested that it offers the following lessons to other organizations: first, its high performance is due to the close alignment of product market strategy and organizational culture, and secondly, its policy mix has played a major role in both shaping and reinforcing a certain type of culture. These studies of strong culture organizations have stimulated a great deal of practitioner and researcher interest in the concept at the present time. Practitioners are particularly interested in the questions of how an organizational culture is created, institutionalized or changed, whereas researchers have tended to focus more on matters such as how the concept is most appropriately measured and studied. Unfortunately the US literature can provide relatively few definite answers to these (and other) questions concerning organizational culture. This is because the literature contains a disproportionate number of articles concerned with defining the term (and here only a relatively limited consensus is apparent) and describing the details or individual components of particularly strong culture organizations, such as Hewlett-Packard. Indeed, among the few relatively clear messages to emerge from the organizational culture literature to date are, first, that the values of the founder (and early senior managers) of the organization are especially important in shaping a particular culture (Schein, 1983), and secondly, that the concept can only be usefully studied by multi-method techniques (Duncan, 1989). This is because an organizational culture is not simply and easily captured by a set of formal stated objectives and purposes (such as those set out in Table 3), but is a much more qualitative, subjective notion in which relatively intangible items (for example, myths, symbols and labels) are particularly influential in the learning, sharing and transmission processes of culture dissemination. The weaknesses of the existing literature have

Table 3   *The organizational culture of Hewlett-Packard*

Objective 1: To achieve sufficient profit to finance our company growth and to provide the resources we need to achieve our other corporate objectives.

Objective 2: To provide products and services of the greatest possible value to our customers, thereby gaining and holding their respect and loyalty.

Objective 3: To enter new fields only when the ideas we have, together with our technical, manufacturing and marketing skills, assure that we can make a needed and profitable contribution to the field.

Objective 4: To let our growth be limited only by our profits and our ability to develop and produce technical products that satisfy real customer needs.

Objective 5: To help HP people share in the company's success, which they make possible; to provide job security based on their performance; to recognize their individual achievements; and to ensure the personal satisfaction that comes from a sense of accomplishment in their work.

Objective 6: To foster initiative and creativity by allowing the individual great freedom of action in attaining well-defined objectives.

Objective 7: To honour obligations to society by being an economic, intellectual and social asset to each nation and each community in which we operate.

Source: Ouchi (1981: 226–33).

predictably produced some perspectives critical of the concept itself, with some individuals commenting on its potentially manipulative capacities and others questioning its essential relevance and applicability in organizational settings (Meek, 1988).

The second major theme in the HRM literature in the US concerns the linkage (or lack of linkage) between business planning and human resource management planning. The basic messages in this predominantly prescriptive body of literature are that human resource issues should be considered in the formulation of business plans, and that human resource issues are particularly important in strategic planning/long-range business planning which is aimed at achieving a major change in an organization's direction or emphasis, although the human resource planning input is also important at other levels within the organization (Walker, 1980). Table 4 helps to illustrate the sort of *ideal* linkages which *should* exist, according to advocates of the above view. Although a good deal of the HRM planning literature is heavily techniques orientated (that is, which statistical techniques should be used to establish future human resource flows), the sort of prescriptive framework set out in Table 4 has stimulated interest in the question of the extent to which human resource plans are actually integrated into the business plans of organizations. This research has involved a mixture of survey and case-study work. For example, a survey of some 220 large companies in the mid-1980s reported that nearly 40 per cent of them included a human resource component in their longer-term business plans, although when the companies were categorized (according

Table 4   *Links between business planning and human resource planning*

	Strategic planning: long-range perspective	Operational planning: middle-range perspective	Budgeting: annual perspective
Business planning process	Corporate philosophy Environmental scan Strengths and constraints Objectives and goals Strategies	Planned programs Resources required Organizational strategies Plans for entry into new business, acquisitions, divestitures	Budgets Unit, individual performance goals Program scheduling, and assignment Monitoring and control of results
	Issues analysis	Forecasting requirements	Action plans
Human resource planning process	Business needs External factors Internal supply analysis Management implications	Staffing levels Staffing mix (qualitative) Organization and job design Available projected resources Net requirements	Staffing authorizations Recruitment Promotions and transfers Organizational changes Training and development Compensation and benefits Labor relations

Source: James W. Walker, in Kochan and Barocci (1985: 115)

to, among other things, the degree to which human resource plans were integrated into the business plan) on a 1–5 scale (ranging from little to advanced human resource planning) only some 22 per cent fell into the advanced categories (Quinn, 1985). Some other survey work in the US (Fombrun et al., 1984: 22) has also suggested that the prescriptive message of Table 4 (which is very much based on an essentially rational, non-political decision-making paradigm) does not appear to have been anything like fully absorbed and assimilated in actual organization practice: this is because only a minority of large firms actually report a relatively close integration between human resource and strategic planning activities. A recent, more detailed study of this issue in eight case-study organizations reported the following findings (Buller, 1988):

1 there was a greater degree of integration in firms operating in more dynamic, less stable environments;
2 there were notable differences, within individual organizations, between the views of planning and human resource management respondents concerning the actual degree of integration;
3 the degree of integration was influenced by an organization's overall culture and philosophy towards human resources, including the traditional level of regard for the personnel function;
4 in organizations where the senior human resource management executives had considerable line management experience there was a relatively higher level of integration.

The latter two points are particularly important in suggesting that the 'internal politics' of managerial decision-making processes within individual organizations plays a far from insubstantial role in helping to bring about (or not) a relatively close linkage between human resource and business strategy planning; this is important because, as we shall see below, the HRM literature in the US has involved very much an apolitical view of organizational decision-making processes.

Some question marks over the US HRM literature

The key messages or terms in the US HRM literature are a strategic focus, the need for HRM policies and practices to be consistent with overall business strategy, the need for individual components of an HRM package to reinforce each other and be consistent with corporate culture, while the individual components of the HRM package should particularly emphasize teamwork, flexibility, employee involvement and commitment. Perhaps not surprisingly, a body of literature with a message along these lines has attracted an above-average number of sceptics, not to say critics. In this section we review some of the leading reservations expressed about, or question marks raised concerning, this body of literature.

To some individuals there is nothing terribly new about HRM in that it is simply the latest stage in the development of a body of thought which began with 'human relations' (*à la* Elton Mayo) in the 1930s and has evolved through the organization development and change literature of the 1960s and 1970s (see the earlier reference to the discussion of Strauss). Commentators who subscribe to this sort of view are likely variously to suggest that

1 HRM embodies some of the leading assumptions of the human relations school of thought (for example high job satisfaction levels lead to high productivity levels), which empirical research has not tended to substantiate (Dunham and Smith, 1979);
2 the stress on the need to successfully integrate human resource and technological developments is little more than the basic message of socio-technical systems theory (Trist, 1981);
3 the major emphasis on the importance of a competitive, unstable product market environment in stimulating the need for flexible work practices and a close individual employee–organization identification process is simply rediscovering the organic management systems theory of Burns and Stalker (1961).

A second line of criticism of HRM is basically that the academic literature is running well ahead of actual organizational practice. That is, individual researchers are simply retitling their textbooks (personnel management becomes HRM), whereas in reality most organizations do not closely integrate human resource and strategic planning. Individual HRM changes in most organizations do not add up to a consistent, integrated package deriving from a long-run, coherent management strategy, and the case studies of sophisticated HRM policies are based on a very small group of atypical organizations such as those which operate on greenfield site locations, have above-average levels of organizational resources or 'slack', or are ones which had particularly charismatic founders or early leaders who imprinted from the inception of the organizations an unusual culture on them. In short, the basic contention of some individuals is that the potential applicability of HRM, at least beyond certain individual practices, is essentially limited to a not unimportant, but certainly relatively small, non-representative group of organizations where either above-average opportunities for change exist or else HRM is but a short step away from their existing policies and practices.

A third line of argument, which draws to some extent on those above, is that HRM is most applicable in non-union organizations, may be difficult to introduce (as a result of union opposition) in highly unionized firms, but if it is introduced in the latter, may have some significant anti-union implications. Advocates of this school of thought can variously point to the fact(s) that sophisticated HRM systems were essentially developed in the non-union sector in the US in the 1970s and 1980s, are designed to produce a strong individual employee–organization identification process that has the potential to limit the presence and extent of job dissatisfaction which tends to trigger a demand for union representation, and may substitute for, rather than complement, existing collective bargaining arrangements by permitting employers to communicate directly with (and so influence) individual employees rather than communicating indirectly with them through union channels. In short, academic advocates of HRM may urge the need for senior managers to adopt a multiple-stakeholder (including employees and unions) perspective when formulating their HRM strategy (Beer and Spector, 1985: 5), but its heavy line management orientation and essential aim (that is, a 'good' HRM system involves an alignment of the goals and objectives of individual employees with those of the organization) embody strong (if subtle) managerial control and 'unitarist' assumptions and implications. Some more detailed arguments and findings concerning the implications of HRM for industrial relations are presented in the next section.

Another set of criticisms of the HRM literature in the US concerns its highly descriptive and prescriptive nature, a label I have frequently used throughout this review. There are two essential sub-elements to this line of argument. The first is that the literature is very 'politically naive' in the sense that it is based very largely on a rational decision-making paradigm which almost totally ignores the all-important realities of organizational politics and differential sub-unit power within the management hierarchy. As a result, questions concerning the practical means of implementing new, innovative HRM policies in organizations are very largely neglected; the literature simply suggests or implies that the very weight of environmental forces (particularly in the product market) will necessarily convince senior management of the need for such a change, particularly if a human resource management audit has been conducted (Fombrun et al., 1984: 235–48). The second element of criticism is that the HRM literature claims to be very 'bottom-line' orientated, and certainly there are many assertions in it to the effect that HRM activities have a major, positive impact on productivity levels and overall levels of organizational performance. However, claims to this effect need to be seen in the light of the fact that the whole question of just how one measures organizational effectiveness is a highly controversial one: indeed there is remarkably little consensus in the literature on this subject (Scott, 1977). Existing studies of individual HRM practices, particularly employee involvement ones, tend to reveal relatively few strong relationships with various measures of organizational performance (Lewin, 1989). Furthermore, there have been remarkably few systematic empirical studies of the relationship between a package of HRM practices and larger organizational performance, with the positive findings of Gomez-Mejia's (1988) survey study being almost the only one which can be cited in this regard.

One should not immediately leap to the conclusion that all of these reservations about, and criticisms of, the HRM literature in the US are equally valid and strong. Nevertheless, there is undoubtedly some merit in

a number of them, and the very fact that such concerns and criticisms
have been expressed should help caution any reader against the belief that
the US HRM literature consists of a body of prescriptions and recommendations that are well grounded in the results of systematic, empirical
research. Indeed, the major challenge for HRM researchers in the US
(and elsewhere) in the future is to make the above statement obsolete.

HRM and industrial relations

In the previous section reference was made to the potentially anti-union
implications of HRM practice and the associated tendency of much of the
HRM literature in the US to ignore the presence and role of trade unions.
Currently at least three concerns are being expressed in the US about the
relationship between HRM and industrial relations. The first is the
concern of industrial relations researchers and teachers in the US that
HRM is increasingly replacing collective bargaining as the popular (in
terms of student numbers) core subject matter of industrial relations
teaching programmes; allied to this concern is the reduced external
funding available for research on collective bargaining topics. This
change, which needs to be seen against the background of the substantial
fall in the overall level of union density and collective bargaining coverage
in the US (particularly in the private sector) in recent decades, has raised
a number of important questions and debates in the industrial relations
research community in the US in recent years. For example, can industrial
relations researchers depart from their traditional concentration on collective bargaining and usefully and legitimately begin to study the employment practices and arrangements of non-union firms? Can industrial
relations researchers, relative to labour economists and OB researchers,
usefully contribute to an understanding of the strategic and workplace
(i.e. non-collective bargaining) levels of decision-making, with their
increasingly important implications for HRM developments, in unionized
firms? And if the latter does not occur, will the distinctive contribution
of industrial relations researchers to an understanding of the employment
relationship (that is, an inherent conflict of interest between employees
and employers) increasingly be lost, in both teaching and practitioner
circles, relative to the 'efficiency' and 'co-operation' emphasis of
economists and behavioural scientists respectively? In other words, will
the concerns of 'due process' and 'equity' not figure prominently in the
HRM literature?

A second, related concern of both industrial relations researchers and
trade unionists in the US is whether the introduction and diffusion of
HRM practices will increasingly 'substitute' for the union role, and thus
help to maintain and increase the size of the non-union employment
sector in the US. As noted in the previous section, the 'household name'
HRM firms in the US are frequently non-union ones, and the concern

here is that the spread of these practices will increasingly limit the ability of unions to successfully organize firms operating with these types of employment packages. There is some survey evidence in the US which indicates that the presence of HRM arrangements along the lines we have discussed is significantly associated with organizations successfully retaining their non-union status in the course of the 1980s (Kochan et al., 1986).

The third concern is that management in the unionized sector in the US, in order to try to compete effectively with non-unionized organizations, will increasingly seek to emulate and introduce the HRM practices which have been pioneered in the non-union sector. And here the concern in union circles is that HRM practices, with their emphasis on teamwork, flexibility and individual employee commitment, will 'individualize' industrial relations, and drive a wedge between the union and its membership. This concern is particularly evident in relation to employee involvement and participation arrangements which have increasingly spread throughout the unionized sector in the US in the 1980s, and have been viewed as the 'leading edge' of modern HRM. Although some national unions have positively endorsed such programmes, others remain more cautious and sceptical, while others have been actively opposed to them. Some of the worries expressed about these involvement/participation programmes within the union movements in the US are that individual employees will increasingly identify with the organization, the workforce will become increasingly divided, grievance procedures and shop steward systems will be ignored, and there will be reduced interest, commitment and activity in the union (Easton, 1990). Indeed a major effect of the national union leadership of the UAW accepting team working arrangements in GM has been the rise of the 'new directions' movement, a group of local union officers who are contesting internal union elections on a programme of opposition to team-working arrangements.

In summary, HRM developments in the US are viewed as having a very awkward, essentially negative relationship with industrial relations from the teacher, researcher and practitioner points of view. This is because they are seen to threaten the position of collective bargaining as the traditional centrepiece of industrial relations research, teaching and practice and raise a variety of difficult questions for unions, namely, how to organize new members in the essential absence of job dissatisfaction and how to maintain the loyalty and commitment of existing members.

The future of HRM in the US

The management-driven, strategic HRM literature very much dominated the scene in the US in the 1980s. Is this likely to be the case in the 1990s? I suspect it will not be completely so, for two major reasons. Firstly, I think there is a recognition that the so-called 'bottom-line' orientation of this literature is far from well established in practice. As a consequence the nature of this particular stream of literature will need to change considerably, so as to provide more systematic empirical evidence of the positive relationship between HRM and larger organizational performance; prescription, description and special case study situations will increasingly become less acceptable elements of that literature. Secondly, there is a small, but growing, body of HRM literature grounded more in the assumptions and values of institutional economists and sociologists (particularly those working on the development of internal labour markets) and mainstream industrial relations researchers. The latter are likely to occupy a relatively more influential role in the HRM literature of the 1990s as a result of a number of developments and occurrences, such as changes in labour market demographics which, in principle, should increase the power of individual employees (or at least certain sub-groups of them), the growing debate over the nature of organizational governance arrangements in the US (with the multiple-stakeholder perspective becoming more prominent) and some of the increasing criticism of the actions of senior management as being inconsistent with values and behaviour of the 'high trust' HRM systems they espouse. Both of the above are developments which I not only expect, but hope to see occur in substantial measure.

Note

A number of helpful discussions with Tom Kochan are gratefully acknowledged.

References

Beer, Michael and Spector, Bert (eds) (1985) *Readings in Human Resource Management*. New York: Free Press.

Buller, Paul F. (1988) 'Successful partnerships: HR and strategic planning at eight top firms', *Organizational Dynamics*, Autumn: 27–43.

Burns, T. and Stalker, G.M. (1961) *The Management of Innovation*. London: Tavistock.

Dertouzos, Michael L., Lester, Richard K. and Solow, Robert M. (1989) *Made in America: Regaining the Productive Edge*. Cambridge, Mass.: MIT Press.

Duncan, W. Jack (1989) 'Organizational culture: getting a fix on the elusive concept', *Academy of Management Executive*. 3 (3) August: 229–38.

Dunham, Randall B. and Smith, Frank J. (1979) *Organizational Surveys*. Glenview, Ill.: Scott, Foresman.

Easton, Adrienne E. (1990) 'The extent and determinants of local union control of participative programs', *Industrial and Labour Relations Review*, 43 (5) July: 604–20.

Fombrun, Charles, Tichy, Noel and Devanna, Mary Anne (1984) *Strategic Human Resource Management*. New York: Wiley and Sons. Chapters 3, 14 and 15.

Gomez-Mejia, Luis R. (1988) 'The role of human resources strategy in export performance: a longitudinal study', *Strategic Management Journal*, 9: 493–505.

Guest, David E. (1987) 'Human resource management and industrial relations', *Journal of Management Studies*, 24 (5) Sept.: 503–22.

Harris, Stanley (1984) 'Hewlett-Packard: shaping the corporate culture', in C.J. Fombrun, N.M. Tichy and M.A. Devanna, *Strategic Human Resource Management*. New York: John Wiley. pp. 217–33.

Kochan, Thomas A. and Barocci, Thomas A. (1985) *Human Resource Management and Industrial Relations: Text, Readings and Cases*. Boston: Little Brown.

Kochan, Thomas A., Katz, Harry C. and McKersie, Robert B. (1986) *The Transformation of American Industrial Relations*. New York: Basic Books.

Lawler, Edward E. (1982) 'Increasing worker involvement to enhance organizational effectiveness', in Paul S. Goodman (ed.), *Change in Organizations*. San Francisco: Jossey-Bass.

Lewin, David (1989) 'The future of employee involvement/participation in the United States', *Proceedings of the Industrial Relations Research Association* (University of Wisconsin: Madison) Spring: 470–5.

Mahoney, Thomas A. and Deckop, John R. (1986) 'Evolution of concept and practice in personnel administration/human resource management', *Journal of Management* 12 (2): 223–41.

Meek, V. Lynn (1988) 'Organizational culture: origins and weaknesses', *Organization Studies*, 9 (4): 453–73. Reprinted as Chapter 12 of the present book.

Mitroff, Ian, Mohrman, Susan and Little, Geoffrey (1987) *The Global Situation*. San Francisco: Jossey-Bass.

Ouchi, William (1981) *Theory Z*. Reading, Mass.: Addison-Wesley.

Peters, T.J. and Waterman, R.H. (1982) *In Search of Excellence*. New York: Harper & Row.

Quinn, Mills D. (1985) 'Planning with people in mind', *Harvard Business Review*, July–August: 97–105.

Schein, Edgar H. (1983) 'The role of the founder in creating organizational culture', *Organization Dynamics*, Summer: 13–28.

Schein, Edgar H. (ed.) (1987) *The Art of Managing Human Resources*. New York: Oxford University Press.

Schuler, Randall S. and Jackson, Susan E. (1987) 'Linking competitive strategies with human resource management practices', *Academy of Management Executive*, 1 (3) August: 207–19.

Scott, W. Richard (1977) 'Effectiveness of organizational effectiveness studies', in Paul S. Goodman and Johannes M. Pennings (eds), *New Perspectives on Organizational Effectiveness*. San Francisco: Jossey-Bass.

Strauss, George (1986) 'Human relations – 1968 style', *Industrial Relations*, 7 (May): 262–76.

Trist, Eric (1981) 'The evolution of socio-technical systems as a conceptual framework and as an action research program', in A. Van de Van and W. Joyce (eds), *Perspectives on Organization Design and Behaviour*. New York: Wiley. pp. 17–75.

Walker, James W. (1980) *Human Resource Planning*. New York: McGraw-Hill.

3

What business can learn from nonprofits

Peter F. Drucker

The Girl Scouts, the Red Cross, the pastoral churches – our nonprofit organizations – are becoming America's management leaders. In two areas, strategy and the effectiveness of the board, they are practicing what most American businesses only preach. And in the most crucial area – the motivation and productivity of knowledge workers – they are truly pioneers, working out the policies and practices that business will have to learn tomorrow.

Few people are aware that the nonprofit sector is by far America's largest employer. Every other adult – a total of 80 million plus people – works as a volunteer, giving on average nearly five hours each week to one or several nonprofit organizations. This is equal to 10 million full-time jobs. Were volunteers paid, their wages, even at minimum rate, would amount to some $150 billion, or 5% of GNP. And volunteer work is changing fast. To be sure, what many do requires little skill or judgement: collecting in the neighbourhood for the Community Chest one Saturday afternoon a year, chaperoning youngsters selling Girl Scout cookies door to door, driving old people to the doctor. But more and more volunteers are becoming 'unpaid staff', taking over the professional and managerial tasks in their organizations.

Not all nonprofits have been doing well, of course. A good many community hospitals are in dire straits. Traditional churches and synagogues of all persuasions – liberal, conservative, evangelical, fundamentalist – are still steadily losing members. Indeed, the sector overall has not expanded in the last 10 or 15 years, either in terms of the money it raises (when adjusted for inflation) or in the number of volunteers. Yet in its productivity, in the scope of its work and in its contribution to American society, the nonprofit sector has grown tremendously in the last two decades.

The Salvation Army is an example. People convicted to their first prison term in Florida, mostly very poor black or Hispanic youths, are now paroled into the Salvation Army's custody – about 25,000 each year.

Reprinted with permission from the *Harvard Business Review*, July–Aug. 1989, pp. 88–93.

Statistics show that if these young men and women go to jail the majority will become habitual criminals. But the Salvation Army has been able to rehabilitate 80% of them through a strict work program run largely by volunteers. And the program costs a fraction of what it would to keep the offenders behind bars.

Underlying this program and many other effective nonprofit endeavors is a commitment to management. Twenty years ago, management was a dirty word for those involved in nonprofit organizations. It meant business, and nonprofits prided themselves on being free of the taint of commercialism and above such sordid considerations as the bottom line. Now most of them have learned that nonprofits need management even more than business does, precisely because they lack the discipline of the bottom line. The nonprofits are, of course, still dedicated to 'doing good.' But they also realize that good intentions are no substitute for organization and leadership, for accountability, performance, and results. Those require management and that, in turn, begins with the organization's mission.

As a rule, nonprofits are more money-conscious than business enterprises are. They talk and worry about money much of the time because it is so hard to raise and because they always have so much less of it than they need. But nonprofits do not base their strategy on money, nor do they make it the center of their plans, as so many corporate executives do. 'The businesses I work with start their planning with financial returns', says one well-known CEO who sits on both business and nonprofits boards. 'The nonprofits start with the performance of their mission.'

Starting with the mission and its requirements may be the first lesson business can learn from successful nonprofits. It focuses the organization on action. It defines the specific strategies needed to attain the crucial goals. It creates a disciplined organization. It alone can prevent the most common degenerative disease of organizations, especially large ones: splintering their always limited resources on things that are 'interesting' or look 'profitable' rather than concentrating them on a very small number of productive efforts.

The best nonprofits devote a great deal of thought to defining their organization's mission. They avoid sweeping statements full of good intentions and focus, instead, on objectives that have clear-cut implications for the work their members perform – staff and volunteers both. The Salvation Army's goal, for example, is to turn society's rejects – alcoholics, criminals, derelicts – into citizens. The Girl Scouts help youngsters to become confident, capable young women who respect themselves and other people. The Nature Conservancy preserves the diversity of nature's fauna and flora. Nonprofits also start with the environment, the community, the 'customers' to be; they do not, as American businesses tend to do, start with the inside, that is, with the organization or with financial returns.

Willowcreek Community Church in South Barrington, Illinois, outside

Chicago, has become the nation's largest church – some 13,000 parishioners. Yet it is barely 15 years old. Bill Hybels, in his early twenties when he founded the church, chose the community because it had relatively few church-goers, though the population was growing fast and churches were plentiful. He went from door to door asking, 'Why don't you go to church?' Then he designed a church to answer the potential customers' needs: for instance, it offers full services on Wednesday evenings because many working parents need Sunday to spend with their children. Moreover, Hybels continues to listen and react. The pastor's sermon is taped while it is being delivered and instantly reproduced so that parishioners can pick up a cassette when they leave the building because he was told again and again, 'I need to listen when I drive home or drive to work so that I can build the message into my life.' But he was also told: 'The sermon always tells me to change my life but never how to do it.' So now every one of Hybel's sermons ends with specific action recommendations.

A well-defined mission serves as a constant reminder of the need to look outside the organization not only for 'customers' but also for measures of success. The temptation to content oneself with the 'goodness of our cause' – and thus to substitute good intentions for results – always exists in nonprofit organizations. It is precisely because of this that the successful and performing nonprofits have learned to define clearly what changes *outside* the organization constitute 'results' and to focus on them.

The experience of one large Catholic hospital chain in the Southwest shows how productive a clear sense of mission and a focus on results can be. Despite the sharp cuts in Medicare payments and hospital stays during the past eight years, this chain has increased revenues by 15% (thereby managing to break even) while greatly expanding its services and raising both patient-care and medical standards. It has done so because the nun who is its CEO understood that she and her staff are in the business of delivering health care (especially to the poor), not running hospitals.

As a result, when health care delivery began moving out of hospitals for medical rather than economic reasons about ten years ago, the chain promoted the trend instead of fighting it. It founded ambulatory surgery centers, rehabilitation centers, X-ray and lab networks, HMOs, and so on. The chain's motto was: 'If it's in the patient's interest, we have to promote it; it's then our job to make it pay.' Paradoxically, the policy has filled the chain's hospitals; the free-standing facilities are so popular they generate a steady stream of referrals.

This is, of course, not so different from the marketing strategy of successful Japanese companies. But it is very different indeed from the way most Western businesses think and operate. And the difference is that the Catholic nuns – and the Japanese – start with the mission rather than with their own rewards, and with what they have to make happen outside themselves, in the marketplace, to deserve a reward.

Finally, a clearly defined mission will foster innovative ideas and help others understand why they need to be implemented – however much they fly in the face of tradition. To illustrate, consider the Daisy Scouts, a program for five-year-olds which the Girl Scouts initiated a few years back. For 75 years, first grade had been the minimum age for entry into a Brownie troop, and many Girl Scout councils wanted to keep it that way. Others, however, looked at demographics and saw the growing numbers of working women with 'latch key' kids. They also looked at the children and realized that they were far more sophisticated than their predecessors a generation ago (largely thanks to TV).

Today the Daisy Scouts are 100,000 strong and growing fast. It is by far the most successful of the many programs for preschoolers that have been started these last 20 years, and far more successful than any of the very expensive government programs. Moreover, it is so far the only program that has seen these critical demographic changes and children's exposure to long hours of TV viewing as an opportunity.

Many nonprofits now have what is still the exception in business – a functioning board. They also have something even rarer: a CEO who is clearly accountable to the board and whose performance is reviewed annually by a board committee. And they have what is rarer still: a board whose performance is reviewed annually against preset performance objectives. Effective use of the board is thus a second area in which business can learn from the nonprofit sector.

In US law, the board of directors is still considered the 'managing' organ of the corporation. Management authors and scholars agree that strong boards are essential and have been writing to that effect for more than 20 years, beginning with Myles Mace's pioneering work.[1] Nevertheless, the top managements of our large companies have been whittling away at the director's role, power, and independence for more than half a century. In every single business failure of a large company in the last few decades, the board was the last to realize that things were going wrong. To find a truly effective board, you are much better advised to look in the nonprofit sector than in our public corporations.

In part, this difference is a product of history. Traditionally, the board has run the shop in nonprofit organizations – or tried to. In fact, it is only because nonprofits have grown too big and complex to be run by part-time outsiders, meeting for three hours a month, that so many have shifted to professional management. The American Red Cross is probably the largest nongovernmental agency in the world and certainly one of the most complex. It is responsible for worldwide disaster relief; it runs thousands of blood banks as well as the bone and skin banks in hospitals; it conducts training in cardiac and respiratory rescue nationwide; and it gives first-aid courses in thousands of schools. Yet it did not have a paid chief executive until 1950, and its first professional CEO came only with the Reagan era.

But however common professional management becomes – and professional CEOs are now found in most nonprofits and all the bigger ones –

nonprofit boards cannot, as a rule, be rendered impotent the way so many business boards have been. No matter how much nonprofit CEOs would welcome it – and quite a few surely would – nonprofit boards cannot become their rubber stamp. Money is one reason. Few directors in publicly held corporations are substantial shareholders, whereas directors on nonprofit boards very often contribute large sums themselves, and are expected to bring in donors as well. But also, nonprofit directors tend to have a personal commitment to the organization's cause. Few people sit on a church vestry or on a school board unless they deeply care about religion or education. Moreover, nonprofit board members typically have served as volunteers themselves for a good many years and are deeply knowledgeable about the organization, unlike outside directors in a business.

Precisely because the nonprofit board is so committed and active, its relationship with the CEO tends to be highly contentious and full of potential for friction. Nonprofit CEOs complain that their board 'meddles.' The directors, in turn, complain that management 'usurps' the board's function. This has forced an increasing number of nonprofits to realize that neither board nor CEO is 'the boss.' They are colleagues, working for the same goal but each having a different task. And they have learned that it is the CEO's responsibility to define the tasks of each, the board's and his or her own.

For example, a large electric co-op in the Pacific Northwest created ten board committees, one for every member. Each has a specific work assignment: community relations, electricity rates, personnel, service standards, and so on. Together with the co-op's volunteer chairman and its paid CEO, each of these one-person committees defines its one-year and three-year objectives and the work needed to attain them, which usually requires five to eight days a year from the board member. The chairman reviews each member's work and performance every year, and a member whose performance is found wanting two years in a row cannot stand for reelection. In addition, the chairman, together with three other board members, annually reviews the performance of the entire board and of the CEO.

The key to making a board effective, as this example suggests, is not to talk about its function but to organize its work. More and more nonprofits are doing just that, among them half a dozen fair-sized liberal arts colleges, a leading theological seminary, and some large research hospitals and museums. Ironically, these approaches reinvent the way the first nonprofit board in America was set up 300 years ago: the Harvard University Board of Overseers. Each member is assigned as a 'visitor' to one area in the university – the Medical School, the Astronomy Department, the investment of the endowment – and acts as both a source of knowledge to that area and as a critic of its performance. It is a common saying in American academia that Harvard has the only board that makes a difference.

The weakening of the large corporation's board would, many of us predicted (beginning with Myles Mace), weaken management rather than strengthen it. It would diffuse management's accountability for performance and results; and indeed, it is the rare big-company board that reviews the CEO's performance against preset business objectives. Weakening the board would also, we predicted, deprive top management of effective and credible support if it were attacked. These predictions have been borne out amply in the recent rash of hostile takeovers.

To restore management's ability to manage we will have to make boards effective again – and that should be considered a responsibility of the CEO. A few first steps have been taken. The audit committee in most companies now has a real rather than a make-believe job responsibility. A few companies – though so far almost no large ones – have a small board committee on succession and executive development, which regularly meets with senior executives to discuss their performance and their plans. But I know of no company so far where there are work plans for the board and any kind of review of the board's performance. And few do what the larger nonprofits now do routinely: put a new board member through systematic training.

Nonprofits used to say, 'We don't pay volunteers so we cannot make demands upon them.' Now they are more likely to say, 'Volunteers must get far greater satisfaction from their accomplishments and make a greater contribution precisely because they do not get a paycheck.' The steady transformation of the volunteer from well-meaning amateur to trained, professional, unpaid staff member is the most significant development in the nonprofit sector – as well as the one with the most far-reaching implications for tomorrow's businesses.

A Midwestern Catholic diocese may have come further in this process. It now has fewer than half the priests and nuns it had only 15 years ago. Yet it has greatly expanded its activities – in some cases, such as help for the homeless and for drug abusers, more than doubling them. It still has many traditional volunteers like the Altar Guild members who arrange flowers. But now it is also being served by some 2,000 part-time unpaid staff who run the Catholic charities, perform administrative jobs in parochial schools, and organize youth activities, college Newman clubs, and even some retreats.

A similar change has taken place at the First Baptist Church in Richmond, Virginia, one of the largest and oldest churches in the Southern Baptist Convention. When Dr Peter James Flamming took over five years ago, the church had been going downhill for many years, as is typical of old, inner-city churches. Today it again has 4,000 communicants and runs a dozen community outreach programs as well as a full complement of in-church ministries. The church has only nine paid full-time employees. But of its 4,000 communicants, 1,000 serve as unpaid staff.

This development is by no means confined to religious organizations. The American Heart Association has chapters in every city of any size throughout the country. Yet its paid staff is limited to those at national headquarters, with just a few traveling troubleshooters serving the field. Volunteers manage and staff the chapters, with full responsibility for community health education as well as fund raising.

These changes are, in part, a response to need. With close to half the adult population already serving as volunteers, their overall number is unlikely to grow. And with money always in short supply, the nonprofits cannot add paid staff. If they want to add to their activities – and needs are growing – they have to make volunteers more productive, have to give them more work, and more responsibility. But the major impetus for the change in the volunteer's role has come from the volunteers themselves.

More and more volunteers are educated people in managerial or professional jobs – some preretirement men and women in their fifties, even more baby-boomers who are reaching their mid-thirties or forties. These people are not satisfied with being helpers. They are knowledge workers in the jobs in which they earn their living, and they want to be knowledge workers in the jobs in which they contribute to society – that is, their volunteer work. If nonprofit organizations want to attract and hold them, they have to put their competence and knowledge to work. They have to offer meaningful achievement.

Many nonprofits systematically recruit for such people. Seasoned volunteers are assigned to scan the newcomers – the new member in a church or synagogue, the neighbor who collects for the Red Cross – to find those with leadership talent and persuade them to try themselves in more demanding assignments. Then senior staff (either a full-timer on the payroll or a seasoned volunteer) interviews the newcomers to assess their strengths and place them accordingly. Volunteers may also be assigned both a mentor and a supervisor with whom they work out their performance goals. These advisers are two different people, as a rule, and both, ordinarily, volunteers themselves.

The Girl Scouts, which employs 730,000 volunteers and only 6,000 paid staff for 3½ million girl members, works this way. A volunteer typically starts by driving youngsters once a week to a meeting. Then a more seasoned volunteer draws her into other work – accompanying Girl Scouts selling cookies door-to-door, assisting a Brownie leader on a camping trip. Out of this step-by-step process evolve the volunteer boards of the local councils and, eventually, the Girl Scouts' governing organ, the National Board. Each step, even the very first, has its own compulsory training program, usually conducted by a woman who is herself a volunteer. Each has specific performance standards and performance goals.

What do these unpaid people themselves demand? What makes them stay – and, of course, they can leave at any time. Their first and most important demand is that the nonprofit have a clear mission, one that drives everything the organization does. A senior vice-president in a large regional bank has two small children. Yet she just took over as chair of the state chapter of Nature Conservancy, which finds, buys, and manages endangered natural ecologies. 'I love my job,' she said, when I asked her why she took on such heavy additional work, 'and of course the bank has a creed. But it doesn't really know what it contributes. At Nature Conservancy, I know what I am here for.'

The second thing this new breed requires, indeed demands, is training, training, and more training. And, in turn, the most effective way to motivate and hold veterans is to recognize their expertise and use them to train newcomers. Then these knowledge workers demand responsibility – above all, for thinking through and setting their own performance goals. They expect to be consulted and to participate in making decisions that affect their work and the work of the organization as a whole. And they expect opportunities for advancement, that is, a chance to take on more demanding assignments and more responsibility as their performance warrants. That is why a good many nonprofits have developed career ladders for their volunteers.

Supporting all this activity is accountability. Many of today's knowledge-worker volunteers insist on having their performance reviewed against preset objectives at least once a year. And increasingly, they expect their organizations to remove nonperformers by moving them to other assignments that better fit their capacities or by counseling them to leave. 'It's worse than the Marine Corps boot camp,' says the priest in charge of volunteers in the Midwestern diocese, 'but we have 400 people on the waiting list.' One large and growing Midwestern art museum requires of its volunteers – board members, fundraisers, docents, and the people who edit the museum's newsletter – that they set their goals each year, appraise themselves against these goals each year, and resign when they fail to meet their goals two years in a row. So does a fair-sized Jewish organization working on college campuses.

These volunteer professionals are still a minority, but a significant one – perhaps a tenth of the total volunteer population. And they are growing in numbers and, more important, in their impact on the nonprofit sector. Increasingly, nonprofits say what the minister in a large pastoral church says: 'There is no laity in this church; there are only pastors, a few paid, most unpaid.'

This move from nonprofit volunteer to unpaid professional may be the most important development in American society today. We hear a great deal about the decay and dissolution of family and community and about the loss of values. And, of course, there is reason for concern. But the nonprofits are generating a powerful countercurrent. They are forging new bonds of community, a new commitment to active citizenship, to social responsibility, to values. And surely what the nonprofit contributes to the volunteer is as important as what the volunteer contributes to the nonprofit. Indeed, it may be fully as important as the service, whether religious, educational, or welfare related, that the nonprofit provides in the community.

This development also carries a clear lesson for business. Managing the knowledge worker for productivity is the challenge ahead for American management. The nonprofits are showing us how to do that. It requires a clear mission, careful placement and continuous learning and teaching, management by objectives and self-control, high demands but corresponding responsibility, and accountability for performance and results.

There is also, however, a clear warning to American business in this transformation of volunteer work. The students in the program for senior and middle-level executives in which I teach work in a wide diversity of businesses: banks and insurance companies, large retail chains, aerospace and computer companies, real estate developers, and many others. But most of them also serve as volunteers in nonprofits – in a church, on the board of the college they graduated from, as scout leaders, with the YMCA or the Community Chest or the local symphony orchestra. When I ask them why they do it, far too many give the same answer: Because in my job there isn't much challenge, not enough achievement, not enough responsibility; and there is no mission, there is only expediency.

Note

1 A good example is Myles Mace, 'The president and the board of directors,' *Harvard Business Review*, March–April 1972: 37.

4

Human resource management in the public sector

John Storey

The basic underlying debate in industrial relations throughout most of this decade has turned on the nature and extent of change in the practice of contemporary industrial relations. At first sight, the facts seem fairly obvious: strike incidence has been reduced; union membership has declined; management appears to be in the ascendant and labour productivity has increased significantly. All of these changes to the 'system' of industrial relations are, moreover, equally evidently embedded in a markedly different 'environment'. Most notably, the legal framework has been altered, the winds of competition (domestic and global) have been felt more keenly, and the political climate under 'Thatcherism' has been radically transformed.

Against such a backcloth, conventional wisdom would seem to dictate that the main, if not the only point of interest, from a public sector standpoint would be the extent to which the revised managerial practices, honed, it is believed, in the private sector, have 'spilled over' into the public sector. However, the situation is far less straightforward than this depiction would imply.

The first difficulty to be encountered is that the issue is far from being a simple factual one: on the contrary, it is clouded with ideological overtones and so is highly charged politically. Thus, for example, it has to be noted that it is undoubtedly part of the Government's intention to 'tell the story' in the way implied above. The party-line is that overmighty trade unions were confronted unflinchingly, that, following legislation and the 'taking' of major strikes, in steel and coal for example, the unions were vanquished. Moreover, the story continues, the promised 'rolling back of the State' has progressed and the laggardly and cosseted public sector has been subject, and will be further subject, to the disciplines customarily experienced by the more efficient private sector.

A second difficulty is the extent to which, even in the private sector, there has been the kind of transformation implied above. This has been a hotly contested issue. Third, while the preferred 'official' view of management practice may depict the relationship of the private and public sectors as

Reprinted by permission of Basil Blackwell Ltd from *Public Money and Management*, 9(3) 1989: 19–24.

'leader' and 'lagger' respectively, this assumption should not go unquestioned. The underlying logic of requiring a more 'commercial' orientation within the public sector in itself tends to suggest the inherent superiority of such an approach and also again implies that the public sector is following the private sector and has much to learn from it.

The analysis which follows will question these common assumptions through an examination of the nature and extent of change in employment management across the private and public sectors – but with primary attention directed towards the latter. The chapter is divided into four sections. First, the meaning and nature of 'human resource management' is discussed; in the second and third sections, evidence of transition towards human resource management in both sectors is examined; finally, we explore the factors which may constrain the adoption of the full-blown model in the public sector. Much of the data upon which this article draws was collected from 15 large organisations in both sectors between Spring 1986 and Autumn 1987.

Definitions and key features

Human resource management is commonly used in both a generic sense simply as a loose synonym for 'personnel management', and in a more specific way when it is intended to denote the adoption of a particular kind of approach to managing labour. It is when this second usage is adopted or implied that the label becomes interesting. Current fascination with the term stems from the idea that it may be used as the signifier for the (possibly interconnected) web of recent managerial initiatives with regard to employee relations and indeed the whole management of the 'human side of enterprise' which are frequently reported as 'leading edge' cases in the management journals and, from time to time, in the national press.

So what are the hallmarks of this 'particular approach' and, furthermore, is it 'better' than those which have preceded it? There is, in fact, no agreed definition of human resource management but a constellation of elements can be constructed which, in broad terms, reflects what many commentators seem to want to signal by their use of the phrase. Perhaps the key point is that, whatever the finer details, it suggests a decisive break with the emergent conventional wisdom of post-Donovan proceduralism (Donovan, 1968), that is, the prescription to 'formalise' rules, agreements and relationships which had erstwhile been 'informal', and, in the case of the US, a break with the long-standing 'New Deal' forged in the Roosevelt years (Kochan et al., 1986).

As an ideal type it may be suggested that the main pillars of the 'new approach' are fourfold. First, that the sense of direction for the way in which the human resource is to be managed stems, quite explicitly, from the corporate strategy. In other words, human resource management is supposed to be better 'integrated' – both internally in the sense that selection, appraisal, reward systems and so on are in greater alignment than was typically the case under conventional personnel and industrial relations management, and 'externally' in the sense that the whole philosophy or approach is in turn emergent from the business plan.

A second feature is that the objective is to elicit the commitment of employees and not merely secure their compliance. Third, that the means of so doing are seen as attainable through a more systematic and careful approach to recruitment, selection, appraisal, training, reward and communication. That is, managerial attention is fundamentally shifted from reliance on 'collective' forms of accommodation with labour to more 'individualistic' ones.

Finally, unlike personnel management and industrial relations, human resource management is 'owned' by line managers and not by personnel specialists. This, in itself, might be presumed to foster the integration referred to above.

Taken together, these four features might be expected to bring about a more strategic and long-term approach to labour management in contrast to the short-term, ad hoc, pragmatic approach which has been noted as characteristic of most personnel and industrial relations management in the British context (Purcell and Sisson, 1983; Thurley, 1981). The classic complaint about the *ancien régime* was that it was marked by 'firefighting' – that is, it was too reactive; the new order is supposedly quintessentially pro-active. In so far as management in recent years would appear to have been not only in a position to, but in actuality to have, 'taken the initiative' then to this extent at least there would be some grounds for believing that there has been some measure of change.

Nonetheless, there is considerable scepticism surrounding human resource management. At one level, this merely arises out of ill-informed comment. Human resource management is thought to be merely 'about quality circles' and other 'flavour of the month' initiatives (though, incidentally, it would be wrong to think that all quality circles are of this ilk). On a more serious plane, there is ample scope for doubt when the prescriptive, idealised statements concerning human resource management are set alongside similar earnest statements that have frequently been made about personnel management. Legge (1989) has undertaken just such an exercise and having systematically compared sets of prescriptions finds little cause to declare a new dawn. Legge constructs what is undoubtedly the most convincing critique of the celebratory tone often found surrounding this concept and the associated 'excellence' literature (Peters and Waterman, 1982; Goldsmith and Clutterbuck, 1984). What surely matters most, however, is what is happening, in practice, rather than what may or may not have been espoused.

The evidence which has so far been published concerning change in industrial relations and personnel management in the 1980s in Britain, tends, on the whole, to give little support to the notion that a 'new industrial relations' has dawned (Batstone, 1984; MacInnes, 1987; WIRS 2, 1986; Marginson et al., 1988). But much of the survey work has been directed towards detecting any major abandonment of or departures from prevailing collective procedures. This is precisely the site of a major ambiguity in the pattern of change which our 15-case research project revealed. Even in those cases where extensive initiatives by management on selection, individual communication, the establishment of problem-solving groups and the like had been established, management had, in the main, kept their high-profile human resource management policies institutionally separate from 'old fashioned industrial relations'. Thus, unions have typically not been de-recognised, collective bargaining machinery was still 'maintained', but the centre of gravity had shifted. The time, energy and other resources given by management was undoubtedly directed in favour of the former set of approaches to 'people management' and not to the latter. It is one thing to 'maintain' negotiation machinery; using it in the same way as before may be quite a different matter.

This brings us to the other question which was raised earlier; is human resource management 'better' than traditional personnel and industrial relations? David Guest (1987) expressed the conventional academic view on such matters when he argued that no one approach can be recommended as 'best practice' in all circumstances. What is 'best' is contingent upon the particular circumstances: for example, the objectives of the key players, the prevailing labour and product market conditions, and so on. Even so, there has been a persistent undercurrent to a considerable amount of recent comment, which, in lamenting British managers' failure to invest in human resource development, to take a long-term strategic view, to communicate effectively with employees, systematically to select, appraise, and reward in an integrated way, in effect, is tantamount to recommending large parts of the human resource management programme. Indeed, Guest (1989: 55) has explicitly stated that for British industry to catch up further with its international competitors will require 'a shift in emphasis away from the industrial relations system towards human resource management policies as the main path to improved performance'.

Private sector model

Arguably, the fullest expressions of what the human resource management model looks like in practice are to be found in certain cases of Japanese and US companies operating in Britain – for example, Nissan (Wickens, 1987) and companies such as IBM and Hewlett-Packard. The main British instances of human resource management which are usually cited, such as Marks and Spencer, tend to be non-union. Moreover, whether unionised or not, there has always been a perception of 'exceptional' cases – exceptions that is, to the perceived pragmatic mainstream of British employment practice. Hence, it may be asked, what is new?

Evidence would suggest that a number of far-reaching changes are in process. There is space here only to give a flavour of some of the more important indicators. For this purpose it is appropriate to select companies within an industry sector which has been especially notorious for its traditional and entrenched industrial relations practices. Hence, the illustrations given here are drawn from the British motor industry.

In Austin Rover, Ford, Jaguar and Peugeot alike, managerial energy has been poured into 'alternative' initiatives such as direct communication with employees, joint problem-solving groups, flexible working, more systematic selection (including the use of psychometric tests for manual recruits), the introduction or reintroduction of appraisal and evaluation systems; an increased attention to training; and a move towards linking reward to performance.

Each of these companies has consciously sought to project line managers into a higher-profile role with regard to labour management. This new assertiveness for the line manager is evident at all levels: from supervision and first line management, through the much neglected middle management levels and right up to the now familiar emphasis on the strategic responsibilities of the chief executive.

At the previously neglected middle level the newly-created general 'area', 'zone' or 'manufacturing' managers have increasingly become responsible not only for the production function but for the total range of activities such as quality assurance, maintenance, cleaning, and supply of materials. Crucial to each and every one of these it should be noted, is the assumed responsibility and capability to manage the human resource. Thus, steps have been taken to 'free-up' the line manager so that he or she will take personal responsibility for the deployment of labour, its reward, its upgrading through training, its motivation and the provision of a sense of direction through direct and effective communications. This emphasis on the re-invigoration of the line or core operation manager turned out to be a key theme in nearly all of the case studies across a range of different industries, including those in the service sectors as well as manufacturing.

Before turning to consider developments in the public sector there is one other important point that must be borne in mind. The most crucial developments in the way the human resource is managed are frequently neither designed nor presented as specifically human resource management initiatives. The thrust of change may come, for example, in the form of a 'total quality management' programme. Alternatively, it may derive from a perceived need to enhance the organisation's image in the area of customer care. Such a push is likely to entail 'people issues' in respect of training, in appraisal, selection and reward – and in the mode of supervision or even teamworking.

Public sector trends

There is a range of ways in which tendencies in the public sector seem to have echoed the developments towards human resource management in the private sector. Indeed, at first sight at least, what is most striking is the degree of commonality. In order to explore these we will again make use of our four-part conceptual framework.

Integration

As in the private sector, attempts have been made to derive the direction for the management of people from 'corporate objectives' rather than from some 'professional' tenets. The shift towards a view of local authorities as 'corporate entities' stems, in no small measure, from the work of the Bains Committee. The idea from the start was to have these new bodies headed by a chief executive, mirroring the position in private sector companies. (The same notion is reflected in the transmogrification of polytechnic directors into chief executives.) At the same time, the integrative concept of 'general management' was being pressed by Stewart (1973). This would facilitate integrative strategic planning at corporate rather than departmental level.

An influential catalyst on this front has been the Audit Commission. Its insistent message is that bureaucracy is no longer an appropriate organisational mode for today's environment. What is currently required, it suggests, is flexibility and responsiveness. An example of its thinking is its publication *Good Management in Local Government* (Audit Commission, 1985). The emphasis is on the management of change 'rather than administering standstill or growth'. It talks of developing a 'vision' and deriving from this strategies, plans and budgets. These are to be followed up with systems for performance review.

Bradford, under its last Labour administration, is a good example of a large metropolitan council which sought to transform its people management approach by taking the lead from an elaborated corporate strategy. This, which the Council labelled its 'Social Strategy', was a policy document which aimed to orientate the whole range of Council activities in what was claimed to be a 'customer-led way'. The Personnel Directorate reassessed its total approach so as to engineer compatibility with this corporate plan. The plan stated, in true mission statement style, that 'Bradford Council is committed to putting people first'. But it added an unusual rider: namely, 'particularly those who are most in need'. This later priority indicates the kind of *adaptation* of currently fashionable ideas which deserves further exploration.

In line with the private sector practice of high-profile, direct communication with the workforce, the council leader, Phil Beeley, issued a series of letters and documents with his by-line and photograph. This was a way of firmly establishing a sense of corporate identity and central leadership which also characterised the approach by Len Peach as chairman of the NHS Management Board. Indeed, the parallels with the initiatives in the health service go much further as a reading of the NHS Training Authority report, *Better Management: Better Health* (1986), clearly demonstrates.

Commitment and responsiveness

These aims find expression through devolved management and flexibility. The key to these has been identified as that rather elusive phenomenon: sustained commitment. 'Committed' employee behaviour rather than 'mere' observance of formal procedure is, in many ways, at the heart of human resource management. For organisations which, in the recent past, have often had the greatest difficulty in gaining 'disciplined' behaviour (attendance rather than absence, punctuality rather than lateness, application rather than dilatory behaviour) this may seem an overly-ambitious objective. But conditions of heightened competitiveness and straitened budgetary circumstances have led many managers to believe that, however unlikely, it simply has to be the adopted objective. Expectations have certainly been raised.

The methods adopted in both the private and public sectors have been similar. Any self-regarding top team has long since forged its mission statement. Chief executives and key line managers have accepted responsibility for communicating the 'message'. Videos abound with chief executives spelling out targets and progress towards those targets. Newsletters have been launched and noticeboards tidied. Meanwhile, commitment has also been sought by 'involving' staff. A key device here has been the quality circle. Even when this term is not used for local political reasons, similar methods such as problem-solving teams have been widely in evidence. It is notable that health authority units and districts make up one of the largest client groups of the National Society of Quality Circles.

Relatedly, few health authorities can have avoided some programme or other directed towards treating patients as 'customers'. This has implied quality initiatives which, in turn, put the spotlight on the need for staff training and the need for a committed workforce rather than one which merely follows the rules and acts according to procedure. A key example is Trent Regional Health Authority's 'personal service' initiative and its associated training programmes.

In each case, whether the method has been unit-based customer-service initiatives or devolved budgeting (in education and local government) the underlying idea has been to mark a departure from overt centralised control through formal rules to a more localised form of control involving flexible response, self-control and commitment. It has been realised that in order to effect such a shift a host of human resource levers would also have to be activated.

Collectivism to individualism

In the 1960s and 1970s following the Royal Commission on Trades Unions & Employers' Associations (the Donovan Commission) the conventional wisdom dictated a greater formalisation of relations with employees on a collective basis. The personnel function was to become more established and specialised, and this led to a growth of personnel departments. Workplace trade union representatives (shop stewards) were to be formally recognised and provided with facilities – including time off for trade union duties. Most importantly, domestic arrangements were to be formalised. In total, relations with workers generally were put on a more proceduralised footing. The rapidly expanding personnel departments set about producing written procedures to cover every eventuality. This 'proceduralisation' was nowhere so marked as in the NHS and in local government.

In the 1980s the emphasis shifted radically. While outright de-recognition may not have widely occurred nor the outright abandonment of agreements and procedures, the emphasis lent to them was significantly reduced. To the fore instead have come a raft of devices which reach out to the employee on an individual basis. Key among these has been a far more systematic approach to selection so that organisational entry is more effectively controlled.

Similarly, there has been widespread use of individual performance appraisal. This is frequently wedded to individual goal setting and the more systematic measurement of performance. From here it is a short step to performance-related pay – again on an individual basis. British Rail offers just one apposite example of an organisation which is cascading this constellation of measures from senior managers steadily through the rest of the organisation. Indeed, in the case of British Rail and the NHS we have seen the further development of the movement of senior managers on to individualised contracts. One consequence in British Rail is that the union which represents managerial grades (the TSSA) has declared that it is, in effect, no longer engaged in the collective negotiation of terms and conditions.

Line managers

In the NHS the rise of the general managers following the Griffiths Report has been quite marked. Len Peach as the first chief executive of the NHS Management Board and Sir Roy Griffiths as a member of that Board have both emphasised the importance of clear and definite 'leadership' from managers in the new health service. Down through the organisation at regional, district and unit management levels, many have interpreted the central theme of change in the past four years to have been precisely this: to secure general management and line management control over an organisation which was previously built around a federal-like structure of loosely co-ordinated self-governing professions and semi-professions. Together, they reached some modicum of order via consensus-seeking. Under the new regime human resource management was to mean a more managerially directed utilisation of staff and other resources. First, clinical budgeting was tried and then 'resource management'. Line managers began to study their accountancy texts and began to regard their accountant as the key member of their management team.

The premier part played by line and general managers in human resource management is particularly evident in the market-trading parts of the public sector. Top management in Austin Rover (before it was sold to British Aerospace) and in British Rail made it clear that the direction for people management would be set not by industrial relations and personnel specialists but by the key operational managers. This found expression both in terms of devising and deriving the new forms of management and in the delivery at local level via, for example, team briefings. In the market-trading parts of the public sector just as in the private sector the emphasis has been placed on the concept of 'managerial leadership'.

A common element across the sectors has been the seizing of the initiative by line managers on the issue of how human resources should be utilised. In British Rail not only have they 'contracted' for a certain level of service for a certain price but they are also intruding into the details of precisely how the personnel specialist function goes about its business. It is perhaps not surprising therefore that traditional assumptions about how people management should be conducted are coming under radical reappraisal.

Constraining factors

While reappraisal and experimentation are proceeding apace, this does not necessarily translate into a systemic transformation. Here we examine some of the main factors which would seem to be constraining a more widespread adoption of human resource management in Britain – particularly in the public sector.

A major consideration arises out of the distinctive nature of management in the public sector. As Stewart and Ranson (1988: 17) have cogently argued:

> One reason why models drawn from other sectors distort the nature of management is that they assume the dilemmas (which characterise management in the public domain) do not exist or do not have the depth implied, because they do not do so in other sectors.

These dilemmas derive from the unbounded demands within the public domain; they derive also from the inherently political nature of the values and objectives which must inescapably govern the direction taken by public sector managers. Bureaucracy in public service is not easily discarded. While it undoubtedly impedes responsiveness of service, it none the less offers a way to achieve consistency, equity and impartiality of service – all of which rightly command high priority in public service organisations. Whether they are compatible with the full-blown human resource management approach is more questionable.

Another factor turns on the interplay between 'strategic human resource management' and the political nature of strategic objectives in the public sector. As noted earlier, a defining feature of human resource management is the idea that it takes its cue from the corporate plan. Now, it might be argued that public sector organisations such as local authorities also have their own corporate plans but, as Stewart and Ranson (1988: 17) argue, 'strategic planning' in the public domain is of a subtly different character from its private sector counterpart. While it is possible to devise human resource plans in, for example, a local authority, these will always be contingent not upon an accurate reading of the market but upon political programmes and the retention of power.

Hence, successful human resource management in the public sector requires not only top management support but also political support from elected politicians. The adversarial nature of the party political system puts the continuity of support into jeopardy. The massive reversal of Bradford Council's social strategy and its attendant human resource management approach is a case in point. In recent years the force of this point has, if anything, been strengthened by the 'politicisation' of local government administration – a feature recorded, for example, in the research for the Widdicombe Enquiry (Leach et al., 1986). And in their analysis of the role of performance indicators in central government, Flynn et al. (1988) show how the use of these in the public domain is inevitably shaped by political constraints.

Another brake on the widespread adoption of a fully-fledged human resource management approach in Britain arises from the comparatively poor education and training of managers. A range of recent reports (Mangham and Silver, 1986; Constable and McCormick, 1987; Mumford et al., 1987; Handy, 1987) have accumulated a substantial body of evidence which demonstrates that, in comparison with major advanced competitor countries, British managers are grossly under-trained – especially in management. In consequence, relatively few managers have had sufficient exposure to the formal processes of planning: to many, planning is associated, at best, with financial planning and budgeting. This is likely to be an obstacle in the private and public sector alike.

Although the private sector model has been influential – not least in its powerful impact on 'marketing' and 'customer care' – there are limits to the validity of this model in public sector organisations. While British Rail managers may (enthusiastically) attend 'aggressive marketing' seminars and while the concept of the 'customer' has suffused the NHS, recipients and employees of public service organisations are, in truth, enveloped in a much more complex web of relationships than simple customer– provider. A further problem is that decisions about human resource utilisation and levels of reward cannot be governed solely by market factors. The comparability principle has, at least for the time being, effectively been discarded. None the less, the problem it was designed to solve has not gone away.

The high level of unionisation in the public sector also needs to be taken into account. British trade unions have, in the main, failed to formulate a thought-through response to human resource management initiatives. One consequence has been that initiatives are often taken without union involvement of any kind; an associated factor is the inchoate character of the resulting package of employment policies. Restructuring has not been halted but it has been slowed. In the public sector with, for the foreseeable future, its continued high union density, the implied 'dualism' of an ongoing industrial relations system and a separate set of human resource policies and practices, all this suggests a problematical path for human resource management.

A final consideration which ought to counsel caution in the way in which techniques are 'borrowed' from the private sector derives from the diverse composition of the human resource in organisations such as the NHS. Clinical staff and para-medics maintain a professional orientation and frequently a deep-seated personal commitment to patient care. In addition, they have been used to a collegiate approach to problem analysis. In such a setting the unadapted paraphernalia of 'customer care' lapel badges, comic videos and the like have been known to strike a counterproductive chord among such staff.

This final point of caution carries a wider implication for the analysis presented here. The constraints upon a widespread adoption of human resource management in the public sector should not necessarily be seen as insurmountable barriers. Rather, they should be seen for what they are: indicators that principles and approaches, refined originally within large and exceptional private sector organisations, such as IBM, should not be expected to translate easily into organisations in very different settings. This being so, it is perhaps not surprising that the overall verdict on the state of play for human resource management in the public sector at the present time has to be one which declares: extensive discussion and diverse experimentation but as yet, with a somewhat limited impact upon staff attitudes and behaviour.

References

Audit Commission (1985) *Good Management in Local Government*. London: HMSO.

Batstone, E. (1984) *Working Order: Workplace Industrial Relations Over Two Decades*. Oxford: Blackwell.

Constable, J. and McCormick, R. (1987) *The Making of British Managers: A Report for the BIM and CBI into Management Training, Education and Development*. London: BIM.

Donovan (1968), Royal Commission on Trades Unions and Employers' Associations (1968) Report, Cmnd no 3623. London: HMSO.

Flynn, A. et al. (1988) 'Making indicators perform', *Public Money & Management*, Winter.

Goldsmith, W. and Clutterbuck, D. (1984) *The Winning Streak*. Harmondsworth: Penguin.

Guest, D. (1987) 'Human resource management and industrial relations', *Journal of Management Studies*, 24(5).

Guest, D. (1989) 'Human resource management: its implications for industrial relations and trade unions', in J. Storey (ed.), *New Perspectives on Human Resource Management*. London: Routledge.

Handy, C. (1987) *The Making of Managers: A Report on Management Education, Training and Development in the United States, West Germany, France, Japan and the UK*. London: NEDO.

Kochan, T.A., Katz, H.C. and McKersie, R.B. (1986) *The Transformation of American Industrial Relations*. New York: Basic Books.

Leach, S. et al. (1986) *The Political Organisation of Local Authorities*, Report of the Committee of Enquiry into the Conduct of Local Authority Business, Chairman: D. Widdicombe, Q.C., Cmnd no 9798. London: HMSO.

Legge, K. (1989) 'Human resource management: a critical analysis', in J. Storey (ed.), *New Perspectives on Human Resource Management*. London: Routledge.

MacInnes, J. (1987) *Thatcherism at Work*, Milton Keynes: Open University Press.

Mangham, I. and Silver, M.S. (1986) *Management Training: Context and Process*. London: ESRC.

Marginson, P., Sisson, K., Martin, R. and Edwards, P. (1988) *Beyond the Workplace*. Oxford: Blackwell.

Millward, N. and Stevens, M. (1986) *British Workplace Industrial Relations*. The DE/ESRC/ACAS Survey, Aldershot: Gower.

Mumford, A., Robinson, G. and Stradling, D. (1987) *Developing Directors: The Learning Processes*. Sheffield: MSC.

Peters, T.J. and Waterman, R.H. (1982) *In Search of Excellence: Lessons from America's Best Run Companies*. New York: Harper & Row.

Purcell, J. and Sisson, K. (1983) 'Strategies and practice in the management of industrial relations', in G. Bain (ed.), *Industrial Relations in Britain*. Oxford: Blackwell.

Stewart, J.D. (1973) *New Approaches to Management in Local Government*. London: Local Government Chronicle pamphlet.

Stewart, J. and Ranson, S. (1988) 'Management in the public domain', *Public Money & Management*, Spring/Summer.

Thurley, K. (1981) 'Personnel management in the UK: a case for urgent treatment?', *Personnel Management*, August: 24–30.

Wickens, P. (1987) *The Road to Nissan*. London: Macmillan.

5

The impact of corporate strategy on human resource management

John Purcell

The particular concern of this chapter is the impact of corporate strategy on the management of human resources. The focus is large multidivisional companies. It seems sensible to ask how the behaviour of these firms influences the management of people at work by the corporate strategies they adopt, and by the controls they exercise on the behaviour of business units and subsidiary companies. The corporate office in many enterprises has four major roles: the development and execution of corporate strategies, the monitoring of divisional and operating subsidiaries' performance, the allocation of internal capital, and the treasury function managing relations with the external capital and money markets. All four, to a greater or lesser extent, impact on the management of human resources as this chapter seeks to illustrate. In the first section consideration is given to the position of large enterprises in the British economy, indicating a concentration of economic power in excess of that found in many other industrialized nations.

A model of corporate strategy is developed in the second section derived from the well-known distinction between strategy and structure developed by Chandler (1962). Here three levels of strategy are identified. Decisions on long-run goals and the scope of activities constitute first-order strategy. These, in the normative model, directly affect and lead to decisions on the way the enterprise is structured to achieve its goals, what is termed second-order strategy. Both first-order and second-order strategy provide the critical context in which functional strategies are developed. Our concern is with those to do with human resource management, what are termed third-order strategies. The term strategy is used throughout to indicate that the focus is on those decisions which have a major and long-term effect on the behaviour of the firm (Hickson et al., 1986) as opposed to day-to-day operating decisions. The rest of the chapter attempts to trace the effect that first- and second-order strategies have on human resource management, especially in relation to subordinate, non-managerial employees.

Reprinted from John Storey (ed.) *New Perspectives on Human Resource Management*, pp. 67–91. (London and New York: Routledge, 1989).

Strategy

The distinctive feature of multi-divisionals is that their internal operating procedures are more refined and differentiated than those found in functional or holding companies. The decision to move to a multi-divisional structure from, say, a centralized functional firm or to adapt the configuration to emphasize local profit centres, is a strategic decision of substantial importance in its consequences for employee relations, as discussed later. The decision to reorganize might have been triggered by strategic decisions taken earlier, for example, to diversify. One useful way of distinguishing between types of strategic decisions is in terms of upstream and downstream. 'Upstream', first-order decisions are concerned with the long-term direction of the enterprise or the scope of its activities. Clearly these decisions will have implications for the type of people employed, the size of the firm and the technology required. If an upstream decision is made to acquire a going concern a second set of considerations apply concerning the extent to which the new firm is to be kept apart from or integrated with existing operations, and about the nature of the acquired firm's relationship with its new owner. These can be classified as more downstream, or second-order, strategic decisions. This is similar to Chandler's (1962) distinction between strategy and structure and his oft-quoted dictum that structure follows (i.e. is downstream from) strategy. The difference here is that decisions on strategy (the type of business undertaken now and in the future) and on structures (how the firm is organized to meet its goals) are both of strategic importance in that they have long-run implications for organizational behaviour, are taken in conditions of uncertainty and commit resources of people, time and money to their attainment.

It is in the context of downstream strategic decisions on organizational structure that choices on human resource structures and approaches come to be made. These are themselves strategic since they establish the basic parameters of employee relations management in the firm, but are likely to be deeply influenced by first and second decisions as well as by environmental factors of law, trade unions and external labour markets. These are termed here third-order strategic decisions. At its simplest therefore three levels of strategy are evident as seen in Figure 1. The concern of this chapter is primarily with first- and second-order strategies, not with strategies *within* human resource management (see Ahlstrand and Purcell, 1988) nor with the outcomes, nor the environmental forces which provide the context in which strategies are formulated and implanted. It will be appreciated, as the model implies, that the actual conduct of human resource management, let alone employee-relations behaviour, is influenced by an enormous variety of forces interacting in a complex and dynamic way. The purpose of the chapter is to draw attention to the impact of corporate strategies which, with a few exceptions (Thurley and Wood, 1983; Batstone et al., 1984) has been largely ignored.

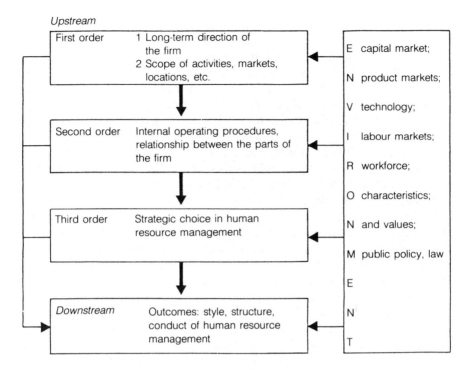

Figure 1 *Three levels of strategic decision making*

In theory in this idealized, normative model, strategy in human resource management is determined in the context of first-order, long-run decisions on the direction and scope of the firms' activities and purpose (location, technology, skill requirements, etc.) and second-order decisions on the structure of the firm seen in its internal operating procedures (levels of authority, control systems, profit centres, etc.). What actually happens in employee relations will be determined by decisions at all three levels and by the willingness and ability of local management to do what is intended in the context of specific environment conditions and forces.

One principal objection needs to be raised on the nature of the model. Like many such models it implies rationality in the process of decision making: a carefully planned series of decisions where human resource management is designed to mesh with organizational structures which in turn derives from first-order strategies. But strategic decisions are characterized by the need to cope with uncertainty, to integrate management activity in various fields, and are concerned with change. A political process model to strategic decisions is more appropriate. 'Strategic decisions,' writes Johnson, 'are characterized by the political hurly-burly of organizational life with a high incidence of bargaining, a trading off of costs and benefits of one interest group against another, all within a notable lack of clarity in terms of environmental influences and objectives'

(1987: 21). The process is especially complicated in the area of human resource management. Since it is difficult to determine the ends (what is the purpose of human resource management?) and the means to achieve these uncertain ends, it is also difficult to measure whether the firm is successful in its personnel or human resources policies.

One of the problems with the rational, normative model of strategy formulation as described and prescribed by many books on corporate strategy is that it tends to de-personalize and reduce analysis to a common currency of figures and hard data of markets, shares, discounted cash flows and rates of return. Questions of values or purpose beyond the 'bottom line' are acutely uncomfortable to strategic decision makers. In the rational model, phenomena which cannot be reduced to figures such as 'motivation', 'good industrial relations' or 'good employment standards' are easily discounted or ignored. If it were possible to prove that 'enlightened or progressive' approaches to the management of people at work were invariably associated with higher productivity, lower unit cost and improved profit, and that exploitative, coercive systems failed, life for the social science researcher and human resource executive would be easier. As it is, little can be conclusively proved because of the complexity of variables and the impossibility of monitoring and measuring all the relevant dynamics and relations. If some 'proof' is obtained over a short period of time in specific circumstances, it is often found to be impossible to replicate. This ambiguity in human resource management, and the relative weakness of the function in the corporate corridors of power (Hegarty and Hoffman, 1987), often leads to a situation where decisions on first- and second-order strategy are taken without consideration of their effects on the conduct of human resource management. Third-order strategy concerned with the management of people is increasingly required to fit the strategies and structures of the firm especially as countervailing requirements in the environment (trade union power, industrial democracy proposals, income policy and labour law) appear to have receded in the 1980s. It is more difficult to argue 'we can't do that because . . .' than it was a decade ago.

We need now to consider how trends in first-order and second-order strategy, especially towards diversification and decentralization, affect the management of human resources. Our concern is first to trace the logical consequences which flow from first-order strategies on the scope of the enterprise activities for employee relations. This will entail an examination of portfolio planning techniques. Next, within the multi-divisional form the critical question is second-order strategy concerning the relationship between parts of the business and the management of interrelationships. This will take us into a discussion of different types of multi-divisional companies seen in terms of integration or separation of divisions and centralization or decentralization within divisions. We will also consider the evidence for profitability and effectiveness and the link with employee relations. Thirdly, there is a need to consider the relationship between the corporate office and business units. How are different styles and approaches likely to impact on human resource management?

First-order strategy: portfolio planning

There is a growing tendency for large companies to be diversified. One of the critical issues facing the corporate office, especially the chief executive officer (CEO) is the allocation of capital to the various parts of the business and the identification of growth areas within the portfolio and outside for possible acquisition. This involves the use of portfolio planning developed as a means of identifying the attractiveness of various parts of the portfolio of businesses as an aid to capital allocation and determining the appropriate mix of businesses held by the enterprise. It is based on two prime premises. First, there is an experience curve: 'average costs will decline as the accumulated experience associated with selling, producing, engineering and financing [a] product increases' (Hamermesh, 1986: 10). Among the most common reasons for this proven relationship are:

> economies of scale (or scope) in manufacturing, marketing, engineering, and financing; labour efficiencies; product standardisation and process improvements. The strategic implications . . . are that the company with the most accumulated experience can have the lower costs and therefore a company should invest rapidly and early to accumulate experience. (ibid.)

The experience curve is associated with market share. In theory the company with the highest market share will have the greatest accumulated experience and the lowest cost and therefore generate the most profit. Secondly, market growth is not constant. Eventually – and the time scale can vary enormously – most markets for a given product reach a mature state of slow growth and may then decline. Firms with a dominant share of a mature market are likely to wish to diversify by switching cash from the mature business into new markets with growth potential and gain early experience to build market share and invest heavily to keep it. Portfolio planning is defined by Hamermesh as 'those analytic techniques that aid in the classification of a firm's businesses for resource allocation purposes and for selecting a competitive strategy on the basis of the growth potential of each business and of the financial resources that will be either consumed or produced by the business' (ibid.). It was estimated in 1982 that half of the Fortune 500 companies in the USA use some form of portfolio planning (Haspeslagh, 1982). Goold and Campbell (1987) in their study of sixteen major British diversified companies showed that while the formal statistical use of the techniques was not widespread, the thinking behind portfolio planning was often employed.

The most well known system is that developed by the Boston Consulting Group (1970; Hedley, 1977) if only because of its mnemonic qualities: cash cow, star, dog, and wild cat (or question mark) as shown in Figure 2. The purpose of the model is to help the strategic planners

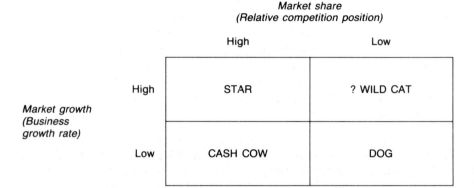

Figure 2 *Portfolio planning growth-share matrix*

classify the various business units in the portfolio in terms of their potential for cash generation or cash usage. High market-share businesses, assuming the experience curve, will have lower costs than their competitors with smaller shares and should be able to generate more profit. Market growth indicates the likely demands for investment. When there is high growth there will be substantial demands for investment in terms of new plant, equipment and technical innovation. Low-growth markets require less investment. The model combines the two axes and leads to generalization about corporate and business strategy.

Stars (high-share, high-growth) are in an advantageous position. While they require high levels of investment their dominant position in the market often allows them to produce sufficient profits to finance further growth.

Cash cows (high-share, low-growth) produce large profits and positive cash flows. They require modest amounts of capital to maintain their market share, renew equipment and to keep in step with technological change. The cash surplus is used to finance the stars where necessary and particularly to help develop new business ventures in growth markets, the wild cat or question-mark businesses.

Wild cat, question mark (low-share, high-growth) businesses compete in rapidly growing markets with the aim of moving up the experience curve ahead of the competition. Market growth in new markets is difficult to predict and the gaining of experience and efficiency in situations of uncertainty can be difficult. These businesses are therefore uncertain and require substantial investment in excess of their own profitability.

Dogs (low-share, low-growth) do not produce much profit and are not worth investing in. Two options exist: either divest the business or act to pare costs down to the minimum to squeeze out the surplus value.

A slightly more sophisticated version of the portfolio-planning model is the nine-box matrix originally developed in the General Electric Company in the USA. Industry attractiveness includes market growth by covering other factors such as industry profitability and market potential and size. Market share is included as one of the factors in business-unit position but this will include an assessment of the unit's technological base, actual profitability, and size (for more detail see Hax and Majluf, 1983). In both models

> the purpose of the strategic mandates is to create a pattern of capital spending whereby a business receives funding early in its life so that it achieves a strong [i.e. profitable] competitive position. Then, as its market matures the business will produce the cash flow that will find other, more rapidly growing businesses . . . [and] facilitate the creation of a portfolio of businesses in which the sources and uses of funds are nearly balanced. (Hamermesh, 1986: 16)

It is not our concern to debate the strengths and weaknesses of portfolio planning for strategic management (see Hamermesh, 1986 for a useful analysis and more recently Porter, 1987). The question of concern here is the implications that flow from it in terms of second-order strategies and third-order human resource matters. At a general level the most important implication is that the enterprise is seen not as a unified business but a collection of businesses. Portfolio planning says nothing about the long-term aims or purposes of the firm and by its analytical methods finds no place for history, tradition or cultures. Firms excessively committed to portfolio planning tend to ignore or find difficulty with that aspect of corporate strategy which determines 'the kind of economic and human organization it is or intends to be, and the nature of the economic and non-economic contribution it intends to make to its shareholders, employees, customers, and communities' (Andrews, 1980: 18). Hamermesh refers to this as 'institutional strategy', others use terms such as goals, values, missions. In employee relations we refer to it as 'management style', being the preferred way of managing employees: see, for example, in corporate philosophy statements Purcell (1987). Portfolio planning tends to drive out, or at least drive down, questions of style and non-economic issues *and* positively encourages different approaches to employee relations in different segments of the business (Schuler and Jackson, 1987).

This comes about in two ways. First, the identification of business units as the prime unit of analysis (sometimes referred to as strategic business units or SBUs for short) is a critical feature in the creation of the multi-divisional company. Business-unit managers are given responsibility for the determination of their success within the confines of the strategic mandate. Corporate office rules and regulations which limit unit managers' freedom of action come to be resented, are seen as an unnecessary overhead cost and are often too general to be applied in detail in each unit. Thus, what may be termed the *administrative control system* of head

office rules and regulations, symbolized in human resource management
by the personnel manual, tends to be out of place, resented or ignored by
profit-responsible unit managers facing different circumstances. If
centralized rules cannot be applied and if, in their place, there is no
guiding logic or set of standards on appropriate employee-relations
management, then the requirements of the financial targets set by
corporate headquarters will dominate unit management behaviour. This
performance control system (Mintzberg, 1979) establishes, through annual
budgeting and monthly reporting (often reinforced by incentive pay and
stock options for unit managers), appropriate financial targets for the unit
within an agreed mandate for capital expenditure. How the unit manager
achieves this is up to him or her. We will look at the effect of different
types of performance-control systems later. Here we note the implication
of separating the enterprise into quasi-independent units and a tendency
for central standards on non-economic conduct to be weakened or abandoned altogether.

There is nothing inherently wrong in separation and decentralization
and there are many advantages to be gained from avoiding over-
centralized, bureaucratic systems, allowing unit managers to design their
own employee-relations strategies for their circumstances. There are two
difficulties, however. First, the implication is that inter-unit comparisons
drawn by trade unions and employees themselves are to be avoided or
minimized and employee involvement in strategic affairs through
corporate consultative committees and collective bargaining, employee
trustees in pension funds, and worker director schemes are out of place.
If the logic of portfolio planning is a separation of business units (second-
order strategy) then employee relations similarly needs to be separated and
decentralized. Employees and the unions which represent them must,
from a management point of view, adopt a unit perspective and be
concerned with the parochial needs of the unit, not the strategic thrust of
the enterprise.

The need for boundary maintenance becomes critical if the enterprise
seeks to implement the logical consequences of portfolio planning for its
human resource strategies. This is not simply because unit managers are
given responsibility for profit generation and business strategies in their
unit but because the types of employee-relations needs are likely to differ
substantially between different segments of the matrix. This is hardly ever
discussed in the analysis of portfolio-planning methods. One small exception came from Arthur D. Little, the major American consulting firm, in
their development of the concept of strategy centres. They suggest that the
wild cat requires an 'entrepreneur' with a free-form or task-force structure
and an informal or tailor-made communication system. Stars need a
sophisticated manager, managing a semi-permanent task force or product
divisional structure with more formal, tailor-made communication
systems. Cash cows place emphasis on administration within a business
divisional structure and with a formal or uniform communication system.

The dog has a manager who is an 'opportunist milker' in a pared-down division. The communication system is 'little or none . . . [a] command system' (Brown and O'Connor, 1974: 21). Brown and O'Connor in their review of corporate planning are even more explicit, suggesting that 'Dog businesses should be run by tough, hard-bitten individuals who are prepared to liquidate people and facilities' (ibid.: 16).[1]

Clearly the type of human resource management will vary considerably. This variety is likely to be greater if, as is probable, the size of the business units varies according to the product market life cycle and the unit's share of the market. Cash cows are likely to be large stable units; wild cats small and experimental; stars medium to large and growing; dogs medium-sized and declining.

It is likely that *wild cat business* units will wish to avoid most of the rigidities associated with larger, stable firms. What is required is a flexible operation with employees willing and able to work in a variety of areas and with broad skills. Overhead costs associated with personnel departments, formal job-grading schemes and work study are expensive for small units in growing markets when change is likely to be both continuous and unpredictable (for a further exploration of these issues in high-technology firms see Kochan and Chalykoff, 1987).

Star businesses face the problem of managing larger and growing units. It is likely that there will be a growth in occupational differentiation with skilled, semi-skilled, clerical, technical and professional staff, because of the adoption in some businesses of sophisticated, technically advanced dedicated technology. At the same time the high rates of investment and technical change require continued flexibility and co-operation in the management of change. As demand grows the need for continuous operations is likely to develop in order both to meet market need and to utilize capital equipment as effectively as possible. The free-form structure of the wild cat is likely to be replaced with more formal structured systems with the growth of sophisticated human resource managemcnt designed by professional staff but implemented and managed by the line managers. If there is strategic thinking in human resource management these units are likely to wish to develop employee-relations policies based on high individualism paying above market rates to recruit and retain the best labour, careful selection and recruitment systems to ensure high quality and skill potential, emphasis on internal training schemes to develop potential for further growth, a payment system designed to reward individual performance and co-operation, performance and appraisal reviews, and strong emphasis on team work and communications. At the same time, as in many greenfield sites, careful consideration will be given to questions of unionization and it is here in new plants (implying heavy capital investment typical of stars) that we might find single-union deals, pendulum arbitration, and new forms of employee representation. In short, technical and capital investment is matched by human resource investments, at times reaching near the ideals of human resource management. The assumption is that the future is good for star businesses provided the market continues to grow and their share of it continues to be high.

Market maturity and the management of *cash cows* brings a need for order, stability and predictability: in short, structured systems of collective bargaining, job evaluation, work study, and the adoption of the modern sophisticated method of managing a highly unionized workforce. The need is to ensure continuing high rates of return on investment sufficient to meet the corporate need for profit generation for use elsewhere in the enterprise. Depending on the tightness of the performance-control system and the profit requirements of head office, cash cows can, however, sometimes slip into forms of indulgency patterns (Gouldner, 1954) or management slack in discretionary behaviour (Williamson, 1975). Here there is tolerance of over-manning, restrictive practices and general inefficiency since the unit is profitable; there is little pressure for change and the costs associated with removing these customs and practices might be deemed too high. Given the size of the unit and the fact that it has been in business for a number of years or decades it is also likely that various overhead costs linked to employee relations will exist such as sports and social clubs, subsidized canteens, employee discount shops, and various welfare services. We might expect to find elements of paternalism. Other costs might well be seen in office facilities and time-off arrangements for shop stewards, especially full-time shop stewards and conveners and a sizeable personnel department. These are affordable because of high profits, are likely to have grown up over a period, and are justified on the grounds of their contribution to labour peace and harmonious labour relations. The requirement is for management to maintain the cash cow, not to be innovative and entrepreneurial, or pare costs down to such an extent that there is a hostile reaction while earning high profits. At the same time, given market maturity, profit improvements are less likely to come from marketing and sales expenditure than from improved efficiency and resource usage, especially labour productivity (McMillan et al., 1982).

Clearly such business units are vulnerable to market changes and they may slip into a *dog mode*. Either they lose market share because of better performance by competitors, perhaps triggered by entry into the market by overseas companies or technical or product innovations developed elsewhere – for example Japanese competition – or they are caught by a general decline and instability in the market as in the recession of the early 1980s. While:

> occasionally it is possible to restore a dog to viability by a creative business segmentation strategy, rationalizing and specializing into a small niche . . . (usually) the only prospect for obtaining a return from a dog is to manage it for cash, cutting off all investment in the business. (Hedley, 1977: 11–12)[2]

In short, action is required to 'harvest' as it is euphemistically called in the nine-box matrix, through a management acting as an 'opportunist milker', the term used by Arthur D. Little. Since there is little prospect of increasing market share, attention is turned to the business unit itself to cut costs in order to improve margins. This might require the use of a 'command system' of communications (another Arthur D. Little term) where vigorous efforts are made to improve productivity, not through investment but by work intensification, reduction of 'surplus' labour, cutting overhead costs like welfare benefits and concession bargaining. 'Turnaround management' can emphasize employee involvement as a means of achieving productivity improvements without investment. The alternative is to sell or liquidate the business (and a hostile reaction by the workforce to cost-cutting measures is likely to accelerate the closure). This may in any case be the obvious course of action even if profitability and productivity improve since a better price can be obtained for a going concern and rationalization costs such as redundancy payments can be offset against profit on corporation tax. The most important consideration is to ensure that there is no form of cross-subsidy to the dog from the cash cow either in investment, corporate subsidy in loss making, or in 'artificially' supported rates of pay. It may well be appropriate to allow earnings to rise in the star and cash cows but dogs need to be treated as an independent, stand-alone unit where pay movements are linked to ability to pay, and ability to pay is a function of cost reduction not price improvement. This separation of units is one way to reduce the size of the exit barrier (Harrigan, 1980). It has also been noted that 'a sense of obligation to workers in plants which would be closed by liquidation of a dog business may also seem as a barrier to exit' (Christiansen et al., 1982).

In sum, different businesses in the portfolio require different types of employee relations and must thus be treated as separate units. This differentiation and the emphasis on market share tends to drive out corporate institutional strategies concerned with non-economic matters such as values, standards and social responsibility. The management of human resources thus becomes an operational responsibility and brings with it the need to weaken or inhibit cross-unit comparisons and trade-union interest in strategic management, while developing local, unit-based loyalties.

Second-order strategy: internal operating procedures

The implication of portfolio planning was seen first in the need to develop a variety of businesses in different segments of the product-market life-cycles and secondly to manage these differently according to market need and position. This has considerable influence on second-order strategies concerning the structuring of the enterprise, in the preference for performance-control systems and difficulty in imposing administrative controls and institutional strategy. One of the difficulties associated with product-portfolio systems is the definition of the business unit. What exactly is the market the unit is designed to serve? The term multi-divisional company portrays an image of relatively large organizational structures designed to trade in general markets. Hill and Pickering noted in their study of 144 British companies that while most had opted for the divisional form the tendency was for the number of divisions to be relatively small. Each division was likely to have a number of operating subsidiaries (on average 10.4 per division). It was therefore by 'no means valid to assume that there is a direct one-to-one relationship between a division, one distinct business and one end market' (1986: 31). They go on to note that 'as companies have become more diverse, rather than increasing the number of divisions they have increased the number of activities within each division' (ibid.: 33). It could be argued that the existence of large, complex divisional structures inhibits the full logic of portfolio planning since in each division there is likely to be a variety of businesses within the various segments of the portfolio grid.

A further difficulty is that these large divisions were liable, by their very size, to exert political and economic power at the corporate level. They 'had become so powerful that they restricted the power of head office, limiting its ability to impose strict financial discipline' (ibid.: 35–6). Thus, the critical advantages of portfolio planning specifically, and multi-divisional companies generally, were not being fully realized either in the structuring of business units or in the separation of strategic management (especially capital allocation and financial control) at head office from operational management at unit level. A growing response noted by Hill and Pickering to these difficulties has been a further twist in the internal operating procedures to decentralize and reduce the power of the divisional tier:

> Several companies had moved away from a structure where the divisional tier mattered as a management unit . . . towards one where [it] only had a minor role. This downgrading of the divisional tier was accompanied by a further decentralisation of short-run decision making power to subsidiaries within divisions . . . while long-term strategic functions and financial control functions were centralised at head office. (ibid.)

Hill and Pickering asked their corporate office respondents to indicate, across a range of decisions, which level in the enterprise had responsibility for decision making. At head-office level a reasonably clear picture emerged with responsibilities for legal functions, relations with financial institutions, long-term planning, investment decisions and acquisitions largely placed in the corporate office. Head offices often were involved in, but shared the responsibility with lower levels, decisions on financial control, public relations, management development, and personnel. They were rarely involved in marketing, production, buying or industrial-relations matters.

The responsibilities of operating subsidiaries was the reverse of head offices with prime responsibility for marketing, production, buying and industrial relations, and a shared responsibility for personnel and management development, financial control, public relations and investment. Divisional offices were in a curious position:

> No decision taking area was identified where, overall, it could be said the divisional head office had the main responsibility . . . . This does perhaps raise questions about the appropriate role of divisional head offices . . . and whether the issue in organisational design is not so much about divisionalisation as about decentralisation. (ibid.: 39)

The authors go on to note that there is a tendency for divisional head offices to be over-involved in the operating affairs of subsidiary companies and that this is associated with slow decision making, intra-organizational conflict and a lack of accountability and control.

The implication of Hill and Pickering's study is first that decentralization not divisionalization is the key attribute of diversified firms with a clear separation of strategic from operational responsibilities. Secondly, strong divisional offices appear to increase complexity and rigidity both upward through interference with strategy and downward through involvement in operating subsidiary affairs. Thirdly, and of particular interest here, industrial relations and to a lesser extent personnel is defined in most multi-divisional companies as an operational responsibility. This takes on particular significance in looking at the effect of these factors on profits measured by rate of return on sales:

> Companies which allowed a stronger head office involvement in operating decisions tended to be less profitable. Similarly companies that involved their divisional head office in operating decisions also tended to be less profitable. These findings suggest that for optimum performance, operating functions should be decentralised down to the level of the operating subsidiaries. This view received support from the evidence of a positive relation between the responsibility of operating subsidiaries and profit in the case of buying, industrial relations and personnel decisions but, surprisingly, not in the case of production and marketing where no statistically significant relation was found but the sign of the coefficient in each case was positive as expected. (Hill and Pickering, 1986: 47)

The data reported here related to the years 1978–80. Since then a number of enterprises have reorganized to remove or significantly weaken the divisional tier, for example, Tube Investments and GKN (Marginson et al., 1988) and restructured into smaller business units and operating subsidiaries. Some centralized firms have moved to create divisional structures and business units like BAA and British Telecom. At the same time there is evidence of further decentralization in collective bargaining to the local level, the break-up of corporate-wide job evaluation systems and a reduction in the size and role of corporate personnel departments. If further testing shows Hill and Pickering's findings to be largely correct (some caveats must be noted such as a response rate of only 28.8 per cent from the sample of *The Times* 500 companies) then it is likely not only that large firms will seek to create a multi-divisional structure but that further reorganization and restructuring will proceed to push for decentralization. This change in second-order strategies and the link between decentralized employee relations and profitability has profound implications for third-order human resource strategies in large firms.

Diversities in second-order strategies

Thus far we have assumed that multi-divisional firms will be generally similar in their behaviour and approach. Two further issues need to be addressed, indicating variety and choice. The first of these relates to the approach taken by the corporate office in managing business units, what is termed by Goold and Campbell (1987) as strategy and style. The second looks more closely at the relationship between business units. The assumption of portfolio planning is that units can be managed as though they are unrelated to each other except in an ownership sense. We saw earlier that the growth of the multi-divisional firm has been particularly marked in related areas of business and this has been argued by Porter (1987) as a more appropriate growth strategy than a collection of unrelated businesses managed in the portfolio method. Once units are related and are to a greater or lesser extent dependent on each other for the provision of goods and services (i.e. vertically integrated) then the pure logic of portfolio planning is harder to implement and may well be inappropriate. This in turn will have implications for third-order employee relations strategies.

Corporate office control

The question asked by Goold and Campbell in their study of sixteen British-owned diversified companies was: how does the corporate office manage its relationship with business units to ensure that value is added to the unit's performance? In their research model they identified two critical features of this process. The first is the extent to which the corporate office had *planning influence*. This 'concerns the centre's efforts to shape strategies as they emerge and before decisions are taken . . . . It is through planning influence that the centre seeks to improve the quality of thinking that surrounds major decisions' (1987: 36). The second was the *control influence* which 'concerns the way in which the centre reacts to results achieved . . . . Control influence arises from the targets that the centre agrees with its business units, the way the centre reacts to poor performance, and the frequency with which the centre monitors results' (ibid.). Three types of control influence were identified: flexible strategic control; tight strategic control and tight financial control. The critical differences are the amount of attention given to annual budget targets and monthly monitoring of results – i.e. the strength of the performance control system and the extent to which there are penalties for failure and rewards for success in target attainment.

These two dimensions are combined to produce three main categories which the authors summarize (ibid.: 10) as follows:

Strategic planning companies push for maximum competitive advantage in the businesses in their portfolio. They seek to build their portfolios around a small number of 'core' businesses, often with co-ordinated global strategies. The style leads to a wide search for the best strategy options, and tenacious pursuit of ambitious long-term goals. But decisions tend to be slower, reaction to poor performance is less decisive and there is less ownership of strategy at the business-unit level. Financial performance is typically strong with fast organic growth, but, from time to time, setbacks are encountered. Companies with this style were BOC, BP, Cadbury Schweppes, Lex, STC and UB.

Financial control companies focus more on financial performance than competitive position. They expand their portfolios more through acquisitions than through growing market share. The style provides clear success criteria, timely reaction to events, and strong motivation at the business level resulting in strong profit performance. But it can cause risk aversion, reduce concern for underlying competitive advantage, and limit investment where the payoff is long term. Although financial performance in these companies has been excellent, with rapid share price growth, there has been less long-term organic business building. Companies with this style were BTR, Ferranti, Hanson Trust and Tarmac.

Strategic control companies balance competitive and financial ambitions. They support growth in strategically sound and profitable businesses, but rationalize their portfolios by closing down or divesting other businesses. The style focuses on the quality of thinking about strategy, permits businesses to adopt long-term strategies, and fuels the motivation of business-unit managers. But there is a danger that planning processes can become superficial and bureaucratic, and that ambiguous objectives can cause confusion, risk aversion and 'political' manoeuvring. Strategic control companies have achieved profitability improvement and share price recovery, but have seen less growth and fewer major initiatives. Companies with this style were Courtaulds, ICI, Imperial, Plessy and Vickers.

The importance of strategy and style was vividly illustrated in the winter of 1986–7 in the hostile bid by BTR (a financial control company) for Pilkington (a strategic planning company). Pilkington is the world's leading glass-maker, which invented float glass in the 1950s and continues to invest heavily in R&D, developing global strategies, and making investments for strategic reasons even if the rate of return might be uncertain: a strategic planning approach. Interestingly the trade unions, and the St Helens community, the home town of Pilkington in north-west England, were active in defence of Pilkington and eventually, after the share price rose substantially, BTR withdrew their bid. What the unions and community feared was that if BTR were successful it would impose its particular management philosophy on Pilkington, which would involve reducing costs[3] and pushing up margins for the benefit of the shareholder (BTR out-performed all but two of the quoted UK companies in terms of return to shareholders in the period 1974–86) but at the expense of jobs, community involvement and long-term development.[4]

The critical question is not whether the firm is profit-maximizing but over what period profits are expected or required to be achieved and, more contentiously, who gains from the profits. Much of the literature on corporate strategy assumes that the only purpose is to service the needs of the shareholder. Other stakeholders – employees, communities, dependent suppliers, and customers – are irrelevant. Not all companies take this view. In particular the strategic planners with long-term aims and objectives are the firms most likely to have a defined sense of purpose. In Hamermesh's terms these are the firms most likely to have an institutional strategy which includes non-economic values and benefits. This is not to imply that they are soft companies or poorly managed, unable to take firm action when necessary, but their approach to unit management is likely to be more benign and their capacity to design and inculcate a management style or corporate culture greater than other companies. Guest has suggested that only strategic planning companies have the capacity and commitment to develop human resource management (1987: 518).

Goold and Campbell, like so many authors in corporate strategy, say virtually nothing about human resource management, assuming it to be an operational responsibility of unit managers. But the way these managers are themselves managed and motivated and the freedom they have within financial targets is likely to influence their approach to employees and the extent to which they can invest in human resource programmes. The authors provide some fascinating insights here aided by quotes from their respondents. The two extremes, strategic planning and financial control, are contrasted.

Strategic planning companies

The centre acts as a sort of buffer to the capital market, protecting the business units from the need to satisfy the short-term performance criteria applied by the outside investor. This allows business managers to concentrate on building their business rather than trimming their sales with a view to making half year earnings targets. . . . But lacking both market disciplines and clear internal targets . . . can mean that flexibility becomes tolerance and tolerance becomes looseness. (1987: 198–9)

Although there are ultimate sanctions for non-performers, we did not get the impression . . . that managers who failed to hit their targets were in any imminent danger of serious reprisals. (p. 68)

One of the features of these companies is their willingness to support subsidiaries that produce poor performance over long periods. (p. 160)

Quoting Sir Hector Laing, CEO of United Biscuits, 'if things are going wrong you identify with management and help them out. At these times control should get more friendly not more fierce.' (p. 68)

UB does not reward it managers with performance bonuses. Bonuses of that sort would jar with UB's culture which values family feeling and working for

UB above individual effort. (p. 68)

Financial control companies

There is no attempt to buffer the businesses from the requirements for short-term profits . . . by exposing all individual investments to this test, it goes much further than the capital market in applying tough standards. (p. 207)

These companies have no formal planning systems, are concerned mainly with the financial results, control only against annual targets and apply strict short-term (2–4 year) pay-back criteria to investment decisions. (p. 111)

They are willing to act speedily to exit from the businesses that are not performing or do not fit [p. 126] . . . [and] are quicker to replace managers fiercer in applying pressure through the monitoring process and more effective in recognising and acclaiming good performance [p. 132] . . . . Taken to extremes the style can encourage managers to milk their businesses by cutting back too far on investments [p. 202] . . . [and the centre] has no wholly satisfactory means of ensuring this does not happen [p. 138] . . . . The style can cause risk aversion, reduce concern for underlying competitive advantage and limit investment where the payoff is long-term. (p. 10)

In GEC 'we peer at the business through numbers' [p. 118] . . . . In any one year there are 20 managers who leave the budget review shaking in their shoes [p. 132] . . . . We asked Malcolm Bates of GEC how many years a manager could fail to meet his budget before expecting to lose his job. His response was telling and only partly tongue in cheek: 'How many years? You mean how many months. He might last for six months or he might not.' (p. 129)

A quote from Tarmac: 'A division chief executive can only revise his budget downwards if he goes through some personal trauma. We can't stand the confessional . . . if they don't deliver they should feel very bad. They should feel that they have failed themselves and that life is awful. On the other hand if they succeed they will feel like winners. They will be basking. And they are rewarded.' (p. 131)

The authors go on to claim that financial-control companies 'generate high levels of motivation and satisfaction in their management' (p. 136) but offer no evidence for this. At the heart of this is a fundamental clash of values between long-term integrated 'family feeling' management teams and aggressive, short-run financially motivated managers (as in 'If you succeed, you are rewarded. If you don't you are out', p. 132). Presumably 'those who are out' or 'leave a review meeting shaking in their shoes' do not feel highly motivated – or rather they feel the motivation of fear. In many ways financial-control companies adopt the logic of portfolio planning in that interdependencies between businesses are ignored and each business unit is given substantial independence within the confines of tight financial control. But the management style adopted within the unit is likely to be analogous to that found in the dog companies where cost cutting is emphasized, margins are pushed up and investment avoided unless there are clear pay-backs over short periods.

It is understandable that in periods of financial stringency and market

instability pressure is placed on firms to improve performance by decen-
tralizing to business units, applying demanding performance standards
and closing down loss-making units. In effect, emphasis is placed more on
control and less on planning (Hill and Hoskisson, 1987). This, in turn,
encourages further decentralization especially in terms of the administrative control system. Strategic shifts towards performance control are
associated with structural shifts in internal operating procedures towards
further decentralization, leading to similar trends in human resource
management strategies. But tight financial control systems and short-term
investment pay-back requirements also tend to drive out long-term
employee-relations investment at the unit level and destroy the basis of
human resource management as part of corporate strategy.

Financial-control companies, even when they gain abundant cash, do
not appear to move back to the strategic planning style (ibid.: 235) and
once a financial-control style is in place it is applied to all units irrespective of their market position and is unlikely to change until forced to by
the shareholders. However, the capital markets approve strongly of financial control companies, for good reason. They:

> produce the best all round financial performance. They substantially out-
> perform the industrial average. They have high profitability ratios and growth
> rates (achieved by acquisitions). Their main weakness is in organic growth,
> where fixed asset growth (4 per cent per year) has been less than inflation and
> less than half that of strategic planning companies (10 per cent per year). (ibid.:
> 161)

In short, financial-control companies produce excellent results for the
shareholder, but few jobs are created and many disposed of through
rationalization and restructuring. In contrast, strategic-planning
companies with strong sales growth have created more jobs and, by their
willingness to support subsidiaries with poor results over long periods,
have disposed of fewer jobs in the recession than might otherwise have
been the case. The returns to the shareholder, however, have been less
good since 'strategic planning companies have the lowest stock growth
. . . and earnings per share growth have been less satisfactory' (ibid.:
160). It is this that makes such firms more liable than others to hostile
bids and acquisition battles like Pilkington with BTR.

Financial-control companies and increasingly pure finance companies
and merchant banks like Merril Lynch and Morgan Stanley find it easy
to raise the equity to engage in leverage buy-outs even after the stock
market crash in the autumn of 1987. According to *Fortune* magazine
these financial buyers:

> have moved into control of corporations because they see opportunities for
> restructuring, cost cutting, divesting – and for squeezing out record cash flows.
> Growth isn't on their minds and neither are capital expenditures . . . . Because
> the financiers are obsessed with reducing debt and getting their money out, they
> are expert in thinking about *today* . . . but . . . the financiers seldom care much

about the company as an institution (and are poor) at encouraging innovation and preserving 'core skills' .... Most financiers insist that the efficiency they're injecting into these companies is a social good. They are generally frank to admit, however, that social utility is not why they got into this business. Money is. (*Fortune*, 1988: 16–32)

Before we leave strategic styles it is worth noting that international comparisons provided by Goold and Campbell indicate that institutional strategy is not inevitably driven out. They argue that the Japanese giant enterprise, Matsushita, is in most respects a financial-control company but:

finance, personnel and training are all fully centralised .... Personnel and training exist to create 'harmony' .... In other words the central role of these two functions is to help build and maintain the Matsushita culture .... [In this enterprise] people are seen as *the* critical resource. (ibid.: 283, emphasis in the original)

Looking at all the overseas companies they cite (IBM, Hewlett-Packard, GE, and Matsushita) they conclude, in analysing their success, that

perhaps most importantly, there are a series of things concerned with corporate objectives and culture that seem to matter. Agreement on basic directions for the long-term development of the business, and on how to treat people within the firm, are perhaps the most essential common features of these companies. (ibid.: 281)

This is a critical part of first-order strategy but, for reasons they do not analyse, is not widespread in Britain or the USA. Here, stock-market emphasis on short-term financial results makes the adoption of non-economic values as part of corporate strategy less likely. In such circumstances professional human resource management comes under increasing pressure.

It is important to note that the well-known examples of sophisticated human resource management embedded in corporate strategy (IBM, Hewlett-Packard, Marks and Spencer) are exceptions which prove the rule. In these companies the values and approach of the founders of the company are much in evidence (as is the case in Matsushita) and they tend not to have deviated much from their core businesses. By 'sticking to the knitting' (Peters and Waterman, 1982) and growing organically they have been able to maintain and articulate core values as part of their strategy. This raises the critical question of the distinction between diversified and undiversified, or critical function firms.

Related businesses, vertical integration, and diversification

One factor which makes it more likely that a strategic planning style exists and that corporate value statements have meaning is the relatedness and extent of vertical integration and interdependence of business units. Hill and Hoskisson (1987) distinguish between financial, synergistic, and vertical economies in the way multi-divisional firms are structured. Financial economies are found when the superior allocative properties of the internal capital market are maximized by choice of style and strategy. These enterprises are likely to diversify into unrelated or loosely related activities and take on the attributes of financial-control, and to a degree strategic-control, companies. They are likely, out of choice, to ignore the interdependencies which happen to exist between parts of the enterprise (Goold and Campbell, 1987: 118). For example subsidiaries are not required to trade with other parts of the enterprise, or to offer preferential terms.

Synergistic economies exist where common techniques, skills or market knowledge are utilized across a range of products. These companies are capable of organizing around a core activity or critical business and are usually concerned that acquisitions match and enhance their business mission and core philosophies. Vertical integration is where a closely co-ordinated and integrated chain of activities from raw material sourcing to final distribution allow for vertical economies to be realized. Banking and multiple retailing companies exhibit some of these properties. Computer companies like IBM and Hewlett-Packard are also organized around base skills and integration mechanisms. Such companies can emphasize administrative co-ordination. They can be decentralized in the sense of giving substantial responsibility to unit managers for the implementation of strategies and policy and for profits but in the context of co-ordinated integrating structures. Internal labour markets can be organized across the firm, not just within the unit. They are more likely to have well organized personnel departments in the corporate office (Sisson and Scullion, 1985) than others and they are capable of emphasizing core values in the way in which employees, customers and suppliers are to be treated. They are much more capable than others of being 'value driven', of 'respecting the individual', of 'viewing themselves as an extended family' and of following the dictum that 'customer relations simply mirrors employee relations' (Peters and Waterman, 1982). The important point here is that the *potential* for strategic human resource management is greater in such companies. This is not to imply that the potential is realized.

This type of firm is, however, becoming rarer, at least among large enterprises. Channon has observed that the pattern of diversification has grown substantially and:

> today large companies tend in the main to be highly diversified both by range of business and by geography . . . . Diversification was continuing amongst many of the organizations engaged in related businesses which seemed likely to make them unrelated concerns in the future. (1982: 79)

There is counter evidence to this as some firms like BET, Cadbury Schweppes and Dalgety have sought to divest businesses which do not fit a slimmed-down version of the portfolio organized around a broad core business. However, there is little evidence to suggest that these firms have at the same time changed the nature of their internal control structures: the dominance of performance-control systems appears to remain intact.

Conclusion

Hill and Hoskisson have hypothesized that:

> as firms grow by vertical integration or related diversification, they will become increasingly constrained by information processing requirements to focus on attaining financial economies. [And that] under conditions of either high or increasing uncertainty, vertically integrated firms will focus on realizing financial economies. (1987: 338, 340)

The 1980s have been marked by uncertainty in product markets and, as we have seen, short-run pressures in the capital market have generated unprecedented uncertainty even for the largest firms. In these conditions corporate strategy increasingly is focused on ways of realizing financial economies. Firms that emphasize the achievement of financial economies are 'characterized by relatively high degrees of decentralization of decisions to divisions, decomposition between divisions, and consequently, high accountability for divisional profits' (ibid.: 334). It is these firms which emphasize the performance-control system; which often examine their businesses along the lines suggested by portfolio-planning principles and which tend towards financial control, reducing the emphasis on long-run strategic planning. These types of first-order strategies and second-order strategic decisions on the structuring of internal operating procedures come to exert a strong influence on third-order human resource management policies. It becomes harder to develop integrated and meaningful institutional strategies or management style at the corporate level, and – to the degree that short-run rates of return on investment, emphasis on margin improvement, and tight financial controls are imposed on unit managers – harder at the unit level to develop and maintain long-run human resource policies.

This pessimistic conclusion is difficult to avoid. It is the contention of this chapter that current trends in corporate strategy in many large diversified companies renders the ideals of human resource management, as specified by Guest (1987), unobtainable. There is nothing new in this. Herman, in his study of corporate power, concluded that 'The present state of evolution in economic freedom has produced an environment dominated by vast impersonal organisations that pride themselves on their ruthlessness and respond only to material incentives' (Herman, 1981: 32). Mintzberg noted that 'the control system of the divisionalised [company] drives it to act, at best, socially unresponsively, at worst socially irresponsibly. Forced to concentrate on the economic consequences of his decisions, the divisional manager comes to ignore their social consequences' (Mintzberg, 1979: 424).

The criticism of diversified companies is not restricted to their economic power and damaging social consequences. Porter (1987) has attacked portfolio planning and argued forcibly for a renewed emphasis on inter-relationships between units and horizontal strategy. Piore and Sabel (1984) have argued that the economic consequences of conglomerates and their search for multinational diversification has had damaging consequences for the US economy. The criticism of the effects of diversified, multi-divisional companies on employee relations presented here is another twist to a familiar story. It is odd, then, that the current wave of interest in human resource management is so optimistic and implies that a major reconsideration of personnel practice is underway. The belief is that corporate executives and line managers have discovered the need to encourage employee involvement, team work, and integrated reward systems (ideas which have been around for a long time) as a crucial element of their corporate and business-unit strategies. Changes are, of course, taking place and there is much experimentation, some very exciting, as the old order crumbles. But in many diversified firms, in Britain at least, the material conditions for these to be translated into long-run strategic decisions placing human resource management as the, or even a, critical function in corporate strategy, do not exist. What ought to happen, as prescribed by the burgeoning literature, is a long way from being realized.

Notes

1 This might seem the ultimate self-sacrifice for the manager if his or her job is to go also. However, 'as a practical matter, it takes some time, perhaps two or three years to liquidate a dog business. At the end of this period there will undoubtedly be other oppor-tunities in the organization for its manager and his staff' (ibid.).
2 Brown and O'Connor are, again, rather more explicit 'for dog businesses an early demise is the appropriate policy. Needless to say, they should receive no investment, not even to repair a leaking roof in the factory. If possible such a business should be sold to an organisation that does not realise it is a dog; if not, it should be abandoned' (1974: 16).
3 Hanson Trust, a very similar company to BTR, has cut, on average, 25 per cent of labour costs out of acquired companies (Porter, 1987).
4 BTR, through a subsidiary company, acquired the major Australian firm ACI in 1988. Within three months the whole of the human resource planning department at head office was closed down. No opportunity was given to the director of human resource planning to present a human resource strategy.

References

Ahlstrand, B. and Purcell, J. (1988)'Employee relations strategy in the multi-divisional company', *Personnel Review*, 17, (3).
Andrews, K.R. (1980) *The Concept of Corporate Strategy*. Homewood, Ill.: Irwin.
Batstone, E., Ferner, A. and Terry, M. (1984) *Consent and Efficiency*. Oxford: Blackwell.
Boston Consulting Group (1970) *The Product Portfolio Concept*, Perspective no. 66. Boston, Mass.: Boston Consulting Group.

Brown, J.K. and O'Connor, R. (1974) *Planning and the Corporate Director*, Report no. 627. New York: Conference Board.

Chandler, A.D. (1962) *Strategy and Structure*. Cambridge, Mass.: MIT Press.

Channon, D. (1982) 'Industrial structure', *Long Range Planning*, 15 (5).

Christiansen, H., Cooper, A.C. and Dekluyver, C.A. (1982) 'The dog business: a re-examination', *Business Horizons*, November/December.

Fortune (1988) 'Corporate strategy for the 1990s', 29 February.

Goold, M. and Campbell, A. (1987) *Strategies and Styles: The Role of the Centre in Managing Diversified Corporations*. Oxford: Blackwell.

Gouldner, A. (1954) *Wild Cat Strike*. New York: Harper & Row.

Guest, D. (1987) 'Human resource management and industrial relations', *Journal of Management Studies*, 24 (5).

Hamermesh, R.G. (1986) *Making Strategy Work: How Senior Managers Produce Results*. New York: Wiley.

Harrigan, K.R. (1980) *Strategies for Declining Businesses*. Lexington, Mass.: D.C. Heath.

Haspeslagh, P. (1982) 'Portfolio planning: uses and limits', *Harvard Business Review*, Jan.-Feb.

Hax, A.C. and Majluf, N.S. (1983) 'The use of the industry attractiveness–business strength matrix in strategic planning', *Interfaces*, April.

Hedley, B. (1977) 'Strategy and the business portfolio', *Long Range Planning*, 10 (1).

Hegarty, W.H. and Hoffman, R.G. (1987) 'Who influences strategic decisions?', *Long Range Planning*, 20 (2).

Hickson, D.J., Butler, R.J., Cray, D., Mallory, G.R. and Wilson, D.G. (1986) *Top Decisions: Strategic Decision Making in Organisations*. Oxford: Blackwell.

Hill, C.W.L. and Hoskisson, R.E. (1987) 'Strategy and structure in the multiproduct firm', *Academy of Management Review*, 12 (2).

Hill, C.W.L. and Pickering, J.F. (1986) 'Divisionalisation, decentralisation and performance of large United Kingdom companies', *Journal of Management Studies*, 23 (1).

Johnson, G. (1987) *Strategic Change and the Management Process*. Oxford: Blackwell.

Kochan, T.A. and Chalykoff, J.B. (1987) 'Human resource management and business life cycles: some preliminary propositions', in A. Kleingartner and C.S. Anderson (eds), *Human Resource Management in High Technology Firms*. Lexington, Mass.: Lexington Books.

McMillan, I.C., Hambrick, D.C. and Day, D.L. (1982) 'The product portfolio and profitability – a PIMS based analysis of industrial-product businesses', *Academy of Management Journal*, 25 (4).

Marginson, P., Edwards, P., Martin, R., Purcell, J. and Sisson, K. (1988) *Beyond the Workplace*. Oxford: Blackwell.

Mintzberg, J. (1979) *The Structuring of Organisations*. Englewood Cliffs, NJ: Prentice-Hall.

Peters, T. and Waterman, R. (1982) *In Search of Excellence*. New York: Harper & Row.

Piore, M.J. and Sabel, C.F. (1984) *The Second Industrial Divide: Possibilities for Prosperity*. New York: Basic Books.

Porter, M.E. (1987) 'From competitive advantage to corporate strategy', *Harvard Business Review*, May–June.

Purcell, J. (1987) 'Mapping management styles in employee relations', *Journal of Management Studies*, 24 (5).

Schuler, R.S. and Jackson, S.E. (1987) 'Organizational strategy and organizational level as determinants of human resource management practices', *Human Resource Planning*, 10 (3).

Sisson, K. and Scullion, H. (1985) 'Putting the corporate personnel department in its place', *Personnel Management*, December.

Thurley, K. and Wood, S. (1983) 'Business strategy and industrial relations strategy', in K. Thurley and S. Wood (eds), *Industrial Relations and Management Strategy*. Cambridge: Cambridge University Press.

Williamson, O.E. (1975) *Markets and Hierarchies*. New York: Free Press.

6

A leadership dilemma: skilled incompetence

Chris Argyris

Most of us dread incompetence. We do not wish to perform poorly or to undercut our objectives. Yet perhaps the most frustrating incompetence of all is that which is repetitive. As one CEO stated: 'In my opinion, the best sign of an incompetent executive, or organisation for that matter, is one who keeps producing consequences that he or she does not intend.'

Ordinarily we attribute such repeated failure to a lack of skill. But in this chapter I am going to argue just the opposite. I hope to show that the incompetence that is most difficult to correct is tightly coupled with skilfulness.

In particular, I will focus on those occasions when executives try to solve problems that are potentially threatening, and they try to do so in a way that communicates caring and respect for the other. In handling these problems, the executives use highly honed skills yet create consequences they do not intend. Hence, their skilfulness is tightly coupled with incompetence. Moreover, this skilled incompetence not only operates at the individual level, it permeates the entire organisational culture as well.

During the past decade, I have been studying small- to medium-sized, fast-growing organisations. Typically they have been started by an entrepreneur who brought together a bright, dedicated, hard-working group of colleagues to market a new service or a new product. All of them have grown and some continue to grow, at high rates, ranging from 30 to 60 per cent per year.

Not surprisingly, they all reach a stage when they must try to manage their growth and their organisation more rationally or many of them will burn out and their company could get into deep administrative trouble. The CEO of one such company said recently:

> Right now we offer products that clients can use that are prepackaged, off the shelf. The people serving those products are primarily sales oriented. We also offer custom-designed professional services. The people producing these services are oriented toward professional help.
>
> The product side is more profitable than the custom side. Yet the custom side

Reprinted by permission of Business and Economics Review from *Business and Economics Review* 1 (Summer 1987): 4–11.

is more challenging and helps us to design and produce new and better products. Our major problem is to decide what kind of company we are going to be. We need a vision and a strategic plan.

I met with the CEO and his immediate reportees. They agree with him that they must develop a vision and make some strategic decisions. They also told me that they have already held several long meetings. Unfortunately, the meetings ended up in no agreement and no choice. 'We end up drawing up lists of issues but not deciding,' said one vice-president. Another added, 'And it gets pretty discouraging when this happens every time we meet.' A third warned, 'If you think we are discouraged, how do you think the people below us feel who watch us repeatedly fail?'

This is a group of executives who are at the top; who respect each other; who are highly committed; and who agree that developing a viable vision and strategy is long overdue. Yet whenever they meet, they repeatedly fail to create the vision and the strategy they desire.

If we go back to the criterion of incompetence described at the outset, their actions are incompetent in the sense that they produce what they do not intend, and they do so repeatedly, even though no one is forcing them to do so.

The executives explanation of their difficulties

At first, the executives believed that the reason they could not formulate and implement a viable strategic plan was that they lacked sound financial data. They hired a senior financial executive who, everyone agrees, has done a superb job.

The financial vice-president reports, 'Our problem is not the lack of financial data. I can flood them with data. We lack a vision of what kind of company we want to be and a strategy. Once we produce those, I can supply the necessary data.' The other executives agreed.

After several more meetings of failure, a second explanation emerged. It had to do with the personalities of the individuals and the way they work with each other when they meet. As the CEO said:

> This is a group of loveable guys with very strong egos. They are competitive, bright, candid, and dedicated. When we meet, we seem to go in circles; we're great at telling the others how wrong they are or how to solve the problem, but we are not prepared to give in a bit and make the necessary compromises.

I question the usefulness and validity of this explanation. For example, should the top management develop weaker egos or become less competitive? Maybe these are the qualities that helped to build the company in the competitive marketplace.

Next, how valid is it? We have studied top management groups that are not good at problem solving and decision making precisely because the participants have weak egos and are uncomfortable with competition.

More important is that executives have learned to act more effectively without taking the personality route.[1]

The best that I can say for a personality explanation is that it prevents executives from thinking about changing their behaviour, because it understandably makes little sense for them to undergo some kind of therapy. It is an explanation, in other words, that may inhibit learning, while at the same time, it may overprotect the executives.

A different explanation: the source of the incompetent consequences is skill

Let us begin by asking: Is the behaviour that is counter-productive also natural and routine? Does every player seem to be acting genuinely? Do they get in trouble even though the players are not trying to be manipulative and political in the negative sense of the word?

The answer to all these questions, for the executive group, is yes. That means that their motives are clean and their actions represent their personal best. If it is the best that they can do, then their actions are skilful in the sense that they are produced in milliseconds, and that they are spontaneous, automatic, and unrehearsed.

How can skilful actions be counter-productive? Skill is usually associated with producing what we intend. One explanation is that the skills they use help not to upset each other. However, these very skills may inhibit working through the important intellectual issues embedded in developing the strategy. Therefore, the meetings end up with lists and no decision.

This conclusion is not only true for this group of executives. It is true for executives in all kinds of organisations regardless of age, gender, educational background, wealth, or position in the hierarchy.[2] Let me illustrate with another example that involves the entire organisational culture at the upper levels.

Organisational defensive routines[3]

One of the most powerful ways people deal with potential embarrassment is to create organisational defensive routines. I define these as any action or policy that prevents human beings from experiencing negative surprises, embarrassment, or threat, and simultaneously prevents the organisation from reducing or eliminating the causes of the surprises, embarrassment, and threat. Organisational defensive routines are anti-learning and overprotective.

These defensive routines are organisational in the sense that individuals with different personalities behave in the same way; and people leave and new ones come into the organisation, yet the defensive routines remain intact.

Now to the example: Built into genuine decentralisation is the age-old tug between autonomy and control. Subordinates want to be left alone while their superiors want no suprises. The subordinates push for autonomy, asserting that by letting them alone, top management will show its trust. They want management to trust them at a distance. The superiors, on the other hand, wanting no surprises, use information systems as controls. The subordinates see the control device as confirming mistrust.

Many executives I observed deal with this dilemma by acting in a way that they believe will lead to productive consequences. They send mixed messages. They keep communicating, 'We mean it – you are running the show.' The division heads concur that the message is credible up to the point that a very important issue is at stake and they want to prove their mettle; then headquarters begins to interfere. In the eyes of top management, they intervene precisely when they can be of most help, that is, when the issue 'requires a corporate perspective'.

In order to design and send an intentionally ambiguous message and have it look as if this is not the case requires skill. The sender has to follow four rules about designing and delivering mixed messages.

1   Design a message that is ambiguous and clearly so; that is imprecise and precisely so.

For example, 'Be innovative and take risks, but be careful about upsetting others' is a message that says in effect, 'Don't get into trouble.' But the designer is careful not to specify exactly what will and will not upset others. The ambiguity and imprecision are necessary to cover the designer. It is also necessary because it is difficult for the designer to be precise ahead of time.

The ambiguity and imprecision, on the other hand, are clearly and precisely understood by the receiver. Indeed, a request for more precision would likely be interpreted as a sign of immaturity or inexperience. Moreover, the receivers may some day want to use the imprecision and ambiguity to their advantage.

2   Act as if the message is not inconsistent.

When individuals communicate mixed messages, they usually do it spontaneously and with no sign that the message is mixed. Indeed, if they did appear to be hesitant because of the mixedness in the message, that could be seen as a weakness.

3   Make the ambiguity and inconsistency in the message undiscussable.

It is rare indeed for an executive to design and state a mixed message and then ask, 'Do you find my message inconsistent and ambiguous?' The message is made undiscussable by the very natural way it is carried out and by the absence of any inquiry.

4   Make the undiscussability of the undiscussable also undiscussable.

It is even more rare to observe individuals while they are producing mixed messages during a meeting reflecting on their actions and the features of the organisational culture that makes the undiscussable

undiscussable. Such a discussion is more likely to occur after a meeting, when some of the players are having a post mortem, and of course, when the 'other side' is not present.

Individuals follow such rules all the time and do so without having to pay attention to them. In this sense they have become highly skilful at enacting such rules. The paradox is that this skilfulness is inextricably intertwined with incompetence. As the next section shows, the skilful use of mixed messages leads to a range of unintended and counter-productive consequences.

Inconsistencies and dilemmas created by defensive routines

To see the impact the defensive routines are having, let's return to the division heads who are being managed by mixed messages. The division managers must find ways to explain the existence of mixed messages to themselves and to their subordinates. These explanations often sound like this:

'Corporate never *really* meant decentralisation.'

'Corporate is willing to trust divisions when the going is smooth, but not when it's rough.'

'Corporate is concerned more about Wall Street than us.'

The managers rarely test their hypotheses about corporate motives with top managers. If discussing mixed messages would be embarrassing, then publicly testing for the validity of these explanations would be even more so. But now division heads are in a double bind. On the one hand, if they go along unquestioningly they may lose their autonomy, and their subordinates will see them as not having significant influence with corporate. On the other hand, if the division executives do not comply; headquarters will think they are recalcitrant, and if it continues long enough, disloyal.

Top management is in a similar predicament. It senses that division managers are both suspicious of their motives and covering up their suspicions. If the top were to accuse the subordinates of being suspicious and covering up their suspiciousness, that could clearly upset the division heads. If the top does not say anything, they could be acting as if there is full agreement when there is not. Most often, the top covers up its bind in the name of keeping up good relationships.

Soon, people in the divisions learn to live with their binds by generating further explanations. For example, they believe corporate encourages open discussions, but basically they are not influenceable. They may actually conclude that openness is actually a strategy top management has devised to cover up its impermeability to influence.

Since this conclusion assumes that corporate is covering up, managers won't test it either. Since neither headquarters nor division executives discuss or resolve either the attributions or the frustrations, both may eventually begin to distance themselves from each other. A climate of mistrust arises that, once in place, makes it more likely that the issues become undiscussable.

Now both headquarters and division managers have attitudes, assumptions, and actions that create self-fulfilling and self-sealing processes, that each sees the other creating, but work from both the top and the bottom.

Under these conditions, it is not surprising to find that superiors and subordinates hold optimistic and pessimistic views about each other. For example, they may say about each other:

They are bright people and well intentioned
but
They are narrow and have a parochial view
They are interested in the financial health of the company
but
They do not understand how they are harming earnings in the long run.
They are interested in people
but
They do not pay enough attention to the development of the company.

It is unlikely that there is a way to build on the positive features without overcoming the negative features. But in order to begin to overcome what we don't like, we must be able to discuss it, and this violates the undiscussability rules embedded in the organisational defensive routines.

Back to the idea of skilled incompetence. Producing mixed messages, we have seen, requires highly honed skills. The mixed messages, in turn, produce unintended, counter-productive consequences that create the incompetence.

All too familiar routines

Wherever I have described these results, I get instant recognition from executives. They are able to give examples from their own organisations. Many ask, 'Is there any organisation that does not have these hang-ups?'

Recently, numbers of researchers have made pleas to managers to get back to basics and be continually alert to counter-productive actions. They provide many, many stories of organisational rigidity and poor performance.[4]

The stories are excellent examples of organisational defensive routines. It is important, as the authors suggest, to correct the errors caused by the defensive routines.[5] But, they do not go far enough. They do not deal with the organisational defensive routines.

For example, in one story, an organisation required a new item to go through some 270 checks before production, which understandably cut into its capacity to innovate. After isolating those checks for which no good reason, business or not, could be found, management reduced the checks to fewer than 75. Because it solved a business problem, the reduction was a step forward. But it didn't go far enough. The authors do not ask why the players adhered to and implemented these unnecessary checks in the first place.

As we all know, management learns a lot by talking directly with customers. Often the outcome is so rewarding, managers wonder why they never thought of doing it before. But what are the organisational and personal defensive routines that prevented them from talking to customers in the first place? What norms did people learn that would blind them to the obvious?

I can see why the authors place much of the responsibility for reducing organisational defensive routines on the CEO. Without the support of people at the top, no one is likely to confront organisational defensive routines.

The freedom to question and to confront is crucial, but it is inadequate. To overcome skilled incompetence, people have to learn new skills, to ask the question behind the question. When CEO's I observed declared war against organisational defensive routines and demanded that people get back to basics, most often the new ideas were implemented with the old skills. People changed whatever they could and learned to cover their asses even more skilfully.

Defensive routines exist; they are undiscussable; they proliferate and grow in an underground manner; the social pollution is hard to identify until something occurs that blows things open. If the defensive routines then surface, it is difficult for those with the stewardship to do much about them. They have been skilful at going along with, not at questioning or confronting the routines.

We do not have the choice to ignore the organisational problems that these self-sealing loops are creating. Management today may be able to get away with it, but it is creating a legacy for those who will have to manage organisations in the future.

What can be done

The top management group with which we began this chapter decided to begin to change their organisational defensive routines by beginning with the ones that they create in their own meetings.

The first step toward change was a two-day session away from the office. The agenda of the sessions were the cases that they were asked to write ahead of time.

The purpose of these cases was twofold. First, they allowed us to develop a collage of the kinds of problem thought to be critical by the group. Not surprisingly, in this particular group, a least half wrote on issues related to product versus customer service. Secondly, the cases provided a kind of window into the prevailing rules and routines used by the executives.

The form of the cases was as follows:

1 In one paragraph describe a key organisational problem as you see it.
2 Assume you could talk to whomever you wish to begin to solve the problem. Describe in a paragraph or so, the strategy that you would use in this meeting.
3 Next split your page into two columns. On the right-hand side write how you would begin the meeting; what you would actually say. Then write what you believe the other(s) would say. Then write your response to their response. Continue writing this scenario for two or so double-spaced typewritten pages.
4 On the left-hand column write any idea or feeling that you would have that you would not communicate for whatever reason.

In short the case includes:

* A statement of the problem.
* The intended strategy to begin to solve the problem.
* The actual conversation that would ensue as envisioned by the writer.
* The information that the writer would not communicate for whatever reason.

The executives reported that they became highly involved in writing the cases. Some said that the very writing of the case was an eye opener. Moreover, once the cases were distributed to each member, the reactions were jocular. The men were enjoying them:

'That's just like . . .'
'Great . . . does this all the time.'
'Oh, there's a familiar one.'
'All salesmen and no listeners.'
'Oh my God, this is us.'

Cases as an intervention tool

What is the advantage of using the cases? The cases, crafted and written by the executives themselves, become vivid examples of skilled incompetence. They vividly illustrate the skill with which each executive tried not to upset the other and to persuade them to change their position. They also vividly illustrate the incompetence component because the results, by their own analysis, were to upset the others and make it less likely that their views would prevail.

The cases are also very important learning devices. It is difficult for anyone to slow down the behaviour that they produce in milliseconds during a real meeting in order to reflect on it and change it. The danger is that others will grab the air time and run with it. Moreover, it is

difficult for the human mind to pay attention to the interpersonal actions
and to the substantive issues at the same time.

Why not have an outside person act as a facilitator to make the conversation more effective? I did act as a facilitator for a while. But this is not
a sound solution for several reasons.

If the facilitator is successful, it is because he acts as a traffic cop; he
rephrases the conversation whenever it is necessary; he clarifies issues; he
points out messages that may be upsetting others, and so on. This is a
short-term solution. The long-term solution is for the executives to learn
to do these things well. In other words, a facilitator is ultimately a person
who helps the group bypass its defensive routines instead of helping them
to learn to engage them in order to get rid of them.

Why not have the group sit down and talk about the strategy issues?
The answer is that they told us that they tried this several times and it did
not work.

One reason for this lack of success may be that it is unlikely that
individuals will make public, in a regular meeting, what is on their left-
hand columns. Yet, as we shall see, what individuals choose to censor has
an important impact, because the individuals not only cover up that they
are censoring something they also strive to cover up the cover up. The
irony is that the others sense this but they too cover up that they sense
it, and they too cover up their cover up.

Here is a collage from several cases. It was written by individuals who
believed the company should place a greater emphasis on customer
service.

Thoughts and feelings not communicated	*Actual conversation*
He's not going to like this topic, but we have to discuss it. I doubt that he will take a company perspective, but I should be positive.	I: Hi Bill. I appreciate having the opportunity to talk with you about this problem of custom service versus product. I am sure that both of us want to resolve it in the best interests of the company. Bill: I'm always glad to talk about it, as you well know.
I better go slow. Let me ease-in.	I: There are an increasing number of situations where our clients are asking for custom service and rejecting the off-the-shelf proucts. My fear is that your sales people will play an increasingly peripheral role in the future. Bill: I don't understand. Tell me more.
Like hell you don't understand. I wish there was a way I could be more gentle.	I: Bill, I'm sure you are aware of the changes [and explains]. Bill: No, I do not see it that way. It's my sales people that are the key to the future.
There he goes, thinking as a salesman and not as a corporate officer.	I: Well, let's explore that a bit . . .

The dialogue continues with each person stating his views candidly but not being influenced by what the other says. To give you a flavour of what happened, here are some further left-hand column comments:

'He's doing a great job supporting his people.'
'This guy is not really listening.'
'I wonder if he's influenceable.'
'This is beginning to piss me off.'
'There he goes getting defensive. I better back off and wait for another day.'

If I presented a collage of the cases written by individuals who support the product strategy, it would not differ significantly. They too would be trying to persuade, sell, cajole their fellow officers. Their left-hand columns would be similar.

Reflecting on the cases

In analysing their left-hand columns, the executives found that each side blamed the other side for the difficulties, and they used the same reasons. For example, each side said about the other side:

'You do not *really* understand the issues.'
'If you insist on your position, you will harm the morale that I have built.'
'Don't hand me that line. You know what I am talking about.'
'Why don't you take off your blinkers and wear a company hat?'
'It upsets me when I think of how they think.'
'I'm really trying hard, but I'm beginning to feel this is hopeless.'

These results illustrate once more the features of skilled incompetence. Crafting the cases with the intention not to upset others while trying to change their minds requires skill. Yet, as we have seen, the skilled behaviour they used in the cases had the opposite effect. The others in the case became upset and dug in their heels about changing their minds.

I can now add an additional finding. These individuals and all the others we have studied to date should not be able to prevent the counter-productive consequences until and unless they learn new skills. Nor will it work to bypass the skilled incompetence by focusing on the business problems, such as, in this case, developing a business strategy.

Several executives in this group did not agree. The dialogue began with one asking: 'Okay, so what's new? This is exactly what I have been saying for years.' 'That's right,' added another, 'no surprises.'

'What surprises me,' said the CEO, 'is how these cases have captured the issues beautifully. That's us and that's what we must work on.'

'No, I do not agree with you,' responded another officer to the CEO. 'If we are not to waste the two days, we ought to focus on something concrete. We ought to focus on the practical and urgent business problems we have of managing our growth and creating a business strategy that will unite us.'

The group split into two factions. About half agreed with the executive above. The other half agreed with the CEO. Their view was represented by one executive who said:

'But how are we ever going to listen to each other if we hold the views that we have about each other, and if we talk the way we talk to each other the way we do in the cases?'

Note the executives are recreating the dynamics that get them into difficulty. I intervened and made a suggestion. Let us begin by trying to answer the question about what kind of company they wish to be, and what should be their strategy. If that did not work, then they could change to examining their cases.

The executives agreed and asked that I act as the facilitator. As the reader might expect, I had my hands full acting like a traffic cop. I did succeed a bit in keeping some degree of order, asking clarifying questions, and clearing up misunderstandings. The executives did begin to listen to each other more effectively. However, some unexpected results occurred. Every time a concrete suggestion was made that they agreed on, someone would point out that the system, policy, or financial information just requested was already in place or something similar could easily be in place. If so, then why were they having these problems?

One explanation that they discovered was that the policy, rule, or system in place was often violated in the name of meeting a deadline or breaking a blockage. Often the violations were not discussed with all those involved because there was no time to meet or people were out of town. Later when the 'other' side was told, they often did not agree with the way it was handled or even that it was a crisis.

Redesigning their actions

The next step was to begin to redesign their actions. The executives turned to their cases. Each executive selected an episode that he wished to redesign so that it would not have negative consequences. As an aid in their redesign, the executives were given some handouts that described a different set of behaviours. The first thing they realised was that they would have to slow things down. They could not produce a new conversation in the milliseconds that they were accustomed to. This troubled them a bit because they were impatient to learn. They kept reminding themselves that learning new skills does require that they slow down.

One technique they used was that each individual crafted by himself a new conversation to help the writer of the episode. After taking five or so minutes, they shared their designs with the writer. In the process of discussing these, the writer learned much about how to redesign his words. But, the designers also learned much as they discovered the snags in their suggestions and the way they made them.

The dialogue was very constructive, co-operative and helpful. Typical comments were:

'If you want to reach me, try it the way Joe just said.'

'I realise your intentions are clean, but those words push my button (for such and such a reason).'

'I understand what you are trying to say, but it doesn't work for me because . . . How about trying it this way?'

'I'm impressed as to how my new designs have some of the old messages. This will take time.'

Practice is important. Most people required as much practice as is required to play a not-so-decent game of tennis. But, it does not need to occur all at once. The practice can occur in actual business meetings where they set aside some time to make it possible to reflect on their actions and to correct them. An outside facilitator could help them examine and redesign their actions just as a tennis coach might do. But, as in the case of a good tennis coach, the facilitator should be replaced by the group. He might be brought in for periodic boosters or to help when the problem is in the degree of difficulty and intensity not experienced before.

There are several consequences of this type of change programme. First, the executives begin to experience each other as more supportive and constructive. People still work very hard during meetings, but their conversation begins to become additive; it flows to conclusions that they all can own and implement. Crises begin to be reduced. Soon the behavioural change leads to new values and the new structures and policies to mirror the new values.

This in turn leads to more effective problem solving and decision making. In the case of this group, they were able to define the questions related to strategy, to conduct their own inquiries, to have staff people conduct some relevant research, to have three individuals organise it into a presentation that was ultimately approved and owned by the top group. The top group also built in a process of involving their immediate reports so that they could develop a sense of ownership, thereby increasing the probability that all involved will work at making it successful.

Notes

1 Chris Argyris, *Reasoning, learning and action*. San Francisco: Jossey-Bass, 1982.
2 Chris Argyris, 'Double-loop learning in organisations'. *Harvard Business Review*. September–October 1977, 55(5), 115–25.

3 For a more detailed description, see Chris Argyris, *Strategy, change, and defensive routines*. Boston: Ballinger, 1985.

4 Thomas Peters and Robert H. Waterman, *In search of excellence*. New York, Harper and Row, 1982.

5 Thomas Peters and Nancy Austin, *A passion for excellence*, New York, Random House, 1985.

7

A model for the executive management of transformational change

Richard Beckhard

The focus of this chapter is the management of a transformational-change effort in a significant system or a complex organization. The management of this type of change is distinctly different in a number of ways from the management of change in many other arenas that concern human resource development (HRD) practitioners daily. A transformational change is orchestrated by the organization's executive managers, who must have access to a model that enables them to diagnose and manage the change process. In addition, employing such a model effectively is dependent on the managers' understanding of a number of important issues: the nature of transformation, the implications of transformational change, the organizational conditions and behavioral changes that are necessary for transformation to succeed, and the challenges and dilemmas that are likely to be encountered. This chapter presents a model for transformational change that HRD practitioners may suggest to managers facing this difficult task, and it provides useful information that practitioners can pass along to managers to help them develop the understanding of the process that is so critical to success.

The nature of transformation

The definition of transformation in Webster's is 'A change in the shape, structure, nature of something.' This definition coordinates well with the needs and practices of organizations involved in transformational change. There is no question that there is an increasing need for a complex organization in today's world to change its *shape* to accommodate changing demands; an organization faces a heavy responsibility in attempting to determine the shape, in terms of both size and complexity, that will allow it to function effectively in the dynamic world in which it operates.

Reprinted by permission of University Associates, Inc. from *The 1989 Annual: Developing Human Resources*, ed. J. William Pfeiffer, pp. 255–64.

Merely altering the configuration or writing new job descriptions is an inadequate and possibly even inappropriate response, given the difficulty of the task.

Transformation in an organization can also address *structure*, or the basic parts of the organization that are responsible for its character or its *nature*. Structure includes values, beliefs, reward systems, ownership, patterns, and so on. Sometimes environmental factors change and necessitate significant reappraisals of the organization's nature: consumer interests and demands, work force, technology, telecommunication, and competition.

However, an in-depth assessment of shape, structure, character or nature, and environment – difficult and essential as that task may be – is insufficient of itself. Undertaking transformational change also necessitates re-examining the organization's mission and creating a vision or desired future state as well as the strategies by which the organization can move toward that vision. The strategic issues involved in formulating an organization's mission and vision are quite different from those involved in 'running the store', or increasing profits in the short term, and HRD practitioners need to ensure that executive managers who attempt transformation are aware of these differences.

The types of organizational change that can be called transformational are as follows:

1 *A change in what drives the organization.* For example, a change from being production driven or technology driven to being market driven is transformational.
2 *A fundamental change in the relationships between or among organizational parts.* Examples include redefining staff roles and moving from central management to decentralized management or from executive management to strategic management.
3 *A major change in the ways of doing work.* Such transformational changes include moving from low-technology to high-technology manufacturing systems, implementing computers and telecommunications, and redesigning the customer interface (for example, by providing salespeople with lap computers so that they can interact directly with both customers and suppliers).
4 *A basic cultural change in norms, values, or reward systems.* An example of a cultural change is moving from standardized incentive rewards to individualized ones.

Organizational prerequisites

The following ten conditions or elements, which are discussed in order of priority, must exist before transformational change can be achieved in an organization.

Prerequisite 1: committed top leaders

One or more of the organization's top leaders, including the chief executive officer (CEO), must be committed champions of the change. In assisting executive managers with transformational change, the HRD practitioner cannot overemphasize the importance of top-level commitment and the visibility of that commitment. Those at lower organizational levels who will be responsible for implementing various aspects of the change cannot be expected to commit to the effort until they see for themselves that the organizational leadership is similarly committed. Although it is possible to achieve some degree of change without top-level commitment, that change is likely to be ephemeral at best.

Prerequisite 2: written description of the changed organization

It is essential to have a statement, written in behavioral terms, of how the changed organization will function. This statement should include a description of the basic organizational character, policies, values, and priorities that will exist as a result of the transformational change. The HRD practitioner should stress that this statement is not a list of short-term objectives and should monitor the writing process carefully to ensure that the statement is sufficiently detailed and focused on behavior.

Prerequisite 3: conditions that preclude maintenance of the status quo

Another critical prerequisite is the existence of a set of external conditions that makes the choice of maintaining the status quo either unlikely or impossible. The HRD practitioner should explain to the executive managers that the transformation will not occur unless people are feeling so much pain in the present situation that they are motivated to change it; in the absence of such pain, resistance will take over and make the change difficult or even impossible.

Prerequisite 4: likelihood of a critical mass of support

The organizational situation should be studied carefully to determine the potential that a critical mass of support for the change will develop. The HRD practitioner can assist in this task through the use of such means as surveys and interviews. The key players involved in the change, both inside the hierarchical system and in the immediate environment, must be identified and their commitment to the change solicited and obtained.

Prerequisite 5: a medium- to long-term perspective

Transformational changes take years, not months; it is important that the executive managers understand and accept this time perspective. The HRD practitioner might want to cite examples from his or her own experience of the fact that 'quick-fix' changes tend to be just that – first-aid treatments that do not have a base for perpetuation. However, it should also be stressed that it is sometimes necessary in the turbulent transitional environment to make quick, dramatic changes in the organization's character. When this is the case, a trap is to mistake such an event for the completion of the entire change effort; instead, it represents only the beginning of the change-management process. Executive managers may need help in discerning the difference between the individual changes that take place during transformation and the completion of the transformation itself. They also may need help in developing a clear strategy for managing the tension between the need for stability – the need to 'run the store' – and the need for change.

Prerequisite 6: awareness of resistance and the need to honor it

Those managing a transformational change need to be helped to understand and accept resistance to that change. It is essential to devise strategies for working with rather than against resistance. Many executive managers assume that resistance is a representation of 'the enemy,' whereas the reality is that no change can occur without it. Resistance is the process of internalizing, taking on and letting go, and moving into the new state. This process is totally normal, not neurotic. The tension between the status quo and change is an inherent part of transformation. The appropriate response is to set up ways to manage the resistance productively and to ensure that its effects further the organization's progress in its journey from here to there.

Prerequisite 7: awareness of the need for education

The executive managers must develop awareness of the need to educate the people and groups involved in or affected by the change. This education may go well beyond simply fostering understanding of the change itself; it may include needs assessment and subsequent training in the skills and knowledge that are shown to be essential to functioning successfully in the changed environment. Education is also one of the best tools for reducing resistance and obtaining commitment to a change. The HRD practitioner can play a vital role in developing awareness of the need, pinpointing the kinds of education required, and providing such education through various training programs.

Prerequisite 8: the conviction that the change must be tried

This conviction on the part of executive management should include a willingness to sustain an experimental attitude throughout the change effort and to stick with the effort. Inherent in this willingness is the assumption that occasional failures will be experienced and will be accepted as a normal part of the learning process that accompanies change. Intolerance of such failures will convince those implementing the change that executive management is not, in fact, committed to the change process and that the old ways of doing things are safer. It is essential that management reward rather than punish the risk taking required in abandoning the old and trying the new. The HRD practitioner can assist in assessing people's orientations towards risk, fostering risk-taking behaviors, and developing an appropriate reward system.

Prerequisite 9: willingness to use resources

Executive management must be willing to 'put its money where its mouth is' and use all kinds of resources – technical, consultative, and expert – in support of the change effort. Those responsible for implementing the change will be thwarted in their efforts if they cannot have access to the resources they need. The HRD practitioner can provide useful assistance in specifying the resources that are needed, in serving as a resource, in identifying other internal and external resources, and in encouraging people to generate creative ways of using resources.

Prerequisite 10: commitment to maintaining the flow of information

From the outset of a transformational-change effort, information must flow freely between and among the different parts of the organization. All employees must receive explicit information about the vision, values, priorities, and rewards that will govern the new state or condition. This often means issuing such information before all of the details are complete. In addition, information about the progress of the effort and about what has worked and what has not worked is extremely valuable. When information is not shared appropriately, mistakes can be repeated and valuable time and other resources can be wasted. Inadequate information also can lead to morale problems. The HRD practitioner can help by stressing the importance of communication; by suggesting appropriate ways to communicate; and by recommending, setting up, and/or conducting training in communication if necessary.

A model of transformational change

The process of transforming inputs (needs and raw materials) into outputs (goods and services) is the 'work' of an organization. When an organization needs to transform itself, it is, in fact, transforming its work. In any such change, there are three states that must be dealt with: (1) the *present state*, which is things as they are; (2) the *future state*, which is what the changed condition will be; and (3) the *transitional state*, which is the one that exists when evolving from the present to the future – the state during which the actual changing takes place.

The author's model addresses the critical relationships among these three states as well as the ten prerequisites previously discussed. It consists of the following steps:

Designing the future state. The future state can be defined as the vision for the organization or the strategic objectives of the change. It includes not only the end state but also an intermediate state, which, for example, might be a year or two from the time during which the future state is being planned. The model assumes that for either the end state or the intermediate state, a scenario is needed – a written description of the envisioned behavior of the operation at some point in time. Generally the existing situation is seen as a problem and the future state as the solution to that problem.

Diagnosing the present state. This diagnosis is performed in the context of the future state. The model suggests that during this step the entire gamut of issues embedded in the defined change problem must be identified, analyzed, and prioritized in terms of any probable domino effects.

Extrapolating what is required to go from the present state to the transitional state. This step consists of identifying in detail what is required to get from here to there: the activities that must be completed, the resources that must be allocated, the relationships that must be in place, the management structures that are necessary for the transition, and the rewards that must exist. These requirements should be listed in sequence and some time frame established for meeting them.

Analyzing the work that occurs during the transitional state. This step consists of formulating a complete picture of how the organization will function during the transitional state.

Defining the system that is affecting the problem. This step does not necessarily mean that everyone affected by the problem must be identified. What is essential is to identify a 'critical mass' of people inside and directly outside the organization who must be committed to the change in order for it to succeed. The smallest number of people or groups is the optimum.

Analyzing each of the members of the critical mass with regard to readiness and capability. Readiness refers to an individual's attitude towards the change, and capability refers to an individual's capacity to do whatever the change requires of him or her. This step is important in that organizational transformation always necessitates the need for changes in the behavior of those who hold key roles in the organization. For example, the types of decision making that are appropriate for a functionally controlled organization are inappropriate for a matrix organization or an organization driven by business areas.

When managing a transformational change, the CEO must behave in ways that indicate commitment to the new state; demonstrating such commitment may be a new and unfamiliar form of behavior. In addition, the goals, priorities, and even activities of the human resource manager may require major modification as a result of transformational change; he or she may need to switch from controlling to facilitating, from providing services only to leading the change, and/or from simply implementing policies to actively initiating new mechanisms like improved reward systems. Finally a transformation can involve agonizing changes in the power structure, expectations about performance, and the control wielded by heads of major staffs in their own functional areas. The staff heads may have to develop new relationships among themselves and with the business leaders; new rewards must be negotiated; and many questions must be answered. The staff heads, who are accustomed to functioning as 'experts' in their particular functions, may need to become supporters, facilitators, and leaders in long-range thinking – a major change requiring behavioral modification. It is a good idea to know at the outset whether the members of the critical mass will be willing and able to respond appropriately to the change; then, if it is determined that certain members are unwilling or unable, that situation can be planned for and dealt with.

Identifying the power relationships and resources necessary to ensure the perpetuation of the change. It is not enough to carefully analyze what is required to get from here to there; it is equally important to analyze and provide what is necessary to make the change stick.

Setting up an organization (or structure or system) to manage the transformation. The company's executive managers are responsible for managing the organization that is set up, not necessarily for managing the change work itself. In the absence of such a setup, the transformational effort may deteriorate into a series of undocumented experiments from which people fail to learn.

Examples of the model at work

Case 1: a cultural change initiated within the organization

The large, multinational chemical company that is the subject of Case 1 had facilities in over eighty countries and produced a variety of products from pharmaceuticals to heavy chemicals. It operated in many markets, and its competitors were all over the world. Its ownership relationships varied from a wholly owned territory to joint ventures to a partnership.

The company was organized in approximately ten areas of business, each of which had its own board of directors and its own CEO, but all of which were wholly owned by the parent company. The enterprise governance was achieved through a board of directors, half of whom were designated as *executive* directors who provided the company's active leadership and half of whom were designated as *nonexecutive* (external) directors who fulfilled the more traditional board functions. The organization had historically operated through executive management in which the executive directors were the CEOs of the individual businesses as well as the heads of the territories and the functions, such as finance and personnel.

This organization was a leading part of the economy of its home country. It was traditional, highly people oriented, somewhat paternalistic, and a comfortable place to work. Relations with the trade unions were excellent; the company was one of the first to start joint consultations many years ago.

Eventually it became apparent to several members of both the main board and the heads of businesses that the technically controlled, decentralized divisions, which were primarily local in nature, were not appropriate for addressing the market of the future. Technical innovation had slipped; markets had been eroded in various ways; some of the products were too mature for growth.

Some of the members of the executive board decided to rethink the organizational culture with the following aims:

1 To focus on moving toward a world-wide business;
2 To place the authority for running the businesses with the heads of those businesses rather than with the central directors;
3 To reduce the central directorate to a small number of enterprise directors and to limit their influence;
4 To revitalize research and development and relate it more to the businesses, replacing the highly centralized research effort with a smaller central effort.

For a number of years the efforts of those who were proponents of this vision were either contained or circumvented by the majority, who resisted such a massive change. The resistance followed classic patterns. For example, commissions and study groups were set up to study organizational changes and changes in board functioning. Through various tactics such as postponing, returning reports for further clarification, and stalling based on excuses like 'bad timing,' the change efforts were effectively squashed.

A few proponents of the change effort saw themselves as having to provide the executive leadership for the change and having to develop a strategy for doing so. Two or three of them who were on the main board solicited support from other board members; they worked even harder to obtain commitment from the heads of the businesses, who would soon be board members. Over a six-year period the board membership moved from a minority of three people who supported the change to a 'critical mass' of individuals who were firmly committed to the change and concerned only about how to implement it.

As some of the leaders of this effort moved into top positions, they began to strengthen the division leadership and to exert their influence in various meetings of the leaders of the businesses around the world. They engaged in goal setting and envisioning for the enterprise and changed the methodology by which the business heads reported to control groups from the center. They began to institute the actual changes that were necessary:

1 They reduced the number of board members to seven and granted group control to all members.
2 They redefined the role of the business head to that of CEO with control over all of his or her resources.
3 They changed to a strategy-management mode in which each of the business heads met with the entire executive board once a year to define strategic objectives and once a year to establish a budget. No other contact with the board was required of the business heads, although each had a contact on the board who provided ongoing support.
4 They revised the budget process.
5 They significantly reduced overhead by combining various subheadquarters of related businesses, thereby eliminating well over 20,000 overhead positions. With the new, smaller board, they were able to reduce the support staff. The smaller staff allowed them to move their headquarters to a building half the size, thus providing one more visual symbol of the change in the organizational culture.

Despite all of these changes, the leaders of the change effort consciously supported and maintained those values and ways of work that had been productive in the past, such as joint consultation with the unions. They set up specific change-management systems that were administered by committees, subgroups of board members, and special study groups, and closely monitored the resulting efforts.

In this case the driving force for transformational change came from within the organization and was led by the top leadership. For the last several years the transformation has been led by one particular member of that leadership, who was designated the 'project manager' of the entire change effort. He used his position power to effect the critical mass that was necessary to make the change.

Case 2: a change induced by competitor activity

For many years the large consumer-goods enterprise that is the subject of Case 2 had a virtual monopoly on its products. It sold world-wide, was a household name, and had virtually no competition. It was driven primarily by technology, the making of its products, and the quality of those products. Although there were stores all over the world, manufacturing and distribution were highly centralized; most of the products were made in one giant plant. The majority of the company's employees worked at this home plant, with relatively few workers located at other plants. The function of research and development was very active, constantly upgrading product quality and in recent years moving into related products.

The organization was humanistic, caring, and paternalistic. Employees were never fired; a job at the company was a career for life that paid very well, included excellent benefits, and afforded a nice place to work.

The organization's market share had been relatively stable for a long time and even growing in concert with the growth in world economies. However, it suddenly began to erode as a result of the emergence of a Japanese competitor that managed to produce a product that was not only competitively priced but also of comparable or better quality. This situation had never existed before. For a time the company failed to acknowledge the problem until the numbers began to be serious, at which time the management decided to 'regroup, become leaner, and work differently.' As is often the case, the first thing the management planned to do was to eliminate people. Programs were instituted to reduce 20 per cent of the workforce, and these programs were implemented in various ways – generally in a humanitarian manner.

At this point the manufacturing entity, which was the largest facet of the organization in terms of people, initiated a change effort that was very creatively managed. Although the starting point was the requirement of reducing numbers of employees, this requirement was translated into a productivity-improvement program that was implemented under the leadership of a transition-management team composed of high-potential managers. The team members solicited improvement suggestions from the entire organization, received several hundred, and culled these to approximately fifteen. Then they set up fifteen study groups, each of which was charged with designing a new state for one of the fifteen suggestions. When the study-group reports and recommendations had been submitted and approved by the hierarchy, transition teams were established to manage the process of implementing the recommendations. Finally the new states began to emerge.

This change process enabled the manufacturing entity to effect not only the required reduction in numbers of employees, but also an improvement in operation. With many fewer people, ideas that had been considered impossible, such as combinations of major functions, were now implemented successfully. For example, five levels of management were cut; this development sent a message to the work force that the required reductions were not to take place only at the lower levels of the hierarchy.

Other parts of the enterprise made cuts, but not as radically. However, top management became aware that all of the work-force reductions, although necessary, were not attacking the basic problem: the organization had been designed for another time in history rather than for the competitive world in which it now lived. The business was not driving the organization; instead, the organization was driving the business.

It became apparent that the company needed to reorganize fundamentally. After consultation and planning, the company set up the organization in approximately fifteen lines of business, each representing a separate product line and each with a general manager. Clusters of these general managers reported to three group vice-presidents. The manufacturing, technical, sales, and other staffs were matrixed. Part of each functional staff was now dedicated to the new businesses, but significant parts were kept functional in order to achieve the synergy necessary for certain processes to occur.

As it is easy to imagine, these changes produced a whole new set of issues. It became necessary to develop a number of change-management organizations to cope with the various matrices and to move the company toward some of the major changes that were essential to the total transformation. Ultimately, the transition state led to several thousand new jobs, important shifts in management, and a test of top management's commitment.

To achieve the critical mass, it was necessary to accomplish the following:

1 Make changes among the key leaders in the organization;
2 Provide new, highly committed leadership that would coordinate all manufacturing efforts;
3 Make changes in the leadership of the various parts of the manufacturing process, the sales process, the advertising process, and so on.

It took a year to train a group of people to function as the general managers. A task force was set up to provide the training, most of which occurred on the job.

This case presents a situation in which the commitment for change was high at the top; but the methods of achieving the change were confused at first, and not enough effort was expended to infuse the total organizational environment with commitment. Each of the organizational parts was working on its specific concerns, and no one analyzed the domino effect. Subsequently the organization centralized the management of the change effort and instituted information linkages among the parts. Today the change tends to be managed in a more system-wide way than it was previously. The critical dimensions of the transformational effort were starting with a vision that was at first unclear or at least insufficiently communicated, focusing too much on cost reduction and not enough on developing a new state, trying to function without adequate transition-management structures, and consciously intervening in the matrix-management issues until they became acute.

The challenges of transformational change

As discussed in this chapter, a number of challenges must be met any time a transformational change is attempted:

1 Ensuring the commitment of the CEO and key leaders;
2 Ensuring that adequate resources are allocated to support the change and to maintain it once it has been achieved;
3 Reaching an appropriate balance between managing the change and managing the stability of the organization;
4 Ensuring appropriate use of special roles, temporary systems, study groups, consultants, and transition teams;
5 Continually evaluating both the total effort and its individual parts in terms of planning improvement;
6 Establishing and maintaining continuity of leadership during the change process;
7 Appropriately allocating rewards (and punishments) consistent with the priority of the change effort;
8 Ensuring adequate information flow among various parts of the organization;
9 Constantly monitoring the system to ensure that people know what is happening during the change, understand their roles in the process, and comprehend the total effort rather than only isolated elements of it.

This impressive list could be quite intimidating to any executive managers faced with planning and implementing an organizational transformation. Consequently, the HRD practitioner's role in helping managers meet these challenges can be extremely useful and challenging in its own way.

8

Competitive strategies and organizational change

Alan McKinlay and Ken Starkey

The enormous environmental turbulence of the 1970s called into serious question one of the established verities of organizational behaviour; namely, that structure was the critical change dimension. The inadequacy of structural responses to a crisis such as decentralization and matrix management stimulated the slow emergence of what Waterman et al. (1981) term 'a new consensus' in organization studies. Central to this 'new consensus' was a concern with the complex and multi-layered nature of organizations which makes the very possibility of rational decision-making problematic. From this perspective, organizations are characterized by inertia, slothful and adaptive change, and the chronic attachment to buried assumptions and routine behaviour. In such contexts, organizational decision-making is far removed from the ideal image of planning, organizing, motivating and controlling so beloved of classical management theorists. Indeed, such is the complexity of behaviour in organizations, its multiple layerings and non-rational features that the dominant stress on structure was both theoretically unfounded and, in an increasingly unstable environment, potentially damaging in practice.

Waterman et al.'s (1981) alternative to structural change in isolation is a broader change agenda encompassing, strategy, structure, systems, style, staff, skills and superordinate goals. Profound organizational change requires the symbiotic realignment of all seven factors (Waterman et al., 1981: 63). The success of change initiatives is dependent upon senior management harnessing the social forces of organization through their role of shaping and guiding values to create, maintain and modify organizational cultures. Faced with environmental turbulence the key managerial concern is to achieve forms of organizing which permit rapidity and flexibility of response. 'At the same time they [managers] were acutely aware of their people's need for a stable, unifying value system – a foundation for long-term continuity. Their task, as they saw it, was largely one of preserving internal stability while adroitly guiding the organization's response to fast-paced external change' (Waterman et

Reprinted by permission of Organization Studies, from *Organization Studies* 9(4) 1988: 555–71.

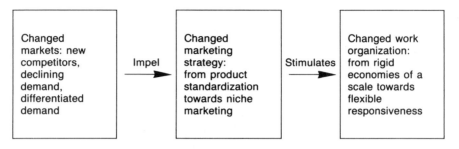

Figure 1   *Trajectory of change*

al., 1981: 51). In short, successful organizations require a responsive capability nested in a stable culture.

The prime mover of contemporary organizational innovation has been the changed conditions of international competition, specifically the decline and fragmentation of previously stable mass markets. Confronted with the entrance of significant new competitors, the secular decline and progressive decomposition of mass demand, innovative manufacturers are experimenting with methods of increasing productive flexibility, reducing the total cost of producing an extended and shifting product range for particular market niches rather than minimizing the average output cost of a narrow range of standardized commodities (Sabel, 1982). This is not to say that mass markets have disintegrated or that economies of scale are irrelevant to competitive performance. Rather, the balance between workforce rationalization, the intensification of inherited work practices and the pursuit of new flexible patterns of work organization is dependent upon the scale, scope and speed of the decline and decomposition of demand for an enterprise's core standardized products. The precise nature of this balance hinges upon a series of strategic choices linking novel and established marketing and production priorities within an overall change agenda. The trajectory of change is schematically represented in Figure 1.

We broadly accept the proposals of the 'new consensus' but would also include technology and work organization as crucial change dimensions. Indeed, we shall stress the importance of work organization in change agendas geared towards securing competitive advantage in uncertain market environments. The volatile market conditions of the 1980s posed an enormous organizational challenge for each of our three case study firms in Britain; Pilkingtons, Rank Xerox and Ford UK. Between 1960 and 1980 Pilkingtons dominated its core markets, glass and insulation, a dominance underpinned by the company's technological superiority in product and process. Rapid market growth and sector under-capacity encouraged Pilkingtons to expand and attracted new entrants to the marketplace without adverse effects on profits. The continuing decline of the domestic motor industry and a sharp downturn in the insulation market then plunged Pilkingtons' core business into severe difficulties in 1980–2. Pilkingtons' marketing response has been the rapid renewal of this technological lead in its basic products and diversification through speciality, high value-added products. Rank Xerox (RX) experienced a similar pattern of prolonged market leadership, partially protected by patents, followed by a rapid decline in demand and profit growth from 1975. The significant, and growing, incursions by Far Eastern competitors into the copier market stimulated the development of a proactive, niche marketing policy centred on meeting customer specifications for integrated office systems rather than maximizing sales of standard products. Similarly, Ford's post-1980 experience stands in marked contrast to the 'rich complacency' of the 1970s: the company's entire product spectrum was directly challenged by Continental European and Japanese competition. Ford's post-1980 marketing response has been twofold: first, heavy discounting to maintain domestic market share, a policy which inevitably depressed profit levels; secondly, initiating a radical redefinition of their central marketing strategy from mass production of standardized vehicles to a conception of the market as a complex amalgam of distinct segments demanding specific products (Lorenz, 1986: 90–1; Clark and Starkey, 1987). This combination of high-volume production and niche marketing based on accelerated product renewal and differentiation through model derivatives has established the parameters of the change process at Ford since 1980 (Willman, 1986: 211).

Despite the broad similarities of the changed market conditions which impelled organizational change, Pilkingtons, RX and Ford each pursued distinctive change strategies. In contrast to Pilkingtons, vital conceptual ingredients of the other two firms' change initiatives were derived from organizational links with multinational corporations. As a result, the experimental, deductive approach of Pilkingtons can be contrasted to the programmatic, inductive rationales which characterized both the Anglo-Japanese strategy of RX and the Anglo-American initiative of Ford. Our intention is to demonstrate that work organization has been a central strand of each of the otherwise contrasting change strategies; namely, the evolutionary development of Pilkingtons, the total process perspective of RX, and Employee Involvement with Ford. The conception and management of change in these organizations confirms the inadequacy of the structure–strategy paradigm either as a heuristic for understanding the process of innovatory change or as a prescriptive tool for enterprises searching for durable competitive advantage in volatile markets.

Our data is extracted from the final project of the Work Organization Research Centre's programme. The WORC programme adopted a longitudinal, comparative focus based on eight in-depth studies of firms and their work organization in their sectoral environments. In this project, we selected firms whose representatives constituted the Organization of Work panel of the British Institute of Management, companies which were self-consciously experimenting with new patterns of work organization (British Institute of Management, 1985). Each of these representatives, all of whom were personnel directors or senior managers reporting directly to the board, participated in a structured interview (see Appendix for details) which focused on the stimuli, dynamics and politics of the change process. In particular, we investigated the internal and external sources of the change strategy, the political strength of its principal patrons and opponents, and shifts in marketing strategy. Similarly, we established the main processes of structural, cultural and work organization change, from workforce rationalization and job redesign to shifts in formal and informal managerial hierarchies. Further, the interview schedule also identified those members of headquarters, divisional and operational managements whom the respondent considered particularly committed to the change programme. By this method, we tapped into informal networks of innovators within the organization. In turn, members of the innovatory networks identified individual managers or particular functions whose overt opposition to, or lack of enthusiasm for the change strategy seriously hindered its progress. The same structured interview was administered by the WORC research team on a face-to-face basis at each organizational level to approximately forty senior managers. This allowed us to identify, for example, differing levels of commitment to particular change initiatives, perceptions of the overall change strategy, and the difficulties experienced by different managerial groups. The interview data were contextualized by internal company documents, the business press and other published academic studies. The three cases are now described.

Pilkington Brothers

For Pilkingtons, change was necessary not only to meet adverse market conditions but also because the company was at a disadvantage compared with competitors producing similar products with similar technology. Internal productivity benchmarking to indicate improvements in work organization was defined as the key to restoring competitiveness. Greengate, a greenfield plant opened in 1981, was to serve as the template for change throughout the company. Greengate proved to be almost four times as efficient as any other Pilkingtons glass plant. For senior management, the key to these productivity gains was not primarily technological but the introduction of new working practices based on fewer, more flexible job descriptions. Jobs were amalgamated into three operator and two craft-maintenance categories (Income Data Services, 1984: 26). Above all, new principles of work organization were introduced: fewer jobs but bigger jobs with increased responsibility and accountability; an emphasis on 'back to the line' with fewer specialists; and fewer layers of accountability. During the long period of growth, management had gradually stripped production workers of responsibility for product quality and process operations by creating an elaborate technical hierarchy. This incurred penalties in both cost and motivational terms. By returning responsibility for quality and efficiency to individual workers, Pilkingtons improved routine problem-solving communications between plant management and the shopfloor without the distorting effect of technical intermediaries.

The task now confronting Pilkingtons' senior management was to diffuse the working practices pioneered at Greengate throughout the corporation. Both the prevailing company culture and industrial bargaining structure were barriers to this. Such pervasive changes could not be negotiated centrally through a national agreement but required the decentralization of industrial relations to plan level. In 1983, Pilkingtons management bypassed stalled central negotiations to install new plant-specific negotiating procedures over the unions' heads. An unintended consequence and major benefit of the prolonged negotiation process was the widespread acceptance of the need for major changes by the work-force. A sea change in labour attitudes was indicated by the cooperation of shop stewards in developing the new localized bargaining processes. Fundamentally, bargains on wage and skill flexibility and training were struck locally, and reflected the market position and relative efficiency of particular plants rather than of Pilkingtons as a whole. Equally, divisional management could now bargain as stand-alone units, freed from corporate direction. Localized wage bargaining was symbolic of the decentralization of decision-making in general, a process involving a profound change in managerial culture.

The defining elements of Pilkingtons' management culture had been technical excellence and centralism. Before 1980, managerial expertise was concentrated in technical areas, the operation of complex chemical and manufacturing processes; operational management regarded finance and marketing as secondary to their primary functions. Business expertise, in the 'entrepreneurial, cutting costs, getting things done' sense had been low (Pilkington, 1985). The success of the change process depended upon reorientating all levels of management from reliance on hierarchies towards greater market sensitivity. Cultural change in divisional and operational managements was accelerated not only through their crucial role in the participative process of work reorganization but also by the widening of their responsibilities to include important plant-level finance and marketing decisions. The 'slow but intense' process of shifting management culture was an integral element of the overall change process, a participative process in which work reorganization was explicitly linked to fulfilling plant plans.

The principal vehicle for implementing change was the dissemination of the company plan mapping out the route to cost competitiveness through work reorganization. The business plan was used as a point of departure, a vehicle for commitment and a reference point for all change initiatives. The goal was to establish a participative cultural and structural framework for future change; and 'enabling architecture' premised on a strong sense of site and business identity. The business plan was the basis for discussion with the unions on changes in job numbers and job design. By scheduling rationalization to avoid compulsory redundancies and by offering employment security in return for skill flexibility, Pilkingtons purposefully mobilized workforce commitment to the change process. The reconstruction and simplification of job profiles, 60 replacing 250, to enable optimum flexibility and mobility of employees was negotiated at plant level. Putting the idea of work reorganization into practice was achieved by small joint management–union teams who analyzed individual jobs and workgroup divisions of labour. The ultimate aim was to replace a highly differentiated workforce by single-status, multi-disciplinary process craftsmen responsible for all appropriate ancillary, maintenance and quality inspection functions. The participative nature of Pilkingtons' job analysis was vital in managing the change process because it ensured the practicality of work reorganization, while positive gains were made in commitment by relying on employee representatives. For senior management an important lesson was the trade unions' capacity to absorb change *and* to become its agents. The profound learning experience which occurred during the early 1980s has established a style of operation and a mutual receptivity to change which Pilkingtons believe will transform the company from a reactive to a proactive organization capable of dealing with market uncertainty.

The stimulus for organizational change in Pilkingtons was the profound business crisis of the early 1980s, a crisis which was also important in facilitating acceptance of major and pervasive change. For corporate management, cost and productivity benchmarking identified work organization as the key to regaining their competitive advantage. The business plan was the vehicle for communicating the strategic necessity for rationalization and work reorganization to the workforce while the participative job evaluation process maximized employee commitment to this strategic goal. The process of work reorganization was and is inseparable from the shift in management culture, particularly the subordination of technical questions to those of finance and marketing. In an important sense, the expansion of managerial responsibilities was the corollary of the move towards a more flexible process operator. Whilst the change process was vital to a return to competitiveness and profitability in 1985, perhaps the most important consequence of the realignment of the early 1980s was the establishment of patterns of managerial organizing geared towards change as an on-going process. Significant changes have been achieved in work organization without having to create additional permanent structures to maintain the momentum of change. In large part, this reflects Pilkingtons' distinctively British approach to organizational change, based on pragmatism and learning through experience. The task now confronting Pilkingtons' senior management is to develop a conceptual understanding of their experience, and to create processes to extend the scope of change. Our next two examples are of innovating organizations which drew essential conceptual elements of their change agendas from their organizational links with foreign firms.

Rank Xerox

A central element in RX's change strategy has been competitive benchmarking, a process in which its liaison with Fuji–Xerox has given it a vital window on Japanese best practice in manufacturing and marketing. The salience of the Fuji–Xerox exemplar was reinforced by the close parallels between the trajectory of Fuji–Xerox and the Far Eastern copier market and RX and European markets, including the maturation and intensification of competition in the mid-1970s. In the context of the smaller-volume and more highly segmented Far Eastern markets, competitive advantage hinged upon increasing customer sensitivity and decreasing the costs of model change (Porter, 1986: 51). In short, the critical balance lay between efficient exploitation of economies of scale on the one hand, and frequent product change across a range of models on the other. For Fuji–Xerox, business turnaround began in 1976 with the New Xerox Movement, a total quality-control process centred on statistical quality control, teamwork and participative management. Unlike Pilkingtons' benchmarking exercise, which was based on crude physical output measures, RX's emulative benchmarking involved identifying competitive gaps in engineering costs, product quality, product lead times, inventory levels and, most informatively, in routine business administration. Competitive benchmarking across the organization was the prelude to 'one of the company's most innovative decisions' (Hornby, 1986): the decision to initiate a massive training programme as the vehicle for a profound company-wide change process. Before 1979, 90 per cent of RX business had been in copier rental: capital realized by the sale of these machines was to be reinvested in training. If the scale of this investment demonstrated the seriousness of RX's intent, then the source of the finance confirmed the company's new marketing strategy and the centrality of organizational change to this new business direction.

Structural change within RX involved two main elements. First, International Headquarters, which coordinates RX's worldwide network, was reorganized into a Strategic Business Unit structure based on different market segments. In contrast to the directive role retained by Pilkingtons' headquarters throughout the change process, RX's corporate headquarters deliberately adopted an enabling function which entailed the rapid devolution of authority to the operational level, now directly accountable for business results. Secondly, purchased materials represent 80 per cent of product cost, a fact which forced RX to include their supplier network in the change process (Grikitis, 1985). From 1980, the supplier base has been progressively consolidated from over 5000 to 300 companies awarded long-term contracts for worldwide volume. By involving its suppliers in product design and development and in the implementation of 'Just In Time' management, RX is progressively transforming its relationships with suppliers from low-trust spot bargaining to high-trust inter-dependence based on long-term single sourcing. The impact of this major modification of the firm's external boundaries has been compounded by internal realignment, specifically the withdrawal of the guaranteed privileged status previously accorded RX's own manufacturing plants. The introduction of 'Just In Time' management throughout RX and its supplier network has not only had a significant impact on company competitiveness but also accelerated the process of cultural change by exposing individual RX plants and workgroups to real and immediate market pressures *within* the company's value chain. In essence, internal relations previously based on hierarchies and bureaucratic authority are being gradually transformed into actual or surrogate market transactions. Inside RX, the disintegrative potential of these profound structural changes is being counteracted by cultural realignment emphasizing participation and commitment to common goals.

Work reorganization was achieved in Pilkingtons despite the absence of a pre-planned strategy for cultural change. In RX, however, cultural change was an integral element of the company's total process change strategy. The vehicle for cultural change in RX is the Leadership Through Quality (LTQ) programme initiated in 1983 to transform every aspect of the company's routine business processes. LTQ is a long-term, company-wide, on-going process aimed at transforming processes of decision-making, interaction among employees and the company's relationships to its customers. Quality is defined in terms of satisfying customers and the prevention of errors rather than rectification. The costs of quality, and of conformity with customer requirements, include such previously hidden costs as training and additional customer liaison. Against these must be set the costs of non-conformity such as unanticipated design changes, unnecessary maintenance and customer dissatisfaction. The principle of quality costing applies not only to RX's external customers but also to each workgroup's internal customers within the RX value chain. Importantly, quality costing is a collaborative rather than a competitive process in which the participants in the transaction share a common analytical framework, exchange information and recognize their mutual inter-dependence with the overall company strategy.

LTQ is based on five processual mechanisms: standards and measurement; reward and recognition; training; communications; and the use of senior management as role models for the process. A key goal in LTQ training has been the development and dissemination of a common language to articulate company goals and a shared approach to routine problem-solving and personal interaction within the company. The basis of this 'company language' is a range of interpersonal skills based on successful interactions between salesmen and customers. Throughout RX each problem is analysed in the same way, with possible solutions evaluated and prioritized in terms of the relative costs of conformance and non-conformance. The LTQ training programme began at the top of the organization and 'cascaded' downwards with each manager training his or her immediate subordinates in the process. Workgroup-based quality teams are established at each stage to maintain the momentum of change, to ensure that common problem-solving techniques and the LTQ language becomes deeply embedded in daily routines throughout the organization.

The change process has impacted on all levels of the organization. For management, it has involved a shift from a competitive, political managerial ethos to an open management style based on a structured, participative approach to problem-solving and decision-making. On the shopfloor, the strategic choice to abandon standardized mass production for mid-volume specialization has forced work organization and cultural change to the top of the managerial agenda. The successful manufacture of products of widely differing size, complexity and quantity within short time-scales is dependent upon the joint effects of more sophisticated technology, especially testing equipment, and employee commitment. Production workgroups are responsible for their own quality control, reduced production faults results in declining rectification time and higher output (Grikitis, 1985). LTQ techniques have also permitted production staff access to the design process as quasi-customers, an influential as opposed to peripheral input to product design. Strategic choice, technological innovation in product and process, job redesign and employee involvement in the LTQ programme have been mutually rein-forcing factors in the RX change process. As a result, RX has now achieved productivity parity with its Far Eastern competitors.

Change in RX was prompted by the slow growth of the copier market in the later 1970s and anticipated dematurity of the office technology market in the 1980s. From the first, RX recognized that profound organizational change was essential to regaining and maintaining competitive edge rather than incidental to strategic choice. The experience of Fuji–Xerox in similar market conditions was crucial to RX's concep-tualization of the multi-dimensional and multi-temporal nature of successful organizational change. Accordingly, the LTQ programme was conceived of as a series of structural realignments and common processual techniques which is embedding a culture of change as an everyday and on-going process rather than for a specific, limited period. The change process has also blurred the boundaries of the firm. In this respect, interest in the celebrated networks, managerial staff who receive technical support from RX but whose contract is defined solely by time or task, has overshadowed the more important alterations to the relationships between RX and its supplier network (Judkins et al., 1985). This has had a reciprocal impact on RX's internal functioning; reducing what were previously sharp breaks in the RX value chain has consolidated the iden-tification of subsequent workgroups as 'customers' with a degree of choice within the extended RX production network. The deliberate creation of structures and processes specifically geared towards organizational realignment makes change within RX a self-perpetuating process, centrally stimulated but dependent for its momentum on grassroots commitment to the LTQ techniques.

Ford UK

Two major change initiatives dominated Ford's development in the 1980s. The first, the 1981 'After Japan' campaign, was the direct result of growing corporate awareness of the Japanese competitive edge. 'After Japan' was conceived of as a 'trigger factor' signalling critical business objectives in terms of financial targets and European market share (Beynon, 1984: 356). The campaign incorporated work organization themes; inventory reduction, improved quality through self-inspection, and maximizing automated process efficiencies by manpower reductions and more flexible manning practices (Willman, 1986: 210). The intimate link between scale economies and product standardization means that the relative costs of model change and the fluidity of production scheduling are critical for competitive advantage (Abernathy, 1978: 39–47). Ford's product-led competitive strategy entailed capital investments in high-productivity automation capable of coping with increasingly variable product mixes (Williams et al., 1987: 58–9). 'After Japan' also attempted to introduce quality circles into Ford UK to form the communications basis for these work organization changes (Marsden et al., 1985: 115–16). Whereas in RX and Pilkingtons union resistance was either negligible or was transformed into active cooperation, at Ford the quality circles foundered on the unions' dismissal of the initiative as a heavy-handed attempt to short-circuit existing bargaining procedures. Despite this failure, the central message of 'After Japan', the company's massive productivity disadvantage, was pressed home by rationalization, specifically the closure of the Dagenham foundry which signalled the end of totally integrated production in the company's heartland. Ironically, the dismal failure of the labour relations element of the campaign was directly attributable to Ford's attempts to impose quality circles as a structural remedy for relatively poor productivity and quality, rather than introducing them as mechanisms for mobilizing employee commitment to company goals. Even so, the campaign was not entirely counter-productive, as it compelled senior management to recognize that the long history of conflictual, low-trust industrial relations necessitated a gradual, processual approach to modifying company culture rather than structural reorganization alone. In itself, this was a major shift in managerial understanding of the change process and one which has informed subsequent company strategy.

The second, and continuing change initiative at Ford was the two-pronged Employee Involvement, Participative Management campaign, imported from the American mother company. This reflected Ford's role in the major shifts in the nature of labour relations in the US automobile industry between 1979 and 1983, specifically the renegotiation of national wage and work-rule agreements to facilitate increased flexibility of work organization and employee participation in business decision-making (Katz, 1985). Inside Ford, American initiatives are invested with enormous political capital and are typically rapidly refracted throughout the corporation. Employee Involvement is regarded as a long-term attempt to create a more cooperative relationship with employees. As the company recognizes, trust-building in labour relations begins from a very low base. For decades, labour relations within Ford have been regulated by annually negotiated company-wide agreements and tight shopfloor supervision. The symbiotic relationship between low-trust industrial bargaining and a management strategy which sought to maximize productivity through extreme task fragmentation, created massive rigidities in work organization and equally complex institutional barriers to change. The structures of Employee Involvement have only been accepted by salaried staff; shopfloor unions have refused to make a formal commitment to the programme, which is regarded as contrary to the established contractural job-control orientation of workplace trade unions. In contrast to the managerial goals which underpinned the attempted introduction of quality circles, Ford regards the creation of such formal structures as secondary to gradual infusion of employee involvement in routine collective bargaining. Unlike RX the enormous obstacle to negotiated change posed by competitive multi-unionism in the British auto industry prevented Ford UK from replicating American developments, while chronic low-trust labour relations prohibited accelerated evolutionary development similar to Pilkingtons'.

The obverse of Employee Involvement is Participative Management, Ford's attempt to break down the organizational barriers between management hierarchies. Again, Ford's current strategy is to overcome the inflexibilities resulting from a long-established, complex and strictly defined line and staff management structure. In this functional bureaucracy, Ford's top-down management style made decision-making slow and inflexible with a heavy emphasis on short-term financial criteria. Until the early 1980s, the efficiency of Ford's three primary 'organizational chimneys' – finance, production and marketing – was judged by different, and often conflicting, criteria. In manufacturing, for example, the yardstick was output while marketing aimed for market share. The post-1980 company strategic goal of combining scale economies in production with niche marketing based on product differentiation has inevitably caused increased friction between functional hierarchies. Experiments in organizational restructuring designed to increase managerial integration and accountability have progressed furthest in manufacturing, another indication of the centrality of work organization in company strategy. Within Dagenham's body and assembly plants, the number of managerial layers has been reduced from eight to five with the creation of four 'mini plants' and the decentralization of finance and quality-assurance activities (British Institute of Management, 1985). However, Ford stresses the limits to the Participative Management programme, that structural changes have been tentative and marginal while cultural change remains an intention rather than an achievement.

In 1985 Ford pay agreement was a watershed in the development of the company's labour relations system and work organization. The agreement represented a sharp break with the traditional flat-rate basis of earnings, the manual unions accepting productivity bonuses for flexible working practices (Income Data Services, 1985). The agreement sought to break down Ford's rigid bureaucratic system of categorizing semi-skilled production work and the craft demarcations it had inherited from craft unionism. It enabled the reduction of demarcations between electrical and mechanical craftsmen. Production workers' roles were expanded to include such indirect tasks as minor maintenance and quality assurance. The flexibility achieved by extending worker responsibilities and enlarging job cycles reduces idle machine time, the factor identified by Ford's management as the main cause of low British labour and capital productivity compared with the company's continental plants. The increased worker autonomy implicit in work reorganization is monitored and controlled by Ford's management through computerized automated measurement procedures (Pettigrew, 1985). Equally important, the expansion of the responsibilities of production workers creates additional space for building trust within individual plants, outside national collective bargaining channels (Roots, 1986). It is this *potential* for mobilizing worker commitment to change which makes the 1985 agreement a landmark in Ford's industrial relations and work organization.

Change initiatives have formed the core of Ford's response to the new competitive challenges of an automobile industry in the throes of 'dematurization', a process involving the destabilization of previously predictable patterns of consumer demand, and the coming of new production possibilities opened up by technical change (Tolliday and Zeitlin, 1986). Behind Ford's change programmes lies a marketing strategy of product diversity, based on more precise definitions of market segments, more speciality model derivatives, and an acceleration of the model replacement cycle. Given this market context and strategic choice, increasing the flexibility of work organization was crucial in an industry in which the relative cost of model change is a key variable. Changes in collective bargaining structures have enabled local work reorganization, specifically the partial reversal of the Fordist paradigm of task fragmentation and ever-intensifying direct control.

Employee involvement represents Ford's first step in the long-term renegotiation of the psychological contract between the individual worker and the company. In this sense, their post-1980 labour relations initiatives are premised on an implicit understanding that flexibility in work organization is dependent upon worker commitment to company goals, rather than upon sophisticated control techniques (Walton, 1985: 78). Even so, the limits are shown by management's determination to maintain tight control over the terms of the effort bargain in newly extended job roles, both by improved measurement of individual productivities and the retention of strict disciplinary rules on the shopfloor, and by the manual unions' hostility towards the Employee Involvement programme.

In general, Ford's use of Participative Management to promote an ethos of change, and modify a management culture grounded in functional loyalties, is an attempt to shift the terms of company politics in favour of those senior managers supportive of change strategies. Whilst RX's rapid withdrawal from the copier market and the simultaneous launch of the LTQ programme irrevocably committed that organization to the total process change strategy, by contrast, Ford, like Pilkingtons, pursued a dual strategy. This sought to improve productivity and market performance in existing areas while developing new products and highly defined derivatives and more flexible patterns of work organization. For Ford, the virtue of slow change is that it permits retention of the organizational bases of current market strength and profitability, a virtue which outweighs the inevitable tension between the long-term goal of employee involvement and the short-term necessity of maintaining shopfloor discipline. Yet the long dominance of finance specialists with little knowledge of the strategic importance of product development means that at Ford the fine balance between organizational innovation and productivity will be especially difficult to sustain (Halberstam, 1987).

Conclusion

Our three case studies of organizational transition share certain characteristics. Changing work organization stemmed from the perception of rapid shifts in the contours of their core product markets; the decline and resegmentation of consumer demand and the entry of significant new competitors. To some degree, each company has reorientated its business strategy from product standardization for stable, relatively homogeneous markets towards a more refined marketing strategy based on satisfying a range of finer market niches. This strategic reorientation has progressed furthest in RX, which has moved away from copiers as its core business to customer-specified integrated office systems. Strategic choice at Ford has involved an acceleration of the model replacement cycle and the production of high-specification derivatives of basic product ranges. Pilkingtons have initiated a long-term change in strategic direction towards higher value-added products. In this market context, competitive advantage hinges on achieving an optimal balance between the efficiency and responsiveness of work organization, rather than simply maximizing scale economies. In this sense, our case studies support Piore and Sabel's (1984) thesis that the 1980s constituted a transition period in business strategy, the end of 'Fordism' and scientific management as the dominant paradigms of work organization. For Piore and Sabel, the contemporary alternative to Fordism – 'flexible specialization' – is implicit in the competitive strategies and work organization of innovating companies. 'Flexible specialization' refers to an integrated marketing, investment and production strategy which lies at the interface of product standardization and customization. Through the judicious mix of flexible computerized production technologies, upskilling and the subcontracting of standardized component manufacture, innovating companies can better balance economies of scale and economies of scope in novel organizational configurations. In all three cases studied, Pilkingtons, RX and Ford UK, the dominant marketing and production strategies of the 1970s were predicted on product market stability and the maximization of scale economies through a highly integrated division of labour based on dedicated machinery, de-skilling and direct managerial control. But now, the key organizational task confronting innovating companies is the management of a portfolio of associated rather than standardized products in fluctuating batch sizes. In turn, this demands increased work organization flexibility dependent upon the active cooperation of an upskilled, more versatile workforce.

The extent of the company's competitive disadvantage was revealed by internal and external benchmarking against sectoral best practice. Benchmarking represented a period of enforced introspection beginning at the strategic level and percolating through the organization as the change process progressed. At Pilkingtons and Ford, benchmarking exercises were confined to manufacturing costs and work organization, whereas RX instigated a more profound organizational benchmarking, isolating competitive gaps in all aspects of organization not simply as a sporadic trigger exercise to prioritize change areas but as an on-going process. This contrast reflects the conceptual imperatives which underlay change in each company. In RX, change was conceptualized as a total process embracing strategic choice, technical innovation in product and process, work organization and company culture. Self-consciously drawing on the experience of Fuji–Xerox, RX accelerated a pervasive change process through the LTQ programme which propagated a common analytical language to maximize employee commitment to the process. Similarly, Ford's first change initiatives were based on the experience of the US mother company. However, the failure of the 'After Japan' initiative in the context of the British industrial relations system forced Ford UK to retrench, to introduce its long-term Employee Involvement strategy. In itself, this constituted a sharp break with Ford's traditional understanding of change in strictly structural terms. Pilkingtons did not adopt a programmatic approach to change, preferring evolutionary development: Pilkingtons' senior management are currently reviewing their post-1980 experiences with the intention of renewing the momentum of change within the company. Nonetheless, it would be misleading to conclude from the relative momentum of change in the three companies that RX alone represents success, not least because all three did achieve significant business turnaround as a result of organizational realignment.

The means of mobilizing employee consent to the process of change differed markedly between the three companies. RX secured employee consent through the LTQ training programme whose key function was to disseminate a common language with which to understand the necessity for and dynamics of the change process. At Pilkingtons, trust-building was facilitated by the joint union–management work reorganization programme. Ford, by contrast, was forced by the inertia of labour relations institutions to forgo a programme-driven process of obtaining consent. Overcoming the legacy of chronically low-trust industrial relations is necessarily a slow process, though it may be accelerated by the localization of aspects of industrial bargaining through the 1985 agreement. Underlying the work reorganization in each case has been the exposure of line management and shopfloor workers to market pressures, either by organizational restructuring, as in RX, or, as at Pilkingtons and Ford, through the demonstration effects of large-scale rationalization.

To return to our starting point; Waterman et al.'s (1981) critique of structuralist approaches to organizational behaviour is based on a rational economic model of human behaviour. The 'new consensus' emphasizes the importance of non-rational aspects of organizational behaviour, dimensions we have placed at the centre of our analysis of organizational transitions. For innovating organizations responding to the new challenges of industrial dematurity, the key task is to mobilize those intangible social forces which perpetuate organizational inertia. In their different ways, RX, Ford and Pilkingtons recognized the vital importance of harnessing employee commitment to company goals. Equally, corporate managers must be sensitive to the powerful inertial forces inherent in organizational cultures and ascribe as much importance to inc lcating a culture of change throughout the organization as to their marketing or investment strategies. In market situations where the flexibility and responsiveness of work organization is crucial to competitive advantage, successful change strategies cannot be premised on the simplicities of the structure–strategy paradigm.

Appendix

Specimen section of interview schedule

Our research is concerned with new forms of work organization and the problems of their management. We are particularly interested in changes in work organization since 1980 – successes and failures, changes that have worked and innovations that have not.

1. We would like to discuss any changes you have made in the areas of working practices, the relationship between management and labour, and the relationship between various managerial groups. Can you describe any changes made in the following areas?

Working Practices   (i) skills

(*Prompts*: moves towards more flexible use of skills/job redesign/new working practices/breakdown of previous demarcations [between and within trades – between craftsmen and operators – between craftsmen and white-collar staff]/new emphasis on training)
(ii) new technology
(*Prompts*: effects on working practices – deskilling/upskilling/economics of new technology vs. new working practices/flexibility as alternative to capital investment)
(iii) use of sub-contracting/'spinning off'

Rationalization   (*Prompts*: size of organization/lean-ness/intensification/efficiency/closures/redundancies/relocation)

More flexible management practices   1. (*Prompts*: just in time/more flexible organizational structure(s)/alteration to the balance between centralization and decentralization/devolution of control/cultural change, e.g. more participation, more consultation/new thinking about management development/role of the various management groups/stress on generalist management vs. functional specialism?)
2. When were changes introduced? When did they become an important part of the managerial agenda? Was change incremental or was there a sudden, sharp turning point?
3. Why were the changes introduced? What problems were they introduced to solve? To replace what outmoded practices?
(*Prompts*: competition/market-driven/efficiency/quality/flexibility/environment – simple–complex; stable–dynamic; predictable)
4. How much importance was attached to these initiatives in terms of overall company strategy?
5. To recap, then, the goals of the change(s) were . . . and these were new developments for your company.
6. What happened in practice?
(*Prompts*: problems of implementation?/comparison of plants/strategies for introduction – consultative/participative approach?/mechanisms e.g. joint consultative procedures, quality circles, job improvement committees?/formal agreements – with which unions?)
7. What were the key sources of management information? Where did the new ideas come from? Was/were the originator(s) of the ideas the moving force(s) behind the implementation of the change(s)?
8. What resistance did the change(s) meet? (*Prompts*: unions/management – individual or groups?)

9. In what ways are the changes related to changes in the company's business strategy?
10. How do you anticipate the changes proceeding? Do you anticipate new developments in the future?

References

Abernathy, W.J. (1978) *The productivity dilemma: roadblock to innovation in the auto industry*. Baltimore: Johns Hopkins University Press.

Beynon, H. (1984) *Working for Ford*. Harmondsworth: Penguin.

British Institute of Management (1985) *Managing new patterns of work*. London: British Institute of Management.

Clark. P. and Starkey, K. (1987) *Organizational transitions and innovation design*. London: Pinter.

Grikitis, K. (1985) *Rooting out quality problems: electronics and test*. Wellwyn: RX.

Halberstam, D. (1987) *The reckoning*. London: Bloomsbury.

Hornby, D. (1986) 'Innovation into profit: can we teach ourselves to change?', Royal Bank of Scotland Lecture, Aston University.

Income Data Services (1984) Study 312.

Income Data Services (1985) Report 461.

Judkins, P. et al. (1985) *Networking in organizations. The Rank Xerox experiment*. Aldershot: Gower.

Katz, H. (1985) *Changing gears: changing labour relations in the US auto industry*. Cambridge, Mass.: MIT Press.

Lorenz, C. (1986) *The design dimension. Product strategy and the challenge of global marketing*. Oxford: Blackwell.

Marsden, D. et al. (1985) *The car industry. Labour relations and industrial adjustment*. London: Tavistock.

Pettigrew, T.J. (1985) 'Process quality control: the new approach to the management of quality in Ford', *Quality Assurance*, 11: 81–8.

Pilkington, A. (1985) *Financial Times*, 12 June.

Piore, M.J. and Sabel, C. (1984) *The second industrial divide: possibilities for prosperity*. New York: Basic Books.

Porter, M.E. (1986) 'Competition in global industries: a conceptual framework', in *Competition in global industries*, ed. M.E. Porter pp. 15–61. Boston, Mass.: Harvard Business School.

Roots, P. (1986) 'Collective bargaining: opportunities for a new approach', Warwick Papers in Industrial Relations 5.

Sabel, C. (1982) *Work and politics*. Cambridge: Cambridge University Press.

Tolliday, S. and Zeitlin, J. (1986) 'Between Fordism and flexibility', in *The automobile industry and its workers*, ed. S. Tolliday and J. Zeitlin, pp. 1–27. Cambridge: Polity.

Walton, R.E. (1985) 'From control to commitment in the workplace', *Harvard Business Review*, 63: 77–84.

Waterman, R.H., Peters, J.J. and Phillips, J.R. (1981) 'Structure is not organization', in *Experimental organizational behaviors*, ed. T.T. Herbert and P. Lorenzi, pp. 49–63. New York: Macmillan.

Williams, K., Williams J. and Haslam, C. (1987) *The breakdown of Austin Rover*. Leamington Spa: Berg.

Willman, P. (1986) *Technological change, collective bargaining and industrial efficiency*. Oxford: Clarendon.

PART TWO
STRUCTURAL STRATEGIES

Introduction

Sheila Cameron

Organizations, faced with the turbulent and competitive environments and technological developments of the 1990s, are increasingly looking for structural solutions to their problems. Old-style bureaucracy, with its traditional tall-pyramid structure, is being rejected as insufficiently flexible, and alternative ways of organization, using flatter structures or less hierarchical ones, and giving more autonomy to those lower down in the organization are sought. While this might be regarded, particularly by those who remember the Quality of Working Life (QWL) movement of the 1970s as a passing fashion, two of the three papers included in this part of the reader make strong cases to the contrary. Drucker argues convincingly that information technology provides a powerful imperative to structural change within organizations. Since the prime function of many layers of middle management has been to transmit information which can be far more efficiently transmitted by modern technology, there is now no longer any need for their employment. Drucker suggests that in the flatter structures that will result, knowledge requirements at the *bottom* of the organization will be greatly increased, and the use of *task forces* will become prevalent. For this form of structure to work, clear goals and a unified vision will be crucial.

While Drucker is *predicting* a trend rather than describing cases, 'de-layering' is *happening*. In 1990 alone, such exercises included BP's plans to cut 1150 jobs at their headquarters, Boots' to shed 500 supervisory and management jobs, the loss of 900 management support jobs at BHS, BT's plans to reduce eleven layers of management to six and BP's cut from eleven layers to five.

Such de-layering will markedly increase responsibility at lower levels of management and below. In the second chapter in this section the focus is on changes at these levels. Buchanan is arguing that because of environmental pressures, and particularly because of changes in management technology and the need for flexibility, high performance requires organizations to combine flatter structures with a much higher degree of worker control. He describes how the Digital Equipment Corporation at Ayr have pursued quality and flexibility by introducing high performance, self-managing work teams. He makes the point that this represents a *genuine* shift of control, not found in the earlier use of semi-autonomous working groups. As well as creating major development opportunities for team members this shift has a profound influence on managerial work. Once teams are working effectively, managerial effort is freed for more strategic activities.

The final reading looks, as is popular, to the East in search of a more appropriate 'post-modernist' model than the bureaucracy which Clegg sees as the 'modern' form of organization. Drawing primarily on Japan, it describes a situation characterized by flexibility, and the rapid diffusion of new technology. Some of this flexibility is achieved through the JIT system, which, among other advantages, displaces wage costs from the core to the often less expensive periphery. But much of the flexibility stems from the use of self-managing teams, whose members are multi-skilled, and where payment systems reward co-operation rather than competition, and recognize skill acquisition.

Thus far, the Japanese situation seems closely to resemble Buchanan's high performance groups. However, further description of the context in which they operate suggests a range of factors not yet common in the UK. Management rotation is practised, so that managers too can co-operate from a basis of knowledge, and this is reinforced by the 'lifetime employment' model which applies to most of these managers, and allows a considerable degree of company-specific expertise to develop. Japanese businesses tend to be more focused on specific activities than is the case in the West, where mergers and acquisitions typically result in conglomerates of unrelated businesses. The West's capital budgeting system leads short-term considerations to predominate, and makes long-term investment less likely to gain approval than would be the case in Japan. There has been a tradition of networking in Japan since before the Second World War.

While Clegg holds back from suggesting that structure is socio-culturally determined, it is worth considering firstly whether the type of initiative described by Buchanan will be *limited* by the absence of the factors Clegg describes as contributing to Japan's 'post modernity'. If so, what should and can British organizations do in consequence? Some differences, such as a *lower* emphasis on training, may be within their influence. Others may be more difficult to address.

It is worth pondering, too, on the 'losers' Clegg identifies; those workers outside the core labour market who are in a sense paying for the benefits Japanese organizations derive. Middle managers are clearly at risk if Drucker is right, and thought should be given to whether 'letting them go' in large numbers *is* in the organization's longer term interest. The position of part-time and contract workers needs to be considered if there is a shift of employment from core to periphery.

Rather than grasping at current structural prescriptions as a solution to all organizational ills, careful thought needs to be given to the full range of their implications, in the *particular context* to which they are to be applied. The 'prescription' can then be adapted accordingly, so that the intended effect of re-structuring on competitiveness can be achieved and unintended negative consequences avoided.

9

The coming of the new organization

Peter F. Drucker

The typical large business 20 years hence will have fewer than half the levels of management of its counterpart today, and no more than a third the managers. In its structure, and in its management problems and concerns, it will bear little resemblance to the typical manufacturing company, circa 1950, which our textbooks still consider the norm. Instead it is far more likely to resemble organizations that neither the practicing manager nor the management scholar pays much attention to today: the hospital, the university, the symphony orchestra. For like them, the typical business will be knowledge-based, an organization composed largely of specialists who direct and discipline their own performance through organized feedback from colleagues, customers, and headquarters. For this reason, it will be what I call an information-based organization.

Businesses, especially large ones, have little choice but to become information-based. Demographics, for one, demands the shift. The center of gravity in employment is moving fast from manual and clerical workers to knowledge workers who resist the command-and-control model that business took from the military 100 years ago. Economics also dictates change, especially the need for large businesses to innovate and to be entrepreneurs. But above all, information technology demands the shift.

Advanced data-processing technology isn't necessary to create an information-based organization, of course. As we shall see, the British built just such an organization in India when 'information technology' meant the quill pen, and barefoot runners were the 'telecommunications' systems. But as advanced technology becomes more and more prevalent, we have to engage in analysis and diagnosis – that is, in 'information' – even more intensively or risk being swamped by the data we generate.

So far most computer users still use the new technology only to do faster what they have always done before, crunch conventional numbers. But as soon as a company takes the first tentative steps from data to information, its decision processes, management structure, and even the way its work gets done begin to be transformed. In fact this is already happening, quite fast, in a number of companies throughout the world.

We can readily see the first steps in this transformation process when

Reprinted with permission from the *Harvard Business Review*, Jan–Feb. 1988, pp. 45–53.

we consider the impact of computer technology on capital-investment decisions. We have known for a long time that there is no one right way to analyze a proposed capital investment. To understand it we need at least six different analyses: the expected rate of return; the payout period and the investment's expected productive life; the discounted present value of all returns through the productive lifetime of the investment; the risk in not making the investment or deferring it; the cost and risk in case of failure; and finally, the opportunity cost. Every accounting student is taught these concepts. But before the advent of data-processing capacity, the actual analyses would have taken man-years of clerical toil to complete. Now anyone with a spreadsheet should be able to do them in a few hours.

The availability of this information transforms the capital-investment analysis from opinion into diagnosis, that is, into the rational weighing of alternative assumptions. Then the information transforms the capital-investment decision from an opportunistic, financial decision governed by the numbers into a business decision based on the probability of alternative strategic assumptions. So the decision both presupposes a business strategy and challenges that strategy and its assumptions. What was once a budget exercise becomes an analysis of policy.

The second area that is affected when a company focuses its data-processing capacity on producing information is its organization structure. Almost immediately it becomes clear that both the number of management levels and number of managers can be sharply cut. The reason is straightforward: it turns out that whole layers of management neither make decisions nor lead. Instead, their main, if not their only, function is to serve as 'relays' – human boosters for the faint, unfocused signals that pass for communication in the traditional pre-information organization.

One of America's largest defense contractors made this discovery when it asked what information its top corporate and operating managers needed to do their jobs. Where did it come from? What form was it in? How did it flow? The search for answers soon revealed that whole layers of management – perhaps as many as 6 out of a total of 14 – existed only because these questions had not been asked before. The company had had data galore. But it had always used its copious data for control rather than for information.

Information is data endowed with relevance and purpose. Converting data into information thus requires knowledge. And knowledge, by definition, is specialized. (In fact, truly knowledgeable people tend toward overspecialization, whatever their field, precisely because there is always so much more to know.)

The information-based organization requires far more specialists overall than the command-and-control companies we are accustomed to. Moreover, the specialists are found in operations, not at corporate headquarters. Indeed, the operating organization tends to become an organization of specialists of all kinds.

Information-based organizations need central operating work such as legal counsel, public relations, and labor relations as much as ever. But the need for service staffs – that is, for people without operating responsibilities who only advise, counsel, or coordinate – shrinks drastically. In its *central* management, the information-based organization needs few, if any, specialists.

Because of its flatter structure, the large, information-based organization will more closely resemble the businesses of a century ago than today's big companies. Back then, however, all the knowledge, such as it was, lay with the very top people. The rest were helpers or hands, who mostly did the same work and did as they were told. In the information-based organization, the knowledge will be primarily at the bottom, in the minds of the specialists who do different work and direct themselves. So today's typical organization in which knowledge tends to be concentrated in service staffs, perched rather insecurely between top management and the operating people, will likely be labeled a phase, an attempt to infuse knowledge from the top rather than obtain information from below.

Finally, a good deal of work will be done differently in the information-based organization. Traditional departments will serve as guardians of standards, as centers for training and the assignment of specialists; they won't be where the work gets done. That will happen largely in task-focused teams.

This change is already under way in what used to be the most clearly defined of all departments – research. In pharmaceuticals, in telecommunications, in papermaking, the traditional *sequence* of research, development, manufacturing, and marketing, is being replaced by *synchrony*: specialists from all these functions work together as a team, from the inception of research to a product's establishment in the market.

How task forces will develop to tackle other business opportunities and problems remains to be seen. I suspect, however, that the need for a task force, its assignment, its composition, and its leadership will have to be decided on case by case. So the organization that will be developed will go beyond the matrix and may indeed be quite different from it. One thing is clear, though: it will require greater self-discipline and even greater emphasis on individual responsibility for relationships and for communications.

To say that information technology is transforming business enterprises is simple. What this transformation will require of companies and top managements is much harder to decipher. That is why I find it helpful to look for clues in other kinds of information-based organizations, such as the hospital, the symphony orchestra, and the British administration in India.

A fair-sized hospital of about 400 beds will have a staff of several hundred physicians and 1,200 to 1,500 paramedics divided among some 60 medical and paramedical specialists. Each specialty has its own knowledge, its own training, its own language. In each specialty, especially the paramedical ones like the clinical lab and physical therapy, there is a head person who is a working specialist rather than a full-time manager. The head of each specialty reports directly to the top, and there is little middle management. A good deal of the work is done in ad hoc teams as required by an individual patient's diagnosis and condition.

A large symphony orchestra is even more instructive, since for some works there may be a few hundred musicians on stage playing together. According to organization theory then, there should be several group vice-president conductors and perhaps a half-dozen division VP conductors. But that's not how it works. There is only the conductor-CEO – and every one of the musicians plays directly to that person without an intermediary. And each is a high-grade specialist, indeed an artist.

But the best example of a large and successful information-based organization, and one without any middle management at all, is the British civil administration in India.[1]

The British ran the Indian subcontinent for 200 years, from the middle of the eighteenth century through World War II, without making any fundamental changes in organization structure or administrative policy. The Indian civil service never had more than 1,000 members to administer the vast and densely populated subcontinent – a tiny fraction (at most 1 per cent) of the legions of Confucian mandarins and palace eunuchs employed next door to administer a not-much-more populous China. Most of the Britishers were quite young; a 30-year-old was a survivor, especially in the early years. Most lived alone in isolated outposts with the nearest countryman a day or two of travel away, and for the first hundred years there was no telegraph or railroad.

The organization structure was totally flat. Each district officer reported directly to the 'Coo,' the provincial political secretary. And since there were nine provinces, each political secretary had at least 100 people reporting directly to him, many times what the doctrine of the span of control would allow. Nevertheless, the system worked remarkably well, in large part because it was designed to ensure that each of its members had the information he needed to do his job.

Each month the district officer spent a whole day writing a full report to the political secretary in the provincial capital. He discussed each of his principal tasks – there were only four, each clearly delineated. He put down in detail what he had expected would happen with respect to each of them, what actually did happen, and why, if there was a discrepancy, the two differed. Then he wrote down what he expected would happen in the ensuing month with respect to each key task and what he was going to do about it, asked questions about policy, and commented on long-term opportunities, threats, and needs. In turn, the political secretary 'minuted' every one of those reports – that is, he wrote back a full comment.

On the basis of these examples, what can we say about the requirements of the information-based organization? And what are its management problems likely to be? Let's look first at the requirements. Several hundred musicians and their CEO, the conductor, can play together because they all have the same score. It tells both flutist and timpanist what to play and when. And it tells the conductor what to expect from each and when. Similarly, all the specialists in the hospital share a common mission: the care and cure of the sick. The diagnosis is their 'score'; it dictates specific action for the X-ray lab, the dietitian, the physical therapist, and the rest of the medical team.

Information-based organizations, in other words, require clear, simple, common objectives that translate into particular actions. At the same time, however, as these examples indicate, information-based organizations also need concentration on one objective or, at most, on a few.

Because the 'players' in an information-based organization are specialists, they cannot be told how to do their work. There are probably few orchestra conductors who could coax even one note out of a French horn, let alone show the horn player how to do it. But the conductor can focus the horn player's skill and knowledge on the musicians' joint performance. And this focus is what the leaders of an information-based business must be able to achieve.

Yet a business has no 'score' to play by except the score it writes as it plays. And whereas neither a first-rate performance of a symphony nor a miserable one will change what the composer wrote, the performance of a business continually creates new and different scores against which its performance is assessed. So an information-based business must be structured around goals that clearly state management's performance expectations for the enterprise and for each part and specialist and around organized feedback that compares results with these performance expectations so that every member can exercise self-control.

The other requirement of an information-based organization is that everyone takes information responsibility. The bassoonist in the orchestra does so every time she plays a note. Doctors and paramedics work with an elaborate system of reports and an information center, the nurse's station on the patient's floor. The district officer in India acted on this responsibility every time he filed a report.

The key to such a system is that everyone asks: Who in this organization depends on me for what information? And on whom, in turn, do I depend? Each person's list will always include superiors and subordinates. But the most important names on it will be those of colleagues, people with whom one's primary relationship is coordination. The relationship of the internist, the surgeon, and the anesthesiologist is one example. But the relationship of a biochemist, a pharmacologist, the medical director in charge of clinical testing, and a marketing specialist in a pharmaceutical company is no different. It, too, requires each party to take the fullest information responsibility.

Information responsibility to others is increasingly understood, especially in middle-sized companies. But information responsibility to oneself is still largely neglected. That is, everyone in an organization should constantly be thinking through what information he or she needs to do the job and to make a contribution.

This may well be the most radical break with the way even the most highly computerized businesses are still being run today. There, people either assume the more data, the more information – which was a perfectly valid assumption yesterday when data were scarce, but leads to data overload and information blackout now that they are plentiful. Or they believe that information specialists know what data executives and professionals need in order to have information. But information specialists are tool makers. They can tell us what tool to use to hammer upholstery nails into a chair. We need to decide whether we should be upholstering the chair at all.

Executives and professional specialists need to think through what information is for them, what data they need: first, to know what they are doing; then, to be able to decide what they should be doing; and finally, to appraise how well they are doing. Until this happens MIS departments are likely to remain cost centers rather than become the result centers they could be.

Most large businesses have little in common with the examples we have been looking at. Yet to remain competitive – maybe even to survive – they will have to convert themselves into information-based organizations, and fairly quickly. They will have to change old habits and acquire new ones. And the more successful a company has been, the more difficult and painful this process is apt to be. It will threaten the jobs, status, and opportunities of a good many people in the organization, especially the long-serving, middle-aged people in middle management who tend to be the least mobile and to feel most secure in their work, their positions, their relationships, and their behavior.

The information-based organization will also pose its own special management problems. I see as particularly critical:

1 Developing rewards, recognition, and career opportunities for specialists;
2 Creating unified vision in an organization of specialists;
3 Devising the management structure for an organization of task forces;
4 Ensuring the supply, preparation, and testing of top management people.

Bassoonists presumably neither want nor expect to be anything but bassoonists. Their career opportunities consist of moving from second bassoon to first bassoon and perhaps of moving from a second-rank orchestra to a better, more prestigious one. Similarly, many medical technologists neither expect nor want to be anything but medical technologists. Their career opportunities consist of a fairly good chance of moving up to senior technician, and a very slim chance of becoming a lab director. For those who make it to lab director, about 1 out of every 25 or 30 technicians, there is also the opportunity to move to a bigger, richer hospital. The district officer in India had practically no chance for professional growth except possibly to be relocated, after a three-year stint, to a bigger district.

Opportunities for specialists in an information-based business organization should be more plentiful than they are in an orchestra or hospital, let alone in the Indian civil service. But as in these organizations, they will primarily be opportunities for advancement within the specialty, and for limited advancement at that. Advancement into 'management' will be the exception, for the simple reason that there will be far fewer middle-management positions to move into. This contrasts sharply with the traditional organization where, except in the research lab, the main line of advancement in rank is out of the specialty and into general management.

More than 30 years ago General Electric tacked this problem by creating 'parallel opportunities' for 'individual professional contributors.' Many companies have followed this example. But professional specialists themselves have largely rejected it as a solution. To them – and to their management colleagues – the only meaningful opportunities are promotions into management. And the prevailing compensation structure in practically all businesses reinforces this attitude because it is heavily biased towards managerial positions and titles.

There are no easy answers to this problem. Some help may come from looking at large law and consulting firms, where even the most senior partners tend to be specialists, and associates who will not make partner are outplaced fairly early on. But whatever scheme is eventually developed will work only if the values and compensation structure of business are drastically changed.

The second challenge that management faces is giving its organization of specialists a common vision, a view of the whole.

In the Indian civil service, the district officer was expected to see the 'whole' of his district. But to enable him to concentrate on it, the government services that arose one after the other in the nineteenth century (forestry, irrigation, the archaeological survey, public health and sanitation, roads) were organized outside the administrative structure, and had virtually no contact with the district officer. This meant that the district officer became increasingly isolated from the activities that often had the greatest impact on – and the greatest importance for – his district. In the end, only the provincial government or the central government in Delhi had a view of the 'whole' and it was an increasingly abstract one at that.

A business simply cannot function this way. It needs a view of the whole and a focus on the whole to be shared among a great many of its professional specialists, certainly among the senior ones. And yet it will have to accept, indeed will have to foster, the pride and professionalism of its specialists – if only because, in the absence of opportunities to move into middle management, their motivation must come from that pride and professionalism.

One way to foster professionalism, of course, is through assignments to task forces. And the information-based business will use more and more smaller self-governing units, assigning them tasks tidy enough for 'a good man to get his arms around,' as the old phrase has it. But to what extent should information-based businesses rotate performing specialists out of the specialties and into new ones? And to what extent will top management have to accept as its top priority making and maintaining a common vision across professional specialties?

Heavy reliance on task-force teams assuages one problem. But it aggravates another: the management structure of the information-based organization. Who will the business' managers be? Will they be task-force leaders? Or will there be a two-headed monster – a specialist structure, comparable, perhaps, to the way attending physicians function in a hospital, and an administrative structure of task-force leaders?

The decisions we face on the role and function of the task-force leaders are risky and controversial. Is theirs a permanent assignment, analogous to the job of the supervisory nurse in the hospital? Or is it a function of the task that changes as the task does? Is it an assignment or a position? Does it carry any rank at all? And if it does, will the task-force leaders become in time what the product managers have been at Proctor & Gamble: the basic units of management and the company's field officers? Might the task-force leaders eventually replace department heads and vice-presidents?

Signs of every one of these developments exist, but there is neither a clear trend nor much understanding as to what each entails. Yet each would give rise to a different organizational structure from any we are familiar with.

Finally, the toughest problem will probably be to ensure the supply, preparation, and testing of top management people. This is, of course, an old and central dilemma as well as a major reason for the general acceptance of decentralization in large businesses in the last 40 years. But the existing business organization has a great many middle-management positions that are supposed to prepare and test a person. As a result, there are usually a good many people to choose from when filling a senior management slot. With the number of middle-management positions sharply cut, where will the information-based organization's top executives come from? What will be their preparation? How will they have been tested?

Decentralization into autonomous units will surely be even more critical than it is now. Perhaps we will even copy the German *Gruppe* in which the decentralized units are set up as separate companies with their own top managements. The Germans use this model precisely because of their tradition of promoting people in their specialties, especially in research and engineering; if they did not have available commands in near-independent subsidiaries to put people in, they would have little opportunity to train and test their most promising professionals. These subsidiaries are thus somewhat like the farm teams of a major-league baseball club.

We may also find that more and more top management jobs in big companies are filled by hiring people away from smaller companies. This is the way that major orchestras get their conductors – a young conductor earns his or her spurs in a small orchestra or opera house, only to be hired away by a larger one. And the heads of a good many large hospitals have had similar careers.

Can business follow the example of the orchestra and hospital where top management has become a separate career? Conductors and hospital administrators come out of courses in conducting or schools of hospital administration respectively. We see something of this sort in France, where large companies are often run by men who have spent their entire previous careers in government service. But in most countries this would be unacceptable to the organization (only France has the *mystique* of the *grandes écoles*). And even in France, businesses, especially large ones, are becoming too demanding to be run by people without firsthand experience and a proven success record.

Thus the entire top management process – preparation, testing, succession – will become even more problematic than it already is. There will be a growing need for experienced businesspeople to go back to school. And business schools will surely need to work out what successful, professional specialists must know to prepare themselves for high-level positions as *business* executives and *business* leaders.

Since modern business enterprise first arose, after the Civil War in the United States and the Franco-Prussian War in Europe, there have been two major evolutions in the concept and structure of organizations. The first took place in the ten years between 1895 and 1905. It distinguished management from ownership and established management as work and task in its own right. This happened first in Germany, when Georg Siemens, the founder and head of Germany's premier bank, Deutsche Bank, saved the electrical apparatus company his cousin Werner had founded after Werner's sons and heirs had mismanaged it into near collapse. By threatening to cut off the bank's loans, he forced his cousins to turn the company's management over to professionals. A little later, J.P. Morgan, Andrew Carnegie, and John D. Rockefeller, Sr followed suit in their massive restructurings of US railroads and industries.

The second evolutionary change took place 20 years later. The development of what we still see as the modern corporation began with Pierre S. du Pont's restructuring of his family company in the early twenties and continued with Alfred P. Sloan's redesign of General Motors a few years later. This introduced the command-and-control organization of today, with its emphasis on decentralization, central service staffs, personnel management, the whole apparatus of budgets and controls, and the important distinction between policy and operations. This stage culminated in the massive reorganization of General Electric in the early 1950s, an action that perfected the model most big businesses around the world (including Japanese organizations) still follow.[2]

Now we are entering a third period of change: the shift from the command-and-control organization, the organization of departments and divisions, to the information-based organization, the organization of knowledge specialists. We can perceive, though perhaps only dimly, what this organization will look like. We can identify some of its main characteristics and requirements. We can point to central problems of values, structure, and behavior. But the job of actually building the information-based organization is still ahead of us – it is the managerial challenge of the future.

Notes

1 The standard account is Philip Woodruff, *The Men Who Ruled India*, especially the first volume, *The Founders of Modern India* (New York: St Martin's, 1954). How the system worked day by day is charmingly told in *Sowing* (New York: Harcourt Brace Jovanovich, 1962), volume I of the autobiography of Leonard Woolf (Virginia Woolf's husband).

2 Alfred D. Chandler, Jr has masterfully chronicled the process in his two books *Strategy and Structure* (Cambridge, Mass.: MIT Press, 1962) and *The Visible Hand* (Cambridge, Mass.: Harvard University Press, 1977) – surely the best studies of the administrative history of any major institution. The process itself and its results were presented and analyzed in two of my books: *The Concept of the Corporation* (New York: John Day, 1946) and *The Practice of Management* (New York: Harper Brothers, 1954).

10

High performance: new boundaries of acceptability in worker control

David A. Buchanan

The argument

The boundaries of what management once considered acceptable worker control are being expanded by new environmental pressures. Approaches now being implemented give employees considerably more control over work activities, personal skills development and career opportunities, and also offer significant opportunities for improved organizational performance. The motives behind this shift in management practice are different from those which sustained the quality of working life movement in the 1960s and 1970s.

This argument is illustrated by the experience of Digital Equipment Corporation (DEC) in computer manufacturing plants in America and Scotland, with applications of 'high-performance work systems'. Complementary evidence that this represents a wider shift in management practice, not confined to one country, company or sector, is drawn from published accounts of similar developments elsewhere.

The short unhappy history of job enrichment

The 'quality of working life' movement enjoyed apparent popularity throughout the 1960s and 1970s in Europe, Australia and North America. It was based on the work of academics and consultants whose methods offered practical solutions to the problems created by jobs designed in accordance with 'scientific management' principles. Among the most influential commentators were Davis (1966), Hackman et al. (1975), Herzberg (1968) and Davis and Taylor (1976) in America; Cherns (1975), Emery (1963), Trist et al. (1963) and Wild (1975) in Britain; and Emery, Thorsrud and Lange (1965) in Norway.

The movement offered four main techniques: three individual-job oriented, and one group oriented. *Job rotation* involves the systematic

Reprinted from *Job Control and Worker Health*, ed. Steven L. Sauter, Joseph J. Hurrell Jnr and Cary L. Cooper, pp. 255–73. (Chichester: John Wiley and Sons Ltd, 1982).

movement of employees from one task to another, usually to reduce monotony by increasing task variety. *Job enlargement* involves combining tasks that have been fragmented through a scientific management approach, again to increase task variety and meaning in otherwise repetitive work. *Job enrichment* adds what Herzberg called 'vertical job loading factors', and what Hackman renamed 'implementing concepts', giving employees tasks previously performed by inspection and supervisory staff, and increasing discretion and accountability as well as variety and meaning. Finally, *composite autonomous group working* involves giving control of an overall task to a team which is collectively responsible for the work. These teams are 'self-regulating', and work without direct supervisory control.

These techniques were based on theories of human motivation related more or less closely to the work of Maslow (1943). Stated briefly, these theories argued that employees would demonstrate high levels of effort and performance if their social and intellectual growth needs were met in addition to the desire for mere financial reward. The scientific management approach was criticized for its naive preoccupation with financial or extrinsic rewards, and for ignoring intrinsic needs for affiliation, self-esteem and self-actualization.

These antidotes to scientific management were aimed at two management problem areas, concerning moral and operational issues, respectively.

The first involved the social responsibility of management. Much of the early commentary argued that improving the quality of working life was an appropriate social goal for modern industrial economies, where levels of education and affluence had increased living standards and aspiration levels. The second set of problems concerned the high costs of absenteeism, poor timekeeping and labour turnover experienced by many companies in both manufacturing and office contexts. These costs were attributed to job dissatisfaction caused by boring, repetitive work. A senior manager at AT&T, one American organization which experimented extensively with job enrichment, was quoted as saying, 'This company has lost too many people who are still with us' (Ford, 1969). Volvo built its Kalmar car assembly plant to enable the company to recruit Swedish workers in the first place, as well as to retain them (Gyllenhammer, 1977). Management thus had to respond to the rising expectations and social aspirations of a higher paid and better educated workforce, and felt obliged also to reduce the rising costs of apathy induced by meaningless work.

The number of published accounts of these techniques, however, probably exceeded the number of practical applications (Buchanan, 1979). Several successful applications of job enlargement, mainly American, were reported in the 1950s. Applications continued to be reported into the 1970s, but a survey which covered 276 of the 500 largest corporations in America found in 1969 that 80% had never used or considered job enlargement (Schoderbek and Reif, 1969).

Philips experimented with job enlargement and enrichment at plants in Holland, Britain and Australia. ICI in Britain also experimented widely with job enrichment in the 1970s. The autonomous group approaches of the Swedish car manufacturers, Saab Scania and Volvo, have been widely publicized. However, one account estimated that, while over 1000 work redesign experiments had been started in Sweden in the late 1960s and early 1970s, many had failed (Valery, 1974). Autonomous group working was not popular in either America or Britain (Butteriss and Murdoch, 1976), although the approach was used by Shell, Scottish and Newcastle Breweries and some others. Since 1980 there have been very few reports of work design applications or developments.

Work redesign was therefore more popular in management journals than on the shop or office floor. Late twentieth-century work design owes more to scientific management than to Herzberg or Emery. There are probably two reasons why traditional methods have remained in use. First, the approach is plausible, easy to apply and seems to work. Managers with a preference for common-sense practical ideas will turn in this direction and away from 'implementing concepts' and 'socio-technical systems design'. Secondly, some forms of work design – autonomous group work in particular – appear to threaten traditional managerial decision-making prerogatives. Most applications of work design have involved little or no significant changes to organization structure, and have presented few challenges to the traditional role of management.

These limited techniques were applied with limited success to limited organizational problems. The changing economic, political and technological environment presents management with a new set of issues, requiring fresh approaches. In this evolving climate, work redesign techniques are finding new expressions in new applications.

New pressures, new boundaries

A number of commentators in the late 1970s argued that the scope of work design techniques should be widened, to involve more significant organizational design and culture changes, if these approaches were to have a real impact on organizational performance (Buchanan, 1979; Weir, 1976; Wild, 1975). But those arguments were expressed at a time when their implications were seen as inappropriate, unrealistic or unacceptable by many managers. As long as the problems being addressed were limited, the degree of acceptable organizational change was limited. More fundamental extensions of worker control and, thus, to the role of management, were not considered appropriate responses to the set of issues surrounding the vague concept of social responsibility and the annoying costs of absenteeism and turnover.

The argument for a more comprehensive approach to work organization has been set in a new context by developments in product markets, trading conditions and manufacturing technology in the 1980s.

Reich (1983) argues that rapid changes in the technology of products and production demand the development of 'flexible production systems' if American companies are to sustain their competitive advantage. Reich's phrase refers to the adaptability of the 'human capital' employed in production, not to the technology of 'flexible manufacturing systems'. Market segmentation, increasingly informed and demanding consumers, complex and sophisticated product technology and the increased turnover in tastes and fashions, mean that speed and flexibility of response are essential organizational characteristics.

Hirschhorn (1984) similarly argues that, while modern manufacturing systems involve little manual work, the need for employee autonomy and problem-solving skills is enhanced, and that work reorganization based on the socio-technical systems design approach is more effective. Perrow (1983) highlights the dangers in the potentially lethal combination of sophisticated technologies and unskilled employees. Buchanan and Bessant (1985) provide further evidence for the need for a skilled, flexible, motivated workforce in a study of computerized chemicals process control. Schonberger (1986) argues that 'world-class manufacturing' status is not achieved merely by purchasing the latest equipment, and that the key roles of shop-floor operators in equipment set-up, maintenance and quality control need to be recombined. He states, in 'Principle no. 1':

> Do not put in equipment simply to displace labour. Equipment cannot think or solve problems; humans can. Our past failures to use shop floor people as problem-solvers have shaped the view that labour is a problem. The World Competitive Manufacturing view is that equipment is a problem, and labour is an opportunity. (Schonberger, 1986: 75)

Lawler (1986) argues that there are around 200 'new design plants' in American companies adopting harmonized skills-based payment systems, self-managing teams and flat management hierarchies – an approach similar to the high-performance strategy developed by Digital. Walton (1985) claims that at least a thousand plants in America have transformed their workforce strategy in an attempt to move from an organizational culture of control to one based on commitment, although only a few have a comprehensive commitment strategy. In their *Harvard Business Review* article, 'People policies for the new machines', Walton and Susman (1987: 98) argue that 'advanced manufacturing technology [AMT] makes human skills and workers' commitment more important than ever. So, many leading-edge manufacturers are searching for ways to enhance their workers' capabilities and improve labour relations, even as they look to the new technology to cut labour costs as well.' They point out that advanced manufacturing technology can lead to increases in:

interdependencies between functions;
skill requirements;
the speed, scope and costs of error;

the sensitivity of performance to variation in skill, knowledge and attitudes;
the pace of dynamic change and development;
capital investment per employee;
dependence on smaller numbers of skilled people.

In general, Walton and Susman argue that an appropriate management response to these developments has four key ingredients:

1 a highly skilled, flexible, coordinated, committed workforce;
2 a lean, flat, flexible and innovative management;
3 ability to retain experienced people;
4 strong partnership between management and unions.

They argue that appropriate management strategies, or 'people policies', include job enrichment, multi-skilling, teamwork, 'pay for knowledge' systems, reconsideration of the levels at which management decisions are taken, close attention to employee selection and training procedures, and to management development programmes. They conclude:

> We are convinced that managers who develop their human resources in conjunction with implementing AMT [Advanced Manufacturing Technology] will achieve a competitive advantage. It takes many years to perfect and reinforce the practices we saw in these pioneering plants. But companies that are willing to take the time to lay this solid foundation will gain the edge in the long run. (Walton and Susman, 1987: 106)

Renewed interest in worker control is thus based on pressures arising from more turbulent domestic and international market conditions, and from the development of new computerized process technologies in manufacturing, which encourage a reconsideration of work flows and work roles. This revival is not based directly on quality of working-life (QWL) or health issues.

Those new pressures have created new and more pressing management problems, particularly with respect to the development of flexibility in organizations designed to deal with stability, and with lower levels of turbulence. Thus a new climate of acceptability in relation to worker control has been established, in which management's perception of the legitimate boundaries of autonomy have been widened. Approaches now being developed have considerably more impact on employee control and discretion, and also on organizational design and the management function, than most previous applications. Much of the earlier commentary refers ambivalently to 'semi-autonomous' or 'quasi-autonomous' groups. What is now required are current, documented examples to illustrate the nature and direction of the new trend.

The roots of 'high performance'

It appears that the language, theory and practice of contemporary 'high-performance work design' have three main roots.

One of the first references to this approach in the management literature was made by the American academic Peter Vaill (1982). Vaill sought to identify the characteristics of what he described as 'high-performing systems' in organizations, and 'human systems that perform at levels of excellence far beyond those of comparable systems'.

In Vaill's terms, organizations or groups qualify for the title 'high-performing system' if they:

1. Perform excellently against a known external standard.
2. Perform beyond what is assumed to be their potential best.
3. Perform excellently in relation to what they did before.
4. Are judged by informed observers to be substantially better than comparable groups.
5. Are achieving levels of performance with fewer resources than assumed necessary.
6. Are seen to be exemplars, as a source of ideas and inspiration.
7. Are seen to achieve the ideals of the cultures.
8. ' . . . are the only organizations that have been able to do what they do at all, even though it might seem that what they do is not that difficult or mysterious a thing'. (Vaill, 1982: 25)

Vaill also argued that high-performing systems tend to have a number of common characteristics. They have clear long-term and immediate purposes. Members display high levels of energy, motivation and commitment in pursuit of those objectives. Tasks are achieved through integrated teamwork. Leadership is reliable and predictable (although initiative can come from any member). New ideas relevant to the task are quickly adopted, but innovations that would involve crossing task boundaries are handled conservatively. A lot of effort is devoted to maintaining the group's image and its boundaries with the other groups in the wider environment.

High-performance systems are often seen as 'a problem' by other groups around them, who can become annoyed by their apparently unmanageable behaviour. Finally, according to Vaill, high-performing systems 'are systems that have "jelled", even though the phenomenon is very difficult to talk about' (Vaill, 1982: 27). The freedom which members of high-performing systems appear to enjoy is thus not inconsistent with stability of purpose and behaviour.

Vaill's article is concerned with identifying key features of high-performing systems, the behaviour of their members and the qualities of their leadership. His account is anecdotal and descriptive, refers to only one earlier theoretical statement on the topic, and contains no systematic illustration of these ideas in practice. Nevertheless, as will be seen in the following section, the approach developed by Digital Equipment

Corporation in Scotland created work groups with most of the characteristics that Vaill identified.

A second reference to this approach is Perry's account of Digital's experience at one of their American plants, *Enfield: A High-Performance System* (Perry, 1984). Enfield was a 'green field' site for Digital (a 'new design' plant: Lawler, 1986), and started operations in 1983. In the words of Enfield's Plant Manager, Perry offers 'an in-depth account of the struggles and personal stress people have encountered in moving a vision to reality' (Perry, 1984: iii). The implementation of the high-performance approach involves 'commitment to learning and risk taking' and is therefore not a simple, effortless management technique to apply.

The Enfield plant was designed to make printed circuit boards (modules) for the corporation's storage system division. Modules were built in the early 1980s in much the same way as they had been in the late 1960s, with little technical or organizational change. But increased competition, and the knowledge that the product was soon to become obsolete, led the Group Manager of Storage Systems in 1981 to the conclusion that, 'We needed to take the initiative. We took a risk because there's got to be a better way' (Perry, 1984: 3).

In designing Enfield, management wanted 'a quantum leap in productivity', and set specific targets in relation to costs, quality, time to market and asset management. They wanted to achieve a 40% reduction in plant labour and overhead costs, 100% quality from vendors, 100% quality through customers' processes, 25% reduction in time to market, and 14 inventory turns per annum through 'just in time' techniques. Time to market for new products was typically 204 weeks; at Enfield, they wanted to cut that by one year.

Enfield was to be a low- to medium-volume plant, with a new product start-up capability which would lead the business in technology, design, testing, sourcing, quality and competitive superiority. Enfield would produce 30% of the corporation's needs for these modules, and the Singapore plant would produce the balance. Enfield was to be a 'small, responsive, high-performance (productivity and quality) facility' (Perry, 1984: 5).

But the goal behind those specific targets was *flexibility*: 'flexibility – the capacity to respond quickly and effectively to a highly uncertain environment – is central to what Enfield is about . . . change without upheaval will be the norm in this plant' (Perry, 1984: 5). The corporation had previously managed uncertainty by introducing more systems, changing the structure, employing more people, tightening controls, designing 'integrating mechanisms'. These strategies introduced more overheads, created more interfaces, increased the complexity of the organization – and created more uncertainty.

The goals for Enfield were:

as few barriers as possible between people, and between people and work;

maximum of four levels of management hierarchy;
multi-functional work teams;
flow of information towards the work – where the decisions are made;
increased responsiveness;
employee 'ownership' of the approach.

To achieve that ownership, it was considered necessary to establish a high quality of working life in the plant through:

participative management decision making;
a high control, teamwork approach;
an innovative reward system;
career development and planning.

Management did not want to experiment with work reorganization, employee control and management style 'in a corner'. They did, however, want to experience this new approach in isolation and to transfer the lessons. Management and employees had 18 months, including 12 months in the new plant itself, to set up the structure before a module had to be shipped. This helped to minimize the perceived risk.

Perry's account was written one year after Enfield began operations, so there were few clear indications of the impact of the approach on plant performance. The Plant Manager's review indicates that by the end of that year, although there were still a number of issues to be resolved, the following results had been achieved (Perry, 1984: 191):

40% reduction in module manufacturing time;
'just in time' inventory system established;
15 inventory turns per annum;
three levels of structure in the plant;
multi-skilled operating teams;
38% standard cost reduction;
equivalent output with half the people and half the space;
40% reduction in overhead;
break-even at 60% capacity.

Perry describes the difficulties managers experienced in assimilating the changes in their function, behaviour and status, moving to a 'flat' structure with higher worker control. She also identifies the need for what is usefully described as 'transition management', to establish the change through a clearly defined communications strategy, based on a model of the change process. Another key lesson concerned the value of powerful 'visions' in generating high levels of commitment.

A third reference to this approach is the account of Digital's experience (summarized in the following section) at Ayr in Scotland (Buchanan, 1987). Enfield provided a reference site for Ayr, where a similar approach was followed, with similar results. Digital managers in Scotland were also aware that at least two other companies in America – Zilog and Hewlett-Packard – had developed similar strategies and used video programmes from those organizations in their planning and communications (but without copying what they had done). Digital employees use the phrase 'high performance' in preference to Vaill's usage; the former has been adopted here.

The Ayr experience

Digital Equipment Corporation was, in dollar revenues, one of the world's three largest computer manufacturers, and was the largest manufacturer of minicomputers. Digital created the minicomputer market in 1960 with the PDP (programmable data processor) system. The Digital PDP 11 was the most popular minicomputer ever made.

Digital had one production site in Britain, Ayr in Scotland, opened in 1976. In 1986 it employed 670 people and shipped around US $500 million of systems. The initial charter for the site was the final assembly and test of minicomputer systems for European markets. This stage of the manufacturing process involved tailoring complex systems to customer specifications, testing, order consolidation and shipping.

In 1982 75% of Digital installations were in Europe, where sales in 1985 accounted for 30% of global revenue. Like other multinational electronics companies, Digital was under political and commercial pressure to increase 'local sourcing' of components.

As computer systems became more reliable and easier for customers to set up and configure for themselves, the traditional final assembly and test operation became redundant. In 1980 60% of Digital's systems went through this stage. By 1985 only 5% did so, as the final test, order consolidation and shipping operations moved back to American manufacturing plants. The Scottish plant had to change its products, or face serious business decline. The organizational changes at Ayr were thus introduced in the context of this potential crisis.

In 1984 the (Scottish) management team at Ayr secured the charter to manufacture in volume small 'micro PDP 11' computer systems for the European business market, with an extra £4 million investment in the site. The product life of these systems was short, with sales peaking over about 3 years, and product improvements were being introduced continuously. This market was extremely competitive and sales volumes were difficult to forecast accurately. To get this charter, Ayr had to demonstrate that they could manufacture at a 'landed cost' competitive with other Digital plants, particularly those in the Far East. The unit cost of most modern computer systems like these comprised about 80% materials, 15% overheads and 5% labour.

This new product range involved a change from skilled technical configuration and test work to volume assembly, with short cycle times on individual operations. Existing staff were retrained, and there were no redundancies. The new business accounted for 30% of employment on the site in 1986, growing from zero in 1984. The company had no unions, and pay and conditions were superior for the area.

Management had to introduce radical changes rapidly. This was not an effortless process; considerable effort went into making the new operation successful. The account produced after the events obscured the hard work, stress and frustration that made them happen. Management action involved a *package* of changes, necessary to support a considerable increase in worker control through autonomous groups. The other aspects of the package were fundamental to the successful development of a high-performance system, and distinguish this approach from previous applications of quality-of-working-life techniques.

Strategic focus

Management had a clear view of future products, and of the type of organizational design that would be required to manufacture them competitively. This *clarity of vision* was shared with all employees on the site and helped to 'sell' sweeping technical and organizational changes – both to corporate management and to the workforce in Scotland. From a strategic or competitive viewpoint, the two outstanding advantages of the high-performance approach concerned the *quality* of the end products and the *flexibility* of the organization in response to rapid change.

Supportive policies

A new skill-based payment system was designed with employee participation. Job demarcations were rare, and people at all levels were expected and encouraged to develop skills in areas other than those in which they were directly employed. Employee career development was flexible, and management encouraged individuals to pursue their interests and extend their skills in areas where they could make a contribution to the business. Employment policies, particularly with respect to rewards, training, development and career planning, were thus consistent with, and positively supported, the strategic focus of the technical and organizational innovations.

Kit to fit

A capital-intensive, automated manufacturing process would have reduced unit costs only with high production volumes, which could not be guaranteed in an unpredictable market. Management felt also that an automated process would not be able to cope with the rapidly evolving product range and with fundamental changes in product technology, such as the move from dual-in-line packaging to surface mount technology in printed circuit board production. Manual assembly with 'stand alone' automated equipment was less expensive, less risky and more flexible – and was therefore a better fit for the business.

The extent to which process layout would encourage or inhibit social interaction on the shop floor was considered important. So process equipment was located to allow maximum freedom of movement and vision. Support personnel worked in areas adjacent to the production floor, so that they could be contacted instantly when required, and through constant contact keep up to date with the processes which they served.

High-performance teams

Management introduced unsupervised autonomous groups, or 'high-performance teams', each with around a dozen members, with full 'front to back responsibility' for product assembly and test, fault finding and problem solving, as well as some equipment maintenance. The group members used flexitime without clocks and effectively policed their own team discipline. Individual members were encouraged to develop a range of skills and to help others to develop their capabilities on the job. It is important to note that this increase in worker control was reinforced by the other dimensions of the change package. The ten key characteristics of Digital's high-performance teams were as follows:

self-managing, self-organizing, self-regulating;
front to back responsibility for core process;
negotiated production targets;
multi-skilling – no job titles;
shared skills, knowledge, experience and problems;
skills-based payment system;
peer selection, peer review;
open layout, open communications;
support staff on the spot;
commitment to high standards of performance.

Management style

Managers had to adopt a supportive style in their relationships with high-performance teams. Some managers found it 'painful' to relinquish their traditional directive management style and moved to other parts of the company. The teams initially had leaders whose job it was to encourage team autonomy, and to develop problem-solving and decision-making skills to the point where the team leader could withdraw. The need for patience and the ability to stand back and let the groups reach their own decisions became new management skills. Group decision making was slow at first, but with experience groups learned to diagnose and resolve problems rapidly and effectively.

This approach released considerable management time, which enabled management to devote more attention to:

vendor management;
accuracy of sales forecasts;
improvements to operational logistics;
environmental scanning, new techniques, new ideas;
finding new business.

They were thus able to devote more attention to two increasingly critical areas. First, they were able to spend more time looking at the characteristics of the turbulent environment outside the plant and exploring the implications of specific developments for their operation. Secondly, they were able to devote more effort to materials supply and inventory issues inside the plant – areas where considerable savings could be achieved given the product cost structure.

Supportive systems

Management introduced a computer-aided system for materials acquisition and production control. Support groups were located on the shop floor around the high-performance teams which they served. The ways in which the support team was fragmented, and the resultant coordination requirements, made it difficult to develop autonomous high-performance teams in this area to the same degree as with assembly groups. Employee discretion and expectation of skills and career development still applied, however.

Transition management

The process of managing the transition from a conventional manufacturing operation to one based on high-performance system concepts was critical to the success of the approach. One manager was primarily responsible for securing the new product line, and for persuading management colleagues that their novel approach to organizational design and management style was going to be effective. But other senior managers had to convince their colleagues and subordinates of the value of this approach. This involved a time-consuming combination of formal committees and informal conversations with people outside meetings to encourage them to voice their doubts and opinions. This process began early, which gave personnel plenty of time to absorb the new ideas, and the changes in behaviour and attitudes that were required.

This could be described as a 'prophet and disciples' approach to organizational change. The pattern of changes in structure, style, attitudes and behaviour that were eventually achieved would probably not have been possible, or would have taken significantly longer to achieve, in the absence of a critical mass of key individuals who were prepared to devote time and effort to heighten the confidence and enthusiasm of their 'converts' with their positive message.

Involvement

Communication with all those to be affected by change took place early and was sustained. A year before manufacturing began, in 1984, a project team was set up, including managers, engineers and assemblers. The high-performance team idea was explained through a programme which again relied on key personalities, regular meetings and frequent use of the language of the approach – such as 'flexible working', 'product owner-ship' and 'front to back responsibility'. The managers who initiated this approach became 'guardians of the concept' of high performance, and their efforts in this respect were critical to the sustained enthusiasm and commitment of others. The ultimate test of this communication and involvement process was that staff eventually felt that they 'owned' the concepts and techniques which they used.

Competence

Assessment of training needs was carried out early, and training was thorough – covering job skills, problem-solving techniques and 'attitude training' in the concepts of high-performance organizational design. The revised payment and review system, which assemblers had helped to design, also assessed group members on their behaviours and attitudes, as well as work output. Training on new equipment was initially carried out by suppliers, but skilled team members were then expected to train others, particularly new team members.

Assessment

The broad goals of the 'micro PDP 11' business concerned adaptability, profitability, customer satisfaction and inventory management. The high-performance approach had been introduced also to control costs, improve product quality and delivery, and to sustain the quality of work experience with skilled and flexible employees.

The results which management felt had been achieved included improved productivity, reduced time to market for product innovations, decreased inventory and rapid and more effective decision making. Management also felt that the high-performance teams had demonstrated:

ability to respond positively and quickly to change;
how the process layout had improved communications;
'ownership' of actions, and product identification;
the potential for multi-functional career development;
better business understanding and priority setting;
greater flexibility through multi-skilling.

According to one manager at Ayr, the approach had created 'massive personal growth and skills development', particularly in relation to:

analysis and synthesis skills in problem diagnosis;
interpersonal, self-presentation and communication skills;
group problem-solving skills;
group decision-making skills;
group self-management skills;
process design and planning skills.

A survey in June 1987 confirmed these beliefs (Buchanan and McCalman, 1987). Asked how personal development had been affected, responses reveal improvements in self-confidence, social skills and aspirations: 'it has given me extra confidence to speak at meetings, e.g. community council, community association meetings'; 'it has brought out skills I never new I had'; 'I have learned to work closer with people since I joined, which is a new experience for me, and become more tolerant of people's attitudes and ways'; 'I am more aware of my own attitude towards my group'; 'it has given me more confidence in my own ability to learn new skills'; 'made me do things that I thought I was not capable of doing'.

Responses to other open-ended questions in this review survey, however, implied that increased worker control had increased employee commitment to work, which in turn had, in some instances, adverse effects on domestic and social lives. These are issues which require fuller investigation.

This survey indicated that, 3 years after their introduction, the high-performance teams were working as intended, solving their own problems, determining their own work schedules, coordinating their own efforts, and sharing skills, experience and knowledge. Comments expressed in the survey revealed that a return to traditional manufacturing techniques and management styles would not be welcomed.

Management was, however, not satisfied that decisions had been really 'pushed down' into the high-performance teams, and was concerned that production pressures had overridden their concern with group autonomy. The survey confirmed that management interference in team operations had increased, and instances of management decisions being taken without team consultation had also increased. Management thus decided to review their attitudes and behaviours in relation to assembly teams.

Digital's interest in this approach was based on technological and strategic factors. The technology used in the manufacturing process was sophisticated and comparatively expensive, even with the rejection of a more expensive automated system. The product technology was also complex and in a state of constant development. Corporate strategy in manufacturing thus has to take into account the fact that organizations that are able rapidly to adapt to change have a competitive advantage in the face of changing technology and volatile product markets.

Management at Digital wanted employees to change jobs and develop skills as the products and the production process developed. They wanted employees to be able to deal with manufacturing problems on their own initiative, without management intervention. They wanted expensive equipment to be operated effectively and expected faults to be identified and rectified rapidly, within the teams where possible. High-performance work design enabled them to achieve those objectives by increasing flexibility, output quality and effective use of assets.

Does this approach have a wider applicability? The pace of technological innovation in manufacturing does not seem to be slowing down. Domestic and world product markets are becoming increasingly segmented and changeable. Most sectors face aggressive competition, rapidly changing customer needs and fashions, and further technical change. Organizations in this environment must pay attention to flexibility, quality and asset utilization to remain competitive.

Other organizations around the world are adopting this approach. In Britain, Trebor has organized 230 production workers into unsupervised, self-organizing teams with degrees of autonomy and control similar to the high-performance teams at Digital. Trebor management feels that the increased challenge and shop-floor decision making have improved attitudes to the job, the factory and the company. Borg-Warner introduced flexible group working following the collapse of their market in automobile gearboxes, and the need to develop more responsive ways to produce new products – a varied range of industrial and marine transmission systems. Significantly increased autonomy and the removal of traditional demarcations on the shop floor have increased skill levels and enabled the company to give their customers flexibility, high quality, accurate delivery and competitive prices.

IBM adopted teamwork in the manufacture of disk drives and processors at its Havant plant in England, using 'low' technology and human skills. The reasons behind their approach include, again, the need for organizational flexibility and quality of end product (Bolton, 1986).

A number of American companies, in addition to those already mentioned, have adopted similar approaches (Hoerr et al., 1986). With the introduction of autonomous, high-performance teamwork, Shenandoah Life Insurance reports handling 50% more business with 10% fewer people. Cummins Engine Company claims to have improved their 'entrepreneurial spirit' and reduced machine downtime. General Motors, at Saginaw, uses robotic axle assembly, with 38 multi-skilled teamworkers. Proctor & Gamble run 18 team-based plants which are between 30 and 40% more productive and more adaptable than conventional plants. Tektronix Inc. claims that one high-performance team now makes as many defect-free products in 3 days as the whole assembly line used to make in 14 days with twice as many people.

In South Australia, Holden's Motor Company at Elizabeth near Adelaide have since 1986 been introducing sophisticated manufacturing technology, as part of an Australian $350 million investment programme, and establishing 'family cells' – shop-floor groups who organize themselves and monitor their own production performance. These, and other changes to organization structure, have transformed the profitability of the company (*SA Motor*, 1987).

The development of autonomous teamwork at Holden's is central to the company's competitiveness, which relies on constant attention to product quality and reliability. The company's position is that 'People are more important than the equipment, because of the necessity of understanding it, maintaining it, and running it' (*SA Motor*, 1987). Holden's aim is 'to be number one in the market place, and that's where we're headed'; and as part of the strategy to achieve this goal, the increase in shop-floor autonomy has in management's view led to 'staggering changes in attitudes and productivity'.

These findings provide some empirical confirmation of Lawler's (1986: 180–1) speculative comments about the potential results from new design plants, combining high levels of worker control with a 'high-involvement management' style. In the instances reported in this chapter, the high-performance strategy was introduced to existing plants which retained, at least in part, traditional methods of working and managing in some areas, and are thus qualitatively different from new design plants, in Lawler's terminology. This partial strategy had been successfully maintained at Digital in Scotland, but the site had experienced the 'foreign body inside the larger organization' problem which Lawler also identifies.

Is the high-performance approach materially different, or is it just a new label for a set of old ideas? Clearly, it has its roots in, and has much in common with, the job enrichment and semi-autonomous group techniques of the previous two decades. However, the key distinctions between quality-of-working-life techniques of the 1960s and 1970s, and the high-performance approach of the 1980s and 1990s, seems to include the following:

QWL in the 1970s	High performance in the 1990s
— aimed to reduce costs of absenteeism and labour turnover and increase productivity	— aims to improve organizational flexibility and product quality for competitive advantage
— based on argument that increased autonomy improves quality of work experience and employee job satisfaction	— based on argument that increased autonomy improves skills, decision making, adaptability and use of new technology
— had little impact on the management function beyond first line supervision	— involves change in organization culture and redefinition of management function at all levels
— 'quick fix' applied to isolated and problematic work groups	— could take 2-3 years to change attitudes and behaviour throughout the organization
— personnel administration technique	— human resource management strategy

The early quality-of-working-life techniques did not substantially increase worker control and have been criticized for making only cosmetic alterations to the experience of work, increasing discretion in superficial ways at best. In some cases, autonomous groups certainly did achieve higher levels of shop-floor control, but were not widely popular with management, presumably for that reason.

However, the climate of acceptability has changed as the management and organizational problems have changed. The operational problems of the previous 20 years legitimized comparatively limited increases in worker control and attendant changes to the management function. The strategic problems of the next 20 years appear to legitimize more fundamental changes to work design, organization culture and management style. The label 'high performance' may contain a certain amount of 'hype', but it also reflects a major strategic shift in emphasis and scope in the practical application of work organization ideas.

References

Bolton, L. (1986) 'Traditional means to a high tech end', *Computing*, 30 January: 13, 24.

Buchanan, D.A. (1979) *The Development of Job Design Theories and Techniques*. Saxon House, Aldershot.

Buchanan, D.A. (1987) 'Job enrichment is dead: Long live high performance work design', *Personnel Management*, May: 40–3.

Buchanan, D.A. and Bessant, J. (1985) 'Failure, uncertainty and control: The role of operators in a computer integrated production system', *Journal of Management Studies*, 22, 292–308.

Buchanan, D.A. and McCalman, J. (1987) *Micro 11 Survey 1987: Digital Equipment Scotland*. Centre for Technical and Organizational Change, company confidential report, June, Glasgow.

Butteriss, M. and Murdoch, R.D. (1976) 'Work restructuring projects and experiments in the USA', *Work Research Unit Report*, No. 3.

Cherns, A.B. (1975) *The Quality of Working Life* (2 vols). Free Press, New York.

Davis, L.E. (1966) 'The design of jobs', *Industrial Relations*, 6: 21–5.

Davis, L.E. and Taylor, J.C. (1976) 'Technology, organization and job structure', in R. Dubin (ed.), *Handbook of Work, Organization and Society*, pp. 379–419, Rand NcNally, Chicago.

Emery, F.E. (1963) *Some Hypotheses about the Ways in which Tasks may be More Effectively Put Together to Make Jobs*. Tavistock Institute of Human Relations, London.

Emery, F.E., Thorsrud, E. and Lange, K. (1965) *Field Experiments at Christiana Spigerverk*. Industrial Democracy Project Paper no. 2. Phase B, Tavistock Institute of Human Relations Document T807.

Ford, R.N. (1969) *Motivation Through the Work Itself*. American Management Association.

Gyllenhammer, P.G. (1977) *People at Work*. Addison-Wesley, Reading, Mass.

Hackman, J., Oldham, G.R., Jason, R. and Purdy, K. (1975) 'A new strategy for job enrichment', *California Management Review*, 17: 57–71.

Herzberg, F. (1968) 'One more time: How do you motivate employees?', *Harvard Business Review*, 46: 53–62.

Hirschhorn, L. (1984) *Beyond Mechanization*. MIT Press, Cambridge, Mass.

Hoerr, J., Pollock, M.A. and Whiteside, D.E. (1986) 'Management discovers the human side of automation', *Business Week*, 29 September: 60–5.

Lawler, E.E. III (1986) *High Involvement Management: Participative Strategies for Improving Organizational Performance*. Jossey-Bass, San Francisco.

Maslow, A. (1943) 'A theory of motivation', *Psychological Review*, 50: 370–96.

Perrow, C. (1983) 'The organizational context of human factor engineering', *Administrative Science Quarterly*, 28: 5210–41.

Perry, B. (1984) *Enfield: A High-Performance System*. Digital Equipment Corporation, Education Services Development and Publishing, Bedford, Mass.

Reich, R.B. (1983) *The Next American Frontier*. Times Books, New York.

SA Motor (1987) 'Holden's comes home', September: 17.

Schoderbek, P.P. and Reif, W.E. (1969) *Job Enlargement: Key to Improved Performance*. Bureau of Industrial Relations, Graduate School of Business Administration, University of Michigan, Ann Arbor.

Schonberger, R.j. (1986) *World-Class Manufacturing: The Lessons of Simplicity Applied*. Free Press, New York.

Trist, E.L., Higgin, G.W., Murray, H. and Pollock, A.B. (1963) *Organizational Choice: Capabilities of Groups at the Coal Face Under Changing Technologies*. Tavistock, London.

Vaill, P.B. (1982) 'The purposing of high-performing systems', *Organizational Dynamics*, Autumn: 23–39.

Valery, N. (1974) 'Importing the lessons of Swedish workers', *New Scientist*, 62: 27–8.

Walton, R.E. (1985) 'From control to commitment in the workplace', *Harvard Business Review*, March–April: 77–84.

Walton, R.E. and Susman, G.I. (1987) 'People policies for the new machines', *Harvard Business Review*, March–April (2): 98–106.

Weir, M. (1976) 'Redesigning jobs in Scotland', *Work Research Unit Report*, no. 5, February.

Wild, R. (1975) *Work Organization: A Study of Manual Work and Mass Production*. Wiley, New York.

11

Modernist and postmodernist organization

Stewart R. Clegg

Bureaucracy and Fordism: the modernist mix

As a hypothesis one may entertain the idea that the Japanese variant of East Asian enterprise represents a form of organization which stands to earlier bureaucratic forms of organization as does the postmodern to the modern. The entertainment is no more than hypothetical. Elements of actual organizational practice will be the key. To the extent that these may appear antithetical to modernism, not only in practice but also in theory, then we may find ourselves running up against the limits of our modernist frameworks of understanding.

Modernist organizations may be thought of in terms of Weber's typification of bureaucratized, mechanistic structures of control, as these were subsequently erected upon a fully rationalized base of divided and deskilled labour. In contemporary literature, following the lead of Gramsci's (1971) reflections in the *Prison Notebooks*, these foundations are usually referred to as those of 'Fordism'. The Fordist labour process base is semi-automatic assembly-line production on the Detroit model. It developed from the 1920s onwards, particularly for mass consumer goods produced in large production runs, although it spread to the 'production of standardized intermediate components for the manufacture of these means of consumption' (Aglietta, 1979: 117). The labour process base was intensive, mechanized, divided labour. It consisted of the previous achievements of Taylorism in the application of empirical methods to the study, design and 'de-skilling/re-skilling' of work (see Clegg and Dunkerly, 1980: chs 3, 11). However, it added to these what Aglietta (1979: 118) refers to as 'two complementary principles'. These were 'the integration of different segments of the labour process by a system of conveyors and handling devices ensuring the movement of the materials to be transformed and their arrival at the appropriate machine tools'. In other words, it was characterized by the semi-automatic assembly line, organizing work into a straightforward linear flow of transformations

Reprinted from Stewart Clegg, *Modern Organizations*, pp. 176–207. (London: Sage Publications, 1990).

applied to raw materials. The second principle 'was the fixing of workers to jobs whose positions were rigorously determined by the configuration of the machine system'. In such a system individual workers lost control over their own work rhythm, and became fully adjuncts to the machine, repeating those few elementary movements designed by engineering departments as the rationalized sum of their formal organizational existence.

Fordism was a system of mass production based on both the increases in labour productivity and the wage relation that linked real wage and productivity growth which Taylorism made possible. Productivity gains were translated into wages, which enabled the growth of final demand for standardized consumer goods (Albertsen, 1988: 344). Mass workers were also mass consumers in the era of 'consumer capitalism' (Jameson, 1984).

Stretching above the organizational base of Fordist enterprises was a pyramid of control, designed in a classically bureaucratic fashion. At its apex this radiated from the product division to the central organs of calculation and control. In the pyramid of control, according to both the formal theory and the practical application of it in organizational design, authority would reside in individuals by virtue of their incumbency in office and/or their expertise. These offices would be organized hierarchically, with compliance being to superordinate instructions expressed in terms of universal fixed rules. Such rules would be formalized so that any appeal against the rules could be expressed in terms of a 'correspondence principle' linking action and formal rules. The day-to-day principles of control, derived from the hierarchy of offices, would reside in direct surveillance and supervision, as well as the standardized rules and sanctions. Employment would be based on specialized training and formal certification of competence, acquired prior to gaining the job. Great care would be taken with the selection of personnel in order to ensure homogeneity in the organization's reproduction. For these upper levels of control (by contrast to the lower levels of those who were far more controlled than controlling), employment could constitute a career in which either seniority or achievement might be the basis for advancement. The general formality of relations would be buttressed through the ideal of impersonality such that relations would be role based, segmental and instrumental: the primary sources of motivation would be incentive based. This instrumentalism would be carried over into a principle of differential rewards according to the hierarchy of office, in which prestige, privilege and power would be isomorphic with one another.

At the core of the pyramid there would be a maximal division of labour. Intellectual work of design, conception and communication would be differentiated from manual work. The latter would be the work of so many interchangeable 'hands' executing and making possible the designs of superordinate others. These others, the managers, supervisors and administrators of the central work-flow, would be differentiated from the performance tasks. Indeed, in many respects, *differentiation* was the hallmark of the system. There was a maximal specialization of jobs and functions and an extensive differentiation of segmental roles. Forms of expertise would be exclusively held and arranged such that the ideal of the specialist-expert would be the basis for individual or occupational specialist or sub-unit empowerment in the system.

By the 1970s, as Albertsen (1988: 348) puts it,

> the Fordist model began to run out of steam. The crisis of the 1970s turned out to be a crisis of the model itself rather than just another conjunctural swing within its confines. The very conditions which had originally supported the expansion of the model now turned into limits to its further development. A slowdown in productivity growth, fierce international competition, and permanent upward pressures on direct and social wages combined to squeeze the profits and put a brake on the accumulation process. At the same time the downward rigidity of wages prevented social demand from cumulative collapse. So the Fordist model survived, but in a stagnating form marked by a prolonged 'stagflationary' crisis, and also imbued with tendencies working towards its dissolution.

Within organizations productivity slowed down, on this view, because Taylorism had reached its limits – there were no new areas left to rationalize; workers had become more resistant, especially during the prolonged period of post-war full employment, and efficiency gains were being outstripped by increasing costs of surveillance and control assaciated with the rigid separation of mental and managerial labour. There were related changes in the state sphere and a wholesale 'internationalization' and associated 'de-industrialization' of areas and enterprises which had previously been strongholds of Fordism. Existing centre–periphery relations 'broke up as mature corporations began to decentralize units of standardized manual production to dispersed localities also within the advanced nations, while concentrating managerial and financial functions within large metropolitan areas' (Albertsen 1988: 347). Organizational responses to this changing state became evident in the 1980s and it is in order to explicate these that the concept of postmodern organizations has been coined. In terms of the changing centre–periphery relations, as a concept it is oriented particularly towards understanding the nature of Japanese organizations.

Postmodern organizations?

Whatever else, it is clear that a modernist representation would not accurately capture the organizational patterns of contemporary Japanese organization, which have served in the 1980s as if they were a very beacon of postmodernity, given the role that various representations of them have played in recent debates. For this reason these are sometimes referred to as 'post-Fordist' or 'Fujitsuist' organizations (Kenney and Florida, 1988). Mindful of the totality of the picture and not just the technology or work-flow elements, one might prefer to call it postmodernist, in order to index the contrast with Weber's modernist representation. The two tendencies, towards modernism and postmodernism, are not unconnected. Theorists of the 'regulation' school, such as Aglietta (1979), regard Fordism as something which will increasingly be confined to the less developed industries, themselves tending to be located within less developed areas of the world economy, as capitalism becomes ever more institutionalized. Within the core enterprises and countries control will become less authoritarian in the workplace as new forms of market discipline substitute for the external surveillance of supervision, changes fostered by extensive deregulation. Internal markets within large organizations will increasingly be created as cost-centres and profit-centres proliferate, and surveillance will be lessened as more flexible manufacturing systems are adopted within which the collective workers become their own supervisors.

For many writers the phenomena which are under discussion here are part of more global tendencies. Lash and Urry (1987), for instance, write of the break-up of 'organized capitalism' and the development of 'disorganized capitalism', in the variable responses of the United States and some of the West European nations to the end of the post-war boom; Piore and Sabel (1984) write of a 'second industrial divide' opening up in societies as a result of the development of flexible manufacturing systems. What these responses have in common is a focus on some tendencies in the articulation of both production and consumption in some of the advanced capitalist societies. The aim of this analysis is altogether more modest and more specific. It is to focus on these tendencies through the embeddedness of economic action.

What the components of a postmodernist organization might be emerge best in contrast to some familiar features of modernist organization. In common with analyses of postmodernism in other spheres, *de-differentiation* (Lash, 1988) is an important component, at least in production. (In consumption, the postmodernist tendency is very much towards greater differentiation.) De-differentiation refers to the reversal of that differentiation process which observers such as Weber (1978) saw as central to the processes of modernity. Postmodernism points to a more organic, less differentiated enclave of organization than those dominated by the bureaucratic designs of modernity. Some highly general tendencies, which will necessarily be subject to subsequent refinement and caution, can serve to represent the scene.

Where modernist organization was rigid, postmodern organization is flexible. Where modernist consumption was premised on mass forms, postmodernist consumption is premised on niches. Where modernist organization was premised on technological determinism, postmodernist organization is premised on technological choices made possible through 'de-dedicated' microelectronic equipment. Where modernist organization and jobs were highly differentiated, demarcated and de-skilled, postmodernist organization and jobs are highly de-differentiated, de-demarcated and multi-skilled. Employment relations as a fundamental relation of organizations upon which has been constructed a whole discourse of the determinism of size as a contingency variable increasingly gave way to more complex and fragmentary relational forms, such as subcontracting and networking.

If organization were to mirror art (and there is no reason why it should or should not), Williams (1989: 52) would have us rediscover organizational 'community' in the neglected, alternative tradition of the past century. While he would see in these neglected traditions a democratic imperative, it is by no means clear that this should be so. Communitarian concepts of organization have had no locational monopoly within the imagination of reformers of a 'left' persuasion. The familiar image of an imagined organic past can as readily illuminate the contemporary reformers of the 'right'.

Postmodernism does not signal the end of politics or the creation of forms which are emptied of political content. There are for instance, diverse democratic conceptions of this postmodernity. One does not have to be a pessimist to realize that no necessity attaches to the contours that any possible postmodernism might take. An interpretation which sees postmodernist organization as simply another form of totalitarianism may just as well turn out to be appropriate as one which celebrates its pluralism. Eventually these matters will not be decided by analytical judgement alone, but will depend on the triumphs and failures of diverse institutional forms of power/knowledge in the making of the postmodern world. For this reason ideal types of Fordism and post-Fordism, such as that foot-noted by Rustin (1989: 56–7), are somewhat misleading (which, to be fair to Rustin, he clearly acknowledges in the body of his analysis): they prejudge the contexts which will shape, and be shaped by, these tendencies.

Aspects of postmodernist tendencies might in some contexts be dependent upon an anti-trade-union posture, such as the contemporary United States (where unionization of the workforce is now as low as 17 per cent). Such would not be the case in Sweden where unionization stands at 90 per cent. For some other countries, such as Australia, the prognosis is not so clear.

Some states will be faced with more strategic choices than others in the construction of contemporary capitalisms. Recent research by Calmfors and Diffil (1988) suggest that a key contingency in comparing capitalisms is the type of wage bargaining systems which is institutionalized in different national settings. Studies have consistently shown a relationship between this variable and selected macro-economic outcomes such as the levels of unemployment and inflation (Clegg et al., 1986). Three types of arrangement were identified by Calmfors and Diffil (1988). Focusing on inter-employer and inter-union co-operation in wage bargaining they split seventeen OECD countries into those characterized by centralized, decentralized and intermediate bargaining patterns. These types were then related to a range of macro-economic outcomes such as levels of inflation and unemployment. Those countries which were either highly centralized or decentralized in their wage bargaining system consistently out-performed those in the intermediate category. Included in this inter-mediate category were both Australia and New Zealand, as well as West Germany, Holland and Belgium; Britain, they suggest, probably belongs here as well. These countries clearly have considerable incentive to rethink their strategies in terms of either a more or a less centralized wage bargaining system if they are concerned with achieving more effective macro-economic outcomes. Those countries at either end of the spectrum are necessarily more 'locked into' their design by virtue of not only institutional isomorphism but also the performance advantages that this goodness of fit produces. Those countries which are least isomorphic in their institutional arrangements have the greatest freedom of movement and choice either way.

It is as a consequence of the choices facing countries which are in this intermediate category that the postmodernist organizational debate takes on an important policy dimension. To the extent that there is an elision in the terms of debate, and the concept of postmodern arrangements is aligned only with a 'free' labour market variant of organizational forms, which actually means freedom for a few and restriction to much more repressive conditions for the many, then the terms of debate and choice are unnecessarily restricted. Moreover, an interest in alternative pre-scriptions would seem ill advised. Consequently, the discussion of Pacific examples such as Japan and the East Asian NICs needs to be balanced with discussion of less 'economically liberal' and more 'social democratic' possibilities such as those which, for example, prevail in Sweden. When posed in these terms the issue of choice becomes even more acute.

If we concentrate only on Japan and the East Asian NICs, the choices, although somewhat inchoate between national strategies, do appear to have some common elements oriented towards re-casting the organiza-tional and industrial relations arena in terms consonant with those which marked the 1980s revival of neo-conservative liberal analysis. Recipes for success will be sought in deregulation, in de-unionization or enterprise unionism and in state intervention oriented to curbing the excesses of democracy, administrative overload, ungovernability and so on. (For an account of the general arguments consult Clegg et al., 1983: 34–8.) When the political and economic imagination is confronted by the economic success of an example which is in many respects an alternative to those Pacific cases, typified here by reference to Sweden, the implicit choices really do become quite evident.

In Sweden, as in a small number of other OECD countries, there is a relatively well organized labour movement which works through organiza-tions and institutions of bargained corporatism, seeking to impose its policy preferences on employers and government. Lash and Urry (1987: 283) note that

> German and Swedish trade unions have taken a role in the initiation of flex-
> ibility in the workplace, in the promoting of job enrichment through the
> broadening of job classifications. They have in part been able to make flex-
> ibility work for labour. British trade unions in their blanket rejection of such
> change have let employers initiate flexibility in a way that has been very
> damaging to the interests of workers and unions.

The distinctiveness of the Swedish strategy will be seen to hinge on the central notions of citizenship and representation: on the one hand the deepening and extension of these on a universalistic basis in not only the political but also the economic sphere; on the other hand their restriction within not only the economic but also the political sphere. Consequently, it is through consideration of these issues that one might be attracted to what, in any economically liberal conception of possible organizational postmodernism, would hardly be a promising example.

The next section will contrast possible aspects of modernist and postmodernist organization forms. It will do so from a common perspective: that is, how might each of them handle what have been seen as necessary imperatives of organizational action? A particular strategy will be followed in mounting this contrast. Initially the major point of the comparison will be between aspects of contemporary Japanese organization contrasted with a typification of modernist bureaucratic and Fordist organizations. By contrast, occasional reference will be made back to other East Asian examples. It will become clear that the contrast between modernist and putative postmodernist organization has to be conducted across a broad range of dimensions. It concerns not just aspects of skill formation but also capital formation and the way these frame differential possibilities for organizational action through contrasting modes of rationality. As will become evident from consideration of the Japanese case, stability in and of capital formation is a crucial variable entering into the organizational calculations from which modes of rationality are constructed. As will subsequently become evident from the discussion of Swedish developments, there is more than one way to achieve this particular outcome. There usually is, of course, as that savage but homely metaphor concerned with 'skinning a cat' suggests.

Organizational imperatives

All effective forms of organization must be capable of resolving perennial problems which beset any administratively co-ordinated, recurrent
and routine activities that occur between transacting agencies. However,
it is by now clear that there is no 'one best way' of doing so. Systematic

comparison can be fostered greatly by the application of a common template with which different ways of achieving organization can be compared. Blunt (1989) has argued that all organizations have to find some way of achieving solutions to perennial problems. These can be thought of in terms of seven organizational imperatives, which he derives from a larger set constructed by Jacques (1989). The imperatives are:

1 Articulating mission, goals, strategies and main functions;
2 Arranging functional alignments;
3 Identifying mechanisms of co-ordination and control;
4 Constituting accountability and role relationships;
5 Institutionalizing planning and communication;
6 Relating rewards and performance;
7 Achieving effective leadership.

Contemporary Japanese organization can be reviewed under these headings and contrasted with an ideal-type modernist, Weberian organization. The point of doing this is not to suggest that Western organizations are just like the modernist ideal type. On the contrary, they may well have moved much closer to the type which will be referred to as putatively postmodernist. However, to the extent that our assumptions for thinking about them remain within the framework which derives from Weberian thought, we may well not recognize them for what they may be. Instead, we may tend to note rather more what they are not.

Missions, goals, strategies and main functions

With respect to strategy Japanese enterprise groups tend not to adopt the conglomerate model which is more common to large firms in the United States or Britain as the locus of their strategic initiative, preferring instead the *keiretsu* form. This is because Japanese corporations place very little emphasis on merger as a mechanism of growth or diversification of business. As a consequence, as Cool and Lengnick-Hall (1985: 8–9) suggest, organization members *know* what business they are in; they have a deep-rooted and substantive knowledge that a policy of horizontal or vertical acquisitions hardly allows for. One of the reasons why the complex inter-market relations of the *keiretsu* are entered into is to organize those related and ancillary actions which would be internally subject to imperative co-ordination in more typical Western enterprises. In the case of the United States or Britain this centre is likely to be a locus of 'private' calculation which attempts to co-ordinate across a range of economic activities. One consequence of having well focused missions, goals, strategies and main functions, it is suggested, is that there is usually a core technology to the organization which is well understood. In consequence, following Emery and Trist (1960) and Tichy (1981), one can propose that 'Since Japanese firms limit their scope to primarily one basic technology, their internal culture tends to be very homogeneous' (Cool and Lengnick-Hall, 1985: 9).

De-differentiation of what elsewhere are more likely to be imperatively co-ordinated functions will lead to a lessening of the degree of specialization of functions subordinated to the missions and goals of an organization. Whitley (1990: 64) has suggested that specialization, when associated with relative homogeneity in the nature of employees, will minimize transaction costs. Within Japanese enterprises it is secured through company socialization in the guise of firm-specific training, enterprise unionism and tenure of employment for those in the internal labour market. Some researchers, such as Cole and Tominga (1976), argue that these processes operate to such an extent in Japanese enterprises that modernist assumptions about there being an 'occupational structure' are quite inappropriate. In the internal labour market, instead of a commitment to an occupation *per se*, they suggest, one finds that because of permanent employment and seniority payment systems, workers tend to be more committed to their organizations than to their occupations.

Dore (1973) tends to regard the development of this institutional framework in Japanese core enterprises as a result of the 'late development' effect. According to Dore (1979) the later that capitalist development occurs the less likely there will have been established a prior system of free wage labour in a capitalist agricultural sector. Consequently the forms of paternalism signified by feudal relations are more likely to be a recent tradition rather than a distant memory. It is from this tradition that he would see organizational commitment and permanent employment deriving. Cole (1978), in contrast, prefers to see the emergence of permanent employment in terms not so much of a living tradition but of an institutional legacy which organizational innovators were able to draw on.

The internal labour markets which generate organizational commitment are not at all unique to Japan (although the extent of their misrepresentation may be). The misrepresentations are easily gauged. Estimates put as low as 25 per cent the proportion of the labour market which positively benefits from organizational tenure, those male, white-collar, full-time employees of the major, core and big-name enterprises (Hamada, 1980). The function of these labour market arrangements is clear, however: principally they serve to retain workers who embody valuable skill formation for the enterprise (Jacoby, 1979). Retention is achieved through the cumulative advantages which accrue to employees from the higher wages and status flowing from long service under the seniority system. Buttressing these are the scarcity of good job opportunities on the internal labour market and the intense competition that there is for them (Koshiro, 1981). These factors explain both the exclusivity and the articulation of permanent employment with the system of subcontracting and outworking, in which the labour of women and retired workers predominates. (Retirement, although now approaching Western norms, until recently occurred at 55. In the absence of a well developed welfare state, 'retirees' have to work, live off earnings or rely on familial support.) The emphasis placed by writers such as Abegglen (1973) and Drucker (1971) on internalized beliefs and values in culturalist accounts is too great and, it is suggested, unwarranted by the texts which are available to Japanese scholars themselves (see Ishikawa, 1982; Urabe, 1979). Culturalist accounts require replacement with a greater emphasis on a more organizationally materialist context (see Marsh and Mannari, 1977, 1980, 1981).

At the centre of de-differentiated specialization of functions and the growth of organizational rather than occupational commitments are technical aspects of production. Technique is not simply a commodity to be bought, but a vital aspect of organization. This is clear in the sense that applied technique includes the human organization or system that sets equipment to work. Equally importantly the concept includes the physical integration of a new piece of equipment into a production process and its subsequent refinement and modification at the hands of the technically skilled workforce. Many manufacturers have come to grief on the belief that technical solutions can be bought pre-packaged. This is to ignore, precisely, the fact that in operation these are always socio-technical solutions. What is at issue is precisely the 'cultural' context in which these solutions have to work. Studies have shown that equipment users rather than makers develop major process innovations (thus stealing a march on their competitors) and that small, imperceptible 'everyday rationalizations' account for the lion's share of productivity gains in an ongoing manufacturing business. Ergas (1987) has referred to this as a 'deepening' model of technological development, in which 'learning by doing' and making the best organizational and technical use of 'what you've got' are far more important than acquiring the latest 'state of the art' process technology (Ewer et al., 1987: ch. 4). A 'deepening' model of technological development may be contrasted with those discontinuous models of technological development which stress the production of novel technological principles. Discontinuous conceptions of technological change may be termed a 'shifting' model. Kenney and Florida (1988: 140) suggest that in Japan 'the close linkage between production and innovation and a more general legacy of organizational flexibility has resulted in the integration of shifting with deepening'. The achievement of successful integration is very much an institutional question. Where employees have a rooted substantive knowledge of what they are doing, rather than one which is simply a certified mastery of some abstract occupational or analytical techniques, then the institutional conditions appear to be most appropriate for such an achievement.

Japanese organizations achieve integration of research and production through deliberately designed overlapping teams which work in the production complex. Such integration appears to be the key to the simultaneous achievement of 'shifting' and 'deepening'. 'As a result, technologies not only diffuse rapidly and help to rejuvenate mature sectors but large enterprises can quickly penetrate emerging areas either through invention, successful imitation, or knowledge acquisition' (Kenney and Florida 1988: 140). The complex of cross-cutting relations within enterprise groups is used to facilitate this technological innovation. 'Component companies in the corporate family are able to launch joint projects, transfer mutually useful information, and cross-fertilize one another' (ibid.) using networks which incorporate markets rather than vertical integration.

Deepening requires the combination of technical constraints and complexities, on the one hand, with the constant need to adapt to and anticipate changes in processes and products on the other. One particular organizational feature which facilitates this process is a degree of flexibility in work practices and a skilled and constantly re-skillable workforce (Hoshino, 1982c). The organization of enterprises dominated by the modernist characteristics of Fordism, in terms of functional specialization, task fragmentation and assembly line production, is inimical to these requirements. The overlapping work roles, extensive job rotation, team-based work units and relatively flexible production lines which characterize Japan are far more facilitative. Flexibility emerged out of the modes of rationality which were constructed during struggles in Japanese enterprises in the post-war era.

At the centre of this emergent mode of rationality was the negotiation of long-term employment tenure in the immediate post-war years. This minimized many of the employment inflexibilities which were endemic to modernist bureaucratic and Fordist organizations. Tenure guarantees reduce the rational basis for worker and union opposition to moves to automation or work redesign by management. Where the jobs of members are guaranteed then the rationality of opposition retreats. In such a context, then, it is not surprising to find that skill sharing will occur more frequently and easily, and that job rotation may be used to facilitate both formal skill sharing and informal learning amongst employees (Koike, 1981). Long-term employment also allows management to decide rationally to make large-scale investments in upgrading the skills of their workforce and in training them, secure in the knowledge that the investment will earn them a return, rather than accrue to someone else who succeeds in poaching the labour away. Where these guarantees are not in place it is always easier and certainly cheaper not to train and not to rely on a production system which requires highly skilled workers. Instead one would work to the lowest common skill denominator – the basis of modernist organization – and minimize the costs of labour turnover not through minimizing the labour transfers but through minimizing training costs and skills.

Arranging functional alignments

Typically, in Weberian bureaucracies, relationships have been settled by hierarchy, giving rise to many of the most characteristic aspects of organizations as they are currently understood. In the case of Japanese enterprise groups many of these hierarchical relationships are arranged through complex subcontracts and the extensive use of quasi-democratic work teams using horizontal relationships to substitute for functional arrangements which more typically are hierarchical in the modernist bureaucracy.

Rather than market and hierarchy being opposed to types, as in the Williamsonian formulation, it may be more appropriate to see them as alternative solutions to the problem of how to arrange functional alignment within the enterprise. They are not the only solutions. Hierarchy may also be mediated by elements of quasi-democracy in the use of work teams, without market relations being entertained in the construction of this internal democracy. Whitley (1990: 63) has suggested that enterprise structures which are premised on producing a relatively concentrated range of related products will tend, of necessity, to resort to market relations in order to complement this narrow base, an option which more imperatively co-ordinated organizations will not require. Those with more of a penchant for market relations will 'tend to deal with uncertainty by being highly flexible and evolutionary in their patterns of strategic change'. Internally, one way of achieving this is to emphasize greater elements of democracy and self-management, albeit within structural parameters, in organizational work teams. By contrast, those more oriented to hierarchy will handle organizational change 'by reallocating resources to new activities as opportunities arise' (see also Kagono et al., 1985: 57–87), thus contributing to differentiation and further specialization.

Unlike a large divisionalized Western corporation, Japanese enterprises are unlikely to practise vertical integration of their component suppliers, in order to minimize transaction costs. Instead, they are likely to use the 'just-in-time' (JIT) system where complex market relations with component subcontractors are used to ensure that supplies arrive on the premises where they are needed at the appropriate time. Large inventory stocks are dispensed with, and the circulation of capital in 'dead' buffer stock is minimized. In Japan there are large JIT production complexes spatially organized so that subsidiary companies, suppliers and subcontractors are in contiguous relationships with each other, extending through to tertiary subcontracting relations. Quoting Cusamano (1985), one may note that with respect to Toyota there are as many as 30,000 tertiary, 5,000 secondary and 220 primary subcontractors. Of the latter, 80 per cent had plants within the production complex surrounding Toyota in Toyota City.

Kenney and Florida (1988: 137) see a number of distinct advantages

168 Stewart R. Clegg

flowing from the JIT system. One is that it displaces wage costs out of the more expensive core to the somewhat cheaper periphery; another is that it leads to stable long-term relations with suppliers which open up multi-directional flows of information between the partners in the subcontracting network. Personnel as well as ideas are freely exchanged. Innovations can be accelerated through the system.

Japanese work organization is premised on self-managing teams rather than workers striving against each other under an individualistic and competitive payment and production system. In Japanese enterprises the functional alignment of activities is achieved by extensive use of the market principle through subcontracting and a (quasi-) democratic principle through self-managed teamwork. (As it takes place within an overall structure of hierarchy and private ownership it is clear why the principle can only be described as quasi-democratic.) Within the self-managing teams work roles overlap and the task structure is continuous, rather than discontinuous, in which the workers themselves allocate the tasks internationally (see Schonberger, 1982). Production is not accelerated by redesigning work downwards in its skill content, by simplifying it further and separating the workers more one from the other, as in the classical modernist organization under Fordism. This is clear from studies of Japanese organizations in other countries, such as the research by Lincoln et al. (1978) into 54 Japanese-controlled Californian organizations, which found an inverse relationship between functional specialization and Japanese control. Within Japanese organization practices, work in the internal labour market seems to be designed with an eye to the collective worker rather than in opposition to the collective worker. It appears to be designed to facilitate such collective work.

> With work teams, the pace of production can be changed by adding or removing workers, and management and team members can experiment with different configurations for completing specified tasks. In contrast to US mass production where work arrives on a conveyor belt, Japanese workers often move with the production line . . .
> Work groups perform routine quality control. This allows Japanese quality control departments to focus on nonroutine aspects of quality control, such as advanced statistical measurement or even work redesign. There is substantial evidence that work groups detect and remedy mistakes much more quickly than designated 'inspectors', saving considerable rework and scrappage. Japanese work organization has led to the integration of quality control and shopfloor problem solving. (Kenney and Florida, 1988: 132)

Quality circles have been seen as a major achievement of the Japanese system, and not only because they serve as a substitute for quality surveillance as a separate management function. They include both operatives and staff specialists such as engineers in the same circle, oriented towards not only reducing the wastage rate but also making technological and process improvements. Once more this is related to the 'deepening' of technological development. Quality control is not 'externalized', nor is maintenance, to anything like the same degree as in more traditional modernist organizations. Much of the routine preventive maintenance is done by the operators who use the machines. Kenney and Florida (1988: 132) note that 'downtime' is considerably less on machines in Japan than in the United States (the figures cited are 15 per cent compared to 50 per cent downtime). This confirms Hayes's (1981) view that the Japanese succeed because of meticulous attention to every stage of the production process.

The greater flexibility of workers extends to the technological design of work itself. Production lines in Japanese enterprises are organized to be more flexible than the simple linear track of a Fordist factory. They can be easily reconfigured between different product lines (Cohen and Zysman, 1987: ch. 9) and do not necessarily conform to the linear layout. Kenney and Florida (1988: 132–3) note that in some industries the lines may be 'U'-shaped or modular, so that operatives can 'perform a number of tasks on different machines simultaneously while individual machines "mind" themselves'. As they note, for such a strategy to succeed, multi-skilling is essential.

Mechanisms of co-ordination and control

Mechanisms of co-ordination and control of the different functions and alignments of the organization depend, in part, on the strategies of power pursued. There are two aspects to this: power in the organization and power around the organization.

Japanese organizations are not based on familism. Nor are authority relations of co-ordination and control. In Japan superiors are expected to make their subordinates accept the practice of groupism so that trust is constituted which transcends particularlisms, binding each person to the universal love of the enterprise. According to Rohlen (1973), drawing on fieldwork in a Japanese bank, about a third of Japanese organizations give their employees 'spiritual training', akin to techniques of religious conversion, therapy and initiation rites, which emphasize social co-operation, responsibility, reality acceptance and perseverance in one's tasks. Tanaka (1980) also describes similar phenomena of socialization to and indoctrination in company goals. Organizational commitment would not appear to be left to chance in many cases. In the case of Japan, organizational commitment is of most moment for those workers who are secured by the golden chains of the internal labour market. These core employees are securely incorporated as members with benefits. Such benefits are not typically approached where there is a much greater reliance on the external labour market as a source of recruitment. (In some instances, as in the case of skilled labour in New Zealand and Australia for much of the post-war era, this reliance on the external labour market has led to a positive neglect of questions of skill formation.) Where skill formation has not been marginalized, as in the Japanese case of the core internal labour market, then it is important to remember that the benefits are not spread throughout the industrial system. Those workers who are subject to domestic outwork, seasonal working or extended subcontracting will secure none of the benefits of the much vaunted core workers (Dore, 1973; McMillan, 1984), yet it is upon their 'flexibility' that the system rests. It is a system which works well in securing loyal commitment, by virtue of low turnover and dissent, even if it does not produce markedly more satisfied workers than elsewhere.

Empowerment on the shop floor appears to be more widespread in Japanese enterprises than it does in the bureaucratically conceived Fordist structures of Western modernity. This is achieved through mechanisms like extensive firm-specific basic training and learning. In part, this is accomplished through being involved in the work teams with more experienced workers. Job rotation also facilitates this learning. Such rotation takes place not only within the work teams but also more widely in the enterprise.

> Workers sequentially master the complexities of different tasks and grasp the interconnectedness among them. By breaking down the communication barriers among work groups, rotation enhances the flow of information between workers and across functional units. Rotation generates a storehouse of knowledge applicable to a variety of work situations and enhances problem-solving capabilities at the enterprise level. (Kenney and Florida, 1988: 133)

The empowerment strategies of Japanese enterprises have been identified in a generalized commitment to 'learning by doing' (Kenney and Florida 1988: 133–5). The *kanban* system, which is used to co-ordinate work between different work teams, has been seen as a part of this empowerment. Instead of top-down co-ordination of the work-flow in the form of superordinate commands and surveillance, the *kanban* system allows for communication flows which co-ordinate horizontally rather than vertically. Work units use work cards (*kanbans*) to order supplies, to deliver processed materials and to synchronize production activities. Communication is through the cards, laterally rather than vertically, reducing planning and supervision, creating empowerment as workers 'do' for themselves.

Empowerment through widespread use of communication of information has been seen by Clark (1979) to be a key feature of the *ringi-ko* decision-making system, where printed documents circulate widely through the enterprise for comment and discussion. Consequently, when decisions are made after this exposure, snags and sources of opposition will invariably have been 'cooled out', often in ways which are organizationally quite productive. Much the same can be said of the widespread use of 'suggestion schemes', which although not compulsory are so widespread that employees feel obliged to participate in them. (For instance, Kamata [1982], in his exposé of Toyota in the early 1970s, suggested that workers who chose not to 'empower' themselves in this way were punished for it through criticism and smaller bonuses!)

Flexibility and empowerment extend throughout the organization structure. There is a far wider use of management 'generalists' than is typically the case under the Weberian model of specialization and credentialization. Managers will not usually be specialists in accounting or finance, for instance, but will more likely be generalists who can rotate between positions (Kagono et al., 1985). 'Management rotation,' state Kenney and Florida (1988: 134), 'results in flexibility and learning by doing similar to that experienced on the shopfloor. This blurs distinctions between departments, between line and staff managers, and between management and workers.' Through this rotation the commitment to a tenure principle and the prevention of organizational arteriosclerosis are maintained simultaneously. Managers who never leave do not have to wait for another manager to retire or die so that they can fill their shoes. Typically, the enterprise will always leave some management slots vacant. Nominal subordinates may discharge managerial tasks. Job titles are thus denotive of seniority not function. Because of rotation and the fact that promotion of a subordinate is not threatening to the status of a superordinate, internal managerial competition is far less than in the Weberian bureaucracy. Managers tend to cross boundaries and share knowledge far more in the normal course of doing their work where the quite rational anxieties induced by more explicitly 'face-threatening' systems are present (Kagono et al., 1985: 116).

Where the traditional Weberian bureaucracy and Fordist production relations are characterized by highly specialized divisions of formalized power and authority, maintained by highly compartmentalized information flows, the situation is quite different in tendencies towards postmodernist organization:

> Long-term employment and extremely low rate of labour mobility ensure that shared knowledge remains internal to the enterprise and that leakage is minimal. This provides firms with large collective memories. The Japanese remuneration schedule sets up sizable disincentives to careerism based on information hoarding. Since bonuses hinge on overall corporate performance and wage increases take into account group performance, the ability to share information, and the development of multiple skills, there are very strong incentives for interaction and cooperation. The Japanese firm thus becomes an information-laden organization with problem-solving and regenerative capabilities far exceeding its Fordist counterparts. (Kenney and Florida, 1988: 135)

Japanese enterprises have not only developed some productive ways of organizing power internally; they are also somewhat different in terms of their power 'around' the organization, to use Mintzberg's (1983) phrase. Power around the organization concerns the way enterprises are interconnected between their strategic apexes. In the West this takes place primarily through the mechanisms of 'interlocking directorships' and the share market. In these capital-market-based systems long-term horizontal linkages, other than of cross-ownership or predatory behaviour oriented towards that end (or associated strategies), are rare.

Japanese enterprises operate under relatively stable capital market conditions compared to the highly volatile share-transactions of bundles of 'ownership' which characterize British, United States and many other Western stock exchanges. Surprisingly, perhaps, to advocates of 'free' markets, this does not result in a lack of dynamism or a neglect of issues of co-ordination and control at the strategic apexes of industry in Japan. In fact, it is the facility to achieve high degrees of such co-ordination and control in its complex inter-market organization and state-facilitated integration which many commentators have seen as the strategic edge of Japanese capitalism. In Japan, the role of MITI has been of particular importance in vertically co-ordinating enterprises in the achievement of longer-term, macro-economic, industry-wide planning (Dore, 1986). Much of the market uncertainty which has to be organizationally buffered in the West is displaced outside the organization in Japan. The system of financial ownership does not generate as much risk in the first place, while the state handles much of what does occur. Consequently there is no necessity to devise strategies to handle risk or to manage uncertainty which is not likely to occur: resources can be better invested in core activities.

In general, the question of managing state–enterprise relations also arises with respect to power around organizations. No matter how well an organization's strategic actors perceive leadership issues and pursue solutions they must secure organizational dominance and consensus, or at least obedience, for their goals. Moreover, they will have to depend on a national institutional environment if their strategy for the organization is to succeed. The most urgent need will invariably be for sources of long-term credit to finance major new investments, to maintain debt-to-equity ratios consistent with minimal capital costs and to cushion the inevitable destruction of capital that flows from basic innovations in organizational practice. Public policy also enters into this general picture. Financial assistance may be required to meet the 'front end' costs of marketing and establishing distribution and service networks, as well as there being policies to protect the domestic market from other governments' predatory trade strategies, such as dumping and the provision of credit packages on tenders for major development projects. Industrial relations systems that do not put arbitrary limits on technological innovation and the upgrading of work practices will also be required. Finally, technical inputs of equipment and components, as well as the maintenance of markets, will depend upon insertion into a diversified manufacturing sector in which public policy plays a coherent role in establishing and maintaining linkages. These general conditions are derived from intensive studies of a counter-factual case to that of Japan: the example of 'manufacturing decline' which has been charted for core sectors of the British economy in the post-war period (Williams et al., 1983).

The stability of the enterprise conditions of calculation that develop in the East Asian example has not been productive of the formation of high-risk entrepreneurial behaviour as firms launch into speculative and unrelated lines of business. In Japan the role that the state takes in developing industry policy with respect to new and declining branches of industry effectively operates to prevent the arteriosclerosis of national capitalism which might otherwise occur. Despite frequent classically economic liberal claims that government should not be in the business of picking winners, the institutional arrangements for achieving this do seem to work smoothly enough in some countries. The issue is whether or not there should be a strong framework and organizational commitment to instruments of public policy or whether or not there is a belief that such interventions are illegitimate and best left to the mysterious movements of market forces.

Constituting accountability and role relationships

Management involves the accountability for role-related actions which it is the manager's responsibility to produce and facilitate in others. The division of labour that achieves this may be more or less complex and more or less individuated. In each of the East Asian economies there is evidence to suggest that both the level of complexity and the degree of individuation of labour are less than is typically the case in a classical Weberian bureaucracy. De-differentiation appears to be operative. Whitley (1990: 65) has suggested that this is in part because of the way skill formation is more intra-organizationally than individually achieved, and thus located in the context of the overall skilling of work groups rather than just the human capital of a competitive individual. Further supporting this sense of group accountability and relationships is a reward system oriented more to teamwork than to individual work. All this is only possible where multi-skilling and flexible skilling are the norm, rather than restrictive skill defensiveness. Where there is a high degree of skill division then more formalized and externalized co-ordination and control will be required. Individual role relationships will tend to be normalized in the calculations which organization agencies make and so management control will be expressed far more in terms of the accountability of individuals.

Institutionalizing planning and communication

Planning and communication of the enterprise strategy is the fifth imperative which Blunt (1989) identifies as essential for organization. In the manufacturing sectors of Britain, the USA and Australia, conglomerates predominate as a major locus of internalized planning and communication. Whatever the structure, a manufacturing firm's facilities, workforce and distribution network impose their own focus on its technologies and markets, and thus their own limits on rational diversification. Recognizing those limits is a matter of fine judgement; expensive mistakes, resulting from uncoordinated manufacturing strategies and managerial distraction, can occur even in the cases of integration and diversification motivated solely by manufacturing considerations. They occur much more frequently in the case of mergers and takeovers that represent a second best to internal expansion, and the situation is much worse in the usual case where businesses are acquired with no manufacturing rationale at all. Thus arises the typical conglomerate of, say, twenty or thirty unrelated businesses presided over by a single head office which, however, bears ultimate responsibility for their strategic decision-making. Merger and acquisition do not necessarily produce rational reconstruction on divisional lines but can produce conflicting authority structures based on disparate organization cultures and systems resistant to the new locus of control.

In such a situation the head office's necessary lack of insight into the dynamics of the individual businesses is compounded by its over-reliance on the major formally rational means of control over local management and assessment of business prospects – that is, dependence upon financial calculations and accounting techniques premised on the divisional form. The degradation of subsidiary businesses to 'profit centres' in contemporary managerial jargon tells the tale plainly enough. Centralized cost-accounting and capital-budgeting systems are the new organs of control to whose simplistic quantifications all complex technical and organizational questions, as well as future production and marketing imponderables, have to be reduced (Standish, 1990). 'Profit-centre' managers in their turn submit to the iron law of quarterly or annual return-on-investment (ROI) calculation, which hardly encourages them to become far-sighted captains of industry. Thurow's (1984) investigation of a conglomerate with thirty subsidiaries revealed an average time horizon of 2.8 years, hardly adequate for planning investments in processes with lifespans covering several product-generations! Analysts of manufacturing decline almost unanimously pinpoint the rise to prominence of ROI calculations as the immediate cause of the sharp decline in expenditure on new process technologies, facilities and research and development.

The adoption of one or other accounting convention as the basis for planning has real material consequences (Standish, 1990). The most important general example is the use of modified historic-cost accounting in Britain and Australia which systematically overstates profits by understating the value of real capital, and this in turn may lead to inadequate retention of operating surpluses and the winding down of the assets of the business. Another arbitrary – if formally rational – aspect of accounting practice is the choice and weighting of time-frames. Profit is struck on an annual basis, and the time-frame and weighting of anticipated returns can vary greatly. The financial institutions' separation from, and domination of, manufacturers gives yearly accounts a much greater salience than in countries where financial institutions are made more receptive to manufacturer's requirements, and this in turn highlights the artificial distinction between operating costs and capital outlays.

Current ROI calculations and capital budgeting techniques bear a heavy inherent bias to conservative investment behaviour and short-term management of manufacturing enterprise. The quarterly or annual ROI calculation presents an unambiguous case and a very strong influence on local managerial behaviour because it is the main – and often only – form of control of it available, as well as the measure of its success. It is much easier to improve 'performance' on such measures by decreasing the denominator than by increasing the numerator, which can take a long time, involves risk and has to be discounted for taxation. A profit-centre manager can achieve quicker, surer and easier results by delaying replacement of old or worn-out equipment, replacing equipment eventually with technologically dated or inferior substitutes and skimping on maintenance, research and development and personnel development – in other words, by disinvestment and technological stagnation (Hayes and Garvin, 1982: 74; Hayes and Wheelwright, 1984: 11–13). In the 1970s, for instance, robots did not meet ROI criteria in either Japan or the USA in the car industry. The Japanese introduced them anyway and thereupon gained market dominance through the much higher quality achieved. As a result, robots were paying for themselves within two and a half years (Thurow, 1984).

Even more insidious, perhaps, is the rapid acceptance of capital-budgeting techniques, which involve discounting calculations for assessing strategic investments. The amount and timing of future cash flows resulting from a proposed investment are estimated; then they are discounted by the estimated return on an alternative, external investment of the same size and aggregated to produce a 'net present value'. This procedure provides plenty of room for fudging the figures and building in arbitrary assumptions. In particular it relies on estimating the final cost of the investment, the amount and timing of returns, the rate of return on the alternative investment (the 'hurdle rate') and the rate of real deterioration of items of productive capital. Even if used sensibly, capital-budgeting procedures will tend to discourage major initiatives and indicate strategies aimed at short-term returns. In practice, hopelessly unrealistic assumptions and expectations are often built into these 'analyses', like payback periods of three years or less, and very high, rule-of-thumb hurdle rates that bear no relation to the real cost of capital to the business or actual rates achievable from external placements. (Net present value calculations can, however, be bent the other way, to justify massive strategic overkill with catastrophic socio-economic – and political – consequences. Perhaps the best examples of this mistake were the British National Coal Board, British Steel Corporation and British Leyland, all of which had strikingly similar histories: see Higgins and Clegg, 1988.)

Whether one is 'sticking close to the knitting' (Peters and Waterman, 1982; Redding, 1990) by focusing only on what one knows well, in a family business, or whether one is involved in imperatively co-ordinating only a fairly specific range of business-related activity, as in typical Japanese enterprises, leaving the broader picture to the inter-market relations and to state planning, one is certainly involved in a far more restricted and less audacious exercise of planning than one would be in trying to plan the twenty or thirty unrelated businesses of the typical conglomerate. Planning and communication can take place through abstracted techniques of management control but it is by no means clear that the technical reason implicit in the use of these techniques serves to substitute for more substantively based judgements and planning. The greater degree of substantive as opposed to formal rationality evidenced in Japanese organization, in particular, seems to be an important consideration. Under conditions of more stable enterprise relations the forms of short-term economic calculation which are predominant in Western enterprises do not prove so necessary. Knowledge of the business is more rooted in substantive criteria of operational intimacy rather than merely rational techniques. Practitioners of such technically adept management, the new 'professional managers' of United States business schools, have recently been lambasted both for their failure to conceive strategies and to implement them as well as for their systematic choice of self-defeating strategies (Hayes and Abernathy, 1980; see also Hayes and Wheelwright, 1984; Hayes et al., 1988). Unlike their predecessor who typically worked up through the various functional departments and divisions of the enterprise, gaining 'hands-on' experience, the new manager cultivates a 'fast track' career by job-hopping and scoring up quick symbolic 'wins'. Knowledge of the specific business grounded in its local culture is replaced with an analytic detachment born of de-contextualized and portable skills gained at business, accountancy or law school. Apart from the formal accomplishments of law, accountancy and financial management, these skills restrict themselves to formalized consumer analysis, market survey technique, matrixes and learning curves. Ignorance of technical contingency is supplemented with 'technology aversion' and an elitism that prevents either being remedied (Pascale, 1984). Institutionally cultivated individual career strategies for organizational dominance contribute to organizational decline.

Two prominent analysts of the Harvard Business School, Hayes and Abernathy (1980: 74) have branded these new managers as 'pseudo-professionals' who *systematically* mismanage a manufacturing business. They regard plant as an embarrassing constraint on financial manoeuvrability and try to buy pre-packaged solutions, commonly on an inappropriate and grandiose scale. But what they do well is more damaging than what they do badly. 'Managing by the numbers' collapses time-frames: individual businesses have to show quick returns on minimal outlays or be deliberately run down and liquidated as 'cash cows'; in conglomerates, individual businesses are reduced to bargaining chips, quickly acquired and shed. 'A "successful" American manager doesn't plant or harvest,' Thurow (1984: 23) comments, 'he is simply a Viking raider.' Clearly, such individuals are strategically ill equipped to address the substantive issues of manufacturing management; and obsolescence, lack of fit, quality and labour problems result.

For many writers, the investigation of manufacturing decline stops here, and they propose solutions accordingly. At the most extreme, Pascale (1984: 65) suggests that rationality as such is an ethnocentric cul-de-sac, and the standard business-journal exercise of learning-from-the-Japanese for him boils down to a flight from rationality and emulating the inspired but erratic hit-or-miss business behaviour of Soichiro Honda. 'The givens of organization,' he reminds us, 'are ambiguity, uncertainty, imperfection and paradox'; he thus follows the organization theory of March and his associates (Cohen et al., 1972) towards the conviction that strategic and structural responses carry their own falsehood. The more common remedies are no less fanciful and voluntarist, from exhumation of the Schumpeterian entrepreneur to proposals for corporate cultural revivalism (see Ray, 1986) and an evangelical faith in the explanatory purchase of 'economic culture' in its post-Confucian mode, an explanation to which can be attributed both the 'decline of the West' and the rise of East Asia. By contrast, this chapter is recommending consideration of the specificities of substantive practice.

In the case of Japan, writers such as Fox (1980) stress that long-term planning based on market research has been vital in those areas where innovation, and not just importation, of technology has occurred in Japan, such as the consumer electronics industry. Eto (1980) stresses the role of the government in supplying information and technological forecasts, sharing the emphasis which Holden (1980) places on MITI's national industrial policy. In addition, she also stresses the institutional freedom which Japanese firms have to plan long term as well as their emphasis on quality control in the actual production process. (The 'cultural homogeneity' of the workforce is also stressed as being important.) Other writers, such as Hoshino (1982a, 1982b, and especially 1982c and 1982d), while sharing the stress on technological innovation, argue that it is characteristics of the organization structure which enable long-term research planning to occur easily, notably the flexibility of the specialist workforce.

Relating rewards and performance

Performance and reward imperatives may be more or less related. Now, this can be achieved in one or other of two contrasting ways. It may be achieved through complex processes of individualization in effort-related bonus systems. Alston (1982), for instance, has noted how these arrangements may give rise to jealousy and rivalry. Alternatively, it may be done through linking rewards not to individual efforts but to organizational success and service. The latter strategy has characterized Japanese management systems. The payment system has been oriented primarily to improving overall organization performance, by tightly coupling length of service to frequent promotion up a ladder of many small gradations. The seniority-based nature of the wages system in Japan, the *nenko* system, has been the major focus of much discussion of the relation between rewards and performance in Japan (see Sano, 1977). It should be clear that *nenko seido*, the combination of lifetime employment and seniority-based wages systems, applies only to the core employees, almost all of whom will be males (Matsuura, 1981). In common with Matsuura, other writers such as Takeuchi (1982) have argued that the ease of dismissal, low wage and fringe benefit costs and frequent part-time provision of female labour are important in buffering and stabilizing the employment situation of core workers. The basis of flexibility is disproportionately shouldered by female patterns of labour force participation.

Wages in Japan are not simply based on age alone. Performance elements do enter into the equation. However, they do so in a distinctive way. Bonuses are related to overall group or organizational performance (Dore, 1973: 94–110). It has been suggested, for instance, that wages in Japan are determined by mechanisms based largely on profit maximization, while Matsuzuka (1967) has pointed to the closely related variable of organization size in determining wage disparities, as well as age and duration of employment service. One aspect of this size function seems to be that the *nenko* system is surviving in larger firms while it is being eroded in the smaller ones (Tachibanaki, 1982). This stress on organizational aspects in wage determination is picked up by Nakao (1980) in the emphasis given to the correlation between high wages and market share (which is itself related to advertising expenditures).

Alston (1982) has suggested that in practice there are two guidelines or rules at work relating rewards and performance in Japan. First, a single individual is never rewarded alone, but the reward is distributed as equally as possible within the work group. Secondly, he has pointed to the expressive dimension of the reward system, in addition to its instrumental qualities. Group rewards of a symbolic kind like a group photograph or company shield with the group's name on it are important devices used to build up the sense of practical ideological community. However, it is easy to overstress how these rewards relate to job satisfaction. The implicit suggestion is that they do – that non-instrumental rewards are of importance in securing greater commitment, involvement and satisfaction from workers. On these criteria one would anticipate that Japanese workers would exhibit high levels of job satisfaction in comparative surveys. Despite the popular image of Japanese employees as happy and harmonious group workers the reality seems to be that they are not. As Lincoln and McBride (1987: 304) suggest on the basis of their extensive survey of the research literature, a 'particularly perplexing but strong and consistent finding from numerous work attitude surveys is the low level of job satisfaction reported by the Japanese'. This suggests caution in imputing too much in the way of intrinsic superiority from the actor's point of view to Japanese management practices, irrespective of the reasons for this low satisfaction. Interestingly, Cole (1979, 238) suggests that the low rates of Japanese satisfaction are due to the fact that they expect more from work than other nationalities! In view of the available evidence from the questions expressly asked there is little chance of disconfirming this view, although one may be inclined to regard it with a degree of scepticism.

Achieving effective leadership

The global success not only of Japanese enterprise in the 1980s but also of the other NICs of East Asia has been seen by some commentators such as Blunt (1989: 21) as a spur to the renaissance of studies of effective leadership in recent times. Leadership is usually defined in terms which relate a 'vision' of the future to some 'strategies' for achieving it, which are capable of co-opting support, compliance and teamwork in its achievement and serve to motivate and sustain commitment to its purpose (after Kotter, 1988: 25–6). Hamilton and Biggart (1988) have stressed 'institutional aspects' of leadership – that is, the societal 'principles' or 'values' around which the vision can coalesce.

Japan is not like the Western type of professional bureaucracy, with its upper echelons of 'cosmopolitans' well versed in conflicts with their more 'local' compatriots (Gouldner, 1957–8). In fact, Japanese organization is closer in many respects to depictions of an 'organic' structure, where the flexible aspects of the latter are widely distributed over areas of the organization which elsewhere would be more mechanical. The fairly effective neutralization of countervailing sources of leadership from professional bodies and trade unions is an important component of this, as is the considerable attention paid to ensuring that leadership initiatives have broad-based support before they are adopted, through the mechanisms of the *ringi-ko* decision-making structure and the extensive use of generalist managerial job rotation. The 'organic' qualities are clearly important in allowing the adoption of systems of management which, in the absence of less effective leadership in gaining commitment, would hardly be viable. Holding very little in the way of stocks and inventory and relying on components suppliers to supply these 'just in time' for use in production could not operate where supply was liable to frequent bottlenecks, disruption or downright 'guileful' dispositions to milk positions of strategic contingency for what they are worth. The achievement of a situation where this is not the case, in leadership terms, is clearly related to the whole institutional fabric of the enterprise, in terms of phenomena such as the labour market structure and system of rewards.

Some writers, such as Blunt (1989: 22), refer to these institutional aspects of leadership in terms of an extended medical metaphor. Leadership provides organizational values which can serve as a basis for the development of mutual trust and commitment. Organization life which lacks this, which is premised on mistrust, is riddled with cholesterol clogging and incapacitating the system, like an epidemic of modern organizational life. The metaphor is a little too colourful, perhaps, but the general point is quite clear. Those organizations whose members can find no good reason, whatever the basis of the bargain, to trust one another at a modicum will find it extremely hard to work effectively with each other. If nothing else, leadership is about building this basis (Bartolme, 1989).

Organization imperatives and organizational representations

The imperatives of organizations have been discussed in terms of a number of dimensions. Representationally these are arranged as in Figure 1.

The preceding section has suggested some ways in which these dimensions align themselves in Japan. National types of economic embeddedness have not been located on these dimensions, for at least two reasons. First, the descriptive data are, by and large, societal and macro in orientation. They have not been specifically collected as organization-level data, generated from a schema such as this. In this respect the schema is more indicative and sensitizing than anything else – it gives us some clues as to what to look for if we are interested in discovering organization diversities. Secondly, one would very much doubt whether one would find that all organizations aligned themselves neatly on to national patterns. There are likely to be some nationally based organizations which will be deviant cases in terms of some or other dimension of the imperatives, if only because of the effects of more specific organization contingencies of size or technology, neither of which are considered here.

This framework for enquiry suggests several things. First, organizations which are undoubtedly effective in their own national contexts may be fabricated in quite diverse ways, using distinct local resources to construct their particular response to the organizational imperatives. Secondly, some of the typical patterns that emerge, those which tend to be more specialized in mission, goals, strategies and functions and to be more oriented towards market relations to handle their functional alignments, for instance, will tend to be a part of a broader economic system in which the isolation of the focal organization makes only limited analytical sense. Indeed, it may well serve to do some injustice and violence to the integrity of the substantive phenomena.

For the future, research needs to address the extent to which these dimensions of organization imperatives do form coherent patterns; the extent to which the coherent patterns form national clusters; and the extent to which they relate to more common criteria of organizational analysis such as the Aston measures. By asking such questions it ought to

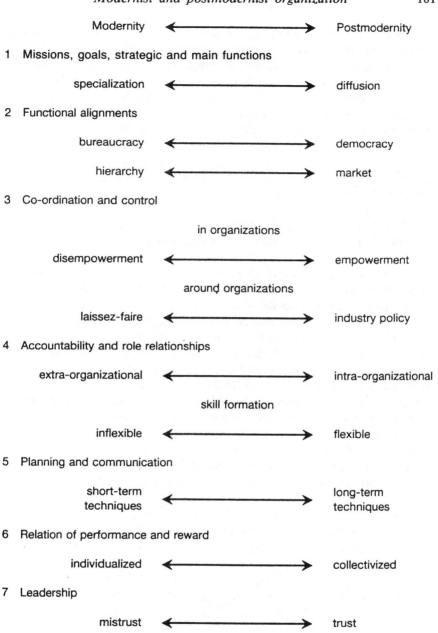

Figure 1 *Organizational dimensions of modernity/postmodernity*

be possible to begin to address systematically some of the sources of organizational diversity which both modernity and postmodernity present to us in their many authentic ways, rather than trying to push them all into a limited number of boxes made to a dominant pattern. Where that national pattern is distinctly modernist and the data under consideration are putatively postmodernist, this analytical strategy should certainly not be preferred. It may be that what is important is not so much 'strategic choice' within national patterns of organization normalization but the patterns themselves, the way they differ from one another and form more or less coherent, nationally contingent entities. Rather than looking for deviations from pattern, perhaps one should be looking at the patterns produced by the modes of rationality which agents typically find it conventional to construct.

Theoretical arguments in organization analysis have tended to be deterministic. The most obvious examples of this are contingency theories of a 'culture-free' variety (Hickson et al., 1974) but it is also the case with certain kinds of institutional theory, such as in Biggart and Hamilton's (1987: 437) hypothesis that '[l]eadership strategies in any one sociocultural setting will have strong underlying similarities'. Against either form of determinism one might instead want to argue that contingencies and institutions should be seen as providing the arena in which power-players will seek to utilize whatever resources are available in constructing local organizational practice, shaped to whatever mode of rationality, against the last of organizational imperatives. Organizations are arenas within which some things will tend to hang together and be adopted by power-players as a bundle, while other forms of combination may be far less likely to occur as a coherent package, perhaps because they are less coherent or because the alliance which could make them so lacks a position in the field of power to be able to constitute the necessity of its choices. Institutional and contingency matters will enter into this determination. The general theoretical model, in a very simplified form, is shown in Figure 2.

The argument of this chapter has been to suggest that a distinctive mode of rationality, which is postmodernist in its opposition to the principles of the Weberian/Fordist organization pattern, may have emerged in

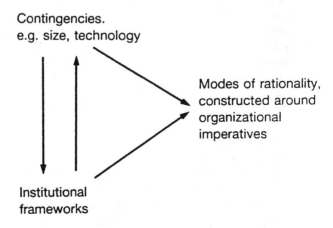

Figure 2   *Framing contingent modes of rationality*

some aspects of post-war Japan. Rather than attribute this either to cultural explanations of an over-socialized kind or to market explanations which are under-socialized, the chapter has built upon the earlier discussion of Japanese specificity in order to develop a power/institutions model for this analysis. Some aspects of the power settlement in post-war Japanese enterprises, particularly the enterprise unions, the wage payment systems and the flexibility which these allowed, have been crucial for the emergence of this putative postmodernist form of organization.

Aspects of the institutional framework of Japanese enterprises developed in the pre-war era, notably the tendency to extensive networking within the *zaibatsu*. This tendency was continued in the post-war era of enterprise groups to shape a framework in which developed a quite distinct set of practices and forms of calculation of economic action. It was out of these that what has been hypothesized as postmodernist organization developed.

If Japan represents one possible path towards postmodernity, it is clear that there have been winners and losers in this development. To recap, the winners have been men who were in internal labour markets in the big-name companies and the enterprise group networks. The losers have been women and those, more than two-thirds of all workers, who are outside the core labour market. With respect to women, the loss derives not just from a low level of labour force participation but from the nature of employment practices. Extended service is a key factor in remuneration, as we have seen. Because there are very few women who have extended lengths of continuous employment with a single employer, male–female wage differentials are large in middle age. It is the nature of the workforce participation which varies, with women's work being largely unskilled because they are not employed in the core enterprises and internal labour market, where continuous training and re-skilling are provided to permanent employees (Koike, 1981). The labour market is relatively highly segmented, with comparatively less rights for labour and a more arduous regime of work than in the more social democratic OECD states. Longer hours and shorter recreation are the norm, with the annual average working hours of a Japanese worker amounting to more than 2,100: by contrast in Britain and the USA the average is 1,800–1,900 hours, with about 1,650 the norm in the Federal Republic of Germany (Deutschmann, 1987). Within the labour market core wages are relatively high, compared internationally – but so are the costs of basic consumer goods and services, with housing, in particular, being inordinately expensive per square metre, compared with OECD averages. Typically, each person occupies far fewer square metres than would be the norm in most other OECD states. Of course, outside Japan, elsewhere in the world, there may also turn out to be losers on a wider scale, those trapped and organizationally outflanked in modernist organization forms as the leading edge turns ever more postmodern.

Conclusion

In this chapter a detailed consideration has been made of the organizational characteristics of the system of economic embeddedness which characterizes contemporary Japanese enterprises. Overall, there appear to be some significant differences when one makes comparison with more typically modernist organizations. Perhaps that is sufficient reason for claiming that postmodern organization forms appear to be implicit in these developments. Certainly, there are evident differences and they may well sketch one political conjecture for postmodern organization premised on stable private capital formation, production-centred strategies of economic calculation and high degrees of labour market segmentation.

References

Abegglen, J.C. (1973) *Management and Worker: The Japanese Solution*. Tokyo: Sophia University Press.

Aglietta, M. (1979) *A Theory of Capitalist Regulation*. London: New Left Books.

Albertsen, N. (1988) 'Postmodernism, post-Fordism, and critical social theory', *Environment and Planning D: Society and Space*, 6: 339–66.

Alston, J.P. (1982) 'Awarding bonuses the Japanese way', *Business Horizons*, 25(5): 46–50.

Bartolme, F. (1989) 'Nobody trusts the boss completely – now what?', *Harvard Business Review*, 67(2): 135–42.

Biggart, N.W. and Hamilton, G.G. (1987) 'An institutional theory of leadership', *Journal of Applied Behavioural Science*, 23(4): 429–41.

Blunt, P. (1989) 'Strategies for human resource development in the Third World', opening address to The International Human Resource Development Conference, University of Manchester, 25–8 June.

Calmfors, L. and Diffil, J. (1988) 'Bargaining structure, corporatism and macro-economic performance', *Economic Policy*, 6(1): 13–62.

Clark, R. (1979) *The Japanese Company*. New Haven, Conn.: Yale University Press.

Clegg, S.R. and Dunkerley, D. (1980) *Organization, Class and Control*. London: Routledge & Kegan Paul.

Clegg, S.R., Boreham, P. and Dow, G. (1983) 'Politics and crisis: the state of the recession', in S.R. Clegg, G. Dow and P. Boreham (eds), *The State, Class and the Recession*. London: Croom Helm. pp. 1–50.

Clegg, S.R., Boreham, P. and Dow, G. (1986) *Class, Politics and the Economy*. London: Routledge & Kegan Paul.

Cohen, M.D., March, J.G. and Olsen, J.P. (1972) 'A garbage can model of organizational choice', *Administrative Science Quarterly*, 17(1): 1–25.

Cohen, S. and Zysman, J. (1987) *Manufacturing Matters: The Myth of Post-Industrial Society*. New York: Basic Books.

Cole, R.E. (1978) 'The late-developer hypothesis: an evaluation of its relevance for Japanese employment practices', *Journal of Japanese Studies*, 4: 247–68.

Cole, R.E. (1979) *Work, Mobility and Participation*. Berkeley, Calif.: University of California Press.

Cole, R.E. and Tominga, K. (1976) 'Japan's changing occupational structure and its significance', in H. Patrick (ed.), *Japanese Industrialization and its Social Consequences*. Berkeley, Calif.: University of California Press. pp. 53–95.

Cool, K.O. and Lengnick-Hall, C.A. (1985) 'Second thoughts on the transferability of the Japanese management style', *Organizational Studies*, 6(1): 1–22.

Cusamano, M. (1985) *The Japanese Automobile Industry: Technology and Management at Nissan and Toyota.* Cambridge, Mass.: Harvard University Press.

Deutschmann, C. (1987) 'The Japanese type of organization as a challenge to the sociological theory of modernization', *Thesis Eleven*, 17: 40–58.

Dore, R. (1973) *British Factory, Japanese Factory: The Origins of National Diversity in Industrial Relations.* London: Allen & Unwin.

Dore, R. (1979) 'More about late development', *Journal of Japanese Studies*, 5: 137–51.

Dore, R. (1986) *Flexible Rigidities.* Stanford, Calif.: Stanford University Press.

Drucker, P.F. (1971) 'What we can learn from Japanese management', *Harvard Business Review*, 49: 110–22.

Emery, F. and Trist, E.J. (1960) 'Socio-technical systems', in C. Churchman and M. Verhulst (eds), *Management Science, Models and Techniques*, Vol. 2. Oxford: Pergamon. pp. 83–97.

Ergas, H. (1987) 'Does technology policy matter?', in B. Guile and H. Brooks (eds), *Technology and Global Industry*, Washington, DC: National Academy Press. pp. 191–245.

Eto, H. (1980) 'Problems and lessons of Japanese technology policy', *R&D Management*, 10(2): 49–59.

Ewer, P., Higgins, W. and Stevens, A. (1987) *Unions and the Future of Australian Manufacturing*, Sydney: Allen & Unwin.

Fox, B. (1980) 'Japan's electronic lesson', *New Scientist*, 88: 517–20.

Gouldner, A.W. (1957–8) 'Cosmopolitans and locals: towards an analysis of latent social roles', *Administrative Science Quarterly*, 2: 281–302; 444–80.

Gramsci, A. (1971) *Selections from the Prison Notebooks.* London: Lawrence & Wishart.

Hamada, T. (1980) 'Winds of change: economic realism and Japanese labor management', *Asian Survey*, 20: 397–406.

Hamilton, G.G. and Biggart, N.W. (1988) 'Market, culture, and authority: a comparative analysis of management and organization in the Far East', in C. Winship and S. Rosen (eds), *Organizations and Institutions: Sociological Approaches to the Analysis of Social Structure. American Journal of Sociology*, 94, supplement. Chicago: University of Chicago Press. pp. 552–95.

Hayes, R.H. (1981) 'Why Japanese factories work', *Harvard Business Review*, 59(4): 56–66.

Hayes, R.H. and Abernathy, W. (1980) 'Managing our way to economic decline', *Harvard Business Review*, 58(4): 67–77.

Hayes, R.H. and Garvin, D.A. (1982) 'Managing as if tomorrow mattered', *Harvard Business Review*, 60(3): 70–80.

Hayes, R.H. and Wheelwright, S.C. (1984) *Restoring our Competitive Edge: Competing through Manufacturing.* New York: Wiley.

Hayes, R.H., Wheelwright, S. and Clark, K. (1988) *Dynamic Manufacturing: Creating the Learning Organization.* New York: Free Press.

Hickson, D.J., Hinings, C.R., McMillan, C.J. and Schwitter, J.P. (1974) 'The culture-free context of organization structure: a tri-national comparison', *Sociology*, 8: 59–80.

Higgins, W. and Clegg, S.R. (1988) 'Enterprise calculation and manufacturing decline', *Organization Studies*, 9(1): 69–89.

Holden, C. (1980) 'Innovation: Japan races ahead as the US falters', *Science*, 210: 751–4.

Hoshino, Y. (1982a) 'The Japanese style of management: technical innovation (Part I)', *Sumitomo Quarterly*, 7: 15–18.

Hoshino, Y. (1982b) 'The Japanese style of management: technical innovation (Part II)', *Sumitomo Quarterly*, 8: 15–18.

Hoshino, Y. (1982c) 'The Japanese style of management: technical innovation (Part III): staff motivation, job mobility are keys to Japanese advance', *Sumitomo Quarterly*, 9: 19–22.

Hoshino, Y. (1982d) 'The Japanese style of management: technical innovation (Part IV): creative technology needs new environment', *Sumitomo Quarterly*, 10: 8–10.

Ishikawa, A. (1982) 'A survey of studies in the Japanese style of management', *Economic and Industrial Democracy*, 3(1): 1–15.

Jacoby, S. (1979) 'Origins of internal labor markets in Japan', *Industrial Relations*, 18(2): 184–96.

Jacques, E. (1989) *Requisite Organizations*. Arlington, Va: Casson Hall.

Jameson, F. (1984) 'Postmodernism, or the cultural logic of late capitalism', *New Left Review*, 146: 53–93.

Kagono, T., Nonaka, I., Satakibara, K. and Okumura, A. (1985) *Strategic vs Evolutionary Management: A US/Japan Comparison of Strategy and Organization*. Amsterdam: North-Holland.

Kamata, S. (1982) *Japan in the Passing Lane*. New York: Pantheon.

Kenney, M. and Florida, R. (1988) 'Beyond mass production: production and the labor process in Japan', *Politics and Society*, 16(1): 121–58.

Koike, K. (1981) 'A Japan–Europe comparison of female labour-force participation and male–female wage differentials', *Japanese Economic Studies*, 9(2): 3–27.

Koshiro, K. (1981) 'The quality of working life in Japan', *The Wheel Extended: A Toyota Quarterly Review*, special supplement, 9: 1–8.

Kotter, J.P. (1988) *The Leadership Factor*. New York: Free Press.

Lash, S. (1988) 'Postmodernism as a regime of signification', *Theory, Culture & Society*, 5(2–3): 311–36.

Lash, S. and Urry, J. (1987) *The End of Organized Capitalism*. Cambridge: Polity Press.

Lincoln, J.R. and McBride, K. (1987) 'Japanese industrial organizations in comparative perspective', *American Review of Sociology*, 13: 289–312.

Lincoln, J.R., Olson, J. and Hanada, M. (1978) 'Cultural effects on organizational structure: the case of Japanese firms in the United States', *American Sociological Review*, 43: 829–47.

Marsh, R.M. and Mannari, H. (1977) 'Organizational commitment and turnover: a prediction study', *Administrative Science Quarterly*, 22(1): 57–75.

Marsh, R.M. and Mannari, H. (1980) 'Technological implications theory: a Japanese test', *Organization Studies*, 1(2): 161–83.

Marsh, R.M. and Mannari, H. (1981) 'Technology and size as determinants of the organizational structure of Japanese factories', *Administration Science Quarterly*, 26(1): 33–57.

Matsuura, N.F. (1981) 'Sexual bias in the *nenko* system of employment', *Journal of Industrial Relations*, 23(3): 310–22.

Matsuzuka, H. (1967) 'Industrialization and the change of wage structure in Japan', in N. Uchida and K. Ikeda (eds), *Social and Economic Aspects of Japan*. Tokyo: Economic Institute of Seijo University. pp. 111–13.

McMillan, C.J. (1984) *The Japanese Industrial System*. Berlin: De Gruyter.

Mintzberg, H. (1983) *Power in and around Organizations*. Englewood Cliffs, NJ: Prentice-Hall.

Nakao, T. (1980) 'Wages and market power in Japan', *British Journal of Industrial Relations*, 18(3): 365–8.

Pascale, T. (1984) 'Perspectives on strategy: the real story behind Honda's success', *Californian Management Review*, 26(3): 47–72.

Peters, T.J. and Waterman, R.H. (1982) *In Search of Excellence*. New York: Harper & Row.

Piore, M.J. and Sabel, C.F. (1984) *The Second Industrial Divide: Possibilities for Prosperity*. New York: Basic Books.

Ray, C. (1986) 'Social innovation at work: the humanization of workers in twentieth century America', PhD, University of California, Santa Cruz.

Redding, S.G. (1990) *The Spirit of Chinese Capitalism*. Berlin: De Gruyter.

Rohlen, T. (1973) '"Spiritual education" in a Japanese bank', *American Anthropologist*, 75: 1542–62.

Rustin, M. (1989) 'The politics of post-Fordism: or, the trouble with "New Times"', *New Left Review*, 175: 54–78.

Sano, Y. (1977) 'Seniority-based wages in Japan – a survey', *Japanese Economic Studies*, 5(3): 48–65.

Schonberger, R.J. (1982) *Japanese Manufacturing Techniques*. New York: Free Press.

Standish, P.E.M. (1990) 'Accounting: the private language of business or an instrument of social communication', in S.R. Clegg and S.G. Redding (eds), with the assistance of M. Cartner, *Capitalism in Contrasting Cultures*. Berlin: De Gruyter. pp. 122–41.

Tachibanaki, T. (1982) 'Further results on Japanese wage differentials: *nenko* wages, hierarchical position, bonuses and working hours', *International Economic Review*, 23(2): 447–62.

Takeuchi, H. (1982) 'Working women in business corporations – the management viewpoint', *Japan Quarterly*, 29(3): 319–23.

Tanaka, H. (1980) 'The Japanese method of preparing today's graduate to become tomorrow's manager', *Personnel Journal*, 59(2): 109–12.

Thurow, L. (1984) 'Revitalizing American industry: managing in a competitive world economy', *Californian Management Review*, 27(1): 9–40.

Tichy, N. (1981) 'Networks in organizations', in P. Nystrom and W. Starbuck (eds), *Handbook of Organization Design*. New York: Oxford University Press. pp. 386–408.

Urabe, K. (1979) 'A critique of theories of the Japanese-style management systems', *Japanese Economic Studies*, 7(4): 33–50.

Weber, M. (1978) *Economy and Society: An Outline of Interpretive Sociology*, 2 vols, ed. G. Roth and C. Wittich. Berkeley, Calif.: University of California Press.

Whitley, R. (1990) 'East Asian enterprise structures and the comparative analysis of forms of business organization', *Organization Studies*, 11(1): 47–74.

Williams, K., Williams, J. and Thomas, D. (1983) *Why Are the British Bad at Manufacturing?* London: Routledge & Kegan Paul.

Williams, R. (1989) 'When was modernism?', *New Left Review*, 175: 48–53.

PART THREE
CULTURAL STRATEGIES

Introduction

Kenneth Thompson

The concept of 'culture' and ideas about 'gaining control of the corporate culture' so as to improve organizational performance have come to prominence in the management literature in recent years, offering the promise of directing and inspiring employees' behaviour and attitudes through the management of meaning and symbols rather than through the unwieldy levers of organizational structures. On the face of it this might seem to be a rather surprising development. After all, culture appears to refer to the more intangible aspects of an organization, such as beliefs, values and norms of behaviour, which contrast with the observable hard facts of structure. Changing organizational structures as part of HRS looks more feasible and straightforward than trying to take hold of something as impalpable as culture. And yet this is precisely what has been attempted in many organizations and it is widely advocated by management consultants who claim to have discovered the secrets behind the success of 'excellence companies'. Clearly, it is worth looking more closely at this approach with a view to discerning its assumptions and ramifications. The three chapters chosen for this section all deal with fundamental questions about culture in organizations, rather than advocating particular strategies for changing organizational cultures. It is our belief that analysis must precede strategy.

Some of the key issues with regard to culture are: what are the various components and levels of organizational cultures? How do these cultures work in organizations? Are some components and levels of culture likely to be more difficult to change than others?

Although cultural analysis is still a fairly recent phenomenon in management literature and is often carried out at a rather superficial level, there is a rich tradition of social scientific analysis to build on. Anthropologists have developed concepts and methods for studying the culture of whole peoples and communities. The sociologist Max Weber (1864–1920) focused on cultural factors in the development of the entrepreneurial personality, the spirit of capitalism, and bureaucracy, in such works as *The Protestant Ethic and the Spirit of Capitalism and Economy and Society*. His French counterpart, Emile Durkheim (1858–1917), laid the foundations of sociological analysis with his studies of *The*

Division of Labour in Society, exploring the relation between changes in organization and changes in 'collective consciousness', and also examining the pathological effects of cultures that are too strong or too weak in *Suicide*. Other notable contributions were Marx's macro-theory of the relationship between economy and ideology, and the micro-sociological theory of symbolic interactionism developed by the social psychologist G.H. Mead (1863–1931) and others of the Chicago School. The subsequent work of anthropologists and sociologists studying the relationships between structure and culture has built on these foundations. The following chapters map out some of the lines of development and their implications for organizational analysis.

The first chapter in this section, by V. Lynn Meek, sets out the background to the concept of culture and discusses the ways in which the concept has been selectively appropriated by management writers. She begins by relating the present prominence of culture in management literature to socio-economic factors in Western societies: the economic downturn, the increase in international competition from Japan and other non-Western economies, and the various structural factors that have put Western institutions under strain. Obviously, it was thought that cultural factors might explain some of these organizational failures and successes. The idea has taken root that culture is something that an organization 'has', in the possession of management, rather than something that an organization 'is' as a result of interactions and negotiations.

Possibly this reflects a period in which the balance of power has tilted in favour of management and against labour, thus fostering the idea that a relatively passive set of individual employees can be easily persuaded to accept management ideas and initiatives. One of the implications of Meek's analysis is that research and strategies which do not take account of cultural differences within an organization may be misleading and ineffectual in the long term.

The second chapter, by Paul Bate, shows how culture can act as an obstacle to change and problem resolution. After an initial discussion of the various components of culture, he concentrates on the fundamental level of shared orientations (what others might call 'meanings' or general beliefs). He draws on his three research studies to identify a range of cultural responses to a set of six issues that face all organizations. In conclusion he seeks to establish a relationship between organizational culture and orientation to change.

Edgar Schein, in the third chapter, sets out to develop a dynamic model of organizational culture. It is a useful attempt to map out the main elements and dimensions of culture, including factors that enter into processes of learning and group dynamics. His definition highlights processes of formation and change around issues of external adaptation and internal integration. He looks at interrelated, patterned sets of basic assumptions that deal with fundamental issues. In order to decipher a given organization's culture he advocates the use of a complex interview, observation, and joint-enquiry approach in which selected members of the organization work with the outsider to uncover the unconscious assumptions that are basic to the culture.

These three chapters give a good indication of the kind of painstaking approach to the study of organizational culture that is a necessary corrective to the superficial views and prescriptions that emerge from hasty attempts to climb on the culture bandwagon.

12

Organizational culture: origins and weaknesses

V. Lynn Meek

The study of organizational culture – the proposition that organizations create myths and legends, engage in rites and rituals, and are governed through shared symbols and customs – is much in vogue. Although the reasons for this are not entirely clear, two issues deserve mention: (1) the effect of political, ideological and socio-economic factors on social theory; (2) the related issue of the scholarly and ideological implications of the selective borrowing of key concepts from one discipline by other fields of study.

The present preoccupation with organizational culture is probably related to socio-economic factors in Western society. Most Western countries have experienced a dramatic downturn in their economies. This, in turn, has helped to emphasize the structural inequalities inherent in these societies and has placed the structure of Western capitalism under severe pressure. It probably is no accident that many scholars are emphasizing cultural problems – particularly where cultural problems are naively operationalized in terms of 'people problems' – at a time when the structures of many Western institutions are under strain.

Some social theorists use the term 'culture' to embrace all that is human within the organization. They emphasize culture, either consciously or unconsciously, in such a way as to blur or hide problems and contradictions inherent in the social structure. Of course, both an organization's culture and its structure are socially created; but that is not what is at issue here. The problem with some studies of organizational culture is that they appear to presume that there exists in a real and tangible sense a collective organizational culture that can be created, measured and manipulated in order to enhance organizational effectiveness. The link between 'culture' and 'effectiveness' has become, recently, quite pronounced, and studies incorporating in their title such phrases as the 'culture of school effectiveness', or the 'culture of corporative effectiveness' abound. It is implied that an ineffective organization can be made effective – a school can produce the 'model citizen', that is, one who can find employment, and the corporation can enhance its profit

Reprinted by permission of Organization Studies from *Organization Studies* 9(4) 1988: 453–73.

margin – if an unhealthy organizational culture can be supplanted with a healthy one. The problem is one of changing people's values, norms and attitudes so that they make the 'right' and necessary contribution to the healthy collective 'culture' despite (or in ignorance of) any inherent conflict of individual and group interest or the way in which power, authority and control are structured in the organization.

Areas of study, such as the study of complex organizations – including educational and corporate administration, management studies, and human relations and interpersonal dynamics – are influenced by concepts that filter down into the ranks of their practitioners from older, well-founded disciplines. The idea of culture in organizations is a concept borrowed mostly from anthropology, although some sociologists, such as Durkheim, have also been influential.

There is nothing wrong with one discipline borrowing concepts from another discipline; this process has resulted in important theoretical innovations. However, there is a danger that, when one area of study borrows key concepts from other disciplines, the concepts become either stereotyped or distorted in the transfer. Also, when concepts are borrowed from other disciplines, they may not be borrowed *in toto*: that is, rather than accepting an entire 'package' – which may include the historical debates surrounding the 'proper' uses of the concepts – people only select aspects of the concepts that suit their interests and thinking at a particular time. This may result either in a slanted and biased application of the concepts or a dilution of their original analytical power.

The concept of organizational culture can be a powerful analytical tool in the analysis and interpretation of human action within complex organizations. Alternatively, it can be misused to reify the social reality of organizational life. It may be timely to have a close look at some of the ways in which the concept of 'culture' has been used in organizational research, paying particular attention to questions concerning what aspects of the concept of culture have been borrowed from anthropology and, to a lesser extent, sociology. It seems that much of the use of culture as a unitary concept expressing, on the one hand, social cohesion and integration, and on the other, organizational effectiveness, is the result of the transfer of the concept of culture to organizational analysis from a particular anthropological and sociological theoretical tradition, that is the 'structural-functional' theoretical paradigm.

Organizational culture is a difficult but seminal concept, and a single paper could neither do justice to all facets of the concept, nor could it analyse all the ways in which it has been employed in empirical research. There is a growing body of literature that critically assesses the study of organizational culture, and it is likely that the debate surrounding the 'proper' use of the concept of culture in organizational analysis will continue for some time (see, in particular, Allaire and Firsirotu, 1984; Gregory, 1983; Smircich, 1983). This chapter contributes to the debate in three limited ways. First, it briefly reviews a few of the consequences of the selective borrowing of the concept of culture. The purpose here is not to debunk past studies of organizational culture, but to attempt to illustrate some of the political and ideological as well as the scholarly effects of viewing culture from a particular theoretical perspective. The chapter then attempts to disentangle the subtle difference between an organization's culture and its social structure, and concludes with a brief discussion of some 'sub-concepts' that comprise the idea of culture. Culture, as a total concept, is too all embracing. It needs to be dissected into manageable proportions so that it can be used in the interpretation of observed behaviour.

The concept borrowed

Some recent studies of organizational or corporate culture have been undertaken by what Turner (1986), drawing on Ott's (1984) terminology, calls 'pop cultural magicians', 'tricksters' who make their living by convincing North American and European corporate executives that they can equal the productivity of Japanese industry through the mechanical manipulation of organizational symbols, myths and customs. Such studies are not much concerned with theory of any sort, but seize upon fads in the realm of ideas. However, many 'honest grapplers' (Turner, 1986) in their approach to corporate culture have produced studies that also seem unduly linked to the interest of management and which promulgate the idea that 'culture' is the collective consciousness of the organization, 'owned' by management and available to management for manipulation. An attempt will be made to illustrate the effects of these weaknesses on the study of corporate culture, not by questioning the integrity of individual researchers, but through examining the theoretical basis on which the idea of corporate culture rests. The argument will explore three interrelated themes:

1 organizational theorists – particularly, though not exclusively, those belonging to the human relations and related schools – have not considered the multiplicity of theories of culture, but have borrowed the concept of culture from only one anthropological tradition: structural-functionalism;
2 although theories of organizational or corporate culture have their 'roots' in structural-functionalism, they have also 'mutated' in the process of application;
3 the equating of corporate culture with a 'natural' force for social integration within the organization – with a unitary organizational collective consciousness that can both be measured and manipulated – seems to flow from the structural-functional tradition from which the concept is borrowed.

Nearly twenty-five years ago, van den Berghe (1963) criticized structural-functional theory for its reliance on a biological metaphor, for its positivistic stance, for its insistence that social order is created and maintained through individuals internalizing dominant social norms and values, for its treatment of people holding alternative norms and values as being socially deviant, and for its assumption that the parts of a society exist in a natural state of equilibrium, functioning efficiently so as to maintain the effectiveness of the total social structure (also see Rex, 1961; Friedrichs, 1970; Gouldner, 1970, 1973). Although, sometimes, it is not realized that rather old arguments are being repeated, similar criticisms are being applied to studies of corporate culture. However, the purpose of this chapter is not to ground contemporary criticisms of corporate culture studies in past criticisms of structural-functionalism. Rather, the intention is to illustrate how studies of corporate culture, because of the structural-functional theoretical legacy, tend to ignore or gloss over inherent conflicts and important structural features of the organization, particularly the structure of power and conflict, structured inequality and the significance of the structure of 'class cultures' (see Turner, 1986). Later in the chapter, an attempt will be made to build the concept of structure and conflict back into a theory of corporate culture.

The structural-functional theoretical framework has had a profound influence on all aspects of the study of complex organizations (Silverman, 1970). Its influence on the concept of organizational culture is particularly notable, which is not surprising since 'structural-functional' theory has its roots in the development of British social anthropology in the 1920s, 1930s and 1940s (Kuper, 1973). While Talcott Parsons transported structural-functionalism across the Atlantic, the British social anthropologists – themselves influenced by the French sociologist Emile Durkheim – gave birth to the theory. Out of the many conceptualizations of culture available, social theorists have been prone to seize – sometimes somewhat uncritically – upon Durkheim's idea of the collective consciousness and upon Radcliffe-Brown's notion that 'cultural patterns are crystallized in social structure "as institutionalized and standardized modes of behaviour and thought whose normal forms are socially recognized in the explicit or implicit rules to which members of a society tend to conform"' (Keesing, 1974: 83). Several studies of organizational culture seem to assume that 'culture' is a unifying force within an organization, that there exists a universal homogeneous culture, and that the task for the researcher is to discover it. A few examples will help illustrate the point.

Kilmann (1982: 11) refers to culture as 'the collective will of members'; it is 'what the corporation *really wants* or what *really counts* in order to get ahead'. According the Schwartz and Davis (1981: 33) culture is 'a pattern of beliefs and expectations shared by the organization's members' that create 'norms that powerfully shape the behaviour of individuals and groups in the organization'. Kilmann et al. (1985a: 2) claim that their

edited book *Gaining Control of the Corporate Culture* represents the
'"state of the art" of corporate culture' and that the contributors are
'those who are the leading edge of this topic'. Chapter after chapter,
definitions of culture are provided that stress the internalization of norms,
social integration and stability, that link culture firmly with the interests
of management, and that treat culture as the collective will or consciousness of the organization. In the Preface, the editors define culture as the
'invisible force behind the tangibles and observables in any organization. . . . Culture is to the organization what personality is to the
individual' (1985a: ix). In the Introduction they state that 'culture can be
defined as the shared philosophies, ideologies, values, assumptions,
beliefs, expectations, attitudes, and norms that knit a community
together' (1985a: 5). In Chapter 2, Schein (1985a: 17) argues that
'"strong" cultures are somehow more likely to be associated with effectiveness than are "weak"cutlures, and that strong cultures can be
deliberately created'. In another chapter, Sapienza (1985: 66–7) states that
'one of the most important facets of organizational culture is the system
of *shared beliefs*'. Lorsch (1985: 84) takes culture to mean 'the beliefs top
managers in a company share about how they should manage themselves
and other employees'. Gordon (1985: 104) chooses to study culture
through an 'upper-level group because we believe that the corporate
values held by management are reflected in behaviour throughout an
organization'. Davis (1985: 138) states that 'corporate culture is the
pattern of shared beliefs and values that shapes the meaning of an institution for its members and provides them with the rules for behaviour'.
According to Martin (1985: 148) 'in many organizations, corporate
cultures are developed from the philosophies of top management and
maintained through the acceptance of these philosophies by the organization's members'. Sathe (1985: 255) sees culture as 'those beliefs and values
people consider to be their own; that is, those they have *internalized*'.
Allen (1985: 334) firmly links culture with the internalization of norms,
with:

> norms encompass[ing] all behaviour that is expected, accepted, or supported by
> the group, whether that behaviour is stated or unstated. The norm is the sanc-
> tioned behaviour, and people are rewarded and encouraged when they follow
> the norms, and chastised, confronted, and ostracized when they violate them.

Those who deviate from the dominant norms are either to be resocialized
or excluded from the organization. According to Kilmann et al. culture
is a 'controllable variable', and 'managing corporate cultures is now
possible' (1985b: 423, 431), and for Kilmann (1985: 351), 'to understand
the essence or soul of the organization requires that we travel below the
charts, rulebooks, machines, and buildings into the underground world of
corporate cultures'.

Gaining Control of the Corporate Culture contains interesting and
valuable information on aspects of the operation of various corporations,

but except for one or two chapters, the theories of culture used by the contributors rest on the premise that the norms, values and beliefs of organizational members are factors that create consensus, predict behaviour and create unity. This leads to conclusions that are little more than statements about managements' responsibility to reward positive behaviour and attitudes, to foster the self-esteem and self-confidence of organizations' members, to encourage allegiance to organizational goals and missions, to inform members of the need for change when it arises, and to create a feeling of *esprit de corps* within the organization. If the book represents the 'state of the art' of corporate culture studies, then it is a state of the art based on a very narrow conceptualization of the idea of culture. The degree to which norms, for example, are internalized and create integrated and stable structures, is, first of all, an empirical question, not something to be assumed through theory. Culture, if it is to have any meaning, needs to be related to the total organization, not regarded as phenomena solely vested in the hands of management. The idea that culture is the collective will of the organization – its personality, an invisible force or the organization's soul – is a metaphysical explanation of behaviour and events that are impossible to observe. Any theory that assumes that culture is the internalization of dominant norms and values must also assume that all members must hold to the dominant value system or else be 'outside culture'. Of course, such a stance flies in the face of reality, particularly when we consider organizations where management tends to belong to one social class and workers to another. In such organizations, values, norms and social meanings are structured by 'class cultures' and are a constant potential source for dispute, with strikes only one example where such disputes become overt conflicts. For example, it would be difficult to explain the 1984 strike of the British coal miners either in terms of the collective will of the corporation or in terms of the internalization of dominant norms and values. As will be discussed later, norms and values have as much potential for creating conflict within organizations as they do for creating social cohesion.

It should be noted that just because organizational theorists may have borrowed the concept of culture from a certain social anthropological tradition, it does not necessarily mean that organizational theorists use the concept of culture in exactly the same way as would social anthropologists. For example, while Radcliffe-Brown and other social anthropologists have treated culture as an integral feature of the structure and function of all societies – relating specific cultures to particular social outcomes – some organizational theorists have been inclined to treat culture as either exotic or 'irrational' behaviour (Kanter, 1977). More importantly, several studies of organizational culture have moved the concept of culture beyond that of a unifying and regulatory mechanism towards it being a form of social control created and manipulated by management. Baker (1980), for example, writes about 'managing organizational culture' and Allen and Kraft (1982) attempt to illustrate 'how to create the corporate culture you want and need'. Schein (1985b: 2) maintains that 'organizational cultures are created by leaders, and one of the most decisive functions of leadership may well be the creation, the management, and – if and when that may become necessary – the destruction of culture'. According to Schein (1985b: 2) 'we must recognize the centrality of this culture management function in the leadership concept'.

Most anthropologists would find the idea that leaders create culture preposterous: leaders do not create culture, it emerges from the collective social interaction of groups and communities. It is unlikely that social anthropologists would postulate that tribal leaders create culture; the chief is as much a part of a local culture as are his tribal or clan compatriots. The link between culture, management and control is not solely due to structural-functional theory *per se*. It is also due to the way in which selective aspects of the concept of culture have been borrowed from the structural-functional tradition, coupled with the propensity (either latent or manifest) of this theoretical paradigm to support the notion that culture can be used by leaders to control others in the achievement of organizational goals.

It has often been noted that one of the crucial weaknesses of structural-functional theory is its reliance on a biological metaphor (see, in particular, Nisbet, 1969). In accordance with the metaphor, the theory assumes that an organization can be understood as either a huge organism or a 'superindividual'; hence, 'culture' is transferred from the individual actors who create and reproduce it to the organization as a whole. Since it is the organic organization that has 'culture', culture, including members' norms, values and beliefs, is necessarily a mechanism that creates organizational unity: the parts of a healthy organism do not work against themselves.

There are numerous examples, as Allaire and Firsirotu (1984: 194) note, where the organization is endowed with biomorphic and/or anthropomorphic characteristics: it is healthy or unhealthy, goes through a life cycle, and has personality, needs and character (see Rice, 1963; Harrison, 1972; Argyris and Schon, 1978; Aldrich, 1979; Kimberly and Miles, 1980). Through the use of the anthropomorphic analogy in particular, the organization is transformed into a 'superindividual', and culture becomes the product of the collective consciousness of the organization's members. As mentioned above, the basic criticism of this approach to organizational culture is that it leads to metaphysical explanations for something that is impossible to observe.

The use of organic simile and the idea that culture can be regarded as the collective consciousness of the group are mostly derived from the theories of Durkheim. Although these theories remain in vogue, it is important to note past criticisms:

The metaphysical concepts of a group mind, collective sensorium or consciousness are due to an apparent antinomy of sociological reality: the psychological nature of human culture on the one hand and on the other the fact that culture transcends the individual. The fallacious solution of this antinomy is the theory that human minds combine or integrate and form a superindividual and yet essentially spiritual being. . . . [S]uch concepts as consciousness of kind or the inevitability of collective imitation, account for the psychological yet superindividual nature of social reality by introducing some theoretical metaphysical short cut. (Malinowski, 1930: 623)

In incorporating the idea of collective consciousness into that of organizational culture many theorists have failed also to incorporate the historical criticisms attached to the original notion.

Individuals create and reproduce culture, but obviously they do not do so in a vacuum. The resources the individual has to draw upon in creating culture are not manufactured by the individual. Language is the classic example: no one person creates language, but we all use language creatively (Giddens, 1982). This point will be examined in more detail below.

The human relations school of 'scientific' management deserves special mention for it was the first body of theorists to explore informal social relations in organizations and to take the concept of organizational culture seriously (see Perrow, 1979 for a review of the history of the human relations school and see Mayo, 1933; Gardner, 1945; Warner and Low, 1947; Richardson and Walker, 1948), but the human relations theorists have approached organizational culture mainly from a behaviourist-oriented psychological framework. The language used by human relations theorists is based on a medical/biological metaphor: they speak of healthy and unhealthy organizational culture or climate and talk about organizational hygiene. Human relations theorists regard culture as something which an organization has and which can be manipulated to serve the ends of management. In summarizing past research efforts of the human relations school, Gregory (1983: 361) argues that the school's 'promanagement position resulted in biased research that studied the "irrational" behaviour of lower ranking personnel and supported unquestioningly the "rational manager" model'. Moreover:

The current corporate culture studies are not substantially different from earlier Human Relations research, in that the goal is still to illustrate the impact of 'irrational' human factors on 'rational' corporate objectives. 'Rational' corporate objectives correspond to management's goals for the organization. Researchers in both areas sought to provide managers with tools to assess and control the organizational culture of their subordinates. (Gregory, 1983: 361)

Despite such criticisms, practitioners, as well as academic researchers, have been intent upon discovering what creates 'healthy' and 'unhealthy' organizational culture. Managers of large corporations have come to think that economic success is somehow linked with the type of organizational culture or climate that they create. The idea of corporate culture has been pursued in such popular forums as *Business Week* and

Fortune Magazine. Ouchi's (1981) work, and the development of 'Theory Z' linking successful and unsuccessful organizational performance to the type of culture created by American and Japanese companies, has gained great popularity (also see Pascale and Athos, 1982). Corporate managers seem to believe that a unifying organizational culture can be created and manipulated, and are prepared to pay good money to back their beliefs: 'the marketing of "corporate culture" is largely underway' (Smircich, 1983: 346).

Those intent upon creating a 'healthy' and 'successful' corporate climate are often blind to 'what is' by their pursuit of 'what should be' (Gregory, 1983; Smircich, 1983; Allaire and Firsirotu, 1984). Corporate success, particularly economic success, is dependent far more upon external environmental influences and the vagaries of the market-place than on internal interpersonal dynamics. More importantly, the assumption that a corporate culture can be created so as to unite members for the effective and efficient attainment of corporate goals flies in the face of almost everyone's experience of organizational life. Organizations are often arenas for dispute and conflict, and one of the main items under dispute is often values. Organizations are not one homogeneous culture, but are 'multi-cultural', and culture can be a source of conflict (Gregory, 1983). Cultural conflict is most obvious in professional organizations – large teaching hospitals, research laboratories, tertiary education institutions. C.P. Snow's thesis of two cultures manifests itself month after month in every meeting of a university's academic board. Several studies have shown that academics may tend to give greater allegiance to their profession than to their college or university, which may produce conflict between the interest of the individual academic and the interests of those who manage the institution (see, in particular, Gouldner, 1958, but see also Meltzer, 1956; Merton, 1957; Box and Cotgrove, 1966; Hind, 1971). Unity within organizational sub-cultures (academic departments, for example) can be a source of conflict as the various sub-cultures compete for both scarce resources and prestige.

Nonetheless, human relations and related fields of study, and their preoccupation with the idea of a healthy or successful corporate culture, need to be taken seriously for two reasons. First, there are successful and not so successful organizations, and there is something about the successful organization that goes beyond explanations based on superior technology, efficient management and an advantageous position in the market-place. There is a certain 'feel' about the successful school, university or large corporation, and the phenomenon, whatever it is and whatever 'success' may mean, deserves investigation.

Second, while organizations may be regarded as forums for conflict and dispute, they also wield power in modern society through what Galbraith (1983) terms their ability to *condition* their own members and the public at large. Organizations have access to the three primary instruments of power: condign power (physical), compensatory power (economic) and conditioned power (belief). According to Galbraith, conditioned power is the most important in modern industrial society, and organization is the locus of conditioned power. It is through 'persuasion, education, or the social commitment to what seems natural, proper or right' that the corporation, educational institution, church and the state 'cause the individual to submit to the will of another or of others' (Galbraith, 1983: 23). Organizations may also enforce their will through the use of physical or economic power. In the past the church was particularly prone to exercise its power through such means, but conditioned power is central 'to the functioning of the modern economy and polity, and in capitalist and socialist countries alike' (Galbraith, 1983: 23). Thus, it is imperative that we understand the beliefs, symbols, myths, ideologies and folklores – the 'culture' – of the modern organization as a form of social control. It is not a form of social control created and manipulated by management, but a process in which management, workers and the community at large participate alike.

Furthermore, Galbraith (1983) argues that there is a symmetric relationship between how power is exercised and how it is challenged: condign power is met with violence, compensatory power is met with the regulation of the market-place, and conditioned power is met with countervailing beliefs and ideologies. Consumer and environmental action groups represent a good example of a symmetric challenge to the conditioned power of modern corporations. In this respect, organizational culture is not a force for social integration, but a phenomenon likely to breed 'counter-cultures'.

An adequate theory of culture needs to be divorced from the direct interests of management and the naive assumption that a 'successful corporate culture' is either 'naturally good and stabilizing' or can be 'consciously manipulated'. Just because group interaction within an organization is based on norms and symbols, it does not necessarily follow that consensus and cohesion, based on shared and internalized value systems, are the result. Hopefully, the structural-functional theoretical assumptions on which the biomorphic, cohesive, integrative and stabilizing characteristics of organizational studies of corporate culture rest have been adequately demonstrated and critiqued, and the need for a theory of culture that more adequately takes account of the contextual richness of social life within the organization as a whole has been illustrated. Before suggesting alternative ways of viewing corporate culture, a few additional words need to be said about the manipulation of culture.

While it is maintained that culture *as a whole* cannot be consciously manipulated by management or any other group, culture is not necessarily static: cultures do change within organizations, and management does have more direct control than other organizational members over certain aspects of the corporate cultures, such as control over logos and officially stated missions and ethos. In this regard, some scholars have expressed concern that certain organizations can foster an allegiance to a corporate ethos that borders on religious fervour, while the ethos itself is of questionable social value (Turner, 1986). The way in which management attempts to intervene in the culture of an organization should be a research priority, particularly in relation to the potential 'conditioned power' of organization. However, empirically assessing the power and ability of management to intervene in the culture of an organization and assuming through theory that management creates, changes and imposes 'culture' on a passive and uncritical membership – that management creates a cultural milieu in which rank-and-file staff are immersed and have no choice but to internalize its embedded norms and values – are quite separate considerations.

If culture emerges from the social interaction of all organizational members (as is argued here), then the way in which management may attempt to manipulate organizational symbols, myths, customs, and so on must be interpreted in relation to the *total* organizational culture of which management itself is only one part. Hitler did not create Nazi Germany by himself. It may be that some organizations are more prone to accept executive control, including control over organizational symbols and meanings, than are other organizations, but again, this is, first of all, an empirical question, not something that can be assumed through theory. Also, power, as Weber maintained, is exercised not merely through its acceptance by others, but rests on having the resources – which flow, at least in part, from one's position in the social structure – to impose one's will on others despite opposition.

While, in practice, questions of power, conflict and culture in the modern organization cannot be divorced, the symbiotic relationship between the phenomena may be more adequately understood if a conceptual distinction is drawn between culture and social structure. We will now look at what consequences such a distinction may have for a theory of organizational or corporate culture.

Towards a theory of culture

While the idea of organizational culture has been approached in a variety of ways, the various theories, basically fall into two camps or schools (Smircich, 1983). First, as was argued above, there are those who treat organizational culture as a variable: it is something that an organization has (see Cummings and Schmidt, 1972; Schwartz and Davis, 1981; Deal and Kennedy, 1982; Peters and Waterman, 1982). Second, there is the view that 'culture is something an organization is' (Smircich, 1983: 347; and see Harris and Cronen, 1979; Weick, 1979; Morgan, 1980; Wacker, 1981). The second approach is much more closely aligned to the way in which anthropologists treat culture. Rather than regarding culture as something imported into an organization from the broader society, or as something created by management, these theorists believe that culture is the product of negotiated and shared symbols and meanings; it emerges from social interaction. In this approach to culture, the researcher is not analysing some 'irrational' or exotic aspect of organizational life. The interpretation of organizational culture must be deeply embedded in the contextual richness of the total social life of organizational members. Culture cannot be treated as incidental to, or outside of, the 'true purpose' of the organization (Gregory, 1983).

Treating culture as emerging from social interaction – treating it as something that the organization 'is', rather than treating it as a variable that can be manipulated by management – has obvious research implications. It also has political implications. If culture is regarded as embedded in social interaction, that is as something that is socially produced and reproduced over time, influencing people's behaviour in relation to the use of language, technology, rules and laws, and knowledge and ideas (including ideas about legitimate authority and leadership), then it cannot be discovered or mechanically manipulated; it can only be described and interpreted. The researcher adopting the social emergent view of culture cannot suggest how it can be created or destroyed; the researcher can only attempt to record and examine how culture may be altered in the process of social reproduction. People do not just passively absorb meanings and symbols; they produce and reproduce culture, and in the process of reproducing it, they may transform it. The social emergent approach to culture also moves the researcher away from the political and ideological interests of management, towards those of the organizational community as a whole.

While it seems necessary to consider culture as something that an organization 'is', rather than something that it 'has' this still begs the question of how (or if) culture is to be demarcated from other social aspects of the organization. The basic question is whether to adopt an inclusive use of the term 'culture' in the tradition of Tylor (1958), or to distinguish culture from social structure?

The debate between those theorists who view culture as meshed into the social system and those who view it as a conceptually distinct ideational system is not confined to organizational studies. It is a debate which has raged in social anthropology over several decades (Singer, 1968: 528).

Social theory which adopts an inclusive view of culture 'tacitly assumes that the social and structural components are (must be) fully integrated, synchronized and consonant with the ideational, symbolic dimensions of the organization' (Allaire and Firsirotu, 1984: 199). One of the problems with this approach to culture is that it does not take account of shifts in the social structure which may occur in the absence of corresponding shifts in members' norms, values and ideologies. Another problem with the inclusive view of culture is that it denies the possibility of conflict between the ideas, ideologies and values of organizational members and the organization's structure (formal and informal). There is evidence to

suggest not only that such conflict may exist, but also that it can be an
essential feature of an organization. For example, in a case study of an
Australian College of Advanced Education, it was concluded that:

> When structures . . . are thought to be in conflict with basic academic norms
> . . . disputes of an ideological nature will follow. This form of conflict can
> rapidly become intractable, with participants basing their actions upon oppos-
> ing sets of values and finding it extremely difficult to communicate with each
> other. Structural changes within [the College] proceeded in the absence of due
> consideration for the normative nature of the enterprise. . . . Severe and
> protracted conflict was the result. (Meek, 1984: 130–1)

On a broader scale, it also seems necessary to draw a distinction between
culture and structure in order to address the question of how the structure
of 'class cultures' in the wider society may cut across individual organizations (see Turner, 1986).

For the purposes of analysis and interpretation, it seems necessary to
distinguish between culture and social structure, but in so doing, two
factors must be kept firmly in mind. First, culture and structure are two
sides of the same coin: they are parallel and complementary and constantly interacting with one another:

> One of the more useful ways – but far from the only one – of distinguishing
> between culture and social system is to see the former as an ordered system of
> meaning and of symbols, in terms of which social interaction takes place; and
> to see the latter as the pattern of social interaction itself. (Geertz, 1973: 144)

Second, both culture and structure are abstractions, not tangible entities:

> The difference between the two concepts is not that one is an abstraction and
> the other a concrete, observable unit of behaviour, for both are abstractions
> of regularities from observations of actual behaviour, whether these
> regularities are implicit and unconscious or explicit and verbalized. (Singer,
> 1968: 533)

The task for the researcher in the field is not to observe culture or structure, but to observe the concrete behaviour of individual actors. Culture
and social structure are not concrete entities; rather they are abstract
concepts that are to be used to interpret behaviour. Geertz' (1973:5)
definition of culture clearly focuses the attention of the researcher on
concrete behaviour:

> Believing, with Max Weber, that man is an animal suspended in webs of
> significance he himself has spun, I take culture to be those webs, and the
> analysis of it to be therefore not an experimental science in search of law but
> an interpretive one in search of meaning.

The task of the social scientist is to observe and describe the actions of
human beings and their characterizations of social reality: social science
is the researcher's constructions of the layman's constructions of what he
and his compatriots are up to (Geertz, 1973: 9). While culture is the webs

of significance spun by man, structure is also the medium and the product of social interaction:

> [Structures] are both the medium and the outcome of interaction. They are the medium, because structures provide the rules and resources individuals must draw on to interact meaningfully. They are its outcome, because rules and resources exist only through being applied and acknowledged in interaction – they have no reality independent of the social practices they constitute. (Riley, 1983: 415)

So far it has been argued that while there is a symbiotic relationship between culture and social structure, in analysis the researcher needs to draw a distinction between the two concepts. However, this still leaves the problem of how to approach 'culture' in empirical research. 'Culture', as a holistic concept, is far too broad to be the main thrust of any research agenda; the concept needs to be dissected into manageable proportions.

The dissection of culture

Most anthropological studies contain one or more of the following 'cultural derivatives': symbol (including language, architecture and artifacts), myth, ideational systems (including ideology), and ritual. While anthropologists and sociologists continue to debate the 'proper' uses and meanings of these concepts, most studies approach them in terms of what motivates individuals and groups to action (Silverman, 1970). There is no space here to discuss each concept in detail. Rather, a brief definition of each will be provided – keeping in mind the preceding argument that culture is neither necessarily an adaptive regulatory mechanism, nor does it necessarily unite individuals and groups into social structures – and some hints on how they may be used in analysis will be offered.

Symbol is the most inclusive of the various cultural derivatives, 'not only because language, ritual, and myth are forms of symbolism but because symbolic analysis is a form of reference, a style of analysis in its own right' (Pettigrew, 1979: 575). Symbols are shared codes of meaning and include a variety of things – words, stories, icons, organizational logos or national flags – that provide 'meanings, evoke emotions, and impel men [and women] to action' (Cohen, 1974: 23). Language is a representation, a symbol, of the real thing. Organizations may be distinguished by the language their members use: academics use jargon to mystify knowledge and computer programmers use a language which mystifies everyone but themselves. The guard tower is a symbol of both the concentration camp and the modern prison, impelling individuals to a form of negative action. Religious icons may, on the one hand, unite the faithful, and on the other, lead them to scourge the infidel.

Organization has itself been defined as being nothing more or less than patterns of symbolic discourse. Within the phenomenology, symbolic interactionism and ethnomethodology schools:

organizations become *figments of participants' interpretation of their organizational experience*; they have no external reality but are merely social creations and construction *emerging* from actors making sense out of ongoing streams of actions and interactions. In what Burrell and Morgan (1979: 260) call their *interpretive paradigm*, 'organizations simply do not exist'. (Allaire and Firsirotu, 1984: 208)

This approach to organizational analysis is in danger of collapsing the social organizational and cultural components of social life into one unitary concept. As argued above, there is a need to maintain a conceptual distinction between culture and social structure, particularly for the purposes of investigating change and conflict. When the socio-structural pattern of human organization is collapsed into being solely a pattern of symbolic discourse, 'the dynamic elements in social change which arise from the failure of cultural patterns to be perfectly congruent with forms of social organization are largely incapable of formation' (Geertz, 1957: 992).

An organization is, of course, a structured association of individuals, and it is individuals who create meanings and symbols. Organization cannot be reduced to the individual, for to do so misinterprets the significance, and the power, of organization. MacIntyre puts the case in relation to the military organization thus:

You cannot characterise an army by referring to the soldiers who belong to it. For to do that you have to identify them as soldiers; and to do that is already to bring in the concept of an army. For a soldier just is an individual who belongs to an army. Thus we see that the characterisation of individuals and of classes [or organizations] has to go together. Essentially these are not two separate tasks. (quoted in Thompson, 1978: 30)

Certainly, symbols are worthy of the researcher's attention. If the symbolic mode of interpretation is to consider the dynamics of change and conflict, then it seems that symbols need to be analysed in terms of a 'dialogue' between actors' sets of meanings and other social organizational aspects of the institution.

Closely related to the idea of culture as patterns of symbolic discourse is the notion of culture as ideational or cognitive systems, that is cultures seen as systems of knowledge (Keesing, 1974). One of the main proponents of this stance in anthropology is Goodenough:

A society's culture consists of whatever it is one has to know or believe in order to operate in a manner acceptable to its members. Culture is not a material phenomenon; it does not consist of things, people, behavior, or emotions. It is rather an organization of these things. It is the form of things that people have in mind, their models for perceiving, relating, and otherwise interpreting them. (quoted in Keesing, 1974: 77)

Obviously, men and women must share some knowledge in common in order to act in concert: organized work would be impossible if people did not share some meanings, knowledge systems and symbols. 'Most occupations . . . operate on the premise that the people who work in them know certain procedures and certain ways of thinking about and responding to typical situations and problems' (Becker, 1982: 522). However, like symbolic interactionism, the ideational or cognitive theory of organizational culture fails when it is elevated to a universal theory that attempts to explain all social organizational phenomena. 'Analyses of cultures as cognitive systems have not progressed very far beyond a mapping of limited and neatly bonded semantic domains' (Keesing, 1974: 78). Organizational culture is too rich and diverse to be amenable to a comprehensive interpretation through ideational codes, however sophisticated their elaboration.

However, the investigation of cognitive systems can be a powerful analytical tool so long as the interpretation of ideas and knowledge is related to, but kept separate from, social structural issues. It is here that the concept of ideology may play an important role. Ideology is not only 'a set of beliefs about the social world and how it operates', but also contains ethical statements 'about the rightness of certain social arrangements' (Wilson, 1973: 91). An ideology may be congruent with the social structure, or it may be expressly divergent from the pattern of social interaction within the organization. Also, an organization may contain a number of ideologies, with ideological groupings in competition with one another over such issues as power and legitimate authority. These are, of course, empirical questions that can be answered only through research.

Contrary to the popular lay definition, myth is not regarded by anthropologists as an erroneous story. Rather,

> a myth is a narrative of events; the narrative has a sacred quality; the sacred communication is made in symbolic form; at least some of the events and objects which occur in the myth neither occur nor exist in the world other than that of myth itself; and the narrative refers in dramatic form to origins or transformations. (Cohen, 1969: 337)

Organizational myths or stories certainly do not constitute all that is 'cultural' in an organization, but the interpretation of organization members' myths and folklores is one angle of attack on the problem of organizational culture that has proved to be fruitful. Creation myths are usually thought of as something belonging to traditional societies, but members of modern organizations also have their stories about how the organization came into being and how it developed over time. Clark terms such folk stories or myths 'organizational sagas':

> Saga . . . has come to mean a narrative of heroic exploits, of a unique development that has deeply stirred the emotions of participants and descendants. Thus, a saga is not simply a story but a story that at some time has had a particular base of believers. (Clark, 1972: 178–9)

The notion of an organizational saga is a useful theoretic tool for the study of certain aspects of symbolic behaviour. As a concept it gives importance to publicly expressed stories about group uniqueness; it is an explanation of what makes an organization unique and distinctive in the eyes of its members. In theory, these stories or 'folk histories' may function as symbolic justifications for members' actions in concrete situations.

Martin et al. (1983: 439), while recognizing the emphasis on uniqueness in organizational stories and sagas, maintain that there are also 'similarities in content and structure' in all such stories: 'a culture's claim to uniqueness is expressed through cultural manifestations that are not in fact unique. This is the uniqueness paradox.' Anthropologists, such as Malinowski, Lévi-Strauss, and others, have also looked at the creation myths of different traditional societies in order to discover similarities in content and structure.

It also needs to be recognized that myths, folklores and sagas may be a source of conflict, particularly in the context of rapid social change. There is evidence to suggest that at least one organization's saga, while appropriate to the development of the institution during a particular historical period, became quite inappropriate and caused disunity, following dramatic changes in the institution's external political environment (Meek, 1982). In another study (Meek, 1984), it was argued that the organization had developed two sets of shared beliefs and ideologies that were in competition with one another: a saga and a counter-saga.

All organizations have forms of ritualized behaviour. A university, for example, would not be a university without the ritual and symbols that surround such events as graduation ceremonies and inaugural lectures. The ritual is as old as the idea of the university itself. At graduation, academics and graduands clothe themselves in medieval garb and speak in foreign tongues – Latin. The procession preceding an inaugural lecture is led by the bearer of arms carrying a mace. Except for historians, most members of the university organization have long forgotten the origin and function of such cultural artifacts as the academic gown and mace, but they all know that these artifacts symbolize the university, and they share a feeling of belonging to an academic community whenever the artifacts are displayed and the ritual is performed.

According to Benedict (1934: 396), ritual simply is the 'prescribed formal behaviour for occasions not given over to technological routine'. This definition is attractive in its simplicity, although it leaves the question of how rituals are to be interpreted unanswered. Anthropologists (Beattie, 1966) and organizational theorists (Pettigrew, 1979) often maintain that what is important is what rituals 'say' not what they 'do'. In this sense, Harrison, (1951) maintained that 'ritual is a dramatization of myth'. However, Leach (1968: 524) argues that 'ritual may "do things" as well as "say things". The most obvious examples are healing rituals which form a vast class and have a world-wide distribution.' Ritualized physical exercise in Japanese industries is both an expression of corporate allegiance and a mechanism for maintaining the health of the workforce.

It is often assumed that rituals legitimize established authority, and 'provide a shared experience of belonging and express and reinforce what is valued' (Pettigrew, 1979: 576). However, as Gluckman (1962) has shown, 'rituals of rebellion' may have the opposite function: they allow people to act out hostilities that may not be expressed in normal everyday social relations.

The interpretation of ritual is just as complicated as any other aspect of cultural behaviour. However, research into the ritualization of behaviour should not assume from the outset that ritual expresses and sanctifies the established social order. It may do this, but ritual may also be a mechanism for maintaining one group in power despite the will of others, or it may be a dramatized expression of rebellion of one group against others. Once again, these are empirical questions, not something that can be assumed through theory.

Summary

There has been a tendency for some researchers to treat organizational culture as a 'variable' that can be controlled and manipulated like any other organizational variable. Culture *as a whole* cannot be manipulated, turned on and off, although it needs to be recognized that some are in a better position than others to attempt to intentionally influence aspects of it. The tendency to assume otherwise results, at least in part, from the selective way in which the concept of culture has been borrowed from anthropology and sociology. The basis of the argument presented in this chapter is that culture should be regarded as something that an organization 'is', not as something that an organization 'has': it is not an independent variable, nor can it be created, discovered or destroyed by the whims of management. Nonetheless, it seems necessary, for the purposes of the interpretation of actors' behaviour, that a conceptual distinction be made between 'culture' and 'social structure'. It must be kept in mind, though, that both culture and structure are abstractions, and have use only in relation to the interpretation of observed concrete behaviour. This chapter, however, does not advance any one elaborate or steadfast theoretical model of cultural interpretation; for 'it is going to take more than one kind of theoretical model to do justice to the variety, complexity, and richness of human culture' (Singer, 1968: 541).

Note

An earlier version of this chapter was presented at the Sociological Association of Australia and New Zealand Conference at the University of New England, July 1986.

References

Aldrich, Howard E. (1979) *Organizations and environments*. Englewood Cliffs, NJ: Prentice-Hall.

Allaire, Yvan, and Firsirotu, Mihaela E. (1984) 'Theories of organizational culture'. *Organizational Studies*, 5/3: 193–226.

Allen, F.R., and Kraft, C. (1982) *The organizational unconscious: how to create the corporate culture you want and need*. Englewood Cliffs, NJ: Prentice-Hall.

Allen, Robert F. (1985) 'Four phases for bringing about cultural change', in *Gaining control of the corporate culture*, ed. Ralph H. Kilmann, Mary J. Saxton and Roy Serpa, pp. 332–50. San Francisco: Jossey-Bass.

Argyris, Chris, and Schon, Donald A. (1978) *Organizational learning: a theory of action perspective*. Reading, MA: Addison-Wesley.

Baker, E.L. (1980) 'Managing organizational culture', *Management Review*, July: 8–13.

Beattie, John (1966) 'Ritual and social change', *Man*, 1: 60–74.

Becker, Howard S. (1982) 'Culture: a sociological view', *Yale Review*, 71: 513–27.

Benedict, Ruth (1934) 'Ritual', *International Encyclopaedia of the Social Sciences*, 13: 396–7.

Box, Steven, and Cotgrove Stephen (1966) 'Scientific identity, occupational selection and role strain', *British Journal of Sociology*, 7: 20–8.

Burrell, Gibson, and Morgan, Gareth (1979) *Sociological paradigms and organizational analysis*. London: Heinemann.

Cohen, Abner (1974) *Two dimensional man: an essay on the anthropology of power and symbolism in complex society*. London: Routledge & Kegan Paul.

Cohen, Percy S. (1969) 'Theories of myth', *Man*, 4: 337–53.

Cummings, L.L., and Schmidt, Stuart M. (1972) 'Managerial attitudes of Greeks; the roles of culture and industrialization', *Administrative Science Quarterly*, 17: 265–72.

Davis, Stanley M. (1985) 'Culture is not just an internal affair', in *Gaining control of the corporate culture*, ed. Ralph H. Kilmann, Mary J. Saxton and Roy Serpa, pp. 137–47. San Francisco: Jossey-Bass.

Deal, Terence E., and Kennedy, Allan A. (1982) *Corporate cultures: the rites and rituals of corporate life*. Reading, MA: Addison-Wesley.

Friedrichs, R.W. (1970) *A sociology of sociology*. New York: Free Press.

Galbraith, John Kenneth (1983) *The anatomy of power*. London: Corgi Books.

Gardner, B. (1945) *Human relations in industry*. Chicago: Irwin.

Geertz, Clifford (1957) 'Ritual and social change: a Javanese example', *American Anthropologist*, 59: 991–1012.

Geertz, Clifford (1973) *The interpretation of culture*. London: Hutchinson.

Giddens, Anthony (1982) *Sociology: a brief but critical introduction*. London: Macmillan.

Gluckman, Max (1962) 'Les rites de passage', in *Essays on the ritual of social relations*, ed. Max Gluckman, pp. 1–52. Manchester: Manchester University Press.

Gordon, George G. (1985) 'The relationship of corporate culture to industry sector and corporate performance', in *Gaining control of the corporate culture*, ed. Ralph H. Kilmann, Mary J. Saxton and Roy Serpa, pp. 103–25. San Francisco: Jossey-Bass.

Gouldner, A. (1958) 'Cosmopolitans and locals: towards an analysis of latent social roles', *Administrative Science Quarterly*, 2: 281–306 and 444–67.

Gouldner, A. (1970) *The coming crisis in western sociology*. London: Heinemann.

Gouldner, A. (1973) *For sociology*. London: Allen Lane.

Gregory, Kathleen L. (1983) 'Native view paradigms; multiple cultures and culture conflicts in organizations', *Administrative Science Quarterly*, 28: 359–77.

Harris, Linda, and Cronen, Vernon (1979) 'A rules-based model for the analysis and evaluation of organizational communication', *Communication Quarterly*, winter: 12–18.

Harrison, Jane E. (1951) *Ancient art and ritual*. New York: Oxford University Press. First published 1913.

Harrison, Roger (1972) 'Understanding your organization's character', *Harvard Business Review*, 5/3: 119–28.
Hind, Robert R. (1971) 'Analysis of a faculty: professionalism, evaluation, and the authority structure', in *Academic governance*, ed. J. Victor Baldridge, pp. 264–92. Berkeley: McCutchan.
Kanter, R.M. (1977) *Men and women of the corporation*. New York: Basic Books.
Keesing, Roger M. (1974) 'Theories of culture', *Annual Review of Anthropology*, 3: 73–97.
Kilmann, Ralph H. (1982) 'Getting control of the corporate culture', *Managing*, 3: 11–17.
Kilmann, Ralph, H. (1985) 'Five steps for closing culture-gaps', in *Gaining control of the corporate culture*, ed. Ralph H. Kilmann, Mary J. Saxton and Roy Serpa, pp. 351–69. San Francisco: Jossey-Bass.
Kilmann, Ralph H., Saxton, Mary J., and Serpa, Roy (eds) (1985a) *Gaining control of the corporate culture*. San Francisco: Jossey-Bass.
Kilmann, Ralph H., Saxton, Mary J., and Serpa, Roy (1985b) 'Conclusion: why culture is not just a fad', in *Gaining control of the corporate culture*, ed. Ralph H. Kilmann, Mary J. Saxton and Roy Serpa, pp. 421–33. San Francisco: Jossey-Bass.
Kimberly, J.R., and Miles, R.M. (1980) *The organizational life-cycle*. San Francisco: Jossey-Bass.
Kuper, Adam (1973) *Anthropologists and anthropology, the British school 1922–72*. London: Penguin.
Leach, Edmund R. (1968) 'Ritual', *International Encyclopaedia of the Social Sciences*, 13: 520–6.
Lorsch, Jay W. (1985) 'Strategic myopia: culture as an invisible barrier to change', in *Gaining control of the corporate culture*, ed. Ralph H. Kilmann, Mary J. Saxton and Roy Serpa, pp. 84–102. San Francisco: Jossey-Bass.
Martin, Harry J. (1985) 'Managing specialized corporate cultures', in *Gaining control of the corporate culture*, ed. Ralph H. Kilmann, Mary J. Saxton and Roy Serpa, pp. 148–62. San Francisco: Jossey-Bass.
Martin, Joanne, Fieldman, Martha S., Hatch, Mary Jo, and Sitkin, Sim B. (1983) 'The uniqueness paradox in organizational stories', *Administrative Science Quarterly*, 28: 438–53.
Mayo, Elton (1933) *The human problems of an industrial civilization*. New York: Macmillan.
Meek, V. Lynn (1982) *The university of Papua New Guinea: a case study in the sociology of higher education*. St Lucia: University of Queensland Press.
Meek, V. Lynn (1984) *Brown coal or Plato?* Hawthorn: Australian Council for Educational Research.
Meltzer, L. (1956) 'Scientific productivity in organizational settings', *Journal of Social Issues*, 12(2): 32–40.
Merton, R.K. (1957) 'The role-set: problems in sociological theory', *British Journal of Sociology*, 8(2): 106–20.
Morgan, Gareth (1980) 'Paradigms, metaphors and puzzle solving in organizational theory', *Administrative Science Quarterly*, 25: 605–22.
Nisbet, R.A. (1969) *Social change and history*. New York: Oxford University Press.
Ott, K.K. (1984) 'Two problems that threaten organizational culture research . . .', paper presented at the first international conference on 'Organizational Symbolism and Corporate Culture', Lund, Sweden, 26–30 June.
Ouchi, W. (1981) *Theory Z*. Reading, Mass.: Addison-Wesley.
Pascale, Richard T., and Athos, A.G. (1981) *The art of Japanese management*. New York: Simon & Schuster.
Perrow, C. (1979) *Complex organizations: a critical essay*, 2nd edn. Glenview, Ill.: Scott-Foresman.
Peters, Thomas, J., and Waterman, Robert H. (1982) *In search of excellence*. New York: Harper & Row.
Pettigrew, Andrew M. (1979) 'On studying organizational cultures', *Administrative Science Quarterly*, 24: 570–81.

Rex, J. (1961) *Key problems in sociological theory*. London: Routledge & Kegan Paul.

Rice, A.K. (1963) *The enterprise and its environment: a system theory of management organization*. London: Tavistock.

Richardson, Friedrich, and Walker, C. (1948) *Human relations in an expanding company*. New Haven, CT: Yale University Press.

Riley, Patricia (1983) 'A structurationist account of political culture', *Administrative Science Quarterly*, 28: 414–37.

Sapienza, Alice M. (1985) 'Believing is seeing: how culture influences the decisions top managers make', in *Gaining control of the corporate culture*, ed. Ralph H. Kilmann, Mary J. Saxton and Roy Serpa, pp. 66–83. San Francisco: Jossey-Bass.

Sathe, Vijay (1985) 'How to decipher and change corporate culture', in *Gaining control of the corporate culture*, ed. Ralph H. Kilmann, Mary J. Saxton and Roy Serpa, pp. 230–61. San Francisco: Jossey-Bass.

Schein, Edgar H. (1985a) 'How culture forms, develops, and changes', in *Gaining control of the corporate culture*, ed. Ralph H. Kilmann, Mary J. Saxton and Roy Serpa, pp. 17–43. San Francisco: Jossey-Bass.

Schein, Edgar H. (1985b) *Organizational culture and leadership*. San Francisco: Jossey-Bass.

Schwartz, H.M., and Davis, S.M. (1981) 'Matching corporate culture and business strategy', *Organizational Dynamics*, summer: 30–48.

Silverman, D. (1970) *The theory of organizations*. London: Heinemann.

Singer, Milton (1968) 'Culture: the concept of culture', *International Encyclopaedia of the Social Sciences*, 3: 527–41.

Smircich, Linda (1983) 'Concepts of culture and organizational analysis', *Administrative Science Quarterly*, 28: 339–59.

Thompson, E.P. (1978) *The poverty of theory*. London: Merlin.

Turner, Barry A. (1986) 'Sociological aspects of organizational symbolism', *Organization Studies*, 7(2): 101–15.

Tylor, E.B. (1958) *Primitive culture: researches into the development of mythology, philosophy, religion, art, and custom*. Gloucester, MA: Smith. First published 1871.

van den Berghe, P. (1963) 'Dialectic and functionalism: toward a theoretical synthesis', *American Sociological Review*, 28: 695–705.

Wacker, Gerald (1981) 'Towards cognitive methodology of organizational assessment', *Journal of Applied Behavioral Science*, 17: 114–29.

Warner, W.L., and Low, J. (1947) *The social system of the modern factory*. New Haven, CT: Yale University Press.

Weick, Karl, E. (1979) *The social psychology of organizing*. Reading, MA: Addison-Wesley.

Wilson, John (1973) *Introduction to social movement*. New York: Basic Books.

13

The impact of organizational culture on approaches to organizational problem-solving

Paul Bate

Organizational culture is a subject which until recently has failed to capture the serious attention of researchers. This neglect has occurred as a result of the organizational culture concept being: (1) simply overlooked as a factor in work behaviour; (2) viewed as a vague or omnibus entity and ignored; (3) considered to be a component of organizational climate and ignored; (4) equated with organizational climate and then ignored; and (5) regarded as a determinant of organizational climate and then ignored. In any case, there has been a failure to come to grips with the cultural component of organizational environments (McNeill, 1979).

Initially the three research studies which now form the basis of this chapter belonged to the first category – that is, they simply failed to take organizational culture into account in early attempts to interpret emerging data and observations. It was only when other concepts proved inadequate that an interest in the amorphous concept of organizational culture began to grow. Some background on this development should provide a suitable basis for defining the aims and subject matter of this chapter.

The studies mentioned above were all carried out in companies in Britain between 1975 and 1981. One began in 1977 and is still continuing, while the other two each ran for five years before recently coming to an end. Two were undertaken in collaboration with colleagues. They were all 'action research' projects in the field of organizational change and development. The main focus of change in the three companies was their decision-making processes, and more particularly the issue of wider employee participation in them. The agreed brief was to survey a wide range of opinion on the present system and future alternatives, feed back the data to the parties concerned, and help to work through desired changes on a collaborative basis. As might be expected with large-scale, long-term programmes of this kind, this brief actually widened out over time to include attempts to change management style, improve work teams, and ameliorate union–management relationships.

Reprinted by permission of Organization Studies from *Organization Studies* 5(1) 1984: 43–66.

The companies themselves are located in the manufacturing sector of the economy. One is a major footwear producer employing nearly 4,000 people throughout the United Kingdom. Another is a multinational chemical company which has several factories in Britain and a head office in Germany. The third is a dairy products company which employs several thousand people in a dozen factories dispersed throughout the country.

One general conclusion reached repeatedly during the course of the work was that organizational change was substantially different in practice from the theory of change – and more difficult. One strand of this theory states that change will take place if and when the following 'preconditions' are present: a problem or problems and a desire or felt need to resolve them; an awareness of the existence and basic nature of the problem; and available information which allows the parties to the problem to define it and make appropriate choices between alternative courses of action (Lippitt et al., 1958; Schein, 1969). In practice it was discovered – initially in the footwear company and later in the others – that change did not always occur even when all of these conditions were in evidence. Something – whatever it may be – was enmeshing people in their problems in a persistent and repetitive way.

Increasingly attention became focused on the question: why were situations allowed to persist when they were accepted by the parties themselves as problematical and undesirable? Gradually a fascinating notion began to emerge that the parties were actively *colluding* in a process which effectively removed all possibility of a resolution to their problems. Closer investigation suggested that at the heart of this collusion process lay the organizational culture. The thesis that resulted from this line of inquiry provides the basis of this chapter. It can be summarized as follows: people in organizations evolve in their daily interactions with one another a system of shared perspectives of 'collectively held and sanctioned definitions of the situation' which make up the culture of these organizations. The culture, once established, prescribes for its creators and inheritors certain ways of believing, thinking and acting which in some circumstances can prevent meaningful interaction and induce a condition of 'learned helplessness' – that is a psychological state in which people are unable to conceptualize their problems in such a way as to be able to resolve them. In short, attempts at problem-solving may become culture-bound.

This chapter looks at that 'something' about organizational culture that has the power to lock people in with their own problems.

What is organizational culture?

The layman's terms for organizational culture are, in their way, just as meaningful as those of the behavioural scientist. They may be found in the everyday conversations of managers and shop-floor personnel.

Reference is made, for example, to the company way of doing things, or more generally to its style, philosophy, spirit, character, or even religion. Most people could (and do) paint a portrait of 'Mr Company' – the organization man who is the perfect embodiment of the company's ethos or culture – and his opposite, the square peg in a round hole whose face for some reason or other doesn't seem to fit. In my view these are everyday expressions about organizational culture in the sense that they spring from a set of generalized assumptions and beliefs about those characteristics of the organization that distinguish it from other organizations. Nevertheless, while providing the essence of the organizational culture phenomenon such expressions are limited in precision and do require further elaboration.

The first important point is that culture is predominantly *implicit* in people's mind; it is not something that is 'out there' with a separate existence of its own; neither is it directly observable. The components of organizational culture are really internalized social constructs – socially produced definitions of the situation that are part of and inseparable from a person's definition of him or herself. These constructs form the basis of that person's 'commonsense' view of her organizational world, something that is notable for its unconscious and unreflecting character. As Silverman (1970: 133) observes in this context, this world is 'a taken-for-granted world governed by what we understand as the laws of nature'.

The deeply embedded nature of culture partly explains why people have difficulty describing it in precise and critical terms. But this is not the only reason: culture forms the very foundation stone of our social existence; it gives meaning in a very literal sense to our social and organizational lives by providing us with a relatively self-contained 'order' or rationale – what Kluckhohn and Kelly (1945) call a design for living. To have this questioned can be both threatening and upsetting, and it is because of this that we defend ourselves by hiding alien values behind stereotypes, restricting our information to selective sources (reading only our 'colour' of newspaper), and limiting our interactions to those with other people of roughly similar outlooks (Hofstede, 1978, 1981).

Another key feature of culture is that it is *shared* – it refers to the ideas, meanings and values people hold in common and to which they subscribe collectively. Durkheim's concept of the 'collective consciousness' would be appropriate here were it not for the fact that a good deal of culture is unconscious and unremarked. While not denying the existence of differences – sometimes numerous and fundamental – in people's outlooks, motivation and interests, the culture concept tends to focus on the commonalities which give a work organization, for example, a recognizable personality and unity – shared perspectives which constitute what Baker (1980: 8) calls 'the social glue holding the company together'. Jaques (1952: 251) places similar emphasis when he defines the culture of the factory as follows:

[It] is its customary and traditional way of thinking and of doing things, which is shared to a greater or lesser degree by all [the factory's] members, and which new members must learn and at least partially accept, in order to be accepted into service in the firm.

The latter part of this quotation identifies a third important characteristic of organizational culture, namely that it is *transmitted* by a process of socialization. People are required to acknowledge and, to a degree at least, conform to patterns of thinking and acting that might stretch far back into an organization's history. This is an issue taken up by Berger (1963) in his portrayal of society as both a prison and a puppet theatre: he points out that people's lives can be dominated by those of men who have been dead for generations and that each situation in which they find themselves is not only defined by their contemporaries but predefined by their predecessors – all of which could apply equally well to organizations. It is organizational culture which acts as the vehicle for transmitting and giving continuity to the past – the 'living history' as Malinowski (1945) graphically describes it.

An issue around which there is a good deal of debate is what culture actually consists of. Some writers (Katz and Kahn, 1966; Hornstein et al., 1971; Silverzweig and Allen, 1976) emphasize its normative dimension by drawing attention to established organizational taboos, folkways, mores and formal rules, all making up a set of expected behaviours which regulate the behaviour of different groups. Kroeber and Kluckhohn (1952) neatly refer to these in the culture context as prescriptions and proscriptions of conduct. Others choose to focus on the values dimension of culture – the morality (Marcuse, 1969) or collective conscience (Durkheim, 1952) of the society or organization. Here the prime concern seems to be to identify the accepted principles of conduct – shared definitions of what is right or wrong, desirable or undesirable, legitimate or illegitimate, and so on (Parsons and Shils, 1951; Morris, 1956). My view is that both of these dimensions are not so much the elements of culture as its product. This view is sustained if one considers organizational culture from the perspective of 'interactionism' (Mead, 1964; Blumer, 1965). The basis of symbolic interactionism is that humanity, from a process of observation, self-interaction, and social interaction, symbolizes or attributes 'meanings' to the surrounding world, and acts in accordance with these meanings. Just as the way that people act arises out of these meanings, so too can values and norms be regarded as having the same derivative. The term 'meaning' thus refers to something which includes but is much wider than actions, values and norms – a conceptual structure of generalizations or contexts, postulates about what is essential, assumptions about what is valuable, attitudes about what is possible, and ideas about what will work effectively. In the organizational context this conceptual structure will encompass one's own roles, the roles of others, rules and institutions, traditional ways of acting, and specific issues such as the nature of authority, leadership and democracy, and many more.

Thus the term 'culture' can be defined as the meanings or aspects of the conceptual structures which people hold in common and which define the social or organizational 'reality'. McNeill (1979: 76) expresses similar sentiments:

> [It] consists of patterns for organizational behaviour that are learned, transmitted, and symbolically derived. These patterns for behaviour constitute a group's characteristic way of perceiving its organizational environment – a group's shared orientations to organizational stimuli. Organizational culture is neither an organizational attribute nor an individual attribute; rather, it is a system of shared orientations to organizational attributes, a 'consensus of perceptions' regarding organizational stimuli.

Superimposed upon these shared orientations are the idiosyncrasies of various individuals' conceptions of the organization. While their existence is recognized they are not the central concern of organizational culture research.

Methodology

A number of instruments purporting to 'measure' culture were found in the literature (Allport et al., 1960; O'Connor and Kinnane, 1961; Caudill and Scarr, 1962; Rokeach, 1973; Harrison, 1978). While many of the concepts contained in these were useful, it was decided that the actual instruments were usually too general to be used in an organizational context, or, more seriously, too culture-bound themselves to have much credibility. It was therefore decided, in the case of this piece of research, to begin the approach from the opposite end first by focusing on the minutiae of culture specifically within the organizational context, and secondly by seeking to describe and understand organizational culture from the viewpoint of the parties to it. The task was to build up a picture from the data of how individuals defined aspects of their work situation, to ascertain from this which meanings or definitions were widely shared in the organization, and finally to try to establish some connections between such observed cultural meanings and human actions (for example approaches to problem-solving).

So much for the theory. In practice, the search for cultural meanings has been far from systematic and straightforward, and it must be stressed that the methodologies stemming from this approach have continually been modified and elaborated in the light of experience. One of the key concerns early on in the research was to adopt an approach which could make full use of data which had already been collected for the purpose of bringing about organizational change and for other research topics. Now, however, the sources of culture data are more clearly established. For example, as already suggested, meanings can be inferred from norms, values and actions. While the latter, particularly joint actions, are readily observable and are a valuable data source, the first two – the 'shoulds' and 'beliefs in' – may be identified in conversations and written communications of various kinds (minutes of meetings, job descriptions, constitutions, workplace agreements and so on). Having immersed myself for relatively long periods of time in the three organizations – observing numerous meetings of various kinds throughout the hierarchy, following specific issues and critical events, interviewing personnel, and surveying records and conversations – I have been able to identify many of the dominant and recurring meanings within them.

The main source of data has been what Pettigrew (1979) calls the 'symbols' of the organization – the myths, legends, rituals and displays which contain, as encoded messages, some of the most sacrosanct of the organization's cultural meanings. Myths and legends permeate, in varying degrees, different levels and groups, and emerge quite naturally in conversations and interviews (particularly with self-confessed 'deviants'). While the core message or story remains the same, the details, points of emphasis and method of presentation may all be quite different. On this latter point, for example, the same myth or legend may appear in different circles as parable or scandal, long-drawn-out story or punchy epigram, gossip or public pronouncement. Rituals and displays may also serve to emphasize some aspect or other about the company's 'way' of doing things or its morality. Customary modes of address, physical appearances and established procedures are some of the main aspects of rituals and displays, and they all provide some clues to the dominant social or organizational meanings.

Language itself is perhaps the most important symbolic offering of culture, containing a wealth of information about social meanings. Recognition of this has been reflected in recent years in the rapid growth of the field of sociolinguistics (Pride and Holmes, 1972; Trudgill, 1974) or linguistic semantics – literally the study of all the different kinds of meanings that are systematically encoded in natural languages (Lyons, 1981). To date, unfortunately, there has been little or no attempt to study the language of organizations – or 'organizational vocabularies' to use Pettigrew's (1979: 575) phrase:

> The study of organizational vocabularies is long overdue. The analysis of their origins and uses and in particular their role in expressing communal values, evoking past experiences, providing seed beds for human action, and legitimating current and evolving distributions of power represent key areas of inquiry in research on the creation and evolution of new organizations.

The claims made in this direction by my own research studies are modest. Unlike many sociolinguists, I have not immersed myself in issues of style, grammar and syntax. I have, however, grasped the essential principle from such language experts as Labov, who states that 'our initial approach to the speech community is governed by the need to obtain large volumes of well-recorded natural speech' (1970: 30). To this end extensive tape recordings of individual interviews and meetings were made in the footwear and dairy products companies. In the case of the former, interviews with more than one hundred people – managers, employees from the shop floor, staff and union officials – ran to nearly 400 hours of tape, while recorded meetings of various kinds ran to nearly 200 hours. Permission to make tapes was not granted in the chemicals company, but a research student was allowed to take shorthand notes of both interviews and meetings over a two-year period. These, too, reflected a cross-section of people from the top to the bottom of the organization.

From repeated readings of the transcripts of these meetings, it has been possible to construct a picture of how people define their work situation – how they symbolize and interpret issues, experiences, events and problems – and how they act and react to this. Since culture, as I have defined it, comprises shared meanings, the major search has been for the commonalities in responses, not necessarily expressed in identical ways but still reflecting shared 'root' constructs. The final step has been to classify and label the different cultural traits that have been identified.

Summary of findings

My main concern was to identify those aspects of each culture that had a strong impact on organizational problem-solving, and it gradually became clear that certain characteristics were present, to a greater or lesser extent and in different forms, in all three organizations. They have been labelled as follows:

Unemotionality
Depersonalization
Subordination
Conservatism
Isolationism
Antipathy

Unemotionality: 'Avoid showing or sharing feelings or emotions'

In two of the companies studied – the footwear manufacturer and the chemicals multinational – and to a lesser degree in the third, there appeared to be a hidden dictate that displays of feeling and emotion were not permitted or were somehow 'bad' for the individual and bad for the organization. This was well captured in the phrase 'civil service mentality' used by one junior manager, who then went on to define it:

> 'Everything is handled in a formal, stiff-upper-lip way. Problems are sterilized and laundered in the company washing machine, and come out whiter than

white. One never need get one's hands wet or dirty. Our meetings are all the same – brisk, businesslike and to the point.'

Unemotionality was also reflected in the apparent superficiality of work relationships. 'Work' and 'personal' relationships were separately defined: 'There are none of them personal friends. The word personal is watered down at work. One's judgement is a bit bland because one is talking about a work rather than total relationship' (senior manager). And, 'I don't think it's part of one's work to form likes or dislikes. I don't find many people sympathetic, nor do I want them to be' (middle manager). And, 'I would rather not have close, socially intimate relationships with people either on whom I depend or who conceivably depend on me as part of their job. I would find that quite difficult' (director).

Such a definition of the work relationship did appear to affect people's ways of dealing with each other:

> 'I suppose on those occasions when I have tried to get close to someone and actually speak my mind, I've sort of sensed the barriers coming down. You known, sort of seen a blank look coming over their face. You see this as a warning signal against getting too close, and begin to back off.' (operator)

The reasons given for playing down feelings and emotions were that it was somehow impolite, embarrassing, or just 'plain useless' to do otherwise: 'Nobody wants to hear about my feelings and problems. And it's not for me to burden others with them' (foreman). And another, 'When somebody blows off steam, everyone else is made to feel uncomfortable. It doesn't really get anyone anywhere at all' (operator). When a female worker was asked why she had not brought her long-standing complaints to the attention of her supervisor, she replied: 'It would cause more trouble than it would solve – a bit like being sick over the floor: first it would upset me, second it would upset him, and third it might lead to me getting a black eye!'

In the case of managers, showing feelings and emotions was construed as a sign of unprofessionalism – a sign of weakness or inefficiency: 'If I blow my top, people will start to brand me an "hysterical woman" and suggest maybe I was working too hard' (female personnel officer). Another said,

> 'You soon learn how to be seen as good at your job – you keep your head down and above all you keep your cool; always keep that little bit of distance; be inscrutable. If you remember this you don't actually have to do anything outstanding to be a high-flier.'

Then there was the issue of vulnerability: 'Once you show that something means a great deal to you people can begin to use it against you. You dare not risk getting personally involved' (senior manager). Unemotionality in this sense is therefore closely connected with the issue of low trust. It is also a protection: a person can 'hide behind his office' when under attack of when having to deal with some volatile or embarrassing issue. A case of being able to say 'I'm only doing my job. I'm sure you appreciate there is nothing personal in this', words which preface announcements of redundancies, strike action, cut-backs in budgets, and so on. What this adds up to is an abdication of personal responsibility in the face of the demands of one's office.

The evidence suggests that, as a result of this orientation, differences between people tended to be repressed (and allowed to smoulder on) or dealt with unsatisfactorily at a 'distance'. There was a fear of bringing true feelings about a problem into the open in case tempers would fray and the situation would become 'unmanageable' (a likely enough outcome in view of people's inexperience of confrontation and openness). Instead, people would tend to 'chew' on their problem for as long as they possibly could, even though this obviously produced a lot of tension and frustration. When the problem could no longer be ducked, the next stage was to approach it in a way that deterred people from opening it up too far. One way in which some senior managers in the footwear company did this was to use junior managers as the first line of defence, and then to issue a written memorandum to the parties involved (the tone of this being vague but firm and conclusive) – in both cases avoiding face-to-face contact. Failing that, one-to-one meetings were held, at which some kind of secret deal was struck – a 'Spanish custom' as it is widely known in the footwear company. Larger meetings were studiously avoided whenever possible except for routine, non-emotive business.

It is not difficult to understand why, in such an environment, joint attempts to deal effectively and creatively with problems often failed miserably. The culture, while having a rationale of sorts, made people inflexible and overcautious. Attempts at exploring issues and using others to collaborate in this would have been regarded – in sensitive areas – as highly dangerous, a case of (to use people's actual words) 'turning over stones and finding the worms' or of 'poking your nose into something that you would do better to keep out of'. People's concern, therefore, was to cope with the situation – *not* to change it – by avoidance and repression strategies, all of which added up to a failure to get to grips with the problems.

People's lack of ability to engage in meaningful interaction was painfully obvious in meetings that did take place: 'We all want to discuss common problems but when we actually get there most of us are fairly mute' (junior manager). And, 'Our meetings? In a word – weak. Lukewarm affairs' (shop steward). 'People never really open up about their concerns. It means that our meetings are pretty dry affairs . . . I suppose we are all fairly reluctant to bring our dirty washing into the open' (personnel officer).

Depersonalization of issues: 'Never point the finger at anyone in particular'

In all three organizations I found a tendency for people at all levels to be publicly vague about the source of their problems or grievances, even when they clearly had in mind a 'blacklist' of culprits and privately discussed this with one or two close colleagues. Confronting or 'naming' individuals was regarded (if regarded is the best word for an unreflecting and natural way of seeing things) as completely out of the question – ungentlemanly, unkind, unnecessary, and often dangerous. The corollary of this was that few people appeared to accept personal responsibility for things that were going wrong: collective responsibility on the lines of a government cabinet was considered to be the order of organizational life.

The following extracts from conversations illustrate the range of different ways people tended to generalize and externalize the sources of their problems: 'You ask why we get upset about things. Well, it's that lot up there – the people at head office up there in London. What do they know about our problems?' When asked whether he was referring to anyone in particular this man – a shop-floor worker – replied, 'No, not really. All them buggers are the same. There's nothing to choose between them.' When pressed further he said that it would not be right to pick out individuals. Employees in the footwear company frequently picked on the 'family' owners as the cause of their difficulties:

> 'It's one thing they all seem to bring with them – a sort of insincerity and lack of positive support . . . no, no one in particular; you've got to remember that they have all come out of the same mould.' (manager)

Only on rare occasions did people differentiate between members of the family. In the case of the chemicals company it was often the parent company in Germany that was behind a problem:

> 'The trouble with that lot is that they can't tell the difference between a safety committee and a participation committee. No wonder we're not getting support in what we want to do.' (director)

> 'We're not really getting on top of things. We respond to changes in the market far too slowly. We are not abreast of new technology, and we are not developing enlightened policies. But you tell me where there's any hope when they are now insisting that even buying a new flag pole requires head office approval.' (manager)

If it was not 'head office' or the 'family' then it was 'the workers', 'the unions', or 'the managers' who were to blame, depending on your standpoint. Even more widely it was often 'the government', 'the recession', or 'the strength of the pound' which were the cause of the problem – but rarely any one individual.

To try to explain this attitude, one must begin with the moral aspects. Widespread in the three organizations was a strong professed belief that to name names was wrong; that there was something uncouth about confronting or even talking about an individual in public. It was, however, a rather odd morality in that it was acceptable to engage in gossip or even smear campaigns behind someone's back. A typical example was a director in the chemicals company who insisted that 'names' should not be put to problems, but who admitted in private that he was keeping secret dossiers on people who weren't pulling their weight – managers and workers whose *bosses* would be shown the contents of such files when the time was ripe!

Several other factors contributed to this attitude: fear, for example – not many people would dare to go to their boss and blame him for any difficulties being experienced; then the view that 'speaking up for yourself' was 'forgetting your place'; it was also regarded as unprofessional to question or criticize individuals (or for individuals to break the party line and take a personal stand on things), and such a course of action was unquestioningly seen to be destructive rather than constructive.

As a result, attempts to resolve problems frequently dissolved into vague discussions which skirted the real issues, or hurried attempts to move on to easier, less contentious ones. In meetings, one would often see the chairman intervening with, 'I really think we should accept that we're not going to get far on this one. I don't think the brief for this meeting is to talk about individuals or individual cases.' Or, 'I'm sure we all know *who* is being referred to here but I'm equally sure we'd all agree that it is better to let sleeping dogs lie.' What is notable – and what emphasizes the collusive side of a culture – is that on these occasions people rarely challenged the chairman on this. There was a conspiracy of silence in a literal and very powerful sense.

An alternative strategy often involved the attribution of a technical (i.e. nonhuman) cause to the problem under discussion, thereby setting in motion the less threatening search for a technical solution. The weaknesses, failings or mistakes of a person or group of people would thus be transformed into 'outdated machinery', 'production pressures', 'design difficulties', and so on.

The evidence suggests that both unemotionality and depersonalization reflected and perpetuated a situation where people were incapable of directness in diagnosing and dealing with their problems. The requirement for diagnostic activities, 'valid information about the status quo, current problems and opportunities, and effects of actions as they relate to goal achievement' (French and Bell, 1973), was not met. 'Valid' information was neither gathered nor discussed; such information as existed was never really evaluated or put to the test – people were allowed to go around with semi-private opinions which might or might not have stood up to public scrutiny. The system also worked in such a way that no one needed to own up to a problem and no one needed to accept responsibility for doing anything about it.

Subordination: 'Never challenge those in authority and always wait for them to take the initiative in resolving your *problems'*

A member of staff in the footwear company pointed out how totally dependent his colleagues had become upon their bosses at the head office: 'All my colleagues now rely on "Mecca" speaking – so if nobody speaks from there nothing happens.' Some of these colleagues to whom he referred also had something to say on this issue: 'X is my boss in the Centre. He should be coming along and saying what needs to be done, and we should be listening to that.'

Leadership was defined – by many leaders and subordinates – as providing the initial impetus for change and problem resolution. The legitimacy of a subordinate doing this was questionable, since 'subordinate' connoted 'following', 'responding', 'carrying out instructions', and similar things. Subordination also symbolized not taking responsibility for solving problems – even if they were your own problems. When resolution was not forthcoming people would tend to suffer in silence or grumble quietly amongst themselves, oblivious to the fact that one of the reasons for the persistence of their problems was their own definition of their role.

Challenging this ingrained way of seeing things, as I encouraged people to do in newly established participative processes, can be an unnatural and painful experience. This was captured well in a comment made by a chargehand-foreman to some of his colleagues:

'I would agree that to begin with we accepted things too easily in our participation committee. It's just a thing you naturally do – you know, there is this feeling that they reserve the final right to say yes or no. You have got to learn how to challenge. You have to get into a way of keeping issues alive. But all this is very embarrassing at times: in meetings the management have tried to get things taken off the agenda. So you have to raise things again and again. It can make the atmosphere pretty icy. It does take a lot of nerve and a very thick skin.'

As with other aspects of culture this subordination was reinforced by sanctions of various kinds applied to deviants. If, for example, someone did challenge authority or take it upon himself to seek a resolution of his own problems, pressures would be applied to make him 'back off'. Such pressures – as evidenced by the following extract from a conversation with some of the workers in the chemicals company – can be very great indeed:

First worker: 'It's all very well and good you telling us to speak up for ourselves at the meetings, but it wouldn't really be worth our while. Our life wouldn't be worth living.'
Researcher: 'What do you mean?'
First worker: 'You would know what I mean if you worked here.'
Second worker: 'Take the people in the warehouse. They have a reputation for sticking up for themselves. And look what happens. If they see you've got

views – are a bit bolshie – they pick on you. You get all the bad jobs.'
First worker: 'And black eyes into the bargain.'
Second worker: 'People need protection.'
First worker: 'It pays to keep your mouth shut.'

In all three companies many of the relationships that were observed between the shop-floor workers and the management were characterized by counterdependence. Workers defined themselves as powerless (which they sometimes were) and grudgingly submitted to management authority. This had the effect of reinforcing the managerial view of this authority, thereby producing a situation where decisions were made without consultation and explanation, and only minimal input was made by workers themselves concerning their problems and anxieties. Consequently, managers were often blissfully unaware that these problems existed and therefore did nothing to search for a solution.

Conservatism: 'Better the devil you know'

Managers and workers alike often had an ingrained conservatism about organizational life that partly stemmed from an underlying scepticism either that 'things will never change', or that if they did the situation might actually become worse than it currently was. The result was that problem-solving was often approached in a half-hearted way, and tended to be superficial or marginal in content. 'What it boils down to is a question of personalities. You'll never change these. What is the point in trying?' (factory manager). And, 'What's the use? Participation is a load of rubbish. If we were to put anything forward it would be squashed – a case of you can't have it, goodbye. There's no point is there?' (operator).

The following example from a recent experience (Bate and Mangham, 1981: 119) shows that such a frame of mind can completely deactivate a change effort. A colleague and I were meeting a group of workers in the chemicals company for the first time to ascertain their views on 'more' participation:

> The operators on the whole were fairly indifferent and off-hand about the whole thing – yes, that would be nice, yes, it sounds a good idea, but well, you know, nothing much will come of it . . . etc. 'What's the supervision like round here?' we asked, trying to stir them into some kind of action. 'Oh, not bad', they replied with a yawn. And taking another tack, 'Do you find things you raise get blocked?' 'Yes', came the reply – followed by another yawn. 'Well, would you like to enlarge on that?' 'Yes, things do get blocked.' 'Oh, thank you. Are there any issues you could raise at the new meetings?' (Yawning) 'Yes, hundreds, but there's not much point, is there?' 'Why not?' 'Well, things get blocked, don't they?'

Similar pockets of scepticism were encountered in the other two organizations, with broadly similar consequences for the change programme.

Isolationism: 'Do your own thing and avoid treading on other people's toes'

In all three companies there was a widely shared belief that one should be able to stake out a personal territory in the organization in which one could 'do one's own thing'. In return one was expected to let others do likewise. This belief had found institutional expression through a highly differentiated organizational structure: each of the three companies was divisionalized, each division was strongly departmentalized, and each department sectionalized. Horizontal and vertical links between people in these areas tended to be weak, and there was little evidence of people working in teams that actually came to decisions. Any approach to problem-solving was highly individualistic: only when a person failed to make progress would he approach his superior for guidance and support, usually on a one-to-one basis. When meetings were held, those who had not been involved would be *informed* of the one-to-one deal that had been struck, but would be discouraged from influencing the matter further. Other people, on the whole, tended to be regarded as more of a hindrance than a help, an obstruction rather than a resource to be tapped, a problem to be 'managed' or avoided. They were also a threat, in so far as they were seen to be competing to take away some of your territory.

> 'I'm trying to involve myself as much as I can. I'm really like a child sitting on the floor with all his toys around him. And I'm trying to do two things. I'm making sure nobody pinches *my* toys, and if any toy passes close to me belonging to somebody else, I'll pinch that if I can. We're all doing the same.' (manager)

And, 'Everyone is fairly jealous of his area – a bit prickly if he feels people are trespassing' (engineer). And, 'I think we all like to run our own thing because the fewer people there are interfering in what you do the easier it is to do it' (manager).

The evidence suggests that the problematical consequences of extreme isolationism are numerous. Information may be withheld, leaving others to piece together a picture of what is happening or to invest considerable energy in 'teasing out' information by various means. Rumour systems may be working overtime to plug the gaps in direct information. Decisions may be made which reflect only one view of a problem and fail to take into account different perceptions of that problem. Available expertise may not be fully utilized. Perhaps more important, long-standing differences between people remain a running sore so long as isolationism is used as a way of avoiding conflicts: 'I for one don't seek criticism or conflict. In fact I'm quite happy if we can actually avoid airing our differences, and establish nonconflicting roles for ourselves' (director). And,

'I suppose the main reason why we haven't sorted out the problems between engineering and ourselves is that we haven't got together and had a good free-for-all. Yes it would clear the air but I'm not sure who is going to take the initiative in setting that up.' (manager)

Antipathy: 'On most things people will be opponents rather than allies'

In view of what has already been said about the superficiality of relationships, low trust, and isolationism, it is not surprising that all three companies – though, in fairness, some factories less than others – were characterized by a particular brand of extreme pluralism. Not only were they, according to the pluralist tradition, 'fractured into a congeries of hundreds of small interest groups, with incompletely overlapping memberships and widely differing power bases' (Polsby, 1963: 25), but many of these groups were engaged in protracted hostilities with each other. Relationships between them were belligerent, distant and untrusting. Meanings attached to intergroup relations were firmly rooted in a 'them' and 'us' tradition. Antipathy was the order of the day.

The multitude of shared meanings that had grown up around such intergroup relations had found expression in the 'adversary principle' of industrial relations and problem-solving. It was assumed by the parties involved – notably (but not exclusively) managers and shop stewards – that all or most of the important issues were of a win–lose nature. Any gains would have to be at the expense of the other party. It was further assumed that there were conflicts of interest over most of the major issues. Even when this was clearly not the case, the parties – ritually and almost instinctively – took up their opposing positions and flatly refused to budge from them. Problems were 'solved' by brinkmanship and confrontation. In one or two factories, relationships had reached a particularly low ebb: nearly all issues were fought over, neither 'side' was prepared to move or look for compromise, and even the most trivial of matters was bitterly contested:

What the parties did have in common was the belief that pluralism of this kind was inevitable – a fact of industrial life:

'The fact is that you can't trust the management an inch. If you turn your back for a moment they'll get you.' (shop steward)

'Frankly, it's essential that I keep my distance. If I lose my independence I lose my integrity – and I'm left with nothing.' (shop steward)

'You have to fight them all the way – fight them as they fight you. It's like a tug-of-war. You all heave like hell, dig your heels in. If you can't win you make sure you don't lose.' (shop steward)

Managers tended to convey the same sentiments in different metaphors:

'It's a bit like a chess game. They're black, you are white! The name of the game is simply to win. Clobber the opposition.' (factory manager)

'It's called "playing the Italian defence" – you hack down the opposition before they get too near your goal, or you run them out at the corner.' (director)

What was not said, but was nonetheless patently obvious, was that this 'way of going about things' actually suited the interests of the parties concerned. A point made by Barbash (1979: 456) is relevant in this regard:

'Management prefers the adversary relationship, because it fears that union collaboration will dilute management authority and thereby impair efficiency. The union prefers it that way, because the adversary relationship is most consistent with the maintenance of the union as a bargaining organization, and bargaining is what the union is all about.'

However, while pluralist conceptions have developed chiefly to preserve the survival interests of the parties this is a very different issue from – and one which may well work against – the need to develop effective problem-solving processes.

Discussion

The findings from the three studies described in this chapter lend support to the view that organizational culture can shape patterns of organizational behaviour (Evan, 1975; Brossard and Maurice, 1976; Child, 1981; Tayeb, 1981; Warner and Sorge, 1981), and in particular that certain cultural orientations can constrain problem-solving behaviour (Argyris, 1962, 1965, 1970; Crozier, 1964, 1969). How does this occur? In what areas does organizational culture exert influence and what processes are involved? One explanation implied throughout this chapter and favoured by Argyris is that the culture affects the type and quality of interpersonal relationships, which in turn affect the approach to joint problem-solving processes. To be more precise, certain shared cultural meanings, once established, define what are acceptable, natural, desirable and effective ways of relating and acting. Taken together, they constitute people's 'dominant relational orientation' to work and to each other (Kluckhohn and Strodtbeck, 1961; Kluckhohn, 1963).

From this we can see that culture has a social consequence, in shaping relationships and interactions. It therefore directly affects the *activity* of joint problem-solving. But this is not the entire picture: my research findings suggest that certain cultural orientations have an important psychological impact, producing a sense of futility and pessimism in people long before they enter the problem-solving arena. The culture induces a condition similar to Seligman's 'learned helplessness' (1975) – a psychological state which results when a person perceives that he can no longer control his own destiny. If this perception finds confirmation in experience – if one learns from trying that one is indeed helpless – 'this saps the motivation to initiate responses' (Seligman, 1975: 74). In other words one simply gives up trying; the energy and will to resolve problems and attain goals drains away.

There is a good deal of data in this chapter to support Seligman's theory: the quotations offer many variations on the theme 'there is no point in trying; there is nothing I can do to change the situation', and in practice there were few if any actual attempts to do so. There is, however, an important difference: whereas Seligman stated that helplessness resulted when a person tried and failed, my findings suggest that an organizational culture can transmit to its members, a priori, the assumption that they are powerless – without them actually having to experience this at all. A state of *socialized* helplessness results, and this becomes an internalized, unquestioned 'fact'. Its reality is never tested and the resulting lack of change reinforces the initial cultural assumption. The culture is confirmed, and the circuit between no action and no motivation is closed. The one predicts the other.

An example of this was mentioned earlier, in the section on subordination where two workers were explaining why they did not air their long-standing problems at meetings. They believed that, as a result, they would end up with all the bad jobs, 'and black eyes into the bargain'. Perhaps this was a realistic assumption but more to the point is that they had never really put it to the test. Helplessness had been socialized, by peers and managers, and had come to be taken for granted. When we challenged them, they confirmed our suspicions:

Self: 'Can I ask you, Maggie, whether in fact anyone has been given a black eye?'
Maggie: 'I can't recall any specific instances – I suppose it's this fear of getting one that prevents it happening.'

How widespread are the six cultural orientations likely to be in organizations elsewhere? There are certainly a great many direct and indirect references to them in the literature: Argyris (1970: 46) refers to cultures that are highly 'cognitively rational':

Feelings and emotions are to be played down. This value influences executives to see cognitive, intellectual discussions as relevant, good, workable, and so on. Emotional and interpersonal discussions tend to be viewed as irrelevant, immature, and not workable. . . . For example, one frequently hears in organizations, 'Let's keep feelings out of the discussion' or 'Look here: our task today is to achieve objective X and not get emotional.'

Crozier (1964) has found unemotionality, subordination, depersonalization and isolationism in the French organizations that he studied (and, interestingly, he claims these traits are uniquely French – a point on which this writer and others [Melcher, 1969; Boddewyn, 1969] would take issue). Tayeb (1981) encountered extreme subordination in Iranian organizations, and this orientation has also been reported by Harbison and Myers (1959:

388) and Child (1981) in Britain, Germany and elsewhere. In Germany, for example, Child found a strong sense of hierarchy and of subordinates knowing their place in organizations, and like Tayeb whose findings in Iran were similar, attributed this to the high level of authoritarianism that existed in the wider society.

Hofstede (1980), in his mammoth 'Hermes' study of more than 100,000 employees in a large multinational company over a period of time, identifies four cultural dimensions that occurred, in varying degrees, in the 40 countries studied. Two of these – 'Power Distance' and 'Individualism' – relate closely to my subordination and isolationism. Hofstede uses various indices to measure and compare different countries on these dimensions. The power distance index, for example, like subordination, is concerned with the degree of subordinate dependence and scope for initiative and responsibility. The individualism index also includes many of the issues described in this chapter – the degree of autonomy, and the extent to which 'caring' is parochial or widely spread.

There is thus a good deal of support for the wider existence of four of my cultural orientations. However, only scant and very general reference has been made to the conservatism and antipathy orientations, thus suggesting that these require further empirical investigation.

At this point I should like to put forward a theory regarding these cultural orientations, based on what may be called a 'universal but variable' thesis of culture, which has its origins in Kluckhohn's (1963, 1964) anthropological studies of numerous different social subcultures. From these studies she concluded that culture 'mirrors at all times an intricate blend of the universal and the variable' (1964: 345). The universal – the features common to all cultures – stemmed from the fact that there was 'a limited number of basic human problems for which all people at all times and in all places must find some solution' (1964: 346). Five 'life problems' were singled out as being of crucial importance to all human groups:

1 What is the character of innate human nature? (human nature orientation)
2 What is the relation of man to nature? (man–nature orientation)
3 What is the temporal focus of life? (time orientation)
4 What is the modality of human activity? (activity orientation)
5 What is the modality of man's relationship to other men? (relational orientation)

Cultural variation stemmed from the infinite number of ways in which people actually came to terms with and resolved these fundamental life problems.

The evidence from this and other studies suggests that this universal-variable thesis might equally well apply to organizational cultures – that here, too, is a limited number of basic problems that are endemic to the

Table 1 *Comparative ratings of each company by cultural orientation*

Orientation	Chemicals company	Footwear company	Dairy products company
Unemotionality	High	High	Medium
Depersonalization	Medium	High	Medium
Subordination	High	High	Low
Conservatism	Medium	Medium	Medium
Isolationism	Low	High	Medium
Antipathy	Medium	High	Low

process of organization, and for which people have to find solutions. Crozier hints at this when he writes 'Organizational systems are cultural answers to the problems encountered by human beings in achieving their collective ends' (1969). Evan (1975) and Child (1981) have gone further, to suggest how variations in Kluckhohn's five orientations will give rise to different characteristics and specific practices in an organization.

We can see in Table 1 how the present study lends support to the 'universal but variable' thesis. This gives my rating of the degree of variation that was observed in the six cultural orientations in the three organizations.

Although it is not possible to show the qualitative differences between the organizations, and while the table is based on a highly subjective assessment, nevertheless it can be seen that the overall profile for each organization is different. Thus, while organizational cultures may hold certain categories of meaning and values in common, they may be unique in the way these are elaborated and given expression. (Incidentally, Hofstede's work offers an interesting perspective on the table: using his power distance index, Great Britain was found to occur half-way down the list of countries, with the Philippines, Venezuela and India ranking the highest. Two of my organizations are rated here as 'high' on subordination, but one wonders how far this would be lowered if an international benchmark that included these countries were to be used.)

Returning now to my six cultural orientations, how do these compare with those of Kluckhohn, or Evan and Child? There are two comments to be made here: first, whereas the latter span the whole range of social and organizational life, mine are almost entirely concerned with only one part of it. They represent a development of Kluckhohn's fifth category – cultural meanings which bear upon people's relationship to others, in organizations. This category dealt chiefly with only one aspect of relationships, namely, the degree of individualism/collectivism preferred by a society, whereas I have included this in my 'isolationism', and have identified five other orientations. Secondly, Kluckhohn and her contemporaries regarded culture as a society or organization's *solution* to the basic 'life problems', implying that the culture has somehow 'got it right'.

Table 2

Basic organization issues	Cultural responses
1 How emotionally bound up do people become with others in the work setting? (Affective orientation)	Unemotionality
2 How far do people attribute responsibility for personal problems to others, or to the system? (Animate-inanimate orientation to causality)	Depersonalization
3 How do people respond to differences in position, role, power and responsibility? (Hierarchical orientation)	Subordination
4 How far are people willing to embark with others on new ventures? (Change orientation)	Conservatism
5 How far do people choose to work alone or with and through others? (Individualist-collectivist orientation)	Isolationism
6 How do people in different interest groups relate to each other? (Unitary-Pluralistic orientation)	Antipathy

I prefer the term *'attempted* solution', since the data in this chapter clearly suggest that the culture has, to some extent, got it wrong, at least with regard to interpersonal relations and problem-solving in organizations. This is perfectly understandable, given the complexity of the issues involved, the resistance of culture to change, and the fact that a culture often merely represents a solution to the 'life problems' of the small number of powerful groups who created it. (Crozier [1964, 1969] similarly claims that French organizations invariably get it wrong – that their cultures have brought about total rigidity and paralysis.)

Thus we come to a vital question: if, to some degree, an organization's culture has 'got it wrong', what are the alternatives? What are the basic organizational 'life problems' to which a solution has to be found? In Table 2 I have suggested six basic organizational issues, in the form of questions, to which my six cultural orientations are the seemingly imperfect solutions.

My argument now is that these six basic issues represent an unavoidable and important range of choices facing people in organizations everywhere: every organization has to find *some* cultural 'solution' to each of the problems. Thus, *some degree* of unemotionality, depersonalization, and so on will be present in every organization. We are back at the 'universal but variable' thesis once more: the choices facing organizations are universal, the solutions are infinitely variable. What exactly do these choices involve, and what are the consequences? Lack of space prevents a detailed discussion here, but some examples will suffice: the first of the basic issues requires evaluations about how emotionally bound up people will become with each other – the degree of intimacy, disclosure of 'self' and feelings. The preferred decision, once made, will influence specific norms such as whether a person is addressed formally or by their Christian name (and by whom), whether one shows feelings in a meeting, whether one should handle a sensitive issue personally or by memorandum, and so on. The sixth item (Unitary-Pluralistic orientation) represents some of the most important issues facing organizations today. These have also tended to be the most contentious and vituperative. The choice, for example, for employers and trade unions is whether to continue to engage in jungle warfare (where, as Cole [1963: 15] has it, the relationship is entered into in a 'spirit of futility and belligerence') or to begin putting into practice 'visions of more constructive, integrative, cooperative problem-solving and trusting relationships' (Barbash, 1979: 455).

The consequences of making some of the many possible 'wrong' choices have been described in this chapter. The data show that the six cultural orientations discussed appear to be linked with the following range of problematical predispositions: a low commitment to and involvement in the change process; a disowning of problems and an abdication of responsibility for the search for solutions; a lack of openness in confronting and dealing jointly with issues; avoidance of data-gathering on the causes of problems; overcaution and a lack of decisiveness and creativity in problem-solving; erection of barriers to change; and a taking of adversary positions on all issues regardless of whether any potential measure of agreement between the parties exists.

Clearly the degree to which some or all of the six cultural orientations is present will greatly affect issues such as problem-solving and an organization's willingness or resistance to change. Argyris (1965: 11) has noted that some relational orientations are more conducive than others to 'interpersonal competence in problem-solving', and suggests that the latter will be low in organizations where the degree of subordination is high and the culture is highly cognitively rational. Arguably we can now include depersonalization, conservatism, isolationism and antipathy in this list. Can change agents therefore be optimistic if they find an organization that is 'low' on some or all of these? Generally speaking, from the results of our studies I feel this to be the case. I have written elsewhere about the many resistances to change encountered in the footwear and chemicals companies (Bate, 1978; Bate and Mangham, 1981); reference to Table 1 shows these rank higher overall in the problem traits than the dairy products company, where on the whole the 'dynamic conservatism' (Schon, 1971: 32) that plagued attempts at innovation elsewhere has been less prevalent, and there had been more rapid progress in implementing new forms of joint problem-solving process. Not that each trait carries equal weight: my impression is that unemotionality, depersonalization and subordination had the greatest impact, since they directly affected the conduct of meetings. Conservatism became less of a problem once a change programme was under way, and isolationism only hinders *joint* attempts at problem-solving. The impact of antipathy will depend on the locus and distribution of power in an organization, and will be greatest when power is distributed equally between the various interest groups.

Nevertheless, despite these qualifications, the evidence remains that the three companies studied showed a leaning towards the same cultural 'solutions' to each of the basic organizational issues, that is a preference for the adversary brand of pluralism, individualism rather than collectivism, and so on. Perhaps, then, there are cultural approaches as yet largely untried which might provide more effective solutions to the problems described above. Perhaps the 'alternative organization' – the commune, the cooperative, the copartnership – has already begun to experiment with alternative cultural solutions (emotionality, personalization, power equalization, and so on). The scope for alternatives is unquestionably great, but whether the existing cultural preferences will allow this scope to be explored is quite another matter.

References

Allport, G.W., Vernon, P.E., and Lindzey, G. (1960) *Study of values: test booklet*, 3rd edn. Cambridge: Riverside Press.

Argyris, C. (1962) *Interpersonal competence and organizational effectiveness*. London: Tavistock.

Argyris, C. (1965) *Organization and innovation*. Homewood, Ill.: Irwin.

Argyris, C. (1970) *Intervention theory and method: behavioral science view*. Reading, Mass: Addison-Wesley.

Baker, E.L. (1980) 'Managing organizational culture', *Management Review*, 69(7): 8–13.

Barbash, J. (1979) 'The American ideology of industrial relations', *Proceedings of Industrial Relations Research Association Spring Meeting*, 30(8): 453–7.

Bate, S.P. (1978) 'Cultural analysis, confrontation, and counter-culture as strategies for organization development', Paper read at XIXth International Congress of Applied Psychology, Munich.

Bate, S.P., and Mangham, I. (1981) *Exploring participation*. Chichester: Wiley.

Berger, P.L. (1963) *Invitation to sociology: humanistic perspective*. Harmondsworth: Penguin.

Blumer, H. (1965) 'Sociological implications of the thought of George Herbert Mead', *American Journal of Sociology*, 71: 535–48.

Boddewyn, J. (1969) 'Ambiguous relationship between culture and organization', in *Modern organizational theory*, ed. A.R. Negandhi, pp. 319–22. Kent, Ohio: Kent State University Press.

Brossard, M., and Maurice, M. (1976) 'Is there a universal model of organization structure?' *International Studies of Management and Organization*, 11: 11–45.

Caudill, W., and Scarr, H.A. (1962) 'Japanese value orientations and culture change', *Ethnology*, 7(1): 53–91.

Child, J. (1981) 'Culture, contingency and capitalism in the cross-national study of organizations', in *Research in organizational behaviour*, vol. 3, ed. L.L. Cummins and B.M. Staw, pp. 303–56. Greenwich, Conn.: JAI Press.

Cole, D.L. (1963) *The quest for industrial peace*. New York: McGraw-Hill.

Crozier, M. (1964) *The bureaucratic phenomenon*. Chicago: University of Chicago Press.

Crozier, M. (1969) 'The cultural determinants of organizational behavior', in *Modern organizational theory*, ed. A.R. Negandhi, pp. 220–8. Kent, Ohio: Kent State University Press.

Durkheim, E. (1952) *The rules of sociological method*. Chicago: Free Press.

Evan, W.M. (1975) 'Measuring the impact of culture on organizations', *International Studies of Management and Organizations*, 5(1): 91–113.

French, W.L., and Bell, C.H. (1973) *Organization development*. Englewood Cliffs, NJ: Prentice-Hall.

Harbison, F., and Myers, C.A. (1959) *Management in the industrial world*. New York: McGraw-Hill.

Harrison, R. (1978) 'Questionnaire on the culture of organizations', in *Gods of management*, ed. C. Handy. London: Souvenir Press.

Hofstede, G. (1978) 'National cultures and work values', Paper read at XIXth International Congress of Applied Psychology, Munich.

Hofstede, G. (1980) *Culture's consequences: international differences in work-related values*. London: Sage.

Hornstein, H.A., Bunker, B.B., and Burke, W.W. (eds) (1971) *Social intervention: a behavioural science approach*. New York: Free Press.

Jaques, E. (1952) *The changing culture of a factory*. London: Tavistock.

Katz, D., and Kahn, R.L. (1966) *The social psychology of organizations*. New York: Wiley.

Kluckhohn, C., and Kelly, W.H. (1945) 'The concept of culture', in *The science of man in world crisis*, ed. R. Linton. New York: Columbia University Press.

Kluckhohn, F.R. (1963) 'Some reflections on the nature of cultural integration and change', in *Sociological theory, values and sociocultural change*, ed. E.A. Tiryakian. New York: Free Press.

Kluckhohn, F.R. (1964) 'Dominant value orientations', in *Personality in nature, society and culture*, ed. C. Kluckhohn and H.A. Murray, pp. 342–57. New York: Knopf.

Kluckhohn, F.R., and Strodtbeck, F.L. (1961) *Variations in value orientations*. New York: Row, Peterson.

Kroeber, A.L., and Kluckhohn, C. (1952) *Culture: a critical review of concepts and definitions*. Cambridge, Mass.: Harvard University Press.

Labov, W. (1970) 'The study of language and its social context', *Studium Generale*, 23: 30–87.

Lippitt, R., Watson, J. and Westley, B. (1958) *The planning of change*. New York: Harcourt Brace.

Lyons, J. (1981) *Language, meaning and context*. London: Fontana.

Malinowski, B. (1945) *The dynamics of culture change*. New Haven, Conn.: Yale University Press.

Marcuse, H. (1969) *An essay on liberation* London: Methuen.

McNeill, J.D., Jr (1979) 'Organization culture: an exploratory taxonomic investigation', PhD thesis, University of Kentucky.

Mead, G.H. (1964) *Selected writings*, ed. A.J. Peck. New York: Bobbs-Merrill.

Melcher, A.J. (1969) 'Comments on Crozier's paper', in *Modern organizational theory*, ed. A.R. Negandhi, pp. 316–19. Kent, Ohio: Kent State University Press.

Morris, C. (1956) *Varieties of human value*. Chicago: University of Chicago Press.

O'Connor, J.P., and Kinnane, J.G. (1961) 'A factor analysis of work values', *Journal of Counselling Psychology*, 8(3): 263–7.

Parsons, T., and Shils, E.A. (1951) *Towards a general theory of action*. Cambridge, Mass.: Harvard University Press.

Pettigrew, A.M. (1979) 'On studying organizational cultures', *Administrative Science Quarterly*, 24: 570–81.

Polsby, N.W. (1963) *Community power and political theory*. New Haven, Conn.: Yale University Press.

Pride, J.B., and Holmes, J. (eds) (1972) *Sociolinguistics: selected readings*. Harmondsworth: Penguin.

Rokeach, M. (1973) *The nature of human values*. New York: Free Press.

Schein, E.H. (1969) *Process consultation: its role in organization development*. Reading, Mass.: Addison-Wesley.

Schon, D.A. (1971) *Beyond the stable state*. London: Smith.

Seligman, M.E.P. (1975) *Helplessness: on depression, development, and death*. San Francisco: Freeman.

Silverman, D. (1970) *The theory of organisations*. London: Heinemann.

Silverzweig, S., and Allen, R.F. (1976) 'Changing the corporate culture', *Sloan Management Review*, 17(3): 33–49.

Tayeb, M.H. (1981) 'Cultural determinants of organizational response to environmental demands', paper read at Workshop on Capitalist–Socialist Dialogues on Organizational Behaviour, Helsinki.

Trudgill, P. (1974) *Sociolinguistics: an introduction*. Harmondsworth: Penguin.

Warner, M., and Sorge, A. (1981) 'Culture, management and manufacturing organization: a study of British and German firms', paper read at Workshop on Capitalist–Socialist Dialogues on Organizational Behaviour, Helsinki.

14

Coming to a new awareness of organizational culture

Edgar H. Schein

The purpose of this chapter is to define the concept of organizational culture in terms of a dynamic model of how culture is learned, passed on, and changed. As many recent efforts argue that organizational culture is the key to organizational excellence, it is critical to define this complex concept in a manner that will provide a common frame of reference for practitioners and researchers. Many definitions simply settle for the notion that culture is a set of shared meanings that make it possible for members of a group to interpret and act upon their environment. I believe we must go beyond this definition: even if we knew an organization well enough to live in it, we would not necessarily know how its culture arose, how it came to be what it is, or how it could be changed if organizational survival were at stake.

The thrust of my argument is that we must understand the dynamic evolutionary forces that govern how culture evolves and changes. My approach to this task will be to lay out a formal definition of what I believe organizational culture is, and to elaborate each element of the definition to make it clear how it works.

Organizational culture: a formal definition

Organizational culture is the *pattern of basic assumptions* that a *given group* has *invented, discovered, or developed in learning to cope* with its *problems of external adaptation and internal integration*, and that have *worked well enough to be considered valid*, and, therefore, to be *taught to new members* as the correct way to *perceive, think, and feel* in relation to those problems.

Pattern of basic assumptions

Organizational culture can be analyzed at several different levels, starting with the *visible artifacts* – the constructed environment of the organization, its architecture, technology, office layout, manner of dress, visible

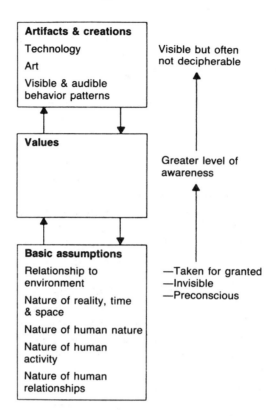

Figure 1   *The levels of culture and their interaction*

or audible behavior patterns, and public documents such as charters, employee orientation materials, stories (see Figure 1). This level of analysis is tricky because the data are easy to obtain but hard to interpret. We can describe 'how' a group constructs its environment and 'what' behavior patterns are discernible among the members, but we often cannot understand the underlying logic – 'why' a group behaves the way it does.

To analyze *why* members behave the way they do, we often look for the *values* that govern behavior, which is the second level in Figure 1. But as values are hard to observe directly, it is often necessary to infer them by interviewing key members of the organization or to content analyze artifacts such as documents and charters.[1] However, in identifying such values, we usually note that they represent accurately only the manifest or *espoused* values of a culture. That is they focus on what people *say* is the reason for their behavior, what they ideally would like those reasons to be, and what are often their rationalizations for their behavior. Yet, the underlying reasons for their behavior remain concealed or unconscious.[2]

To really *understand* a culture and to ascertain more completely the group's values and overt behavior, it is imperative to delve into the *underlying assumptions*, which are typically unconscious but which actually determine how group members perceive, think, and feel.[3] Such assumptions are themselves learned responses that originated as espoused values. But, as a value leads to a behavior, and as that behavior begins to solve the problem which promoted it in the first place, the value gradually is transformed into an underlying assumption about how things really are. As the assumption is increasingly taken for granted, it drops out of awareness.

Taken-for-granted assumptions are so powerful because they are less debatable and confrontable than espoused values. We know we are dealing with an assumption when we encounter in our informants a refusal to discuss something, or when they consider us 'insane' or 'ignorant' for bringing something up. For example, the notion that businesses should be profitable, that schools should educate, or that medicine should prolong life are assumptions, even though they are often considered 'merely' values.

To put it another way, the domain of values can be divided into (1) ultimate, non-debatable, taken-for-granted values, for which the term 'assumptions' is more appropriate; and (2) debatable, overt, espoused values for which the term 'values' is more applicable. In stating that basic assumptions are unconscious, I am not arguing that this is a result of repression. On the contrary, I am arguing that as certain motivational and cognitive processes are repeated and continue to work, they become unconscious. They can be brought back to awareness only through a kind of focused inquiry, similar to that used by anthropologists. What is needed are the efforts of both an insider who makes the unconscious assumptions and an outsider who helps to uncover the assumptions by asking the right kinds of questions.[4]

Cultural paradigms: a need for order and consistency

Because of the human need for order and consistency, assumptions become patterned into what may be termed cultural 'paradigms', which tie together the basic assumptions about humankind, nature, and activities. A cultural paradigm is a set of interrelated assumptions that form a coherent pattern. Not all assumptions are mutually compatible or consistent, however. For example, if a group holds the assumption that all good ideas and products ultimately come from individual effort, it cannot easily assume simultaneously that groups can be held responsible for the results achieved, or that individuals will put a high priority on group loyalty. Or if a group assumes that the way to survive is to conquer nature and to manipulate its environment aggressively, it cannot at the same time assume that the best kind of relationship among group members is one that emphasizes passivity and harmony. If human beings do indeed have a cognitive need for order and consistency, one can then assume that all groups will eventually evolve sets of assumptions that are compatible and consistent.

Table 1   *Basic underlying assumptions around which cultural
paradigms form*

---

1 **The Organization's Relationship to Its Environment.** Reflecting even more basic
assumptions about the relationship of humanity to nature, one can assess whether the
key members of the organization view the relationship as one of dominance, submission,
harmonizing, finding an appropriate niche, and so on.

2 **The Nature of Reality and Truth.** Here are the linguistic and behavioral rules that
define what is real and what is not, what is a 'fact', how truth is ultimately to be
determined, and whether truth is 'revealed' or 'discovered'; basic concepts of time as
linear or cyclical, monochronic or polychronic; basic concepts such as space as limited
or infinite and property as communal or individual; and so forth.

3 **The Nature of Human Nature.** What does it mean to be 'human' and what attributes
are considered intrinsic or ultimate? Is human nature good, evil, or neutral? Are human
beings perfectible or not? Which is better, Theory X or Theory Y?

4 **The Nature of Human Activity.** What is the 'right' thing for human beings to do, on
the basis of the above assumptions about reality, the environment, and human nature;
to be active, passive, self-developmental, fatalistic, or what? What is work and what is
play?

5 **The Nature of Human Relationships.** What is considered to be the 'right' way for
people to relate to each other, to distribute power and love? Is life cooperative or
competitive; individualistic, group collaborative, or communal; based on traditional
lineal authority, law, or charisma; or what?

Source: Reprinted, by permission of the publisher, from 'The Role of the Founder in
Creating Organizational Culture', in Edgar H. Schein, *Organizational Dynamics*. Summer
1983 © 1983 Periodicals Division, American Management Associations. All rights
reserved.

To analyze cultural paradigms, one needs a set of logical categories for
studying assumptions. Table 1 shows such a set based on the original
comparative study of Kluckhohn and Strodtbeck.[5] In applying these
categories broadly to cultures, Kluckhohn and Strodtbeck note that
Western culture tends to be oriented toward an active mastery of nature,
and is based on individualistic competitive relationships. It uses a future-
oriented, linear, monochronic concept of time,[6] views space and
resources as infinite, assumes that human nature is neutral and ultimately
perfectible, and bases reality or ultimate truth on science and pragmatism.

In contrast, some Eastern cultures are passively oriented toward nature.
They seek to harmonize with nature and with each other. They view the
group as more important than the individual, are present or past oriented,
see time as polychronic and cyclical, view space and resources as very
limited, assume that human nature is bad but improvable, and see reality
as based more on revealed truth than on empirical experimentation.

In this light, organizational culture paradigms are adapted versions of
broader cultural paradigms. For example, Dyer notes that the GEM
Corporation operates on the interlocking assumptions that: (1) ideas come
ultimately from individuals; (2) people are responsible, motivated, and
capable of governing themselves; however, truth can only be pragmatically

determined by 'fighting' things out and testing in groups; (3) such fighting is possible because the members of the organization view themselves as a family who will take care of each other. Ultimately, this makes it safe to fight and be competitive.[7]

I have observed another organization that operates on the paradigm that (1) truth comes ultimately from older, wiser, better educated, higher status members; (2) people are capable of loyalty and discipline in carrying out directives; (3) relationships are basically lineal and vertical; (4) each person has a niche that is his or her territory that cannot be invaded; and (5) the organization is a 'solidary unit' that will take care of its members.

Needless to say, the manifest behaviours in these two organizations are totally different. In the first organization, one observes mostly open office landscapes, few offices with closed doors, a high rate of milling about, intense conversations and arguments, and a general air of informality. In the second organization, there is a hush in the air: everyone is in an office and with closed doors. Nothing is done except by appointment and with a prearranged agenda. When people of different ranks are present, one sees real deference rituals and obedience, and a general air of formality permeates everything.

Nonetheless, these behavioral differences make no sense until one has discovered and deciphered the underlying cultural paradigm. To stay at the level of artifacts or values is to deal with the *manifestations* of culture but not with the cultural essence.

A given group

There cannot be a culture unless there is a group that 'owns' it. Culture is embedded in groups, hence the creating group must always be clearly identified. If we want to define a cultural unit, therefore, we must be able to locate a group that is independently defined as the creator, host, or owner of that culture. We must be careful not to define the group in terms of the existence of a culture however tempting that may be, because we then would be creating a completely circular definition.

A given group is a set of people (1) who have been together long enough to have shared significant problems, (2) who have had opportunities to solve those problems and to observe the effects of their solutions, and (3) who have taken in new members. A group's culture cannot be determined unless there is such a definable set of people with a shared history.

The passing on of solutions to new members is required in the definition of culture because the decision to pass something on is itself a very important test of whether a given solution is shared and perceived as valid. If a group passes on with conviction elements of a way of perceiving, thinking, and feeling, we can assume that that group has had enough stability and has shared enough common experiences to have developed a culture. If, on the other hand, a group has not faced the issue of what to pass on in the process of socialization, it has not had a chance to test is own consensus and commitment to a given belief, value, or assumption.

The strength of a culture

The 'strength' or 'amount' of culture can be defined in terms of the *homogeneity* and *stability* of group membership, and the *length* and *intensity* of shared experiences of the group. If a stable group has had a long, varied, intense history (that is, if it has had to cope with many difficult survival problems and has succeeded), it will have a strong and highly differentiated culture. By the same token, if a group has had a constantly shifting membership or has been together only for a short time and has not faced any difficult issues, it will, by definition, have a weak culture. Although individuals within that group may have very strong individual assumptions, there will not be enough shared experiences for the group as a whole to have a defined culture.

By this definition, one would probably assess IBM and the Bell system as having strong cultures, whereas very young companies or ones which have had a high turnover of key executives would be judged as having weak ones. One should also note that once an organization has a strong culture, if the dominant coalition or leadership remains stable, the culture can survive high turnover at lower ranks because new members can be strongly socialized into the organization as, for example, in elite military units.

It is very important to recognize that cultural strength may or may not be correlated with effectiveness. Though some current writers have argued that strength is desirable,[8] it seems clear to me that the relationship is far more complex. The actual content of the culture and the degree to which its solutions fit the problems posed by the environment seem to be the critical variables here, not strength. One can hypothesize that young groups strive for culture strength as a way of creating an identity for themselves, but older groups may be more effective with a weak total culture and diverse subcultures to enable them to be responsive to rapid environmental change.

This way of defining culture makes it specific to a given group. If a total corporation consists of stable functional, divisional, geographic, or rank-based subgroups, then that corporation will have multiple cultures within it. It is perfectly possible for those multiple cultures to be in conflict with each other, such that one could not speak of a single corporate culture. On the other hand, if there has been common corporate experience as well, then one could have a strong corporate culture on top of various subcultures that are based in subunits. The deciphering of a given company's culture then becomes an empirical matter of locating where the stable social units are, what cultures each of those stable units have developed, and how those separate cultures blend into a single whole. The total culture could then be very homogeneous or heterogeneous, according to the degree to which subgroup cultures are similar or different.

It has also been pointed out that some of the cultural assumptions in an organization can come from the occupational background of the members of the organization. This makes it possible to have a managerial culture, an engineering culture, a science culture, a labor union culture, and so on, all of which coexist in a given organization.[9]

Invented, discovered, or developed

Cultural elements are defined as learned solutions to problems. In this section, I will concentrate on the nature of the learning mechanisms that are involved.

Structurally, there are two types of learning situations: positive problem-solving situations that produce positive or negative reinforcement in terms of whether the attempted solution works or not; and anxiety-avoidance situations that produce positive or negative reinforcement in terms of whether the attempted solution does or does not avoid anxiety. In practice, these two types of situation are intertwined, but they are structurally different and, therefore, they must be distinguished.

In the positive problem-solving situation, the group tries out varies responses until something works. The group will then continue to use this response until it ceases to work. The information that it no longer works is visible and clear. By contrast, in the anxiety-avoidance situation, once a response is learned because it successfully avoids anxiety, it is likely to be repeated indefinitely. The reason is that the learner will not willingly test the situation to determine whether the cause of the anxiety is still operating. Thus all rituals, patterns of thinking or feeling, and behaviors that may originally have been motivated by a need to avoid a painful, anxiety-provoking situation are going to be repeated, even if the causes of the original pain are no longer acting, because the avoidance of anxiety is, itself, positively reinforcing.[10]

To fully grasp the importance of anxiety reduction in culture formation, we have to consider, first of all, the human need for cognitive order and consistency, which serves as the ultimate motivator for a common language and shared categories of perception and thought.[11] In the absence of such shared 'cognitive maps', the human organism experiences a basic existential anxiety that is intolerable – an anxiety observed only in extreme situations of isolation or captivity.[12]

Secondly, humans experience the anxiety associated with being exposed to hostile environmental conditions and to the dangers inherent in unstable social relationships, forcing groups to learn ways of coping with such external and internal problems.

A third source of anxiety is associated with occupational roles such as coal mining and nursing. For example, the Tavistock sociotechnical studies have shown clearly that the social structure and ways of operation of such groups can be conceptualized best as a 'defense' against the anxiety that would be unleashed if work were done in another manner.[13]

If an organizational culture is composed of both types of element – those designed to solve problems and those designed to avoid anxiety – it becomes necessary to analyze which is which if one is concerned about changing any of the elements. In the positive-learning situation, one needs innovative sources to find a better solution to the problem; in the anxiety-avoidance situation, one must first find the source of the anxiety and either show the learner that it no longer exists, or provide an alternative source of avoidance. Either of these is difficult to do.

In other words, cultural elements that are based on anxiety reduction will be more stable than those based on positive problem-solving because of the nature of the anxiety-reduction mechanism and the fact that human systems need a certain amount of stability to avoid cognitive and social anxiety.

Where do solutions initially come from? Most cultural solutions in new groups and organizations originate from the founders and early leaders of those organizations.[14] Typically, the solution process is an advocacy of certain ways of doing things that are then tried out and either adopted or rejected, depending on how well they work out. Initially, the founders have the most influence, but, as the group ages and acquires its own experiences, its members will find their own solutions. Ultimately, the process of discovering new solutions will be more a result of interactive, shared experiences. But leadership will always play a key role during those times when the group faces a new problem and must develop new responses to the situation. In fact, one of the crucial functions of leadership is to provide guidance at precisely those times when habitual ways of doing things no longer work, or when a dramatic change in the environment requires new responses.

At those times, leadership must not only insure the invention of new and better solutions, but must also provide some security to help the group tolerate the anxiety of giving up old, stable responses, while new ones are learned and tested. In the Lewinian change framework, this means that the 'unfreezing stage' must involve both enough disconfirmation to motivate change and enough psychological safety to permit the individual or group to pay attention to the disconfirming data.[15]

Problems of external adaptation and internal integration

If culture is a solution to the problems a group faces, what can we say about the nature of those problems? Most group theories agree it is useful

Table 2 *Problems of external adaptation and survival*

Strategy	Developing consensus on the *primary task, core mission, or manifest and latent functions of the group.*
Goals	Developing consensus on *goals*, such goals being the concrete reflection of the core mission.
Means for accomplishing goals	Developing consensus on the *means to be used* in accomplishing the goals – for example, division of labor, organization structure, reward system, and so forth.
Measuring performance	Developing consensus on the *criteria to be used in measuring how well the group is doing against its goal and targets* – for example, information and control systems.
Correction	Developing consensus on *remedial or repair strategies* as needed when the group is not accomplishing its goals

to distinguish between two kinds of problem: (1) those that deal with the group's basic survival, which has been labeled the primary task, basic function, or ultimate mission of the group; and (2) those that deal with the group's ability to function as a group. These problems have been labeled socioemotional, group building and maintenance, or integration problems.[16]

Homans further distinguishes between the *external system* and the *internal system* and notes that the two are interdependent.[17] Even though one can distinguish between the external and internal problems, in practice both systems are highly interrelated.

External adaptation problems

Problems of external adaptation are those that ultimately determine the group's survival in the environment. While a part of the group's environment is 'enacted', in the sense that prior cultural experience predisposes members to perceive the environment in a certain way and even to control that environment to a degree, there will always be elements of the environment (weather, natural circumstances, availability of economic and other resources, political upheavals) that are clearly beyond the control of the group and that will, to a degree, determine the fate of the group.[18] A useful way to categorize the problems of survival is to mirror the stages of the problem-solving cycle as shown in Table 2.[19]

The basic underlying assumptions of the culture from which the founders of the organization come will determine to a large extent the initial formulations of core mission, goals, means, criteria, and remedial strategies, in that those ways of doing things are the only ones with which

Table 3   *Problems of internal integration*

Language	*Common language and conceptual categories.* If members cannot communicate with and understand each other, a group is impossible by definition.
Boundaries	Consensus on *group boundaries and criteria for inclusion and exclusion.* One of the most important areas of culture is the shared consensus on who is in, who is out, and by what criteria one determines membership.
Power & status	Consensus on *criteria for the allocation of power and status.* Every organization must work out its pecking order and its rules for how one gets, maintains, and loses power. This area of consensus is crucial in helping members manage their own feelings of aggression.
Intimacy	Consensus on *criteria for intimacy, friendship, and love.* Every organization must work out its rules of the game for peer relationships, for relationships between the sexes, and for the manner in which openness and intimacy are to be handled in the context of managing the organization's tasks.
Rewards & punishments	Consensus on *criteria for allocation of rewards and punishments.* Every group must know what its heroic and sinful behaviors are; what gets rewarded with property, status, and power; and what gets punished through the withdrawal of rewards and, ultimately, excommunication.
Ideology	Consensus on *ideology and 'religion'.* Every organization, like every society, faces unexplainable events that must be given meaning so that members can respond to them and avoid the anxiety of dealing with the unexplainable and uncontrollable.

Source: Reprinted by permission of the publisher, from Edgar H. Schein, 'The Role of the Founder in Creating Organizational Culture,' in *Organizational Dynamics*, Summer 1983 © 1983 Periodicals Division, American Management Associations. All rights reserved.

the group members will be familiar. But as an organization develops its own life experience, it may begin to modify to some extent its original assumptions. For example, a young company may begin by defining its core mission to be to 'win in the marketplace over all competition', but may at a later stage find that 'owning its own niche in the marketplace', 'coexisting with other companies', or even 'being a silent partner in an oligopolistic industry' is a more workable solution to survival. Thus for each stage of the problem-solving cycle, there will emerge solutions characteristic of that group's own history, and those solutions or ways of doing things based on learned assumptions will make up a major portion of that group's culture.

Internal integration problems

A group or organization cannot survive if it cannot manage itself as a group. External survival and internal integration problems are, therefore, two sides of the same coin. Table 3 outlines the major issues of internal integration around which cultural solutions must be found.

While the nature of the solutions will vary from one organization to another, by definition, every organization will have to face each of these issues and develop some kind of solution. However, because the nature of that solution will reflect the biases of the founders and current leaders, the prior experiences of group members, and the actual events experienced, it is likely that each organizational culture will be unique, even though the underlying issues around which the culture is formed will be common.[20]

An important issue to study across many organizations is whether an organization's growth and evolution follows an inherent evolutionary *trend* (for example, developing societies are seen as evolving from that of a community to more of a bureaucratic, impersonal type of system). One should also study whether organizational cultures reflect in a patterned way the nature of the underlying technology, the age of the organization, the size of the organization, and the nature of the parent culture within which the organization evolves.

Assumptions that work well enough to be considered valid

Culture goes beyond the norms or values of a group in that it is more of an *ultimate* outcome, based on repeated success and a gradual process of taking things for granted. In other words, to me what makes something 'cultural' is this 'taken-for-granted' quality, which makes the underlying assumptions virtually undiscussable.

Culture is perpetually being formed in the sense that there is constantly some kind of learning going on about how to relate to the environment and to manage internal affairs. But this ongoing evolutionary process does not change those things that are so thoroughly learned that they come to be a stable element of the group's life. Since the basic assumptions that make up an organization's culture serve the secondary function of stabilizing much of the internal and external environment for the group, and since that stability is sought as a defense against the anxiety which comes with uncertainty and confusion, these deeper parts of the culture either do not change or change only very slowly.

Taught to new members

Because culture serves the function of stabilizing the external and internal environment for an organization, it must be taught to new members. It would not serve its function if every generation of new members could introduce new perceptions, language, thinking patterns, and rules of interaction. For culture to serve its function, it must be perceived as correct and valid, and if it is perceived that way, it automatically follows that it must be taught to newcomers.

It cannot be overlooked that new members do bring new ideas and do produce culture change, especially if they are brought in at high levels of the organization. It remains to be settled empirically whether and how this happens. For example, does a new member have to be socialized first and accepted into a central and powerful position before he or she can begin to affect change? Or does a new member bring from the onset new ways of perceiving, thinking, feeling, and acting, which produce automatic changes through role innovation?[21] Is the manner in which new members are socialized influential in determining what kind of innovation they will produce?[22] Much of the work on innovation in organizations is confusing because often it is not clear whether the elements that are considered 'new' are actually new assumptions, or simply new artifacts built on old cultural assumptions.

In sum, if culture provides the group members with a paradigm of how the world 'is', it goes without saying that such a paradigm would be passed on without question to new members. It is also the case that the very process of passing on the culture provides an opportunity for testing, ratifying, and reaffirming it. For both of these reasons, the process of socialization (that is, the passing on of the group's culture) is strategically an important process to study if one wants to decipher what the culture is and how it might change.[23]

Perceive, think, and feel

The final element in the definition reminds us that culture is pervasive and ubiquitous. The basic assumptions about nature, humanity, relationships, truth, activity, time, and space cover virtually all human functions. This is not to say that a given organization's culture will develop to the point of totally 'controlling' all of its members' perceptions, thoughts, and feelings. But the process of learning to manage the external and internal environment does involve all of one's cognitive and emotional elements. As cultural learning progresses, more and more of the person's responses will become involved. Therefore, the longer we live in a given culture, and the older the culture is, the more it will influence our perceptions, thoughts, and feelings.

By focusing on perceptions, thoughts, and feelings, I am also stating the importance of those categories relative to the category of *overt behavior*. Can one speak of a culture in terms of just the overt behavior patterns one observes? Culture is *manifested* in overt behavior, but the idea of culture goes deeper than behavior. Indeed, the very reason for elaborating an abstract notion like 'culture' is that it is too difficult to explain what goes on in organizations if we stay at the descriptive behavioral level.

To put it another way, behavior is, to a large extent, a joint function of what the individual brings to the situation and the operating situational forces, which to some degree are unpredictable. To understand the cultural portion of what the individual brings to the situation (as opposed to the idiosyncratic or situational portions), we must examine the individual's pattern of perceptions, thoughts, and feelings. Only after we have reached a consensus at this inner level have we uncovered what is potentially *cultural*.

The study of organizational culture and its implications

Organizational culture as defined here is difficult to study. However, it is not as difficult as studying a different society where language and customs are so different that one needs to live in the society to get any feel for it at all. Organizations exist in a parent culture, and much of what we find in them is derivative from the assumptions of the parent culture. But different organizations will sometimes emphasize or amplify different elements of a parent culture. For example, in the two companies previously mentioned, we find in the first an extreme version of the individual freedom ethic, and in the second one, an extreme version of the authority ethic, *both* of which can be derived from US culture.

The problem of deciphering a particular organization's culture, then, is more a matter of surfacing assumptions, which will be recognizable once they have been uncovered. We will not find alien forms of perceiving, thinking and feeling if the investigator is from the same parent culture as the organization that is being investigated. On the other hand, the particular pattern of assumptions, which we call an organization's cultural paradigm, will not reveal itself easily because it is taken for granted.

How then do we gather data and decipher the paradigm? Basically, there are four approaches that should be used in combination with one another.

Analyzing the process and content of socialization of new members   By interviewing 'socialization agents', such as the supervisors and older peers of new members, one can identify some of the important areas of the culture. But some elements of the culture will not be discovered by this method because they are not revealed to newcomers or lower members.

Analyzing responses to critical incidents in the organization's history   By constructing a careful 'organizational biography' from documents, interviews, and perhaps even surveys of present and past key members, it is possible to identify the major periods of culture formation. For each crisis or incident identified, it is then necessary to determine what was done, why it was done, and what the outcome was. To infer the underlying assumptions of the organization, one would then look for the major themes in the reasons given for the actions taken.

Analyzing beliefs, values and assumptions of 'culture creators or carriers'   When interviewing founders, current leaders, or culture creators or carriers, one should initially make an open-ended chronology of each person's history in the organization – his or her goals, modes of action, and assessment of outcomes. The list of external and internal issues found in Tables 2 and 3 can be used as a checklist later in the interview to cover areas more systematically.

Jointly exploring and analyzing with insiders the anomalies or puzzling features observed or uncovered in interviews   It is the *joint inquiry* that will help to disclose basic assumptions and help determine how they may interrelate to form the cultural paradigm.

The insider must be a representative of the culture and must be interested in disclosing his or her *own* basic assumptions to test whether they are in fact cultural prototypes. This process works best if one acts from observations that puzzle the outsider or that seem like anomalies because the insider's assumptions are most easily surfaced if they are contrasted to the assumptions that the outsider initially holds about what is observed.

While the first three methods mentioned above should enhance and complement one another, at least one of them should systematically cover all of the external adaptation and internal integration issues. In order to discover the underlying basic assumptions and eventually to decipher the paradigm, the fourth method is necessary to help the insider surface his or her own cultural assumptions. This is done through the outsider's probing and searching.[24]

If an organization's total culture is not well developed, or if the organization consists of important stable subgroups, which have developed subcultures, one must modify the above methods to study the various subcultures.[25] Furthermore, the organizational biography might reveal that the organization is at a certain point of its life cycle, and one would hypothesize that the functions that a given kind of culture plays vary with the life-cycle stage.[26]

Implications for culture management and change

If we recognize organizational culture – whether at the level of the group or the total corporation – as a deep phenomenon, what does this tell us about when and how to change or manage culture? First of all, the evolutionary perspective draws our attention to the fact that the culture of a group may serve different functions at different times. When a group is forming and growing, the culture is 'glue' – a source of identity and strength. In other words, young founder-dominated companies need their cultures as a way of holding together their organizations. The culture changes that do occur in a young organization can best be described as clarification, articulation, and elaboration. If the young company's culture is genuinely maladaptive in relation to the external environment, the company will not survive anyway. But even if one identified needed changes, there is little chance at this stage that one could change the culture.

In organizational midlife, culture can be managed and changed, but not without considering all the sources of stability which have been identified above. The large diversified organization probably contains many functional, geographic, and other groups that have cultures of their own – some of which will conflict with each other. Whether the organization needs to enhance the diversity to remain flexible in the face of environmental turbulence, or to create a more homogeneous 'strong' culture (as some advocate) becomes one of the toughest strategy decisions management confronts, especially if senior management is unaware of some of its own cultural assumptions. Some form of outside intervention and 'culture consciousness raising' is probably essential at this stage to facilitate better strategic decisions.

Organizations that have reached a stage of maturity or decline resulting from mature markets and products or from excessive internal stability and comfort that prevents innovation[27] may need to change parts of their culture, provided they can obtain the necessary self-insight. Such managed change will always be a painful process and will elicit strong resistance. Moreover, change may not even be possible without replacing the large numbers of people who wish to hold on to all of the original culture.

No single model of such change exists: managers may successfully orchestrate change through the use of a wide variety of techniques, from outright coercion at one extreme to subtle seduction through the introduction of new technologies at the other extreme.

Summary and Conclusions

I have attempted to construct a formal definition of organizational culture that derives from a dynamic model of learning and group dynamics. The definition highlights that culture: (1) is always in the process of formation and change; (2) tends to cover all aspects of human functioning; (3) is learned around the major issues of external adaptation and internal integration; and (4) is ultimately embodied as an interrelated, patterned set of basic assumptions that deal with ultimate issues, such as the nature of humanity, human relationships, time, space, and the nature of reality and truth itself.

If we are to decipher a given organization's culture, we must use a complex interview, observation, and joint-inquiry approach in which selected members of the group work with the outsider to uncover the unconscious assumptions that are hypothesized to be the essence of the culture. I believe we need to study a large number of organizations using these methods to determine the utility of the concept of organizational culture and to relate cultural variables to other variables, such as strategy, organizational structure, and ultimately, organizational effectiveness.

If such studies show this model of culture to be useful, one of the major implications will be that our theories of organizational change will have to give much more attention to the opportunities and constraints that organizational culture provides. Clearly, if culture is as powerful as I argue in this chapter, it will be easy to make changes that are congruent with present assumptions, and very difficult to make changes that are not. In sum, the understanding of organizational culture would then become integral to the process of management itself.

Notes

1 See J. Martin and C. Siehl, 'Organizational Culture and Counterculture: An Uneasy Symbiosis', *Organizational Dynamics*, Autumn 1983, pp. 52–64.

2 See C. Argyris, 'The Executive Mind and Double-Loop Learning', *Organizational Dynamics*, Autumn 1982, pp. 5–22.

3 See E.H. Schein, 'Does Japanese Management Style Have a Message for American Managers?' *Sloan Management Review*, Fall 1981, pp. 55–68; E.H. Schein, 'The Role of the Founder in Creating Organizational Culture', *Organizational Dynamics*, Summer 1983, pp. 13–28.

4 See R. Evered and M.R. Louis, 'Alternative Perspectives in the Organizational Sciences: "Inquiry from the Inside" and "Inquiry from the Outside"', *Academy of Management Review* (1981): 385–95.

5 See F.R. Kluckhohn and F.L. Strodtbeck, *Variations in Value Orientations* (Evanston, IL: Row Peterson, 1961). An application of these ideas to the study of organizations across cultures, as contrasted with the culture of organizations can be found in W.M. Evan, *Organization Theory* (New York: John Wiley, 1976), ch. 15; other studies of cross-cultural comparisons are not reviewed in detail here. See, for example, G. Hofstede, *Culture's Consequences* (Beverly Hills, CA; Sage Publications, 1980); G.W. England, *The Manager and His Values* (Cambridge, MA: Ballinger, 1975).

6 See E.T. Hall, *The Silent Language* (New York: Doubleday, 1959).

7 W.G. Dyer, Jr, *Culture in Organizations: A Case Study and Analysis* (Cambridge, MA: Sloan School of Management, MIT, Working Paper 1279–82, 1982).

8 See T.E. Deal and A.A. Kennedy, *Corporate Culture* (Reading, MA: Addison-Wesley, 1982); T.J. Peters and R.H. Waterman, Jr, *In Search of Excellence* (New York: Harper and Row, 1982).

9 See J. Van Maanen and S.R. Barley, *Occupational Communities: Culture and Control in Organizations* (Cambridge, MA: Sloan School of Management, November 1982); L. Bailyn, 'Resolving Contradictions in Technical Careers', *Technology Review*, November–December 1982, pp. 40–7.

10 See R.L. Solomon and L.C. Wynne, 'Traumatic Avoidance Learning: The Principles of Anxiety Conservation and Partial Irreversibility', *Psychological Review* 61, 1954, p. 353.

11 See D.O. Hebb 'The Social Significance of Animal Studies', in *Handbook of Social Psychology*, ed. G. Lindzey (Reading, MA: Addison-Wesley, 1954).

12 See E.H. Schein, *Coercive Persuasion* (New York: Norton, 1961).

13 See E.L. Trist and K.W. Bamforth, 'Some Social and Psychological Consequences of the Long-Wall method of Coal Getting', *Human Relations*, 1951, pp. 1–38; I.E.P. Menzies, 'A Case Study in the Functioning of Social Systems as a Defense against Anxiety', *Human Relations*, 1960, pp. 95–121.

14 A.M. Pettigrew, 'On Studying Organizational Cultures', *Administrative Science Quarterly*, 1979, pp. 570–81; Schein (Summer 1983), pp. 13–28.

15 See Schein (1961); E.H. Schein and W.G. Bennis, *Personal and Organizational Change through Group Methods* (New York: John Wiley, 1965).

16 See A.K. Rice, *The Enterprise and Its Environment* (London: Tavistock, 1963); R.F. Bales, *Interaction Process Analysis* (Chicago: University of Chicago Press, 1950); T. Parsons, *The Social System* (Glencoe, IL: Free Press, 1951).

17 See G. Homans, *The Human Group* (New York: Harcourt Brace, 1950).

18 See K.E. Weick, 'Cognitive Processes in Organizations', in *Research in Organizational Behavior*, ed. B. Staw (Greenwich, CT: JAI Press, 1979), pp. 41–74; J. Van Maanen, 'The Self, the Situation, and the Rules of Interpersonal Relations', in *Essays in Interpersonal Dynamics*, W.G. Bennis, J. Van Maanen, E.H. Schein, and F.I. Steele (Homewood, IL: Dorsey Press, 1979).

19 See E.H. Schein, *Process Consultation* (Reading, MA: Addison-Wesley, 1969).

20 When studying different organizations, it is important to determine whether the deeper paradigms that eventually arise in each organizational culture are also unique, or whether they will fit into certain categories such as those that the typological schemes suggest. For example, Handy describes a typology based on Harrison's work that suggests that organizational paradigms will revolve around one of four basic issues: (1) personal connections, power, and politics; (2) role structuring; (3) tasks and efficiency; or (4) existential here and now issues. See C. Handy, *The Gods of Management* (London: Penguin, 1978); R. Harrison, 'How to Describe Your Organization', *Harvard Business Review*, September–October 1972.

21 See E.H. Schein, 'The Role Innovator and His Education', *Technology Review*, October–November 1970, pp 32–8.

22 J. Van Maanen and E.H. Schein, 'Toward a Theory of Organizational Socialization', in *Research in Organizational Behavior*, Vol. 1, ed. B. Staw (Greenwich, CT: JAI Press, 1979).

23 Ibid.

24 See Evered and Louis (1981).

25 See M.R. Louis, 'A Cultural Perspective on Organizations', *Human Systems Management*, 1981, pp. 246–58.

26 See H. Schwartz and S.M. Davis, 'Matching Corporate Culture and Business Strategy', *Organizational Dynamics*, Summer 1981, pp. 30–48; J.R. Kimberly and R.H. Miles, *The Organizational Life Cycle* (San Francisco: Jossey-Bass, 1981).

27 See R. Katz, 'The Effects of Group Longevity of Project Communication and Performance', *Administrative Science Quarterly*, 1982, pp. 27, 81–94.

PART FOUR
PERSONNEL STRATEGIES

Introduction

Paul Iles and Christopher Mabey

Much of the interest in human resource strategies has been stimulated by consideration of the ways recruitment, selection, induction, appraisal, development and reward of employees could be conducted so as to achieve the organization's strategic objectives. This concern with the strategic functioning of what is often conceived of as the traditional domain of 'personnel management' characterizes many of the major US approaches to strategic HRM. In such approaches, implementing a human resource strategy is seen as involving the interrogation of the effectiveness of the various dimensions or components of the HR system as regards their contribution to strategic management. For example, how effective is the recruitment and selection process in ensuring the attraction and placement of staff with appropriate abilities and skills for their positions? How effective is the reward system in sustaining the achievement of organizational objectives? How effective are the systems in ensuring that potential and existing employees are treated equitably and fairly? Answers to such questions require some language or framework within which to discuss organizational roles and human requirements and capabilities and ways of helping bridge the gap between the language of job analysis and the language of personal attributes. One framework holding that promise which grew in popularity throughout the 1980s is the language of occupational *competencies*, and much of the growth in use of a competency language stems from the seminal work of David McClelland and his associate, at McBer consultants in the 1970s, culminating in the summary provided by Boyatzis (1982) in the first chapter in this section.

One difference between the approach of Boyatzis (1982) and the Management Charter Initiative in the UK towards competence lies in the methodologies used to identify the competences. The Boyatzis approach makes extensive use of a form of critical incident interview called a 'behavioural event interview', to identify characteristics distinguishing successful role incumbents from unsuccessful areas. The resulting competences are thus expressed as skills, personal characteristics or behaviours – that is, in language that is 'worker orientated'. The British Management Charter Initiative approach in contrast uses a form of 'task orientated' job analysis called 'functional analysis' to identify the necessary key purpose of the occupational group, followed by the required key roles, elements of competence and performance criteria defining what acceptable performance might be for each element of competence. The description resulting from this is in terms of functions or roles appropriate to the *occupation* rather than in terms of behavioural skills appropriate to the *person*.

In other parts of the book from which this extract was taken, Boyatzis discusses how the management competences might be developed and used, and how periodic assessment of the human resource system can help managers prepare for future needs. He recommends incorporating competency assessment into selection, performance appraisal, succession planning and career pathing systems, and into development programmes. These would involve recognition and understanding of the competences, self-assessment and instrumented feedback, experimentation and practice in using the competences, and application of the competences in job situations.

How can this be done? Increasingly organizations have come to realize the significant advantages that can accrue from using assessment centre technology, and in particular its application for training, development and career development purposes. Such development centres or career development workshops, as they are often called, seem more developed in Great Britain and the Benelux countries than in the United States, as the article by Seegers (1989) makes clear. The assessment centre itself is primarily of German origin but was later taken up, in the 1940s and 1950s, by British public sector organizations, like the armed Second World War forces and the Civil Service. It was then exported to the United Sates via the Office of Strategic Services, and re-imported to Europe in the 1970s, mainly by multinational companies. The approach lays great stress on simulations and situational exercises and tends to use as assessment criteria dimensions of behaviour which often resemble the 'competencies' identified by Boyatzis (1982).

Such 'assessment centres' have often been used to identify potential and aid in the selection or promotion of employees. Much research, some of which is discussed by Seegers (1989), has found that they are probably the most valid predictors of managerial potential in particular. However, they have been increasingly used to identify potential, provide feedback on performance, help in generating tailored personal action plans for individual development and facilitate organizational, rather than individual, development. Some of these uses are discussed by Seegers who gives a full description of the characteristics of the method, the kinds of exercise used, the validity and cost-effectiveness of assessment centres, and the various steps involved in designing, running and evaluating an assessment centre. He also indicates some specific benefits from using assessment centres, such as better selection, more specific training, more effective use of human resources, more effective management, better communication, greater stimulation of development and as a tool to change organizational culture. What he does not discuss in such detail are some of the differences in structure and climate involved in running a 'selection' centre as opposed to a 'development' centre, or some of the ways assessment and development centres can be integrated into the overall human resources strategy of the organization.

Both articles focus very much on *individual* assessment and development, and much discussion in this area involves prescriptions concerning how best to recruit, select, develop and shed individual employees. In the better texts and discussions, a longer term 'career' perspective is taken, in contrast to the 'snapshot' view often promulgated. What is rarely done, however, is to link a discussion of individual career development to an analysis of ways in which different organizations adopt different career systems in response to different business strategies.

Such an analysis is provided by Sonnenfeld et al. (1988) who categorize career systems, the set of policies and practices organizations use to provide staff to meet human resource requirements, according to two basic dimensions, 'supply flow' and 'assignment flow'. These dimensions reflect staff entry and exit and staff development. The authors also use the strategic analysis offered by Porter (1980) to illustrate the ways in which different organizations exhibit different career systems in relation to their basic competitive strategies.

This chapter offers a number of company examples, all taken from American private sector companies, but returns to the individual level of analysis at the end, posing the question of whether individuals also choose the kind of career system in which they want to work. It offers longitudinal data on 125 Harvard MBA graduates to support the view that over time people tend to gravitate to the kind of career system which most matches their personalities and values. This constitutes a welcome rejoinder to the stress on *organizational* assessment offered by Boyatzis (1982) and Seegers (1989), emphasizing the ways *individuals* assess and select organizations. Such an analysis, however, is not wholly convincing. It seems to discount the ways in which individuals with specific personalities or values may have been selected in or out by organizations seeking to match persons to jobs. An analysis of the match between individual *competences* and organizational career systems, in addition to that between career systems and personalities and values, would also be interesting. As the authors themselves note, the links between career systems and organizational or national culture also need consideration.

Career systems and national culture are themes taken up by Keep in his chapter on corporate training strategies. He returns us to the UK where he takes stock of a number of cultural, economic and organizational factors that are either hindering or encouraging investment in training. He argues that a company's active involvement in training is in many ways the litmus test of its commitment to HRM. This is because such investment will be positively interpreted by employees and potential recruits, who will go on to perceive their job in career terms, such loyalty thus justifying money spent by the employer. Indeed, among the several recent HRM trends he cites is the link up of training and development with the wider corporate (business planning, manpower forecasting) and human resource (recruitment, appraisal, career planning) strategies. Keep's assertion that such moves are both recent and confined to a handful of companies is perhaps over-pessimistic. Nevertheless, the unfavourable international comparison of Britain's low levels of education and training is undeniable. What is more, Keep points to some underlying attitudes among British managers – and even personnel managers – that will continue to work against the progressive development of human resources. However, sophisticated HRD and HRM doesn't necessarily imply heavily centralized and formalized systems. We are in an age where most employees – especially well-qualified ones – are less dependent on the organizations to manage their careers, seeking rather to steadily accumulate a portfolio of competencies in a more self-determined fashion. Does this individualistic approach, similar to that expressed by the MBA graduates in Sonnenfeld et al. above, also hold true when it comes to remuneration?

The issue of employee remuneration and the ways pay and reward plans can be used to complement and reinforce changes in strategic orientation is explored in further detail by Mahoney (1989). Reward systems can make substantial contributions to an organization's effectiveness and can have considerable impacts on an organization's ability to attract, retain and motivate staff. Reward systems can also contribute to the overall culture of the organizations and can help influence the kinds of decision-making structure that emerge. Different kinds of business strategy are often claimed to require different behaviours and therefore different reward systems.

In traditional organizations it is the *job* that is evaluated and pay levels are based on the job the person does. An alternative is skill- or knowledge-based pay, where individuals are paid according to the skills and knowledge they have, not the job they do. Such differences signal different kinds of culture and encourage different kinds of flexibility. Increasingly, pay in both the public and private sectors in Britain and much of Europe has come to be based more on individual performance rather than on seniority, though *how* this is done opens up another set of questions, only some of which are explored by Mahoney. Such changes may also generate negative or unintended side-effects, such as the encouragement of short-term behaviour rather than a focus on long-term goals. Mahoney discusses some 'non-traditional' pay plans from an American perspective in terms of the deficiencies of traditional pay plans and whether these new plans can overcome such deficiencies. His overall argument is that, despite the dangers of faddism (not of course confined to this area alone) careful matching of reward systems and organizational systems can provide opportunities to refine organizational strategy.

What such analyses do not fully address is how to put such a framework into operation in the face of the constraints and competing agendas that characterize organizational life. Though Mahoney does touch upon such process issues as the degree of openness of the system to participation and influence and the degree to which information about it is shared or kept secret, he does not deal at length with some of the tensions in recent British discussions of reward systems, such as those between centralization and decentralization, between flexibility and uniformity, and between individual, team or unit based remuneration. Such tensions, and the need to take political realities into account, are not of course confined to the remuneration area alone but also enter into the introduction of a competence-based selection or assessment system, the implementation of assessment centre technology and any realignment in the ways that organizations seek to source the staff necessary to meet constantly changing human resource requirements.

15

Building on competence: the effective use of managerial talent

Richard E. Boyatzis

[This chapter was originally published as Chapter 12, titled 'Summary and Implications' from the book *The Competent Manager* by Richard Boyatzis.]

The efficient and effective use of most of an organization's resources depends on the decisions, actions, and thoughts of its managers. The managers are resources that are as vital to organizational performance as its patented products and processes, capital, or plant. Understanding the manager as a resource (that is, managerial talent) is a prerequisite to organizational improvement efforts whether the focus of these efforts is on strategy, structure, systems, culture, procedures, or whatever. This chapter opens with a description of an empirically derived competency model of managers and a model of effective performance. It then examines how these models and the concept of competence can be used as skeletal structure for an integrated human resource system within an organization.

Effective performance

Effective performance of a job is the attainment of specific results (that is, outcomes) required by the job through specific actions while maintaining or being consistent with policies, procedures, and conditions of the organizational environment.

A competency model

A job competency is 'an underlying characteristic of a person which results in effective and/or superior performance in a job' (Klemp, 1980). An aggregate sample of over 2,000 managers who were in forty-one different management jobs in twelve organizations was used to determine the competencies of managers that were common to those who were effective in their jobs and not to those who were less effective. Of the twenty-one characteristics initially hypothesized to relate to managerial

Table 1 *Summary of competency results*

Cluster	Competency	Threshold competency	No support found
Goal and action management cluster	Efficiency orientation (skill motive, social role)[1] Proactivity (skill, trait, social role) Diagnostic use of concepts (skill, social role) Concern with impact (skill, motive)		
Leadership cluster	Self-confidence (skill, social role) Use of oral presentations (skill, social role) Conceptualization[2] (skill)	Logical thought (skill, social role)	
Human resources management cluster	Use of socialized power (skill, social role) Managing group process[2] (skill, social role)	Accurate self-assessment (skill) Positive regard[3] (skill)	
Directing subordinates cluster	Developing others (skill, social role)	Spontaneity (skill) Use of unilateral power (skill, social role)	
Focus on others cluster	Perceptual objectivity (skill) Self-control[4] (trait) Stamina and adaptability (trait)		Concern with close relationships (skill, motive, social role) Self-control (skill) Stamina and adaptability (skill)
Specialized knowledge		Specialized knowledge (social role)	

[1] Items in parentheses indicate levels of competency for which empirical support was found.
[2] Supported as a competency at middle and executive-level management jobs only.
[3] Supported as a competency at middle-level management jobs only.
[4] Supported as a competency at entry level management jobs only.

effectiveness, thirteen were found to be competencies, as summarized in Table 1. They were: efficiency orientation, proactivity, diagnostic use of concepts, concern with impact, self-confidence, use of oral presentations, conceptualization (for middle and executive-level managers only), use of socialized power, managing group process (for middle and executive-level managers only), developing others, perceptual objectivity, self-control (at the trait level only), and stamina and adaptability (at the trait level only).

Six of the characteristics were found to be threshold competencies. They were: use of unilateral power, accurate self-assessment, positive regard (for middle-level managers only), spontaneity, logical thought and specialized knowledge.

For two of the characteristics, and at the skill levels of two of the other characteristics, either no support was found or the results suggested an inverse relationship to managerial effectiveness. They were: concern with close relationships (at all levels of the characteristic), memory, self-control (at the skill level), and stamina and adaptability (at the skill level).

The competencies and threshold competencies were found to relate to each other at the skill level in a manner that yielded five clusters. These clusters were: the goal and action management cluster, which included efficiency orientation, proactivity, diagnostic use of concepts, and concern with impact; the leadership cluster, which included self-confidence, use of oral presentations, logical thought, and conceptualization; the human resource management cluster, which included use of socialized power, managing group process, accurate self-assessment, and positive regard; the directing subordinates cluster, which included developing others, use of unilateral power, and spontaneity; and the focus on others cluster, which included perceptual objectivity, self-control, stamina and adaptability, and concern with close relationships. The relationships within each cluster and between the clusters were thought to represent primary and secondary relationships, respectively, between the competencies. Although not at the skill level, the sixth cluster, specialized knowledge, is also an integral part of the model.

Differences were found in the degree to which one aspect of the environment in which managers operate demanded, required, or stimulated these competencies, in terms of whether the organizations were located in the public or the private sector. Differences were also found in the degree to which one aspect of the managers' jobs demanded, required, or stimulated these competencies, in terms of entry, middle, or executive-level management jobs.

Analysis of the combined effect of the set of competencies at the skill level was conducted to determine the degree of accuracy they would show in predicting the performance group (that is, poor, average, or superior performers) of the managers. The results indicated that the competencies correctly classified 51 per cent of the managers, as compared to a random prediction that would have correctly classified only 33 per cent of them.

A word of caution is in order regarding the summary and potential application of the findings from this study. First, the study was an initial attempt to determine what a generic competency model of management should include. A precise determination of causality would require additional research through longitudinal studies, as well as replication in other sets of organizations. Since the selection of organizations and jobs included in the study was not random, generalizing from these findings beyond a certain point may not be appropriate. Secondly, development of a comprehensive model of management would require that a similar effort be completed regarding additional job and environment variables not examined in this study.

Linking competencies and job demands

The demands, or requirements, made on a person in a management job can be considered functional requirements of the particular job, situational demands, or specific demands emerging from day-to-day events on the job. Although it would be difficult to propose a framework for the varying day-to-day demands of a management job, the functional requirements of management jobs can be described in terms of five basic functions, planning; organizing; controlling; motivating; and coordinating. Each of these functions can be further examined in terms of the various activities or tasks that constitute the function.

In performing the planning function, the manager is determining the goals and plans for the organization and communicating them to others. The type of planning may vary from management job to management job. An executive may be responsible for determining the strategic direction of the organization. He or she would be determining how the organization will respond to the market place and competitive environment in the years ahead. An entry-level manager may be responsible for determining the performance goals of individual contributors (that is, salespeople, bookkeepers, engineers, production workers) and work units.

Although the specific types of goals and plans for which the manager is responsible may vary, every manager has some degree of responsibility for establishing goals and developing plans for achieving those goals. For some managers, the overall goal may be handed to them and they must establish the activity plan to achieve it. It is the competencies in the goal and action management cluster that will enable a manager to perform these tasks effectively, regardless of whether he or she is determining the goals and plans or working with others to develop them.

The degree to which the manager must communicate the goals and plans and the rationale for the goals and plans to his or her subordinates will also vary from job to job. When this is required of the manager, it is the competencies in the leadership cluster that will enable him or her to communicate this to others most effectively. Through the use of these competencies, the manager is communicating to others in the organization the direction of the organization's efforts and basic expectations as to the level of organizational performance.

In performing the organizing function, the manager is determining what human and other resources are needed and how they should be structured to accomplish the plan and achieve the goals. He or she is also establishing standards of performance for individuals and groups. Since all managers must be prepared to explain the organization of people, other resources, and activities to their subordinates, all managers should at least understand the basis for the organization of resources. Often, it is this understanding that is the basis for day-to-day decisions which the manager must make regarding the use of resources in addressing priorities and changes in priorities.

It is the competencies in the goal and action management cluster that enable the manager to determine effectively what resources are needed, how they should be structured, and what the standards of performance should be. These competencies are needed whether the manager is performing these tasks himself or herself or working with others to perform these tasks. It is the competencies in the leadership cluster that enable a manager to determine how the resources should be structured or organized, what the standards of performance should be, and communicate the rationale for the organization of resources to others. It is the competencies in the human resource management cluster that enable a manager to communicate the rationale and importance for the particular organization of resources to his or her subordinates as well as to other groups in the organization.

In performing the controlling function, a manager is monitoring the performance of individuals and groups, providing feedback on their performance, and rewarding and disciplining them based on their performance. Every manager has some degree of responsibility for monitoring performance of others or an organizational unit, providing feedback to others, and taking appropriate actions (that is, rewarding or disciplining others).

It is the competencies in the goal and action management cluster which enable a manager to perform all of these tasks effectively. Without these competencies, the manager cannot provide the *context* within which others' performance is monitored, nor provide a basis for the rewards given nor disciplinary actions taken. It is the competencies in the directing subordinates cluster and the human resource management cluster that enable a manager to effectively provide performance feedback to others and dispense rewards and punishments.

As with other functions, the way in which the tasks in the controlling function are performed will vary at different levels of management. For example, it is expected that at executive levels, managers will perform the monitoring and feedback tasks more through the use of management information systems than through personal interactions. As the methods of performing these tasks vary, so will the competencies needed by the manager to perform them. At the executive level, where personal performance monitoring and feedback is probably less frequent and possibly less relevant, the competencies in the directing subordinates cluster would be less relevant.

In performing the motivating function, a manager must build commitment, identity, pride, and spirit in the organization. He or she must also stimulate an interest in work and develop capability in his or her subordinates. Building the commitment, identity, and pride of others is a responsibility for the executive which is focused on the organization as a whole. For the middle-level manager, the focus is more on the work group, or groups, reporting to him or her rather than on the organization as a whole. It is the competencies in the human resource management cluster and the leadership cluster that enable the manager to perform these tasks effectively. It is the competencies in the directing subordinates cluster that enable a manager to develop his or her subordinates' capability.

In performing the coordinating function, a manager must stimulate cooperation among departments, divisions, and other work groups. He or she must also negotiate resolution of conflicts or differences that emerge. It is the competencies in the human resource management cluster and the focus-on-others cluster that enable a manager to perform these tasks effectively.

As part of this function, managers are often expected to 'represent' the organization and its products to various groups within the organization, but also to groups external to the organization (that is, the community, the financial community, professional associations, government agencies, consumers and so on). This responsibility is particularly important to managers at executive levels. It is the competencies in the leadership cluster that enable a manager to represent the organization and its products to others effectively.

These relationships are summarized in Table 2. Certain activities, such as communicating and decision making, are essential tasks involved in the performance of each of the five basic functions of management. The competencies within a particular cluster will vary in their importance and relevance to effective performance of the tasks according to both the centrality of the function to the manager's job and the level of management job.

Links to the organizational environment

To complete the integrated model of management, links between the job demands, competencies, and aspects of the organizational environment must be established. It should be noted that when people think about the organizational environment, they usually consider aspects of the environment in which the organization exists (for example, the marketplace, culture, industry). These are aspects of the environment *external* to the

Table 2 *The relationship between management functions and competency clusters*

Tasks	Relevant competency clusters
1 Planning function Determining the goals of the organization Establishing plans of action for achieving those goals Determining how the plan should be accomplished Communicating this to others	Competencies in the Goal and Action Management Cluster Competencies in the Leadership Cluster
2 Organizing function Determining what people and resources are needed to accomplish the plan Determining how these people and resources should be structured to do it Establishing the standards of performance Communicating this to others	Competencies in the Goal and Action Management Cluster Competencies in the Leadership Cluster Competencies in the Human Resource Management Cluster
3 Controlling function Monitoring performance of individuals and groups Providing feedback to individuals and groups Rewarding or disciplining based on performance	Competencies in the Goal and Action Management Cluster Competencies in the Directing Subordinates Cluster and Human Resource Management Cluster
4 Motivating function Building commitment, identity, price, and spirit in the organization Stimulating an interest in work Developing capability in subordinates	Competencies in the Human Resource Management Cluster and the Leadership Cluster Competencies in the Directing Subordinates Cluster
5 Coordinating function Stimulating cooperation between departments, divisions, and other work groups Negotiating resolution of conflicts and differences Representing the organization to outside groups	Competencies in the Human Resource Management Cluster and the Focus on Others Cluster Competencies in the Leadership Cluster

organization. In a model of management rather than a model of organizations, the external environment should be addressed through elements in the organization's *internal* environment. These are the environmental demands over which managers have the most control. They should, and often do, reflect the external conditions. For example, the strategic condition of the industry of which an organization is a part and its position in the industry should be reflected in the organization's strategic plan. The comparability of the wages and benefits offered by an organization and its competitors, or other organizations, should be reflected in the organization's compensation and benefits system. Throughout this section, therefore, organizational environment or environment will refer to the *internal* organizational environment.

There are two elements in the organizational environment that appear most related to the performance of the planning function: the strategic planning process; and the business planning process. The strategic planning process requires assessment of the competitive position of the organization, anticipated changes in the marketplace and environment external to the organization (for example, changes in technology or consumer preferences), and the relative capability of the organization to respond to those changes. The business planning process includes the articulation of specific goals and objectives and can be considered the identification of the tactics associated with the overall strategy chosen. Business planning processes include operational planning (that is, day-to-day or week-to-week establishment of goals and planning of activities).

There is an additional aspect of the organizational environment linked to the planning function: the organizational climate, or organizational culture. This was not listed above because it is not really a separate element in the organizational environment, but reflects the way in which people in the organization perceive and react to the elements listed above. Aspects of the organizational climate should be considered indicators of how the people in the organization are responding to elements in the internal environment related to each of the managerial functions. With respect to the planning function, clarity and standards are particularly important aspects of the climate. The clarity aspect of climate refers to the degree to which people know what is expected of them (that is, performance goals) and why it is expected of them (that is, the rationale for those goals and how they correspond to the corporate objectives) (Klemp, 1975). The standards aspect of climate refers to the degree to which challenging but attainable goals (that is, performance expectations) are established and the degree of emphasis placed on continually improving performance (Klemp 1975).

A manager's ability to effectively address these elements in the organizational environment through performance of the planning function will be a result of: the planning tasks that are a part of his or her job, and the degree to which he or she possesses the corresponding competencies in the goal and action management cluster and the leadership cluster.

There are seven elements in the organizational environment that appear most related to the performance of the organizing function:

organization design
job design
the personnel planning process
the selection and promotion system
the succession planning and career pathing system
the job evaluation system
the financial resource allocation process

The organization design (that is, organization structure) should reflect appropriate flow of goods and information from one organizational unit to another, and the transformation of raw materials from suppliers to the products made available to the customers. The design of jobs addresses the issues of whether the set of demands that constitute each job is meaningful to the job occupant, can be performed by a person, and correspond to the organization design.

The personnel planning process, formerly called the manpower planning process, is essential in determining the number and type of human resources needed to work toward the organization's goals. The selection and promotion system addresses the appropriate placement of personnel into jobs. The succession planning and career pathing system addresses the efficient placement of people into jobs in response to current needs and in anticipation of future needs. The job evaluation system provides the organization with a vehicle for assessing the value of the performance of each job to the accomplishment of its objectives (that is, the relative value of the contribution from people performing each of the jobs). The job evaluation system is most often used for establishing salary scales.

The financial resource allocation process includes allocating the financial and other resources to accomplish the organization's goals. This element is closely linked to the strategic and business planning processes, especially in addressing the formation and use of capital, cash flow, debt management, and similar considerations.

Another aspect of the environment linked to the organizing function is the organizational climate, in particular the responsibility, clarity, and standards aspects of climate. The responsibility aspect of climate refers to the degree and appropriateness of the delegation of decision-making authority to various jobs in the organization and the degree of risk taking encouraged (Klemp, 1975).

A manager's ability to effectively address these elements of the organizational environment through performance of the organizing function will be a result of the organizing tasks that are part of his or her job, and the degree to which he or she possess the competencies in the goal and action management cluster, the human resource management cluster, and the leadership cluster.

There are four elements in the organizational environment that appear most related to the performance of the controlling function:

product and business unit performance review process
individual performance review process
management information system
compensation and benefits system

The product and business unit performance review process and the individual performance review process provide management with an assessment of the performance of products, business units, and individuals toward the corporate objectives. They also provide managers and individual contributors with information on how their own performance is contributing to corporate performance. Through these review processes and the management information system, managers are able to monitor and supervise others and the flow of work.

The compensation and benefits system is associated with performance of the controlling function as a system of rewards and punishments. This would work effectively only if the operation of the compensation and benefits system was directly related to job performance. To the extent that it is related to seniority, tenure, favoritism, or other forms of nonperformance-based discrimination, the compensation and benefits system would not be associated with effective performance of the controlling function.

An additional aspect of the organizational environment linked to the controlling function is the organization climate, in particular the rewards, clarity, and conformity aspects of the climate. The rewards aspect of the climate refers to the degree to which people feel that effective performance is recognized in an equitable manner and that rewards are used more often than punishments and threats (Klemp, 1975). The conformity aspect of climate refers to the amount of rules and regulations that are thought to be unnecessary and the degree to which people are told how to perform their jobs (Klemp, 1975).

A manager's ability to effectively address these elements in the organizational environment through performance of the controlling function will be a result of the controlling tasks which are part of his or her job, and the degree to which he or she possesses the competencies in the goal and action management cluster, the human resource management cluster, and the directing subordinates cluster.

There are four elements in the organizational environment that appear most related to the performance of the motivating function:

the training and development system
the compensation and benefits system
the career planning process
the management information system

The training and development system includes developmental assessment of people's ability, mentoring or guidance, and training programs. All of these activities are oriented toward helping people improve their abilities. The compensation and benefits system is associated with the motivating function to the extent that it operates as an incentive system. The career planning process helps individuals make personal decisions about developmental activities and job changes in the context of long-term personal objectives and organizational needs. The management information system can be an element of the organizational environment related to the motivating function if it provides subordinates with performance information directly (that is, not requiring the personal interpretation of the manager).

Of course, the management information system would only be effective in this context if individuals had clear and meaningful performance goals.

An additional aspect of the organizational environment associated with performance of the motivating function is the organizational climate, in particular the team spirit and rewards aspects of climate. The team spirit aspect of climate refers to the degree to which people feel proud to belong to the organization and have a sense of relationships being warm, friendly, or trusting (Klemp, 1975).

A manager's ability to effectively address these elements in the organizational environment through performance of the motivating function will be a result of the motivating tasks that are part of his or her job, and the degree to which he or she possesses competencies in the human resource management cluster, the leadership cluster, and the directing subordinates cluster.

There are three elements in the organizational environment which appear most related to the performance of the coordinating function:

the public relations program
the grievance procedure
the cross-functional and interdepartmental coordinating process

An appropriate grievance procedure can help establish a framework and setting for resolution of conflicts, whether the conflicts are based on an interpersonal difficulty, a problem with an organizational system or policy, or among organizational units. The cross-functional and interdepartmental coordinating process may be formal or informal. This process is often established on the basis of interpersonal relationships. The process may be supported by existence of 'integrating' jobs, task forces, and other similar vehicles. The process is an important element in the potential of the organization to facilitate cooperation, collaboration, and smooth functioning. The public relations program addresses the representational task in the coordinating function. Aspects of this element may be focused on internal representation, often called internal communications programs. It is usually focused on representing the organization and its products to the world outside the organization.

An additional aspect of the organizational environment associated with the coordinating function is the organizational climate; in particular, the team spirit and clarity aspects of the climate.

A manager's ability to effectively address these elements in the organizational environment through performance of the coordinating function will be a result of the coordinating tasks that are part of his or her job, and the degree to which he or she possesses the competencies in the human resource management cluster, the focus-on-others cluster, and the leadership cluster.

The linkages between competencies, job demands as presented by managerial functions, and the internal organizational environment are summarized in Table 3.

Table 3 *Elements of an integrated model of management*

Competency clusters	Elements in the organizational environment
1 Planning function	
Goal and action management cluster	Strategic planning process
Leadership cluster	Business planning process
	Related climate: clarity, standards
2 Organizing function	
Goal and action management cluster	Organization design
Leadership cluster	Job design
Human resource management cluster	Personnel planning process
	Selection and promotion system
	Succession planning and career pathing systems
	Job evaluation system
	Financial resource allocation process
	Related climate: responsibility, clarity, standards
3 Controlling function	
Goal and action management cluster	Product and business unit performance review process
Directing subordinates cluster	Individual performance review process
Human resource management cluster	Compensation and benefits system
	Management information system
	Related climate: rewards, clarity, conformity
4 Motivating function	
Human resource management cluster	Training and development system
Leadership cluster	Compensation and benefits system
Directing subordinates cluster	Career planning process
	Management information system
	Related climate: team spirit, rewards
5 Coordinating function	
Human resource management cluster	Public relations program
Focus on others cluster	Grievance procedures
Leadership cluster	Crossfunctional and interdepartmental coordinating processes
	Climate: team spirit, clarity

Concluding comments

If you are a part of the scientific management tradition, you may view competencies as the specifications for the human machinery desired to provide maximum organizational efficiency and effectiveness. If you are part of the humanistic management tradition, you may view competencies as the key that unlocks the door to individuals in realizing their maximum potential, developing ethical organizational systems, and providing maximum growth opportunities for personnel. If you are one of the people who work in organizations or one of the people who studies, thinks about, and tries to help organizations utilize their human resources effectively, this model and these findings should provide a needed relief from the eclectic cynicism or parochial optimism concerning management that many of us have developed.

References

Klemp, G.O., Jr (1975) *Technical manual for the organization climate survey questionnaire.* Boston: McBer.

Klemp, G.O., Jr (ed.) (1980) *The assessment of occupational competence.* Report to the National Institute of Education, Washington, DC.

16

Assessment centres for identifying long-term potential and for self-development

Jeroen J.J.L. Seegers

An assessment centre is a procedure (not a location) that uses multiple assessment techniques to evaluate employees for a variety of manpower purposes and decisions (Thornton and Byham, 1982). Assessment differs from psychometric prediction in both measurement techniques utilized and the process of making the prediction.

The assessment approach may use techniques like paper-and-pencil tests, questionnaires, and the use of background information. Particularly important in the assessment approach, however, is the focus on relevant behaviours displayed by the assessee in simulations.

The assessment centre method may be used to identify an individual's growth and development possibilities. The simulations in which the assessed person takes part represent as closely as possible the situations that the incumbent will be encountering in performing the job in question and they portray different aspects of that job. Thus, information is gathered, in a standardized and controllable manner, on behaviour that is representative for future job behaviour. This information is not communicated in psychological terminology, but expressed in terms easily recognized by management. The assessment centre method is conducted strictly step by step, with each phase basically forming an entity of itself. The effectiveness of the assessment centre method has already been proved in practice on numerous occasions, especially in cases concerned with potential assessment and career development.

Assessment centre for identifying potential

The assessment centre method is used with particular success as a method for potential evaluation and management development. Evaluation of potential is based on gathering information on a range of aspects that is

Reprinted from chapter 5.8 in P. Herriot (ed.) *Assessment and Selection in Organizations*. (Chichester: John Wiley and Sons Ltd, 1989).

much wider than with evaluation of achievements and job performance. The latter types of evaluation may be restricted to evaluation of the knowledge, the capacities and skills that are necessary for successful performance of a particular job or of all jobs within a specific department. Potential evaluation should focus on the skills that are required for a great number of positions that may be within the reach of the assessee at some point in the future.

By using an *integrated* evaluation system composed of tests and simulations for the purpose of arriving at the best possible predictions, the assessment centre method is highly effective for the prevention of the most common assessment errors (Byham, 1970).

One of the objectives of application of the assessment centre method is to evaluate the growth potential of individual employees. The primary concern then is not information on the employee's performance of his or her present job and the resulting achievement over the last few months or years, but answering the question of whether he or she would be able to fill other jobs, that is, prediction. So the emphasis is not on the present or the past, but on the future (potential evaluation). The assessment centre method in its application for potential evaluation is based on the following assumptions:

that every employee can develop his or her skills further;
that the development possibilities of the assessees can be established, also those possibilities for which no evidence may be traced in the performance of the present job;
that the organization is continually in need of people who can perform various kinds of jobs.

The organization benefits from using the assessment centre method for potential evaluation in that it offers an opportunity for human resource planning to meet the requirement of an appropriate number of suitable employees. The employees benefit from the potential evaluation in that they are given the opportunity to develop their capacities and use them in work situations.

Career policy

The assessment centre method as a technique to evaluate potential should be considered within the framework of a more comprehensive (career) policy. Career policy is concerned with making three factors agree with each other: the potential skills of individual employees; their personal and professional interests; and the specific needs of the organization itself.

Career planning policy involves the following activities:

determination of the establishment, i.e. the total number of positions of a particular type and level, based on the future organizational structure;
recruitment and selection;

development and training;
potential evaluation.

For potential evaluation the following instruments may be used:

performance appraisal and achievement evaluation;
career interests registration: recording the wishes and aspirations of the
employees regarding their future;
suitability advice;
results of special assignments, such as practical training period and
teaching commitment;
results of assessment exercises;
advice based on psychological tests;
advice based on a medical examination by the company physician.

The term 'suitability advice' denotes the prognosis given by managers
and, if necessary, other personnel about the suitability of the employee to
fill different – mainly higher-level – positions. This suitability advice is
the 'potential evaluation' in a narrower sense. It will be apparent from the
above that there are also other ways to evaluate an employee's potential.
Three types of evaluation have been summarized in Table 1, which shows
that they differ in many respects.

Most assessment methods generally try to establish a person's suitability
to hold a new position on the basis of behaviour and, above all, successful
performance of previous jobs. This approach is workable if the new position does not greatly differ from the old one. However, if it does differ
substantially, prediction of a person's future performance on the basis of
current performance proves to be a tricky business. A brilliant salesman
does not necessarily make a good sales manager. In such cases, the assessment centre method may be applied.

Characteristics of the method

The assessment centre method is not to be looked upon as replacing all
other methods and techniques used in the promotion and selection
processes, such as interviews, psychological tests and performance
appraisals, but as supplementing these tools of assessment. In combination with these traditional methods, assessment exercises supply the
organization with a fairly complete picture of the competence of its
(future) employees.

The term 'assessment centre' may be used to denote:

1 the assessment centre method in general;
2 a specific assessment centre programme designed for selection, evaluation or training purposes;
3 a specific assessment centre meeting in which the actual evaluation of
  the candidates takes place.

Table 1 *Comparison of three types of evaluation*

Type of evaluation evaluation interview	Performance appraisal job performance interview	Achievement evaluation remuneration interview	Potential evaluation assessment centres
General objective	improvement of job performance and work situation	establishment of remuneration	evaluation of growth potential
General question:	how does the employee perform his/her job?	how has the employee performed his/her job?	what other skills does the employee possess?
Motivation of the organization:	employment of available personnel	effective remuneration	securing of future staff
Motive of the employee:	satisfactory job	justified remuneration	motivation for future
Position:	present position	present position	other, mainly higher-level positions
Time perspective:	recent past and near future	recent past	future
Object:	work behaviour	results	behavioural criteria
Aspects:	qualitative aspects	output, effect	predictive aspects
Stress on:	what may be improved	what is (specially) remunerated	what growth potential there may be

Source: Proot and Dragstra, 1982 (adapted)

The following elements are characteristic of the assessment centre method:

To evaluate a person's suitability for a particular position, use is made of previously formulated and defined criteria, resulting from a careful analysis of the job in question.

Different techniques are employed for the establishment of a person's suitability for a specific job. Apart from interviews, tests and exercises may be used.

The exercises are attuned to the content of the future job and they are often simulations of part of the job content (simulation exercises).

A form of group selection is used in which the participants who are considered for a specific job meet and their mutual interaction is observed.

Multiple assessors are involved. They are managers, preferably working in jobs that are several levels higher up in the organizational hierarchy than the job in question.

The final judgement is based on a combination of the different evaluation methods.

In the United States the assessment centre method is used mainly as an alternative selection method. In Europe – where it is most frequently employed in the United Kingdom, the Netherlands, and Germany – the assessment centre method is mainly used as a diagnostic instrument in potential evaluation, career planning, and management development. In particular, larger organizations use the method to give substance and direction to their often extensive training programmes for management trainees and intermediate and higher-level staff.

Assessment centre technology

The assessment centre method or *technology* is characterized, among other things, by the use of multiple instruments:

job practice simulations;
interviews;
tests.

The choice of instrument depends on:

the critical situations in which the future incumbent is supposed to (re)act successfully;
the data available from the participant's work experience;
the criteria that are relevant for the job in question and in relation to which the participant's behaviour is to be assessed.

Table 2 *The use of assessment exercises*

Assessment exercise	Frequency of use (%)
In-basket	95
Assigned-role leaderless group discussion	85
Interview simulation	75
Non-assigned-role leaderless group discussion	45
Scheduling (primarily for supervisory positions)	40
Analysis (primarily for higher-level positions)	35
Management games	10
Background interview (as part of the assessment centre as opposed to being part of a promotion system)	5
Paper-and-pencil tests	
Intellectual	2
Reading	1
Mathematics and arithmetic	1
Personality	1
Projective tests	1

Source: Thornton and Byham (1982).

There is research evidence that a combination of assessment exercises and psychological tests provides a very powerful method for arriving at fairly accurate predictions about a person's future behaviour. The combination of the two instruments leads to considerably higher results than will be the case if only one of them is used (Moses and Byham, 1977). Tests tend to work mainly in-depth and can frequently provide explanations for certain behaviours that have been observed during the assessment meeting. Tests are occasionally also used for the pre-selection of candidates. The information resulting from the tests then forms the basis for the interview with individual candidates.

It is generally true that no single exercise exists that enables the assessment of *all* behavioural criteria. A specific group exercise may say something about a person's persistence, but little about their written skills. It is obvious that the best manner of predicting a person's future behaviour through exercises will be for that person to be put in a situation that closely resembles the future job. If it proves possible to simulate accurately the reality, the yield is a powerful instrument for evaluation. A disadvantage of this instrument is that more experienced candidates may be favoured above those with more talents. Therefore, the assessment centre method makes frequent use of simulated job situations: so-called simulation exercises. In Table 2 the uses of the different types of exercise are listed by percentage (Thornton and Byham, 1982). This list was developed from a review of approximately 500 centres with which the authors have been associated. To be more accurate, it must be stated that the usage of psychological tests is very much larger in the United Kingdom and Benelux countries than in the United States.

The exercises

The in-basket (in-tray)   The exercise that is used most is the in-basket. It is an individual exercise in which the participant is provided with a basket or file containing letters, memos, and other written notes, on the basis of which he or she needs to assess particular problem situations and make a number of decisions to solve the problems involved in a limited time. The problems are true-to-life simulations of everyday job practice. The in-basket may be used to elicit a candidate's management skills, such as planning, organization, written communication skill, and decisiveness. The evaluation of the results is the work of experts, so the results of this exercise are rated by experienced and trained assessors. Next, the assessor writes a report on the candidate's performance. It is often advisable to arrange for interview with the candidate after the assignment has been completed: such interview leads to a better understanding of the candidate's method of handling the different exercise items and greatly contributes to the acceptance of the findings by the candidate. The validity of the in-basket has been studied on numerous occasions (Crooks, 1968; Frederiksen, 1962, 1966).

Management game   A management game is excellently suited for simulation. These games can be designed to reflect the organization's own background. Thus, the candidates may be given the assignment to sell particular products or draw up a policy plan, in cooperation with other members of the group or with the assessors themselves. Differences in professional experience within the group should be avoided. As a management game is fairly complex and extensive it is most effectively used in training situations and less suitable in assessment situations.

Criteria-based interviewing   The interview is conducted on the basis of a list of behavioural criteria. The interviewer puts specific questions to the participant to elicit information about a number of behavioural criteria that are relevant to the job in question.

This type of interviewing must not be confused with so-called 'situational interviews'. One of the major things you would *not* do is to put questions in a form like 'what would you do if . . .?' These questions are theoretical and will give you theoretical answers: 'if I were my boss, I would . . .'. The following questions are examples of wrong questions because they are either leading questions or theoretical questions.

'I suppose you enjoyed working in sales, didn't you?'
'I guess you left that job because you needed more money?'
'What makes you think you can sell?'
'Are you well organized?'

Better questions are those which are non-leading behavioural questions. Examples are:

'What was your biggest decision within the last two months?'
'What did you do when you discovered he was not capable of handling
that person?'
'Tell me about the largest sale you made and how you did it.'

These questions may also relate to the participant's biographical criteria,
such as education, work experience, interests, career progress, ambitions
and aspirations. Such an interview can also be used effectively if a pre-
selection of candidates (those who will and those who will not be invited
to attend an assessment centre meeting) is desired.

Leaderless group discussions There are different types of
leaderless group discussions: those with and those without assigned roles.
On some occasions the participants are asked to solve a number of
problems in playing the part of a consultant; at other times each participant is assigned an individual role and together they must carry out a
specific task. The latter type of group discussion will inevitably call up
more emotions and tension than is the case in group discussions in which
the participants meet informally and which lack the element of competition.

The use of group discussions in which the participants are really competing with each other has frequently been criticized in the Netherlands.
Roe and Daniels (1984) are right in stating that in view of the validity of
the decisions it is fully justified to incorporate this type of exercise in the
assessment programme if successful performance of a particular job
requires the incumbent to act effectively in groups. For additional studies
on the subject the reader is referred to Hinrichs and Haanpera (1974,
1976).

Fact-finding exercises In a fact-finding exercise the participant is
supplied with general information, for example relating to the fact that a
particular employee has been fired. The participant must question a role
player who is well informed and try to come to a judgement about the
correctness of the decision taken in the past, after which he or she has to
affirm or revoke it. No matter what his or her personal decision, it will
subsequently be challenged by the role player. This exercise is an instrument to test the participant's listening skill, stress tolerance, judgement
and problem analysis skill (Pigors and Pigors, 1961).

Analysis exercises In these exercises complex situations and information must be analysed and different alternatives studied. Furthermore,
participants must communicate the findings of their analysis to an
assessor or a group of colleagues by means of a presentation. Here again,
it is possible to simulate situations that occur in real job practice. The
exercise is often followed by a group discussion. In these exercises the
major stress is on analysis and interpretation of written material: stress

which is usually covered less comprehensively in the exercise types mentioned before.

Interview simulation   Candidates are placed in an interview situation in which they are expected to play a specific role, for example that of customer complaint manager, or supervisor or foreman. The opponent is a trained and previously instructed role player. Behaviour relevant to dimensions such as interpersonal skill, behavioural flexibility, and listening skill will be elicited in the course of the exercise.

The validity of assessment exercises

Designing good exercises and simulations that meet the demands is a time-consuming and complex activity. Many times a particular exercise is used without considering if that exercise really does what it ought to do, that is elicit job-relevant behaviour. In this connection it is essential that not only the job activity, but also the practical situation be simulated. Using a group exercise just because it seems a nice thing to do is a wrong approach. A group exercise should only be used if performing in groups constitutes an essential part of the job.

Similarly, a group discussion is not necessarily always required as an exercise in an assessment programme for managers, since it should be borne in mind that many managers seldom find themselves acting in group situations, but most frequently maintain relationships on a person-to-person basis. Therefore, the stress in the assessment programme should be on that type of interaction.

A mistake that is frequently made when designing an exercise is that it proves either too easy or too difficult. The level of the exercise should correspond to the level of the job.

The criterion 'planning and organization' is important both for the job of sales manager and for the job of salesman, but for different reasons: the salesman needs planning and organization skills primarily because he must be able to schedule his sales calls and because he must make his personal list of priorities, whereas the sales manager needs his planning and organization skills primarily to make strategic plans and to set priorities both for his own activities and for those of his subordinates. The difference in level must be reflected in the exercise. Besides, they must be constructed in such a way that every candidate has an equal chance and that company candidates, or candidates who have experience in the type of business, will not be at an advantage over candidates who do not yet know the ins and outs of the organization.

Content validity

One bit of evidence supporting the content validity of assessment centres is provided in a unique study originally conducted by Byham and Byham (1976) and recently updated with new data. Over 1000 assessment reports

Table 3 *Evidence of dimensions observable in several assessment exercises*

Job-related dimensions	Business game	In-basket and interview	Leaderless group discussion (assigned roles)	Leaderless group discussion (non-assigned roles)	Analysis	Scheduling	Background interview	Fact-finding and decision making	Interview simulation	Written presentation	Analysis/oral presentation
1 Impact	√		√	√			√		√		*
2 Oral communication skill		√	*	*			√		*		*
3 Oral presentation skill		*	*							*	*
4 Written communication skill										×	
5 Creativity		√			×		√				
6 Tolerance for stress					×ᵃ	×ᵃ			√ᵇ		
7 Work standards					×						
8 Leadership	√		√	*	√		√	√	*		*
9 Persuasive sales ability			√	*			√		×	×	
10 Sensitivity		*	√					√	√		
11 Behavioral flexibility	×		√						√		
12 Tenacity			√	×	√		√	√	×		
13 Risk taking	√	√		×			√			×	
14 Initiative	√	*	√	*			*		×		√
15 Independence		√					√	×	×	×	

Table 3 *contd.*

16 Planning and organizing	✓	*	×		✓		×	
17 Delegation		*		*	✓		×	
18 Management control		*			✓			
19 Analysis	✓	*	*		✓	*	✓	×
20 Judgement		*	*	*	✓	*	✓	*
21 Decisiveness		*	*		×	*	✓	*
22 Development of subordinates		×			✓		×	×
23 Adaptability	✓				✓			
24 Technical translation		×	×				*	✓
25 Organizational sensitivity		×	×		✓		×	×

Source: 'Effectiveness of Assessment Center Exercises in Producing Behavior' by R.N. Byham and W.C. Byham Assessment & Development. March 1976 9–10 Copyright 1976 by Development Dimensions International. Reprinted by permission.

a Time stress
b interpersonal stress
* observed in 95% of the exercises.
✓ observed in 90% of exercises.
× observed in 90% of certain exercises in category, but not all exercises.

in twelve large companies were examined to identify the number of assessors who were able to make a judgement of the participants' skill levels on the basis of behaviour observed relevant to each of 25 dimensions. In these programmes the assessors were instructed not to rate the dimension if insufficient behaviour was observed. Therefore, the assessment reports contain evidence of whether or not the exercise elicited adequate behaviour relevant to the dimensions. Table 3 presents the findings. A checkmark (ν) means the dimension was observable at least 90 per cent of the time it was sought, a star (*) means the dimension was observable at least 95 per cent of the time and ($\times$) means the dimension was observable at least 90 per cent of the time it was sought, but in only some of the exercises in the category.

Validity and cost effectiveness

Hardly any other psychological tool except tests of aptitude has a research basis as firm as the assessment centre methodology.

In 1970 the assessment centre method was unique in that extensive research had established its validity before it came into popular use. The assessment centre method, in its modern form, came into existence as a result of the AT&T Management Progress Study (Bray et al., 1974). In this study, which began in the late 1950s, individuals entering management positions in Bell Telephone operating companies were assessed and, from then on, their careers were followed up. The study was unusual in that it was pure research. Neither the individuals assessed nor their bosses were given information about their performance in the centre. Nor was this information in any way allowed to affect participants' careers. Participants were assessed soon after they entered management as new college recruits or after being promoted from the ranks. In 1970 a *Harvard Business Review* article presented the results from the first eight years of the study (Byham, 1970).

Additional data from this landmark study are now available. Not only have researchers followed participant advancement over the ensuing years, but a second assessment was conducted eight years after the first (Bray and Howard, 1983). Table 4 shows the validity of both assessment predictions. The criterion used was advancement to the fourth level of management in a seven-level hierarchy. The eight-year prediction is more valid – an expected finding since most individuals would have begun to consolidate their management skills after eight years in management. Yet the original assessment ratings were still valid – even after 20 years. Thornton and Byham (1982) reviewed 29 studies of the validity of assessment centre methodology. The authors found more support for the assessment centre method than for other selection methods, while still lamenting the fact that most of the studies were done by a few large organizations (AT&T, GE, IBM, SOHIO, Sears). In 1985 Thornton and his associates at Colorado State University processed 220 validity coefficients from 50

Table 4 *Ratings at original assessment and eight years later and management level attained at year 20*

	Attained fourth level	
Original assessment rating of potential	N	
Predicted to achieve fourth level or higher	25	60%
Predicted to achieve third level	23	25%
Predicted to remain below third level	89	21%
	137	
Eight-year assessment rating of potential	N	
Predicted to achieve fourth level or higher	30	73%
Predicted to achieve third level	29	38%
Predicted to remain below third level	76	12%
	135	

studies using meta-analysis. They estimated the method's validity at 0.37 (Gaugler et al., 1987). Working independently of Thornton, Cascio and Ramos (1984) arrived at the same figure (0.37) in studying the validity of first-level assessment centres in an operating company of the Bell system. Cascio and Ramos's main interest, however, was to measure the 'bottom-line impact' of promotion decisions based on assessment centre information and decisions based on criteria extracted from other methods.

To determine the dollar impact of assessment centres, Cascio needed more than validity information; he needed cost data (fully loaded costs of the assessment process), plus job performance data expressed in dollars. Over a four-year period he developed a simple methodology for expressing in dollar terms the job-performance levels of managers. Using information provided by more than 700 line managers, Cascio combined data on the validity and cost of the assessment centre with the dollar-valued job performance of first-level managers. With these data, he produced an estimate of the organization's net gain in dollars resulting from the use of assessment centre information in the promotion process. Over a four-year period, the gain to the company in terms of improved job performance of new managers was estimated at $13.4 million, or approximately $2700 each year for each of the 1100 people promoted into first-level management jobs.

Starting up an assessment centre

Basically, the assessment centre method is a very systematic and step-by-step approach (see Figure 1), and that is just the reason why it is so widely applicable. Hereafter each phase will be discussed briefly and commented upon.

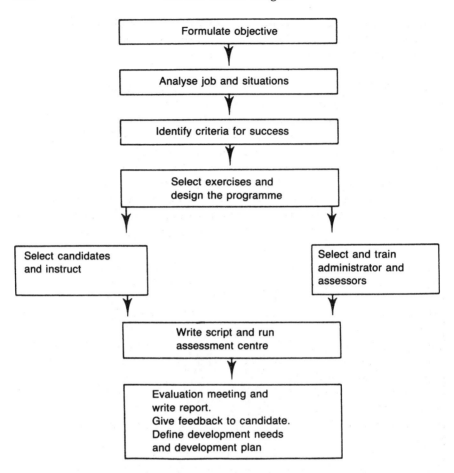

Figure 1   *Starting up an assessment centre: a step-by-step approach*

Inventory phase

Formulate objective   For what purpose is the assessment centre method going to be used: Selection? Management development? Evaluation? Education and training? Each objective calls for its own specific approach.

Introducing the assessment centre method should not be an aim in itself, but a *means* to handle certain processes in the organization more effectively and more efficiently. We do not intend to force an open door but we know from experience that only too frequently organizations are eager to introduce assessment centres because of the novelty, without applying the technique in the way that is best within the organization concerned. As a matter of fact there is no standard approach: every organization requires a specific approach that depends on the formulated objective. For example, an assessment programme for the purpose of selecting from large groups of applicants the best candidates for certain vacancies will be quite different from a programme designed to establish the potential of the current intermediate staff.

Job analysis and criteria   Some questions are crucial to this phase – which target group is involved: salespersons, trainees, specialists, executives? What elements are the jobs concerned made up of, and what are the essential characteristics of each job? About which dimension does the assessor wish to gather information: leadership skill, ability to organize, planning skill, communication skill or stress tolerance? Whether it be a matter of selection of external candidates or evaluation of internal candidates within the framework of management development and promotion, in both cases the criteria on which the candidates are assessed should be chosen in such a way that the crucial job elements may be traced back to them.

The main objective of personal selection and placement is to predict a person's behaviour in a new job. To be able to do so it is a prerequisite that the job in question is understood in all its detail and that the behavioural patterns, that must be shown by the candidate in order to be able to perform his or her future job successfully, are explicitly known. Therefore, when people are evaluated for the purpose of selection and promotion, job analysis should be considered as an essential component of the package of methods to be used. This means that the job analysis should lead to a sound understanding of what I would like to call 'job-related behaviour'. In the description of this behaviour I am concerned with finding out what kind of behaviour is required in any specific work situation.

Often there is confusion about the difference between the criteria that need to be met for successful job performance and the specific 'requirements' that need to be met by the candidate. Criteria are accurate descriptions of the expectations that an organization has regarding a candidate in terms of behaviour, whereas many so-called 'job-requirements' only point in the direction of a criterion. An organization that only wants candidates with a complete academic training presumably looks for such specific recruits not just because it values an academic degree – preferably the highest possible – but primarily because it is interested in criteria such as 'ability to learn' and 'specialist knowledge'.

That a candidate has a college degree is information that may be relevant to these criteria, but no more than that. For most sales positions organizations are not really that much concerned about the length and range of experience that candidates can demonstrate, but basically just want to know if they can sell. Experience from working as a salesperson may be an indication that a person really can sell, but does not necessarily mean that he or she will be able to do so in practice. In view of the above it may be concluded that job requirements should be used only if they are indispensable or if they are needed to restrict the number of applicants,

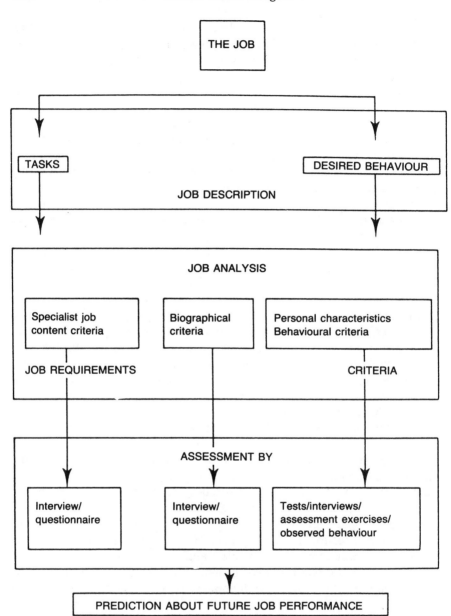

Figure 2 *Derivation of job requirements and behavioural criteria*

and that criteria should always be used as much as possible to describe the job.

Figure 2 shows the manner in which the behavioural criteria and the job requirements are derived from the job in question. The job is divided into tasks (job description): from these tasks different job requirements are derived from the job in question. The desired behaviour, however, leads us to which behavioural criteria are important for success. Finally, various assessment instruments are selected to elicit the behaviours related to each single behavioural criterion.

In summary, the following four 'conditions' related to proper job analysis need to be emphasized:

The method used to analyse the job and identify the criteria must be well elaborated.
The job analysis and criteria identification must have a fixed place in the entire selection or assessment procedure.
The criteria must be defined clearly and unambiguously.
There must be an objective and controllable method of determining the order of importance of the criteria.

Making the system operational

Select exercises and design the programme

Which exercises will be used and why? The exercises to be used in an assessment programme must simulate elements of the future job. They must resemble the actual job practice, that is the problems and situations portrayed in the exercises must be of the same kind, of the same complexity and level of difficulty as encountered in the daily routine of that job.

The exercises are designed to elicit 'job-related behaviour'. This means first of all that the criteria on which the exercises are based should be directly derived from the job and contain all crucial and common elements of the job; secondly, that the exercises must simulate the most important and common job aspects; and, thirdly, that the exercises are constructed in such a way that they are actually able to evoke the desired behaviour, to enable the assessors to make statements on the candidate's behaviour concerning the criteria involved.

Select and train the administrator and the assessors

Which members of management will be assessing? How do you learn to assess purely on the basis of facts (what people do and say) and not on the basis of prejudice and presumptions? Who takes care of the coordination of the entire assessment process? Who controls the data, provides for feedback to the candidates and designs the programme? Most organizations using the assessment centre method employ their own managers as assessors of the candidates. Normally they are managers who work two levels higher up in the organizational hierarchy than the level of the job that the candidates are considered for.

Involving the immediate superior as an assessor is not recommended, as this might pose a threat to both parties. It is important, though, that the assessors are familiar with the job in question. As a rule, there is one assessor for every two candidates.

Sometimes, though, external consultants and psychologists are asked to act as assessors. This is often done when the job considered is top level or when the organization is too small to supply enough trained assessors of its own. Also, when an organization starts working with the assessment centre method for the first time, it will usually be dependent on outside assessment experts. Personnel departments should play a major role in the entire assessment centre process. In most cases, someone from the department is put in charge of the coordination and supervision of the process. From the very moment that the organization decides to start up an assessment programme to the final evaluation together with the candidates, this internal administrator supervises the assessment process. He or she gives advice on the preparation of job analysis and the selection of instruments; takes part in the pre-selection of the candidates; trains, occasionally together with other people, the assessors; controls and clusters all information and provides for follow-up. He or she supervises the final evaluation made by the assessors.

The assessors must receive adequate and thorough training in assessing the candidates. This is an item in the process that should really not be underestimated, because (in combination with the criteria and the exercises) it is a determining factor for the success of the programme. Training the assessor should usually taken from three to five days. Training topics are: What is the aim of the intended programme? Which criteria do we select and why? and so on. The assessors are also asked to participate in all the exercises that will be used in the assessment programme. The results of their participation will be discussed in detail with the trainer.

Observing behaviour, evaluating it in relation to the criteria, writing reports and arriving at the final judgement (which includes establishing a candidate's training needs), are all essential elements of the assessor training.

The assessors must be made familiar with interview techniques and with eliciting behaviour by means of role play exercises. To be proficient in both, the assessor must first of all know the criteria. These criteria must be based on a thorough job analysis which the assessor understands and finds unambiguous. The assessor must learn which behaviour is related to which criterion, and become skilful in observing the often very subtle differences.

Pure observation, without any immediate judgement, is extremely difficult. In translating behaviour into criteria (classification) it is of the utmost importance that the assessor has a clear understanding of the criteria involved. This is the reason why accurate definition of the criteria is of vital importance.

Select and instruct the candidates   Who will be considered for participation in the assessment centre programme? Who will be asked to attend the meeting on how to conduct the pre-selection? Good pre-selection of the candidates for participation in the assessment centre programme is a primary concern. Here again, depending on the aim of the assessment programme, different problems may occur. The problems arising when the assessment method is used for the selection of external candidates are completely different from the problems accompanying use of the method for career planning, which involves internal candidates only.

In the case of external candidates, the problems are relatively limited after the pre-selection. It is possible to arrive at a first selection on the basis of reviewing of the application letters, review of the candidate's curriculum vitae and a first round of interviews. Using a structured criteria-based interview proves to be very helpful at this stage. During the pre-selection of internal candidates a number of problems may arise.

In fact judgements made by the direct superior count heavily in the decision regarding who is going to be considered for a specific development programme or for a certain promotion. It will be obvious that the superior's judgement is based on a mixture of facts, subjective impressions, vague feelings and prejudices.

A primary concern in the pre-selection of internal candidates must be to avoid a person being given the life-long label of either unsuitable for a management position or 'crown prince'. Make sure that the candidates who, at some point in the process, are no longer considered for participation in an assessment meeting or for promotion, are at any rate considered for participation in a different programme.

A psychological test or structured interview may be part of the pre-selection. More and more frequently some types of self-selection are used, in which potential candidates are helped to arrive at their own decision on whether or not they will participate in an assessment programme. Afterwards they may again be considered for an assessment programme.

Implementation

Prepare script for the assessment centre   How will the assessment programme be implemented? How long will it be? Where will it be held? When will the meeting be? After the job has been analysed, when the exercises to be used have been selected, the number of candidates participating is known and an estimate has been made of the overall time involved, it is possible to prepare a script or programme. This script contains information on the day's timetable, the work programme, interviews and feedback discussions, who should be where at what time, and so on. It also contains information about the candidates, the job under consideration, the criteria, and the exercises. It may sometimes be necessary for the assessors to take part in a short refresher course, so that, among other things, they can study and go over the observation forms and evaluation forms once again and can brush up their knowledge and skills required for successful performance of their roles as assessors.

Table 5   *Example of an assessment centre programme*

Programme Day 1	
08.30 a.m.	Reception of candidates + coffee + checking into hotel
09.00 a.m.	General introduction
09.30 a.m.	Participants prepare for in-basket
11.30 a.m.	Participants fill in PEF (participant evaluation form) on in-basket
11.45 a.m.	Participants take part in group tests
	Assessors prepare for in-basket interview
12.45 p.m.	Joint lunch
1.30 p.m.	Participant 1 is interviewed on IB by team AB
	Participant 3 is interviewed on IB by team CD
	Participant 5 is interviewed on IB by team EF
	Participant 7 is interviewed on IB by team GH
	Participant 9 is interviewed on IB by team IJ
	Participant 2 is interviewed by psychologist X
	Participant 8 is interviewed by psychologist Y
2.30 p.m.	Participant 4 is interviewed by psychologist X
	Participant 7 is interviewed by psychologist Y
3.30 p.m.	Participant 3 is interviewed by psychologist X
	Participant 2 is interviewed on IB by team BA
	Participant 4 is interviewed on IB by team DC
	Participant 6 is interviewed on IB by team FE
	Participant 8 is interviewed on IB by team HG
4.10 p.m.	Participant 1 prepares for group discussion
4.30 p.m.	Participant 1 is interviewed by psychologist X
5.10 p.m.	Participants 2 to 9 prepare for group discussion
5.30 p.m.	Participants 1 to 4 conduct group discussion
	Assessors AB and IJ
	Participants 5 to 9 conduct group discussion
	Assessors CD, EF and GH

Programme Day 2	
08.30 a.m.	Participant 2 takes part in interview simulation with team GH
	Participant 4 takes part in interview simulation with team IJ
	Participant 6 takes part in interview simulation with team AB
	Participant 8 takes part in interview simulation with team CD
	Participant 5 is interviewed by psychologist X
09.30 a.m.	Participant 1 takes part in interview simulation with team HG
	Participant 3 takes part in interview simulation with team JI
	Participant 5 takes part in interview simulation with team BA
	Participant 7 takes part in interview simulation with team DC
	Participant 9 takes part in interview simulation with team FE
	Participant 6 is interviewed by psychologist X
10.30 a.m.	Participant 2 takes part in fact-finding with team EF
	Participant 4 takes part in fact-finding with team GH
	Participant 6 takes part in fact-finding with team IJ
	Participant 8 takes part in fact-finding with team AB
	Participant 9 is interviewed by psychologist X
11.30 a.m.	Participant 1 takes part in fact finding with team FE
	Participant 3 takes part in fact finding with team HG
	Participant 5 takes part in fact finding with team JI
	Participant 7 takes part in fact finding with team BA
	Participant 9 takes part in fact finding with team DC
12.45 p.m.	Debriefing and lunch
3.00 p.m.	Assessors meet for evaluation discussion
8.00 p.m.	Closing

Table 5 presents an example of such a script. The choice of accommodation depends on the duration of the assessment centre programme, which may vary from one up to three days. If the session stretches over several days, it will usually be a hotel or conference facilities, although it is not strictly necessary to meet in a place completely secluded from the outside world. On the contrary, the accommodation chosen for an assessment programme should be no different from the place commonly used for training courses.

Evaluation

Final judgement and report writing
How is a joint final decision reached and how is it reported to the candidates and the management? What happens with the information? After all the candidates have completed the exercises, they will be invited to a closing interview. They are informed then about the criteria on which they were assessed and why specific exercises had to be done. They are also told about the manner of report writing and about the time when the individual feedback discussions will take place. During this closing discussion the candidates have the opportunity to express their feelings and ideas about the programme.

All information gathered during the assessment meeting – both from the observations made by the different assessors and from the analysis of the handling of/approach to individual exercises – is clustered and must result in a unanimous final judgement. This final judgement is not necessarily, nor need it be, equivalent to the average of the judgement of the individual assessors. The administrator clusters all information and conducts the discussion with the assessors. This discussion is very useful as it provides an opportunity to gain a good understanding of the weaknesses and strengths of each candidate. Weighing the different judgements against each other is of great importance, for certain criteria may be so crucial that a good score on one of these is an absolute prerequisite, if the candidate is to be considered for the specific job.

The evaluation discussion follows some simple rules:

each individual participant will be discussed;
no comparisons made between participants;
criterion by criterion;
through all exercises;
no average scoring but evaluation based on behavioural evidence.

After the evaluation meeting has been concluded and once the final judgement of each candidate is known to the assessors and the administrator, the latter can start writing the final reports. In each report the candidate's weaknesses and strengths are indicated in a manner readily understandable by the candidate, all based on actually demonstrated behaviour and familiar situations. Afterwards the administrator discusses the report with the candidate. The report may include suggestions for (further) development. Some weaknesses may be such that it will be relatively easy to reach the desired level of adequate behaviour on these dimensions; others may be of a structured nature and not amended so easily.

Careful follow-up and the presentation of alternative development opportunities and a realistic picture of the candidate's further career may ensure that the candidate does not feel badly about the assessment programme. Good follow-up is just as important as good report writing. Follow-up should be a task both for personnel and for management. In particular, management should not neglect its responsibilities in this respect.

Designing a well-balanced system

Common errors

The assessment centre method is used more and more frequently and successfully in different organizations and different forms. The strength of the method lies in the fact that it can always be tailored to the specific purpose envisaged by the organization. If the errors that are made before the actual assessment process starts are not counted, three errors are left that are commonly made in applying the assessment centre method:

1 The assessment centre method is not regarded as an element of a complete package of methods, but as an alternative to other techniques, such as psychological tests or interviews.
2 The criteria on which the evaluations are based are inadequately justified, because in analysing the job in question there has been too little attention to the search for the crucial elements.
3 The exercises used are insufficiently related to the crucial job elements, so that it is impossible to give reliable predictions about future job performance.

In order to establish a well-balanced selection and promotion system it is necessary to base it on the criteria derived from the job. In such a system every method of evaluation will contribute to the overall evaluation.

It will be apparent from Table 6 that there is little sense in holding the same interview more than once, which is often the case. In fact the different general interviews should be replaced by more specific interviews and simulations. In Table 6 an example is given of such a programme containing only one general interview, the other interviews having been replaced by alternative evaluation methods. After all, these alternative methods do not take more assessor time than the traditional interviews did, but because they have been specifically designed to elicit behaviour relevant to certain criteria, they contribute more to the overall evaluation.

Table 6 *Example of a selection or evaluation programme*

Criteria	Structured general interview	Criteria-based interview	Interview simulation	In-basket + interview	Psychological test
				Methods	
Biographical criteria	X				X
(Professional) training	X				X
Practical experience	X				X
Expert knowledge	X				X
Planning and organization			(X)	X	
Delegation					X
Problem analysis			X	X	X
Judgement			X	X	X
Persuasion	(X)		X		
Listening	X		X		X
Flexibility		X			X
Cooperation		X			X
Stress tolerance		X	X	X	X
Achievement motivation		X		X	X
Initiative		X	X	X	
Time	1 hour	1 hour depending on number of criteria	30 minutes	2 hours	depending on number of tests and on whether or not accompanied by interview with psychologist

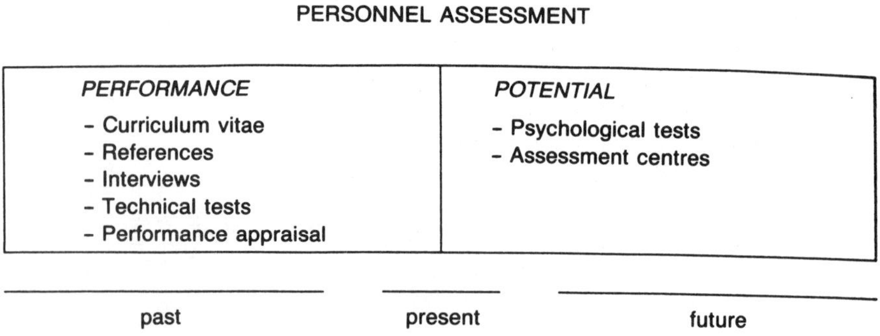

PERSONNEL ASSESSMENT

PERFORMANCE	POTENTIAL
– Curriculum vitae	– Psychological tests
– References	– Assessment centres
– Interviews	
– Technical tests	
– Performance appraisal	

past	present	future

Figure 3   *The assessment centre method as an element of a total process*

So each assessment technique helps to gather the information needed for final evaluation.

Part of a total process

Assessment exercises provide information on specific criteria; interviews, tests and performance appraisals provide information on yet other criteria. It is highly recommended, though, to plan the system in such a way that the same criteria may be observed for assessment on several occasions and to let various persons give their statements about the same set of criteria. This adds to the strength of the selection and promotion system, because there is an opportunity to compare opposite opinions with each other.

If the demands of the job for which the candidates are being assessed are different from those pertaining to the candidates' present positions, the assessment centre method can be very helpful, as the method is eminently suited for the evaluation of potential, that is future capacities. The same holds for psychological tests. This is not the case with methods that are mainly used to evaluate a person's capacities as made explicit in the past, that is to evaluate past job performance and achievements (see Figure 3).

Assessment centres for development

The most widely known application of the assessment centre method is for the selection of managers. Especially in the United States the method has always been used almost exclusively as an instrument in the selection of management personnel (Moses and Byham, 1977), and only recently has it come to be used for management development as well. However, in the United Kingdom and the Benelux countries the method is used mainly as support in the areas of management development, career planning and identification of potential.

The major reason for this may be found in the fact that the assessment centre method provides management with a system and language which allow better identification of the individual needs of employees. The system also enables management to guide and monitor more effectively the individual employee's development.

Basically three different types of programme are distinguished:

assessment centres with outside consultants/assessors;
assessment centres with inside assessors;
assessment centres with self-assessment.

Outside assessors

A number of organizations are using assessment centre programmes in which outside consultants act as independent assessors to the organization. They are usually one- or two-day assessment programmes on an individual basis and are used to obtain a comprehensive picture of the candidate by means of a mix of instruments (tests, simulations, interviews). The positions concerned are usually high-level positions within the organization and for political or practical reasons it is impossible to use inside assessors. The result of this type of comprehensive assessment centre is an overview of individual development needs. This overview will then be discussed with the human resource development manager and translated into an individual development plan. This development plan is more than just an enumeration and description of training courses, task forces and special assignments.

Inside assessors

Assessment centres with inside assessors are frequently used within larger organizations in order to improve the operation of their succession plans. For such organizations it is essential that they can make accurate judgements about the extent of the 'gap' between the individual's present job performance and future job requirements. The system is not only designed to identify future potential, but also creates opportunities for specific development.

In point of design, this type of assessment centre closely resembles the centres for selection purposes. The main difference is that in assessment centres with inside assessors the candidates are already employed in the organization and are assessed in view of a career rather than because they are considered for a specific position. Such a centre calls for a different choice of criteria and exercises.

Peer assessors

The third type involves self-assessment or peer-assessment. In such an assessment centre programme the assessees and assessors are the same persons. At a preliminary stage each candidate analyses his or her job. This analysis is then discussed with the candidate's manager. Next, the assessor takes part in an assessment centre programme. This centre will be videotaped from beginning to end. In the days following the centre the participants receive a 'crash course' assessor training that teaches them to view critically their own videotapes. They are also asked to look at videotapes made of a number of peers and provide feedback to each of these peers. On the basis of this self-assessment and peer assessment, the candidate can now draw up an analysis of his or her personal strengths and weaknesses and formulate a personal development plan. Finally, the candidate and his or her manager will meet to discuss this plan.

This type of programme, of which various versions are known to exist, proves to have a very strong effect. In particular, the 'peer rating' component seems a major influence.

Development: a continuous process of assessment and appraisal

Any development plan or management development process is doomed to fail if management does not commit itself. Several studies have led to the conclusion that training in itself seldom results in changes in behaviour unless there is some sort of reinforcement by management.

If follow-up is not included as part of the development assessment centre programme, the development character of the programme will soon lose its credibility.

Table 7 shows the results of a study by Dulewicz (1985) in which he describes the changes over time in attitudes towards a specific assessment programme called IMPACT (Identification of Management Potential and Counselling Techniques). Around three years after the event, management investigated development recommendations which had not been implemented and took action wherever appropriate.

From the foregoing it may be concluded that an effective system for human resource development should meet a number of primary conditions:

1 As soon as a person is employed by the organization, a specific development plan and introduction programme should be drawn up, both being based on a thorough analysis of the candidate's relative strengths and weaknesses in view of his or her future career.
2 The development plan must be part of the performance assessment and appraisal system within the organization.
3 Managers must be asked to perform different roles, that is of planner and controller, of mentor and of assessor/appraiser. They should be trained in order to be able to perform these roles successfully.
4 Development of employees should be reinforced positively:

Table 7 *Specific attitudes to IMPACT: debriefing and follow-up*

	Highly favourable or favourable	Highly unfavourable or unfavourable
1 Assessments of my performance were accurate		
(immediate survey)	86	2
(follow-up survey)	72	5
2 Feedback information will be/has been valuable for my personal development		
(immediate survey)	75	5
(follow-up survey)	56	20
3 Feedback recommendations on career planning and development will be/have been valuable		
(immediate survey)	83	4
(follow-up survey)	34	31
4 My career will benefit/has benefited from attendance		
(immediate survey)	65	6
(follow-up survey)	36	34
5 In future my career will benefit from attendance		
(follow-up survey)	41	24

(a) towards the employee so that he or she takes initiatives to develop himself/herself (self-motivation and self-assessment);

(b) towards the superior so that he or she will create the conditions that allow the employee to develop and to ensure the superior's mentorship to the employee;

(c) towards the human resource development manager, so that he or she will provide for the appropriate means and resources for development and training.

Advantages and problems

On the basis of practical experience and extensive research the assessment centre method can be said to have the following advantages:

More accurate evaluation The assessment centre method results in more accurate and sharper selection and evaluation of employees, which means that on fewer occasions will the wrong decisions be made with respect to promotion and placement.

More specific training A more clearly criteria-based diagnosis enables more specific training: no investment in people who will not produce a profit after all and no investment in training which is too general.

More effective use of human resources Use of the assessment centre method results in reduced job turnover caused by poor performance or by identifying the presence of potential too late.

More effective management Use of the assessment centre method

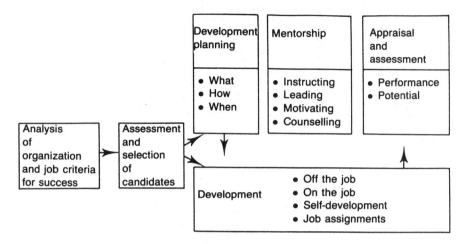

Figure 4   *The derivation of criteria and job requirements*

leads to a better understanding of, and insight into, employee performance, which allows for more effective and more efficient steering by
management. In the assessment centre method managers are trained to
assess people. As a result, their skill in assessing people will improve and
they will feel more strongly involved in the 'people' aspects of their job.
The assessment centre method endows management with the responsibility
for the decisions regarding personal placement, transfers and promotion.
The idea behind it is that the manager possesses a good insight into, and
wide knowledge of, the job concerned, knows how it should be performed, and that the final responsibility for job performance lies with the
manager.

More effective communication   The assessment centre method provides
the organization with a common language for assessment purposes; line
management, and personnel and organization departments will understand each other better.

Stimulation of development   The assessment centre method makes it
easier to give feedback and to stimulate training. Employees understand
what is meant and will more readily accept the message. The assessment
centre method ensures that employees assume part of the responsibility
for their personal development, stimulating self-development through
acceptance. The assessment centre method is more objective and more
just, and therefore the employee is more likely to accept its results. The
candidates can get a feeling of what it is like to perform the job that they
are considered for. Because they take part in simulations they get a better
understanding of what will be expected of them in the future job and it
will be easier for them to make an accurate judgement about whether they
will be able to fulfil these expectations.

Change of organizational culture   The assessment centre method helps
organizations change their work style because the employees are taught to

work in a different manner; thus, the change may be from non-profit to profit-based work.

Again, based on practical experience and research I may mention as main problems:

Acceptance by management How do I convince management that it, and not personnel, is responsible for the assessment?

Fear of the unknown 'Assessment centre' as a term is very obscure: it erroneously calls up visions of large-scale procedures and tremendous costs.

Management time involved Because management time is condensed (in *one* day) the time involvement is made visible and, as a result, may be calculated.

Costs The initial costs of starting up the system are often relatively high: the costs of job analysis, training and simulation development weigh heavily upon the first project. The costs of wrong decisions are often difficult to visualize (money value of personnel). In weighing the costs against the profit there is too much focus on the short-term impact. The yield (cost saving) of properly functioning management is difficult to visualize.

Confusion with performance appraisal The assessment centre focuses primarily on future job behaviour. It is not concerned with appraisal of the candidates' job performance in the past, but with their potential to perform successfully in a future job.

Reactions to feedback By means of the assessment centre method it is possible to make fairly accurate statements about a candidate's weaknesses (development needs). If this knowledge is not used afterwards, for example by providing for a good training programme or coaching by the superior, the person involved will get frustrated.

Absence of policy The assessment centre method as a method is very balanced and as such fits in well with a properly formalized personnel policy. Many organizations are still stuck in the 'bulldozer' phase and are not yet ready for a subtle approach. Absence of innovative thinking in the field of human resources policy acts prohibitively.

References

Bray, D.W. and Howard, A. (1983) *The AT&T Longitudinal Studies of Managers. Longitudinal studies of adult psychological development*. The Guilford Press, New York.

Byham, R.N. and Byham, W.C. (1976) 'Effectiveness of assessment center exercises in producing behavior', *Assessment & Development*, 3(1): 9–10.

Byham, W.C. (1970) 'Assessment center for spotting future managers', *Harvard Business Review*, 48(4): 150–60, plus appendix.

Byham, W.C. (1987) 'Applying a systems approach to personnel activities', *Monograph IX* Development Dimensions International, Pittsburgh.

Cascio, W.F. and Ramos, R.A. (1984) 'Development and application of a new method for assessing job performance in behavioral/economic terms', *Journal of Applied Psychology*.

Crooks, L.A. (1968) 'Issues in the development and validation of in-basket exercises for specific objectives' (Research memo 68–23), Educational Testing Service, Princeton.

Dulewicz, S.V. (1985) 'Assessment Centres: Practical issues and research findings', *Human and Industrial Relations* (Supplement 17).

Frederiksen, N. (1962) 'Factors in in-basket performance', *Psychological Monographs*, 76(22, Whole No. 541).

Frederiksen, N. (1966) 'Validation of a simulation technique', *Organizational Behavior and Human Performance*, 1: 87–109.

Gaugler, B.B., Rosenthal, D.B., Thornton, III, G.C. and Bentson, C. (1987) *Journal of Applied Psychology Monograph: Meta-Analysis of Assessment Center Validity*, 72(3): 493–511.

Hinrichs, J.R. and Haanpera, S. (1974) 'A technical research report on management assessment in IBM World Trade Corporation' (Personnel Research Study, No 18), *IBM Europe*, March.

Hinrichs, J.R. and Haanpera, S. (1976) 'Reliability of measurement in situational exercises: An assessment of the assessment center method', *Personnel Psychology*, 29: 31–40.

Moses, J.L. and Byham, W.C. (eds) (1977) *Applying the Assessment Center Method*. Pergamon Press, New York.

Pigors, P. and Pigors, F. (1961) *Case Method in Human Relations: The incident process*. McGraw-Hill, New York.

Proot, J.R. and Dragstra, H. (1982) *Personeelsbeoordeling*. GITP, Nijmegen.

Roe, R.A. and Daniels, M.J.M. (1984) *Personeelbeoordeling, achtergrond en toepassing*. Van Gorcum, Assen.

Thornton III, G.C. and Byham, W.C. (1982) *Assessment Centers and Managerial Performance*. Academic Press, New York and London.

17

Strategic determinants of managerial labor markets: a career systems view

Jeffrey A. Sonnenfeld, Maury A. Peiperl and John P. Kotter

Executive staffing texts and research reports generally identify best-practice approaches to recruiting development, and exit (Schwab, 1982). The advice drawn from practitioners and researchers is frequently based on the experience of large firms with relatively similar strategic roles. The following two contrasting examples of leading firms in their industries present approaches that are most appropriate to their distinct strategies.

> 'Ten years together on Wall Street . . . is quite amazing' remarked the COO of Wasserstein Perella, the newest firm of merger and acquisition specialists in New York, speaking admiringly of Bruce Wasserstein and Joseph Perella, the company's CEO and chairman. The two recently led a defection of some nineteen investment bankers from First Boston Corp., whose M&A group they headed for that 'amazing' period. 'We expect stability', the COO went on to explain. 'But', he added, 'You're always going to have a superstar who comes with forty clients, who wants to join and you just can't resist. . . . There will always be that talent market around.' (Interview with George Hornig, COO of Wasserstein Perella, 3 November 1988)

The world's largest and most profitable transportation firm, United Parcel Service, provides a different perspective on executive staffing:

> *We Promote From Within.* Whenever possible, we fill managerial positions from our ranks. . . . We fill a vacancy from the outside only when we cannot locate one of our own people who has the capacity or . . . skills . . . which may be required.

This excerpt from the policy manual of this eighty-year-old company leaves no doubt that partnership between the firm and its employees is the cornerstone of its human resource policy. Thirty-nine percent of all full-time employees in 1987 had been with the firm ten years or more, and even people recently hired to fill new skills needs such as information

Reprinted by permission of John Wiley and Sons Inc. *Human Resource Management* 27(4) 1988: 369–88.

systems expressed similar sentiments: '. . . I love it and I won't leave', said one new employee, 'until either I die or they fire me' (Sonnenfeld and Lazo, 1987).

Wasserstein Perella and UPS are both thriving firms in high-stakes service industries, yet they employ very different career systems. In the former industry, people come and go in great numbers over short periods, and ten years can be the length of a career. In the latter, ten years is but a stage or two in an executive's development, in an internal labor market not subject to defections.

We propose to show that diverse approaches to executive staffing exist because the basic business strategies of industries differ. It is business strategy that drives executive labor markets and the career systems in which executive talent develops. By exploring the strategic aspects of executive labor markets, we can shed light on why radically different career systems can be equally effective in different firms. In addition, we will examine whether individual background and personality factors can be used to predict career system choice.

A careers systems typology

Previous research in human resource management has focused on descriptions of fragments of career systems, and has sometimes led to prescriptions for improving the practice of management. But the coordination of these pieces into an overall plan to support a firm's business strategy has not been addressed. The research lacks a theory of the firm as a career system (Sonnenfeld, 1988).

A career system is the set of policies and practices an organization uses to provide staff to meet its human resource requirements. Applying general systems theory to the flow of human resources, we would expect to see input, throughput, and output processes taking place. As an open system, a firm's labor supply is subject to external forces in the processes of input and output (entry and exit), and is internally interdependent among its components in the process of throughput (development) (Miller and Rice, 1967; Mayo, 1933; Barnard, 1938). We can thus combine entry and exit of staff into one dimension, which we will call *supply flow*, and contrast it with development of staff, which we will call *assignment flow*. These external and internal dimensions are not only a means of clustering general systems stages; they also derive from two prominent clusters in the careers literature (Sonnenfeld and Peiperl, 1988). The two dimensions provide us with a classification system for career systems, measured as follows (Sonnenfeld and Peiperl, 1988):

Supply flow may be primarily internal, in which case jobs are filled from the internal labor pool at all but the lowest levels, or it may be external, in which case the firm is at least as likely to hire talent from outside as it is to promote it from within at all levels. Strategically, firms which

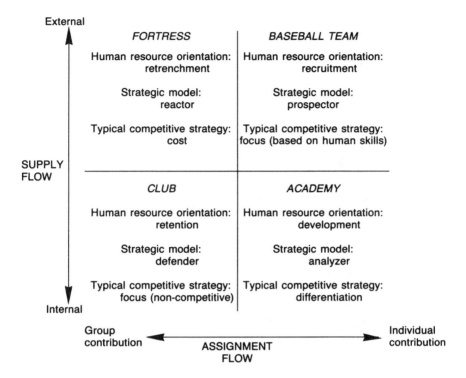

Figure 1   *A typology of career systems*

focus on internal supply flow tend to think of people as assets, with long-term developmental value, rather than costs, which carry an annual expense.

Assignment flow measures the basis on which people are assigned and promoted to new tasks (Rosenbaum, 1979, 1984; Kanter, 1977; Thurow, 1975). It may focus primarily on individual contribution to production or profits, or more on group contribution – support of others, loyalty, tenure, background, status, and the like. Strategically, firms which focus on individual contribution expect people to be continually producing value, while those which focus on group contribution see people as having intrinsic value.

Squaring these dimensions off against one another gives us the four-cell typology depicted in Figure 1. Key characteristics of each type of career system are shown in the figure. The metaphoric names given each of the cells are intended to evoke appropriate organizational imagery (Morgan, 1986). We will examine the human resource aspects of each system first; then we will discuss the competitive characteristics of industries typically exhibiting each of the career system types.

The four types of career systems have distinctly different features:

Academies are firms with internal labor markets, and reward systems based on individual contribution. They are characterized by stability and

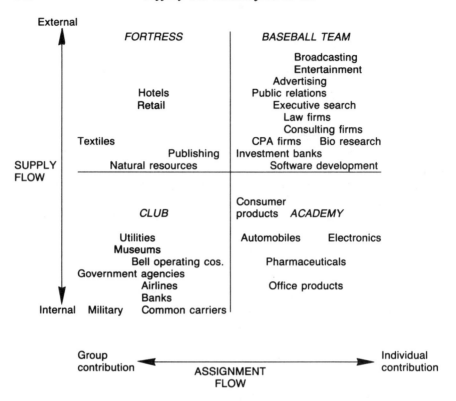

Figure 2   *Career systems – example industries*

low turnover. These companies hire from outside only at entry levels, and expect a large proportion of their employees to stay through to retirement. The key human resource function is development: these firms obtain needed talent, and create barriers to the exit of labor, by developing firm-specific skills and, in many cases, a deep-seated loyalty, in their employees. The internal labor market which develops then becomes the most efficient means of staffing (Chandler, 1962, 1977; Williamson, 1975). Tournaments of the sort described by Rosenbaum (1979, 1984) are often used to determine promotions. Figure 2 shows some industries which often follow the academy model, including consumer products, pharmaceuticals, office products, and electronics manufacturers.

Clubs also employ internal labor markets, but assign and promote more on the basis of group factors than on individual contribution. They are more concerned with seniority, commitment, status, and equal treatment of members than with innovation or profitability. The critical human resource function is retention of the membership: the 'maintenance stage' described by career theorists (Super et al., 1957; Hall and Nougaim, 1968) is the primary mode of operation. Industries containing clubs (Figure 2) include utilities, government agencies, insurance, the military, and, before deregulation, airlines, commercial banks, and common carriers.

Baseball Teams are open to external labor markets at all levels, and seek out those employees who will make the largest individual contributions. The major human resource function is recruitment, to keep the firm fully staffed and performing. Labor here behaves more along the lines of human capital theory, derived from neoclassical economics, which suggests that a labor market represents an open opportunity to all workers. Workers increase their own capital through education and training (Becker, 1964; Blaug, 1970; Mincer, 1974; Wachter, 1974), and through experience. People in baseball teams tend to identify more with their profession than with any firm. Like professional athletes, executives in these firms practice a kind of free agency. Baseball team industries (Figure 2) include accounting, law, and medicine, consulting, advertising and public relations, biotechnology research, software development, investment banking, and entertainment.

Fortresses are firms preoccupied with survival. As such, they cannot afford to focus on individual members, either by promising job security through internal labor markets or by rewarding only on the basis of individual contribution. Fortress recruitment may focus on generalists with turnaround skills, while exits may be based on business imperatives such as cutting product lines, rather than on a person's performance. In the fortress, the good of the many outweighs the good of the few, and group factors dominate in the choice of assignments, promotions, and layoffs. The primary emphasis is retrenchment. Fortress industries (Figure 2) include publishing, textiles, natural resources, and retailing.

A strategic parallel

Miles and Snow (1978) propose four strategic types of firm – 'analyzers', 'defenders', 'prospectors', and 'reactors' – which provide a counterpart to our career systems typology. Analyzers, although not the most innovative group, tend to excel in the delivery of newer products and services, paying close attention to the market. Their career systems must produce people who take moderate risks and strive for freshness while remaining loyal to the firm. They are stable but not entrenched in their market positions.

Defenders are firms with narrow product markets. Their leaders seek mastery over a narrowly defined organization. Their focus is on stability and reliability; thus they must develop loyal members committed to maintaining the institution over the long term.

Prospectors depend on product innovation and the creation of new markets. Their pioneering strategy is to identify new opportunities and emerging trends. They may sacrifice internal efficiency in their effort to stay innovative. Their career systems must continually recruit creative, independent, expert thinkers who will produce new ideas to pursue.

Reactors are firms which are buffeted by their markets. They either have little control over their vital resources or they consistently fail to predict key changes in the competitive system. Their career systems must focus on retrenchment and exit-related activities, as well as the limited recruitment of turnaround experts.

Systems and strategy combined

Combining the two analytical frameworks yields a strategic explanation of career systems:

The analyzer strategy of the academies leads them to survey their competitive context thoroughly and to develop all the necessary skills before deploying staff into new areas. At the same time, innovation in marketing and delivery of products and services keeps these firms in the competitive forefront of their industries, although they rarely lead with new product ideas. Rather, they are skilled at execution and offer better-quality products and services. Their competitive strategy is usually one of differentiation (Porter, 1980, 1985) through marketing and/or support. Human activity may not be the actual product of academies, but is often a source of advantage.

The defender strategy of the clubs reflects a preoccupation with holding their strategic ground instead of seeking newer or better product markets. External barriers to entry such as government regulation, large infrastructures, or general community support are often important. Many clubs, whether public or private, see themselves as public institutions with a service orientation which causes them to feel removed from the concerns of the marketplace. They pursue a focus strategy (Porter, 1980) of non-competition, fulfilling their niche function free from any external threat.

The prospector strategy of the baseball teams includes an implicit decision to 'buy' rather than 'make' talent. The uncertainty of their new product markets makes it impractical to invest in a 'vertically integrated' career system to meet projected talent needs; uncertainty as to demand and the changing technological aspects of the business will militate against this kind of development (Harrigan, 1985, 1986). Baseball teams are often professional service firms which pursue a focus strategy based on skills; analysis and/or human interaction are the value-adding activities. People more than processes confer competitive advantage in these businesses.

The reactor strategy of the fortresses also forces them to forgo 'making' talent. These firms not only 'buy' but often 'sell' labor into the outside market through layoffs, early retirements, and the like. Many fortresses are academies, clubs, or baseball teams which have failed at their mission. Some spend a long time as fortresses before recovering; others make quick and drastic changes in order to turn around; still others never leave fortress mode (Tushman et al., 1986). These semi-permanent fortresses often find themselves competing on the basis of cost (Porter, 1980), but without the means to attain a stable position. They are commodity or other highly competitive businesses in which markets are fragmented or experience large swings.

Company examples

A classic case of an academy is IBM, whose executive labor market is completely internal. The firm rarely recruits at other than college graduate (or in the case of research, PhD graduate) level. Managers are groomed through a succession of assignments across a range of task responsibilities and geographic areas. Assignments and promotions are determined through a system of individual goal setting and evaluation between an employee and his or her immediate superior. Training is offered as a means to performing well in one's current or succeeding assignment; it is a developmental tool used in a focused fashion. Managers are given annual training in developing subordinates. A newly promoted manager at IBM has an 80 percent chance of staying with the firm through to retirement.

IBM is able to foster such an employment system because its business is one of differentiation: it depends on firm-specific skills for the marketing and servicing of its products, the activities from which it gains much of its competitive advantage. It is large enough to provide continually varying career paths, and has successfully maintained a 'no layoffs' policy through retraining and relocation.

Identification with the firm is strong, implying a long-term dedication on the part of employees. This is important in a business in which product development often takes five years or more. Early in their careers, employees decide to make IBM their career 'home', enabling the firm to operate without short-term financial incentives to its people. The cultural tie, supported by generous health and retirement benefits, athletic facilities, and a variety of clubs and activities outside of work (and in the old days by a company songbook, including 'Hail to Thee, IBM') means IBM can get the benefit of its employees' creative ideas without continually paying a premium for them. In 1982, the 'first level invention achievement award', given by the firm for a total of twelve points (where a patent is worth three points and a published paper one point), consisted of $1500 and a certificate. Comparable efforts at many other firms would yield a share of the profits from any resultant products.

United Parcel Service, our introductory example, is a successful example of a club. It hires people very early in their careers – often as part-time workers during their college years – and promotes them through a well-defined series of jobs. Attitude, seniority, and other group-oriented features have a lot to do with assignment and promotion at the firm. Practically all top UPS executives have twenty or more years of service, and remember vividly how Jim Casey, who founded the business in 1907, still came into the office regularly until just before his death in 1981.

The culture at UPS is very strong. Like most clubs the firm has a service mentality, a mission to serve the public interest. There is a pervasive people orientation, founded in part in the close relationship between the firm and the Teamsters Union. Clubs are often unionized or partly unionized firms; in the case of UPS, the foresighted Casey, realizing that labor unions were inevitable, asked the Teamsters to represent the UPS drivers and part-time hourly employees in 1919. Said Casey, 'I think it's possible to be a good UPS member and union member at the same time' (Sonnenfeld and Lazo, 1987). This focus on membership carries over into the ownership structure of the firm, which is owned entirely by its employees. While their salaries may be modest, UPSers who stay with the firm for years can amass substantial wealth through profit sharing and annual distributions of stock, which is carefully managed for continual increases in value.

UPS is able to operate in a club fashion because it has a well-entrenched infrastructure that would be difficult for any other company to duplicate without years of effort and great expense. Its flexible relationship with the Teamsters (with some 110,000 employees, it is the Union's single largest represented company) also contributes to its entrenched position. For years, UPS has focused on ground transport of packages, and continues to be the leader in this industry. In 1986 the company had the highest net income in the transportation industry: $669 million (Sonnenfeld and Lazo, 1987). With the recent deregulation of common carriers, however, it has begun to face some competition, particularly as it expands into air transport. This newer business presents a challenge to the firm's club system, as it requires externally trained talent (for example, pilots, mechanics) and does not include substantial barriers to competition.

Our other introductory example, Wasserstein Perella, is a classic baseball team in that it is the result of human capital seeking the most rewarding outlet for its efforts. A group of highly skilled service professionals left a larger firm (First Boston Corporation) because they felt the value they were producing was being used to subsidize money-losing operations (securities trading, in particular) that played no part in creating that value. They set up their own operation, barely two blocks away, to focus on their area of distinctive competence: mergers and acquisitions. In existence for barely a month, the firm was already closing deals (its first, a $1.2 billion acquisition) and reviewing applications from potential employees.

Financial services firms are legendary for the speed and salaries at which their executives turn over. With the advent of deregulation, many financial firms, especially commercial banks, have found their middle and upper executives unequipped to manage in the new environment (Hill and Sonnenfeld, 1986). Trimming of mid-level staff, turnover of top management, and hiring of young executives trained in more complex financial markets is common. It is also the norm in this industry for top producers to earn the highest rewards: both Bruce Wasserstein and Joseph Perella were earning far more at First Boston than the firm's top executives.

Wasserstein Perella is likely to be a more stable company than many others in its industry. Mergers and acquisitions are still on the rise, and client relationships in this area still hold some longevity, although not as much as they once did. People who stay with the firm will probably do very well for themselves; the wealth they create will be in large part returned to them. Yet the firm is a baseball team in the same way that trading and brokerage operations, with their dizzying turnover rates, are baseball teams: they buy their talent and reward people on the basis of what they produce. They do not train their employees; the employees either come in fully skilled or develop skills very quickly on the job. People are the firm's competitive advantage – people that own the means of value creation and expect to collect the concomitant economic rents.

Continental Airlines is an example of how external changes in the competitive dynamics of an industry can force a firm to become a fortress. With the deregulation of the airline industry in 1978, older carriers who had depended on protected routes and fare structures were at a double disadvantage: they faced an array of new competitors skilled at designing and marketing high-yield routes and fares, and they were laden with costly union contracts that paid more than market wages to employees with very limited job flexibility.

Faced with mounting losses and, so he felt, intractable unions, Texas Air chairman and new Continental chief Frank Lorenzo took the company into Chapter 11 in 1984. The bankruptcy filing allowed Lorenzo to take unilateral action against the unions by abrogating contracts setting wages and work rules. Amid great controversy, Lorenzo's actions were upheld by the courts, and layoffs and salary cuts became the order of the day. The company retrenched and began to restructure itself as a true fortress: a cost-based competitor focusing on survival. In an industry in which labor represented over 70 percent of 'controllable' costs, Lorenzo's actions were defensible. For the time being, Continental could not afford to offer either job security or increased rewards for good performance (Heckscher, 1986).

Continental's career system followed the competitive changes in the airline industry, albeit slowly, into reactor mode. The turnaround which ensued placed the company back on the road to profitability; yet the nature of the industry at present does not provide the carrier with much hope of making the transition to a more stable career system. In addition, Continental's confrontational approach to solving its problems will affect future efforts to foster stability.

Companies in transition

It is not only externalities such as those in the Continental example that cause a shift in companies' career systems. In some cases a firm matures to a stage which requires a different approach to staffing in order to match a changing business strategy. (Various stage theories of a firm's development exist; see, for example, Greiner, 1972.) Two recent examples of companies undergoing such transitions are Apple Computer and the Eastman Kodak Company.

Apple grew up the iconoclastic baseball team, challenging the established computer industry. This attitude was most graphically displayed in a 1984 Super Bowl television commercial, announcing the introduction of the Macintosh, in which a female athlete, colorfully dressed and carrying a sledgehammer, is seen running down a long, sterile hall, pursued by storm-trooper-like guards. She bursts into an auditorium filled with thousands of grey, male drones worshipping a man on a screen. She hurls the hammer at the image and shatters it in a blaze of light, thereby (we presume) breaking the vise-grip that (the unidentified) IBM holds on computer users everywhere.

Apple's early years were filled with change, as described in a case study on the company:

> Apple's early rapid growth meant a constant influx of new employees. For a long time organizational charts were not printed at Apple; they changed too quickly. Frequent reorganizations reflected the conflict between product organization and functional organization. When Apple began, it had only one product and therefore its structure was largely functional. As new products began to develop, each team formed its own division, modelled on the original Apple, each with its own marketing, its own engineering, and so forth. (Gentile et al., 1986).

Given this background, it is all the more remarkable that Apple began to take on many IBM-like aspects. A recent *Wall Street Journal* article described the firm as trying to 'institutionalize inventiveness to produce a steady stream of new products, without inhibiting . . . individual creativity' (Schlender, 1987). It quoted one industry expert as saying that 'Most high-tech companies don't make that transition mainly because they can't overcome conflicts between the geniuses who come up with the ideas and the "doers" – the business people who actually run the company' (William Dowdy of SRI, quoted in Schlender, 1987).

Yet, despite some layoffs in the course of restructuring, Apple is well on the way to becoming an Academy. With well over 6000 employees, it can no longer afford to have dozens of competing 'skunk works' within the firm. Instead, it is focusing on long-term coordinated development. Like IBM, it is instituting research laboratories aimed not at developing products, but at staying abreast of technology. It has also created several positions called 'Apple Fellows', a direct take-off of IBM's 'IBM Fellows', industry and technical experts commissioned to 'evangelize' both inside and outside the company.

Apple's shift makes sense in light of its position in the industry it founded. No longer a one-product company, it must concern itself with the development of firm-specific skills and a loyal workforce that will allow it to pursue a strategy of differentiation. If it can indeed institutionalize inventiveness – a difficult task at best – Apple will be well positioned for the future.

Eastman Kodak, by contrast, is trying to evolve from a club into a baseball team. Said a recent *New York Times* article,

> Kodak is in the throes of a cultural upheaval that could serve as a case study for what happens when an old company faces new groundrules. It has changed its internal power structure, its manufacturing methods, its dealings with suppliers and competitors, almost every aspect of how it does business. (Deutsch, 1988)

The firm's once insular culture, in which employees referred to Kodak as the 'Great Yellow Father' because of the lifelong relationship it fostered with its people, has recently been exposed to the harsh realities of the markets, including fierce competition from Japanese and European companies in film, and wide swings in the price of silver, a key ingredient.

In response, Kodak has begun acting like a true prospector, seeking out new, high-margin businesses. Concurrently, it has instituted a new profit-consciousness in its old product lines. In 1985 it reorganized into 24 business units, each with a general manager responsible for costs, profits, and product quality. Beginning in 1985, it also embarked on a program of joint ventures and acquisitions, which has taken it into 35-mm cameras, floppy disks, pharmaceuticals, credit, medical diagnostics, lithium batteries, electronic photography, biotechnology, information management, and expanded photofinishing. Most recently, in January 1988, Kodak announced that it would acquire Sterling Drug, a maker of prescription and over-the-counter drugs and household cleaning products, for $5.1 billion.

But changing both its supply flow and its assignment flow orientation has been painful for the company. When it reorganized Kodak also shrank, cutting its workforce by 10 percent in 1986. That meant the end of job security and a tradition of trust. And with most of the firm's senior managers steeped in less-than-competitive traditions, assignment and promotion in the new business units had to focus on younger, more competitive executives. 'We had to throw out the seniority process, because we wanted to take the strongest people we had', said Phil Samper, a senior marketing executive (Deutsch, 1988).

Irreversibly shifted from its club traditions, Kodak is now striving to succeed in a number of baseball team, diversified but related businesses. Whether it will do so remains to be seen, but it has at least instituted the kind of career system changes necessary – if not sufficient – to the task.

Career systems and individuals

If companies employ different career systems according to corporate strategy and industry characteristics, do individuals also choose the kind of career system in which they want to work? We might expect that certain kinds of people will thrive in each of academies, clubs, baseball teams, and even fortresses, given certain sets of characteristics.

We have done some initial classification of a group of MBA graduates which indicates that, over time, people gravitate toward the kind of career system which most matches their personality. We used longitudinal data on 125 MBA graduates of the Harvard Business School class of 1974, collected annually over ten years from the same group of subjects, to compare the backgrounds and experiences of people who ended up in each of the four career system groups ten years after business school. The surveys, which have experienced an 85 percent annual response rate, are drawn from two class groups of approximately equal size. Half the respondents are from a typical first-year MBA section demographically reflecting the entire MBA class; half are from a second-year course in career planning – a self-selected sample. The data covered five general areas:

1 Childhood and family;
2 Performance and personality measures during business school;
3 Problems in the first ten years out;
4 Recent priorities and values;
5 Current status (job, family, and net worth).

We classified the respondents' current firms into academies, clubs, baseball teams, and fortresses, based on their industry, corporate strategy, turnover, and their use of individual vs. group factors in deciding on promotions, as reported in Friedman (1984). We found significant differences among the career system groups in each of the five areas. Here are some highlights of characteristics which stood out:

People in academies had parents who valued self-reliance more than those of their peers, but who also valued honesty and considerateness less. These people were less religious than the rest of the sample. They graduated business school with significantly higher grades. In the first ten years out, they were more likely to have problems with subordinates; they were also more likely to have difficulty deciding how many children to have and when.

People in clubs had parents with very different values. These included a higher emphasis on honesty and considerateness, and a lower regard for hard work and self-reliance, than the rest of the sample. People in clubs had higher religious scores, and lower economic scores, than their peers in business school. Also during school, they expressed less interest in money, and claimed to have less difficulty finding a job upon graduation. Nine

Table 1   *Selected data on MBA respondents*

	Average number of organizations worked for 1975–84	Average annual remuneration 1984
Academies	1.9	$107,000
Clubs	1.7	$ 70,000
Baseball teams	2.6	$141,000
Fortresses	2.3	$ 95,000

and ten years out, they cared more about health, family, and security, and less about future income and autonomy, than the other groups. Finally, ten years out, they were less likely to have substantial equity in their firms, and had a lower net worth than their peers.

People in baseball teams described their fathers as unpredictable, relative to the others in the sample. They strongly described themselves as group workers during business school. In the first ten years after school, these people were more likely to have problems planning their careers, which makes sense in light of the fact that they worked for more companies during that period than did their peers. Priorities in recent years included career progress, personal growth, and especially future income. Those in baseball teams also valued security less than the others, were more likely to have equity in their firms, and had, on average, more children.

People in fortresses scored significantly higher than the other groups on only two items: their parents valued curiosity about causes, and they attested to the importance of mentors several years out of school. Strikingly, the fortress members scored significantly lower than their peers in eleven categories, and notably lower in several more. These included independence from and competition with fathers, pressure from mothers, problems in career planning, on-the-job decisions, job implementation, and technical and managerial skills. In addition, this group was less concerned with feelings of belonging, professional growth, future income, and societal contribution.

Table 1 shows two further statistics for executives from our sample. The average number of organizations worked for is exactly what we would expect: clubs are lowest, followed closely by academies; both have an internal supply flow focus. A wider gap separates these from fortresses, which are exceeded only by baseball teams; both of these recruit heavily from outside. Assuming that our MBA sample are highly motivated and capable, we would also expect salaries to vary, with those executives in baseball teams receiving the highest, and academies second highest, remuneration, as these firms reward individual contribution; those in fortresses and clubs should have lower average salaries. Table 1 shows that this is indeed the case.

On the basis of these findings, we believe that there is a self-selection process taking place among this MBA group with regard to the kind of career system in which they work. It is not just the fact that people in each group have certain characteristics in common that argues for the 'sorting-for-fit' theory. It is the nature of many of those characteristics that suggests the validity of the groupings. That academies have people with higher grades and more self-reliance; that clubs have people who care more about considerateness, family, and security, and less about autonomy and future income; that baseball teams have people who care less about security, and more about future income and equity; that fortresses have employees with generally lower scores overall: these indications match our impressions of academies as being concerned with development, clubs with membership, baseball teams with recruitment and stardom, and fortresses with retrenchment. The implications are that people eventually wind up in the career system that matches their personality and experience. This is an important finding for managers, because it suggests that, at least in part, we can predict in which career system a person will work best, given certain background information.

Job changers

After looking at our MBA sample ten years out in order to compare characteristics, we decided to study the movement of people in the sample from their first to their most recent job. We went back to the first year of the study and classified the respondents' initial jobs by career system type, then compared them with the career systems in the jobs they held in the tenth year of the survey. The movement is illustrated in Figure 3.

The most striking change over the ten-year period is the movement away from clubs and towards baseball teams. This movement could mean that many MBAs who initially identified with the work environment and/or the mission of a club later became frustrated, perhaps because of the difficulty of effecting change. They may have perceived little prospect of increased salary and position. Possibly they were discouraged by the clubs' equal treatment of all employees, no matter what their contribution. Whatever the reason, only 25 percent of those in clubs in 1973 were still in clubs in 1984. For baseball teams, that stable percentage was 85 percent. Beside those who stayed in baseball teams, 39 percent of those in other groups chose to join baseball teams by the end of the ten-year period.

Baseball teams, it seems, hold the most promise for MBAs, many of whom want to be rewarded on the basis of their individual contributions and do not like to feel a constraining attachment to any one organization. Academies held a distant second in our sample, but unlike clubs and fortresses, did not decrease in overall membership over the period. We interpret this to mean that development and assignment/promotion based on contribution are more important to our subject group than mobility, although both are concerns.

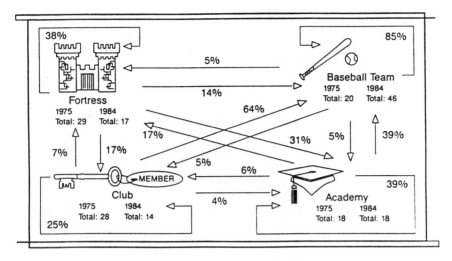

Figure 3 *Job changers*

To support our contention that the shift from one career system to another was indeed a process of 'sorting for fit' and not a random movement, we tested the group of people who had moved from clubs to baseball teams against those who were in clubs at the end of the period and those who were in baseball teams (other than the changers). We measured the groups on all the variables which had been significant in the original tests on the longitudinal data described above. While the changers were significantly different from the clubs (their old group) on fully 38 percent of the characteristics (10 of 26), they differed from the baseball teams (their new group) on only 8 percent (2 of 26).

Conclusion

In this chapter we have questioned the reliance on universalistic approaches to the executive labor market, instead emphasizing different approaches to executive staffing. We therefore proposed a model which matches career systems to strategic roles. This model ultimately links three previously independent fields of inquiry: corporate strategy, corporate career systems, and individual career development.

The underpinnings of the model are based upon two distinct dynamics of the executive labor market: *supply* – the degree of reliance on external vs. internal labor pools; and *assignment* – the criteria used for promotion and placement throughout the firm. Examining the interaction of these two dimensions provides a useful framework for comparing firms, and also helps to reveal a parallel with the strategic model of Miles and Snow (1978).

Implications for research

This model speaks to the need to appreciate different purposes which inspire diverse but equally appropriate approaches to executive staffing. Students and researchers should further question the strategy and career systems of the populations of firms most typically studied, in order to better understand their representativeness and the reasons for their similarities and differences. Contrasting the internal system properties of firms of the same career system type may yield an understanding of what makes that type of career system most effective.

It should also be possible to study the link between career systems and company culture, which in some firms changes less often than strategy and may have a strong effect on staffing policy. Where a strong national culture has an effect on staffing policy, as is the case in Japan, the link between strategy and the internal and external managerial labor markets may not be as strong as in other countries.

Implications for practice

Our work suggests that managers look for consistency between their frequently disjointed staffing activities (recruitment, training, development, promotion, and exit) and corporate strategic objectives. Furthermore, as these objectives are often moving targets, the career system cannot be a rigid structure. The main focus of a firm's career system should be those elements of staffing policy which directly address the firm's strategic needs. For example, baseball teams may want to focus on recruiting and executive search activities, while academies might be more concerned with training, clubs with mentoring, and fortresses with outplacement counseling and locating specific turnaround skills.

Finally, mobility across executive labor markets must be understood by executives, both as leaders of their firms and as individual job seekers and career planners. The patterns of mobility across firms and across industries, as well as the frequency of movement within and across firms, is in part determined by the career context created by the prevailing business strategies of industries.

The original data and recent corporate examples of this chapter are intended to generate new thought about variations in executive labor markets. Future research is needed to test and refine the hypotheses which are suggested by this exploratory work.

References

Barnard, C.I. (1938) *The Functions of the Executive*. Cambridge, MA: Harvard University Press.
Becker, G. (1964) *Human Capital*, New York: Columbia University Press.
Blaug, M. (1970) *An Introduction to the Economics of Education*, Harmondsworth: Penguin.
Chandler, A.D. Jr (1962) *Strategy and Structure*. Cambridge, MA: MIT Press.

Chandler, A.D. Jr (1977) *The Visible Hand*. Cambridge, MA: Belknap/Harvard University Press.

Deutsch, C.H. (1988) 'Kodak Pays the Price for Change', *The New York Times*, March 6, Section 3: 1.

Friedman, S.D. (1984) 'Successful systems and Organizational Performance in Large Corporations', unpublished doctoral dissertation, Ann Arbor, MI.

Gentile, M., Dubinsky, Donna and Apple Computer, Inc. (1986) (A), Harvard Business School case no. 486-083.

Greiner, L.E. (1972) 'Evolution and Revolution as Organizations Grow', *Harvard Business Review*, July–August.

Hall, D.T. and Nougaim, K.E. (1968) 'An Examination of Maslow's Need Hierarchy in an Organizational Setting', *Organizational Behavior and Human Performance*, 3: 12–35.

Harrigan, K.R. (1985) 'Vertical Integration and Corporate Strategy', *Academy of Management Journal*, 2: 397–425.

Harrigan, K.R. (1986) 'Matching Vertical Integration Studies to Competitive Conditions', *Strategic Management Journal*, 535–55.

Heckscher, C. (1986) *Note on the U.S. Airline Industry in the 1980s*. Harvard Business School case no. 486-078.

Hill, L.A. and Sonnenfeld, J.A. (1986) 'Renewal within Financial Service Firms: Managers' Reflections on Retraining', Colloquium on Changes in the Financial Services Industry, May 3.

Kanter, R.M. (1977) *Men and Women of the Corporation*. New York: Basic Books.

Mayo, E. (1933) *The Human Problems of an Industrial Civilization*. New York: Macmillan.

Miles, R.E. and Snow, C.C. (1978) *Organizational Strategy, Structure, and Process*. New York: McGraw-Hill.

Miller, E.J. and Rice, A.K. (1967) *Systems of Organization: The Control of Task and Sentient Boundaries*. London: Tavistock.

Mincer, J. (1974) *Schooling, Experience, and Earnings*. New York: National Bureau of Economic Research.

Morgan, G. (1986) *Images of Organization*, Beverly Hills, CA: Sage.

Porter, M.E. (1980) *Competitive Strategy*. New York: Free Press.

Porter, M.E. (1985) *Competitive Advantage*. New York: Free Press.

Rosenbaum, J.E. (1979) *Career Mobility in a Corporate Hierarchy*. New York: Academic Press.

Rosenbaum, J.E. (1984) 'Tournament Mobility: Career Patterns in a Corporation', *Administrative Science Quarterly*, 24: 220–41.

Schlender, B.R. (1987) 'Apple Computer Tries to Achieve Stability but Remain Creative', *The Wall Street Journal*, July 16: 1.

Schwab, D.P. (1982) 'Recruiting and Organizational Participation', in *Human Resource Management*, ed. K. Rowland and G. Ferris. Boston: Allyn & Bacon.

Sonnenfeld, J. (1988) 'Career Systems Profiles and Strategic Staffing', in *Handbook of Career Theory*, ed. M. Arthur, D.Hall and B. Lawrence. Cambridge and New York: Cambridge University Press (forthcoming).

Sonnenfeld, J. and Lazo, M. (1987) *United Parcel Service (A)*, Harvard Business School case no. 488-016.

Sonnenfeld, J. and Peiperl, M. (1988) 'Staffing Policy as a Strategic Response: A Typology of Career Systems', *Academy of Management Review*, October: 588-600.

Super, D., Crites, J., Hummd, R., Moser, H., Overstreet, P. and Warnath, C. (1957) *Vocational Development: A Framework for Research*. New York: Teachers College Press.

Thurow, L.C. (1975) *Generating Inequality*. New York: Basic Books.

Tushman, M.L., Newman, W.H. and Romanelli, E. (1986) 'Convergence and Upheaval: Managing the Unsteady Pace of Organizational Evolution', *California Management Review*, 1: 29–44.

Wachter, M.L. (1974) 'Primary and Secondary Labor Markets: A Critique of the Dual Approach', *Brookings Papers on Economic Activity*, 3: 637–93.

Williamson, O.E. (1975) *Markets and Hierarchies*. New York: Free Press.

18

Corporate training strategies: the vital component?

Ewart Keep

The purpose of this chapter is to examine the importance of training and development to human resource management policies. Subsumed under the general heading of training will be the issues of selection and recruitment. The interrelationship of training and recruitment strategies is usually a very close one, not least because if an organization wishes to improve the skills of its workforce, it has the choice of either training its existing employees or recruiting pre-skilled labour that has been trained elsewhere. As training and recruitment are to some extent substitutable, it is difficult to study either activity in isolation.

The chapter outlines the importance of investment in training and development as a test of whether an organization is treating its employees as a resource, or as a cost or commodity. The implications of training activity for employee motivation and wider aspects of HRM are discussed. The chapter then examines the evidence that training has an effect on economic performance at both aggregate and company levels, and instances the ways in which international comparisons have acted as a spur to the adoption of HRM in the UK. The types of change in training that have recently taken place are surveyed, and it is argued that the evidence indicates the centrality of these changes to evolving HRM practices. Following on from this, some potential problem areas in current managerial attitudes towards training are discussed, and a number of underlying structural factors adduced to explain these barriers to the widespread adoption of HRM policies. The chapter concludes with some brief remarks about the prospects for the widespread adoption of HRM, and the need for further research on the factors that impede its spread among UK companies.

The importance of training strategies within HRM

The purpose of this chapter is to argue that training and development should be regarded as central to anything that can sensibly be termed

Reprinted from John Storey (ed.) *New Perspectives on Human Resource Management*, pp. 109–25. (London and New York: Routledge, 1989).

HRM. In so doing it is suggested that the loose definition of HRM is not one that helps reliably apportion the motivation for and importance of changes that are taking place in the management of the workforce, in that it tends to act as a 'catch-all' banner under which a huge variety of very different developments can be lumped. The underlying impetus for many of these changes, such as casualization and numerical flexibility, has little to do with a desire to develop the workforce, or to treat employees as a resource.

By contrast, the case that the adoption by companies of a strategic approach towards the training and development of their workforce represents a vital component of any worthwhile or meaningful form of HRM (or HRD) is easily made. If the term human resource management is to be taken as something more than an empty 'buzz phrase', then the word human, in this context, can only relate to the employees, present and future, of the enterprise. The use of the word 'resource', as opposed to commodity or cost, implies investment therein. The word management, for its part, implies that strategies aimed at the motivation, development and deployment of this resource and its associated investment will be directed in such a way as to maximize its potential. Training is a prime investment in human resources that plays a vital role in securing these goals. Companies that, for whatever reasons, are inclined to treat their employees simply as a cost or commodity, and who hence fail to invest in training and development activity cannot meaningfully be said to be practising human resource management.

It can also be argued that there is a solid economic rationale that is likely to bind the incidence of training to the development of wider human resource management policies. If a company has invested in training its workforce, it then makes sense to develop policies that will help to retain these employees and to motivate and develop them in such a way as to put to best use their skills, thereby maximizing the return on investment. With a low-skilled workforce, whose training has mainly been in the form of an unstructured, on-the-job acquisition of experience, there is far less incentive to retain them and their loyalty, as the cost of loss and replacement is likely to be lower.

Furthermore, training and development activities have implications for attempts to motivate and involve the workforce. One of the primary objectives of HRM is the creation of conditions whereby the latent potential of employees will be realized and their commitment to the success of the organization secured. This latent potential is taken to include, not merely the capacity to acquire and utilize new skills and knowledge, but also a hitherto untapped wealth of ideas about how the organization's operations might be better ordered. These motivational aspects of HRM are bound up with investment in training and development insofar as such investment is a powerful signalling device, which enables employers to confirm to their employees that they are being regarded as important to the company's future success. Obversely, there is little use in firms claiming to their workforces that they have become people-centred organizations that regard their employees as important and valuable, if they subsequently refuse to invest in people. Actions speak louder than words and employees have normally not been slow to notice inconsistencies in the messages emanating from management. Thus a failure to treat expenditure on training as a necessary investment can rapidly undermine the credibility of an organization's attempt to adopt HRM practices.

The role of internal comparisons

Above and beyond the abstract logic of this proposition, there is evidence that suggests that training and development activities have an effect upon relative competitiveness and economic performance, at both the aggregate level of the national economy or industrial sector, and at the level of the individual enterprise. In terms of a national policy debate about the need to secure improvement in Britain's training performance, the most important comparative study was *Competence and Competition*, which was undertaken by the Institute of Manpower Studies for the MSC and NEDO (NEDO/MSC, 1984). Other, more detailed studies, undertaken by the National Institute of Economic and Social Research (NIESR), have tended to underline the weakness of specific aspects of the British training effort when compared with that of other European countries (see, for example, Prais and Wagner, 1981, 1988; Prais, 1985; Steedman, 1987).

Other research undertaken by NIESR, using studies of matched plants in two industries, metal-working and kitchen furniture manufacture, in Britain and West Germany, has pointed to the results that spring from the relatively low levels of training and technical competence that were found in the British plants (Daly et al., 1985; Steedman and Wagner, 1987). These deleterious consequences included a slower adoption of new technology, a less adventurous use of it where it was adopted, more frequent breakdowns of machinery and longer periods of down-time as a result. The overall effect was that West German productivity was found to be markedly higher – over 60 per cent greater in both industries. In the case of the kitchen furniture industry it was further suggested that the low skill levels among the British workforce reinforced, as well as reflected, the decision of British manufacturers to abandon the high-quality end of the market to German producers and to concentrate their efforts at the lower, mass-produced end of the market (Steedman and Wagner, 1987: 85–7).

Such international comparisons have formed the major spur to the government and MSC's attempts to improve the quality and quantity of the British training effort, there being in the government's view – to quote a Cabinet minister – 'a clear and well-proven link between training and industrial performance' (*THES*, 9 January 1987). International comparisons have also been one of the main forces motivating change on the part of individual companies, particularly those operating in increasingly competitive international markets. The direct relationship between overseas exemplars of good HRM and training practice and change in British enterprises can be seen in the cases of Lucas Industries, Jaguar Cars, and the British Steel Corporation. These organizations, faced with severe overseas competition, in terms of both price and quality, mounted major study exercises to see what lessons about the motivation, development and deployment of workforces could be drawn from best practice abroad. As an executive at Jaguar put it, 'we were up against the wall in the early 1980s and we had people going overseas, particularly to Germany, to see how and why competitors like BMW and Mercedes managed to be successful' (*Self Development*, November 1986: 1). One of the chief messages that emerged from the visits to Germany was that German companies appeared to 'have a much greater commitment to training and development' than their British counterparts (*Self Development*, November 1986: 2).

In the case of BSC, senior managers looked in detail at HRD methods in Japanese steel-making companies, as well as drawing comparisons with some of its European competitors, most notably the Belgian firm SIDMAR. Another example of a British company's reflections on Japanese personnel and training policies, based on research undertaken in Japan, is given in Brown and Read (1984).

Changing company training strategies

The result of such comparisons, and of the forces for change generated by increased competitive pressures, has been to convince some senior British managers of the need to lay far greater stress upon the importance of HRD activities within their companies. This step change in the importance attached to training and development activity has been accompanied by the equally vital acknowledgement that training needs to be regarded as an investment, rather than as a cost. Thus, according to Peter Nicholson, chairman and chief executive of the Forward Trust, 'Our key investment is in people' (*Self Development*, November 1987: 3), or, as Sir Dennis Rooke, the chairman of British Gas put it: 'We must transform the perception of training expenditure so that it is no longer seen simply as a cost, but is regarded as an investment to be evaluated alongside investments in capital equipment' (ibid.).

As well as supportive statements from company chairmen, there are now a number of companies operating in the UK, usually large employers, that appear to have progressed some way towards successfully developing training and HRD systems that are integrated into wider business planning and strategy. It is these companies that tend to be cited as the leaders of the HRM movement in Britain. Among them can be numbered firms such as Jaguar Cars, Lucas Industries and ICL. They join a select band of companies, such as IBM, Hewlett-Packard, and Marks and Spencer, who have a long-standing commitment to the type of employment practices and strategic consideration of personnel issues that are now styled as constituting HRM.

There is not space to undertake here a detailed analysis of the changes that have been introduced within many of these companies, but even a brief description of developments indicates the basic thrust of HRM in practice, and, in so doing, underlines the centrality of the role afforded to training and development within such changes. The companies cited below have by no means followed a single, uniform pattern of development, but in most cases there are common strands running through the initiatives that they have instituted.

To begin with, the integration of training and development into wider business planning has been seen as crucial. Instead of being activities peripheral to the achievement of corporate objectives, the human resources of the organization are seen as a vital factor in corporate planning, and training and development as able to make an important contribution to the achievement of business objectives. Allied to this has been the clear requirement that such integration, and the heightened profile for HRD activities that goes with it, should command the participation and support of the most senior levels of management (Beattie, 1987; Bowen, 1987: 10; Brady, 1987: 5–6; Hendry and Pettigrew, 1987: 30). Certainly in companies such as Jaguar Cars, British Airways, and British Steel, the message that training and development were to be treated as important has been passed down very firmly from board level.

Apart from a top-down approach, the aim has been to create an integrated and coherent package of complementary measures aimed at altering many aspects of the employment relationship. These include greatly enhanced efforts in the area of corporate manpower planning and forecasting (Beattie, 1987), an area in which British companies have in the past generally tended to be particularly weak. Within this area, the issue of succession planning has assumed considerable importance, particularly in those organizations which, because of large-scale redundancies and recruitment freezes in the past, now find themselves faced with significant age bulges in key sections of their workforces.

Hand in hand with improved manpower planning have come various attempts to upgrade the quality of those being recruited. As one chief executive put it, 'a company is only as good as its personnel – so it's vital to choose and train the best' (Upton, 1987: 29). This outlook has found expression in moves towards the creation of more systematized, sophisticated and objective systems of selection and recruitment (Ballin, 1986: 25–6). These have, for example, included greater interest in the use of psychometric testing, more concerted efforts to specify the skills, competences, qualifications and qualities being sought from applicants, and the increasing use of assessment centres.

Companies' efforts to improve the quality and suitability of those they recruit has in turn given an added impetus to the need to forge closer links with educational institutions at all levels within the education system (Ballin, 1986: 26). Improved contact on a continuing basis with local schools, sixth-form colleges and further education colleges is being seen as an important first stage in the process of shaping and channelling the job choices of prospective young entrants into the local labour markets in which the companies operate. At the level of graduate recruitment, the renewed emphasis upon the crucial importance of managerial expertise as a corporate resource has led to considerable efforts being directed into targeted links with selected higher-education institutions. Demographic trends, in the shape of a major decline in the number of young people coming onto the job market in the first half of the 1990s, means that the priority afforded to industry/education liaison activity is likely to increase still further.

Another common factor among many of the firms that have been identified as having adopted HRM policies has been moves to increase the use of formal performance and/or training needs appraisal procedures (Upton, 1987: 28; Hendry and Pettigrew, 1987: 31–2). In one or two cases, the use of a training-needs appraisal system has been extended downwards to cover the entire shop-floor workforce.

Efforts to upgrade the skills base of the managerial workforce have also usually been high on the agenda of the leading HRM practitioners. That this should be the case is hardly surprising, given the relatively low qualification levels of many British managers and the traditionally poor record of most UK companies in the area of management training and development (an issue to which we will be returning below). Such efforts have often been made in conjunction with measures to enhance career planning and introduce greater use of job rotation and lateral transfers.

On the shop floor there have been a large number of changes, not least in the introduction of training in support of greater functional flexibility. This has frequently meant multi-skilling for craft workers, as well as equipping production operatives with the skills necessary to undertake routine maintenance on the plant that is in their charge. Other developments have included moves to systematize and upgrade the provision and recording of hitherto informal on-the-job training. Another measure, and one that has attracted considerable interest, is the efforts that have gone into the provision of enhanced opportunities for self-development, most notably through investment in computer-based open-learning systems. Probably the best-known example of this has been Jaguar Cars (Simpson, 1986; Richards, 1986), but similar developments can be found in Lucas Industries, the Rover Group, BSC, and a number of other companies.

Increased competition has led some organizations to adopt a strategy of attempting to compete in terms of quality rather than price, and in such cases training has been closely associated with attempts to improve product quality. In manufacturing this has meant not just the introduction of quality circles and statistical process control (SPC) methods, but also various initiatives to build a quality approach into the production process through major improvements in the motivation and competence of the workforce at all levels. One example of this has been within British Steel, which is introducing a package of measures, originally promoted under the title of total quality performance (TQP), aimed at securing competitive advantage through a higher-quality product. The most important training element within TQP has been the decision to identify required standards of competence for every level of activity, and to undertake training and development needs assessments of the corporation's entire workforce against these criteria.

In the services sector the drive for quality has most often been seen in attempts to improve the levels of customer care or customer service. British Airways and British Rail are the two perhaps best-known examples, but there are many others, not least in retailing (Upton, 1987: 26).

This extensive range of activities has normally been accompanied by major financial investment in training and development. This has meant both increased injections of capital, to finance items such as new open-learning centres, and also rises in the general level of recurrent spending on training.

In nearly all the published case studies of companies that have embarked upon such changes, training and development have been seen as an integral part of wider strategies aimed at the creation of new working practices and a better motivated, more self-reliant workforce (Ballin, 1986: 24). Thus, for example, it is often hard to draw firm lines between new methods of training and new forms of communication. Team briefings are an example of management attempting to improve communications with employees, but they can also be used as a training opportunity and as a means of reinforcing the message of team-training exercises. Frequently, many of the wider changes in areas like communications and management structures have carried with them major requirements for training and re-training. Finally, there has been a general acknowledgement that training has acted as an important lever in promoting cultural change within those companies that have been attempting to upgrade the importance attached to the workforce's contribution to organizational success.

Problem areas in the field of training and development

Despite the high-profile examples of good practice on the part of a number of large companies, a great deal of evidence suggests that at aggregate level the broad mass of British employers may not yet have accepted the vital importance of training and development activities and acted accordingly. Given the centrality of training to the success of meaningful forms of HRM, it seems likely that if this evidence is correct it has serious implications for the widespread adoption of HRM in this country.

To begin with, such statistics as are available indicate generally low average per capita spending on training and development by British companies. An MSC-sponsored survey found that, on average, employers were spending only £200 per employee per annum on training, which represented 0.15 per cent of company turnover (MSC, 1985). No less than 24 per cent of the establishments surveyed had provided no training of any kind in the previous 12 months, and 69 per cent of employees had received no training during this period (MSC, 1985: 23). By contrast, it has been alleged that leading employers in West Germany, Japan and the USA spend up to 3 per cent of their turnover on training and development, and that employees in these countries tend to be trained to far higher levels than their counterparts in the UK (NEDO/MSC, 1984). A report prepared in 1985 by Coopers and Lybrand Associates for the MSC and NEDO on British companies' attitudes towards training concluded that:

> few employers think training sufficiently central to their business for it to be a main component in their corporate strategy; the great majority did not see it as an issue of major importance . . . training [was] rarely seen as an investment but either as an overhead which would be cut when profits are under pressure or as something forced on the company as a reaction to other developments. (Coopers and Lybrand, 1985: 4)

Beyond the apparently comparatively low priority afforded to training activity, there are a number of specific areas within the field of British training and development that it can be suggested are likely to prove particularly problematic with regard to the spread of HRM policies and practices. A number of the most important of these problem areas are discussed below.

The very clear example of a potential barrier to the take-up of HRM are current levels of management education and training in the UK. Recent research (Mangham and Silver, 1986; Handy, 1987; Constable and McCormick, 1987) has served to underline the extreme poverty of British practice in this area, with levels of education and training that are very poor by international standards. Mangham and Silver point out that 'over half of all UK companies appear to make no formal provision for the training of their managers', and that in companies employing more than 1,000 people fewer than one in ten senior managers received any training (1986: 1). Handy cites another survey which indicated that 36 per cent of middle managers had received no management training since starting work (1987: 10), and goes on to suggest that 'management training in Britain is too little, too late, for too few' (1987: 11). If HRM means something, one might at the least expect a significant investment in the managerial segment of workforce, but on current evidence this would appear not to be generally the case in much of British industry and commerce.

In the wake of the Handy Report there is currently a flurry of activity in this area, mainly centred on the creation of the Charter Group of two hundred leading companies who are to take the lead in promoting and implementing good practice in management education, training, and development. New qualifications are proposed and a code of practice has been launched. As yet it is too early to judge to what degree these efforts will have any significant impact upon the problem of an under-educated and under-trained managerial workforce, but it must be said that the difficulties experienced by the Charter Group in attempting to agree a firm commitment to an entitlement to a specific number of days off-the-job management training, are not particularly encouraging. Indeed, the fact that the fairly rudimentary provisions that make up the code of prac-tice have been hailed as a landmark in British management education and training is a reflection on the paucity of what has gone before.

Moreover, given the scale of the backlog of training needs among the existing managerial workforce, even the most dramatic improvement in provision will take a considerable length of time to achieve widespread effects. Or, to put the problem another way, John Banham, the director-general of the CBI, admits that current training levels among British management represent 'a relatively blank sheet with which to start to prepare the managers we will need for the 1990s and beyond' (*Personnel Management*, December 1987: 8). The danger is that large areas of the sheet will continue to remain unmarked by progress.

Low levels of management training and development have other, less direct, implications for the widespread adoption of HRM. For, in the light of the limited training opportunities available to management, it is perhaps not altogether surprising that managers have in their turn often tended to regard a lack of training on the part of their workforce as something that does not constitute a serious problem. For example, Steed-man and Wagner's comparative study of matched manufacturing plants in the British and West German kitchen furniture industry (1987), revealed worrying assumptions about training on the part of the British employers that contrasted markedly with those of their West German counterparts. Despite the fact that only 10 per cent of the British workforce held any kind of vocational qualification, as against the 90 per cent of the West German workforce who had passed through a three-year period of craft training (1987: 91–2), British managers appeared unconcerned at the disparity. They were, moreover, apparently willing to accept the limitations that were being imposed by low skill levels upon productivity, product innovation and the ability to adopt and utilize new technology.

The reaction of many companies, particularly in the retail sector, to the introduction of the more advanced, two-year Youth Training Scheme, appeared symptomatic of broadly similar attitudes to the need for and value of extended periods of training for young employees (Pointing, 1986). The MSC's announcement of the decision to extend the duration of YTS from one year to two was greeted with widespread concern on the part of companies that they would be unable to 'fill out' the training to occupy two years (ibid.). These views existed despite the fact that under the widely respected West German dual system of apprenticeships, the vast majority of young entrants to the labour market undergo a 3-year period of training, not only in manufacturing companies, but also in the retail and commercial sectors.

On a wider front, firms' reactions to YTS give even greater cause for concern. The scheme has been hailed as the most important development in British vocational education and training since the 1944 Education Act, and the foundation upon which subsequent improvements in upgrading the quality of the adult workforce can be built (Manpower Services Commission, 1988: 15). Despite these expectations on the part of government and policy makers, the majority of employers are still not participating in YTS (Leadbeater, 1987), and many of those who do still choose to see it as a measure aimed at the young unemployed, rather than as a period of foundation training for all their young employees. The result is that large numbers of YTS trainees leave the scheme to take up a job that carries with it no opportunities for training. The fact that such attitudes towards YTS are held by a significant proportion of British management, it can be argued, reflects a series of limiting assumptions on their part about the levels of knowledge and skill that are required and used by their employees. These assumptions stand in the way of a recognition of the importance of investing in people.

Underlying factors that impede the widespread adoption of HRM

The examples cited above of barriers to the spread of improved training and development, and thereby the spread of successful HRM policies, raise questions about the extent to which HRM is likely to extend beyond what is at present a fairly select group of companies. At another level, these barriers are themselves merely symptomatic of a number of underlying structural factors that inhibit British employers from placing greater emphasis upon the importance of the people they employ, particularly in the area of training. A large number of deep-seated structural explanations have been advanced to explain Britain's poor performance in training and development, and this chapter is not the place to undertake a thoroughgoing exploration of such complex issues. Nevertheless, there is some value in outlining a number that are particularly germane to the adoption or otherwise of HRM policies.

One that has already been touched upon is the variety of other strategies for survival and growth that are available to British employers. It seems reasonable to expect that companies will, at least partly, tailor their approaches to the management of the people they employ on the basis of the product markets in which they compete. For some companies operating in the UK this has meant efforts to compete through mass-volume production and the sale of standardized product lines. The result in terms of skill requirements and people management techniques tends to be a mass of relatively low-skilled operatives, who are managed along more or less Taylorite lines. Examples of those following this type of route would include sectors as diverse as the fast-food chains and parts of the clothing and footwear industry. Companies operating in this way are unlikely to find the full-blown HRM model relevant to their perceived needs.

The growth of the British multi-national, particularly in the wake of the end to exchange-control regulations, has meant the opening up of new avenues for growth. The figures on overseas acquisitions and investment contained in many British company annual reports indicate that there has been a significant move to shift productive capacity and investment overseas. One indicator of the scale of this activity is the fact that in 1987 British companies spent \$31.7 billion on acquisitions in the USA (Rodgers and Tran, 1988). The result has in some cases been to effectively marginalize the importance of the British component of the companies' manufacturing operations. In such circumstances it is open to question whether these companies are going to bother to invest heavily in reskilling their UK workforces, when, through overseas acquisition, they can buy new workforces pre-trained.

Another strategy, and one that has commonly been adopted by some large British companies, has been growth and profitability through a cycle of takeovers, followed by divestment of those parts of the new company that no longer fit the approved product mix, or which are failing to turn in adequate levels of profit in the short term. The food industry is a sector in which such practices have been rife in recent years. It can be argued that companies that follow this path are likely to lack the long-term commitment to their subsidiaries that is a prerequisite to securing a reasonable return from any heavy investment in training and retraining. In this connection it is noticeable that most of the firms cited as leading examples of HRM in Britain tend to be single or closely related product companies, rather than large conglomerates or holding companies.

The counter-pressures against investing in people referred to above are compounded by other factors. For, despite the CBI's recent report on relations between industry and the City, the overwhelming balance of evidence suggests that the relative absence in Britain of the type of long-term relationship that exists between banks, stockholders and company managements in West Germany and Japan, does create damaging pressure that forces companies to adopt a short-term view of the trade-off between investment and profit. These difficulties are compounded by stock market and takeover pressures, which materially affect industry's ability to invest in long-term projects, such as training and research and development, at the expense of short-term profit margins (Dore, 1985; Walker, 1985; Parker, 1986; Fifield, 1987).

These short-term financial pressures assume a still greater significance in the UK because of the dominance of financial management and accounting systems that militate against people-centred investment (Hayes and Garvin, 1983; Allen, 1985; Kaplan, 1985; Benjamin and Benson, 1986). As Jonathan Fox, the director for personnel and corporate affairs at Norsk Hydro, pointed out in a recent article, such systems hinder attempts to change employment practices:

> we have not helped this drive towards innovation by the way we assess our business performance; for if we examine the core of our decision-making process it is based on an accounting system which counts the cost of what we do and ignores the consequences of what we fail to do. We need to know more about the cost of not doing things. The absence of initiative, poor teamwork, under-utilisation of people's talents, quality, safety, are not part of the financial model. (1988: 38)

Added to these difficulties is Britain's persistent failure to evolve and maintain a coherent national system of vocational education and training. In a situation where there is no statutory requirement to train, a policy of recruiting skilled labour rather than developing it internally is an economically rational strategy for individual companies. The threat of seeing skilled labour 'poached' is one that makes it all the harder for those companies that do train to treat training expenditure as an investment.

A final major underlying impediment to the spread of HRM remains to be discussed; that relating to the ability and willingness of many British managers to banish informality in personnel practices. As has been pointed out, the whole tenor of HRM suggests rigour, and a systematic and coherent approach towards managing and developing the productive capacity of the workforce. Unfortunately it can be argued that many of the basic processes and procedures that ought to underpin HRM simply do not have widespread currency among British employers, and often operate very patchily even within organizations that are attempting to formalize their employment management systems.

In this context, the example of recruitment and selection is an instructive one. If HRM indicates the widespread adoption of a more people-centred approach to organizational management, then it might reasonably be expected that significant effort would be made towards obtaining the right basic material, in the form of a workforce endowed with the appropriate qualities, skills, knowledge, and potential for future training. The selection and recruitment of workers best suited to meeting the needs of the organization ought to form a core activity upon which most other HRM policies geared towards development and motivation could be built.

In fact much of the available evidence tends to indicate that there are real problems in this crucial area of personnel management activity. In many organizations, recruitment and selection are apparently conducted in a haphazard and informal fashion, a circumstance which appears to reflect the enormous strength of resistance that exists towards any attempt to institute more thorough, formalized and objective systems. In the past, studies of the recruitment process have pointed to the entrenched traditions of informality (Blackburn and Mann, 1979; Courtney and Hedges, 1977). Wood, in a further study of recruitment practices (1986: 11) has suggested that,

> the new human resource management is concerned to develop the conditions in which new ideas and tacit and diagnostic skills can flourish. This implies far more intensive selection, aimed at gauging both an ability and commitment to harness and develop working knowledge in order constantly to improve performance than appeared to be the norm from the study reported in this article.

Collinson's study (1988) of equal opportunities practices in the recruitment systems in a number of sectors illustrates how deep-seated are the difficulties that face such developments. This research covered a wide variety of jobs, ranging from semi-skilled manual and clerical posts to managerial vacancies in some sixty-four workplaces. The companies in which his investigations were conducted were usually large, including national clearing banks, insurance companies, hi-tech companies, food manufacturing, and the mail-order business. It seems not unreasonable to suggest that some of these organizations, particularly among the banks and insurance companies, would have identified themselves as practitioners of HRM policies.

The picture painted by the case studies however, is one of informal arrangements, often blatant sexual discrimination, and the use of vague and subjective selection criteria, with the result that employees were taken into employment or promoted on grounds that had little or nothing to do with ability or suitability. In two cases (Collinson, 1988: 63–9) informal selection processes allowed candidates who were the least well qualified, or who had scored lowest on the selection tests, to be selected over the heads of better qualified and apparently more able candidates. The earlier study by Wood (1986) found extensive evidence of similar informal practices.

Collinson attributes the prevalence of these informal arrangements to the desire on the part of line managers for autonomy, and the weakness of many personnel departments (1988: 3–4). This weakness was reflected in an inability to implement policies, either due to remoteness from operational levels in the organization, or through subordination to line managers (1988: 4). More depressingly still, the study revealed that 'even many personnel managers had not been trained in selection and interviewing methods' (1988: 3).

If the organizations under study had been small businesses, in unprofitable or declining sectors of the economy, the results might have raised fewer problems for anyone suggesting a widespread adoption of HRM policies and practices by British employers. As it is, of the forty-five companies involved, only three employed fewer than 1,000 people in the UK, and all but two maintained corporate personnel or HRM departments, and had formalized recruitment and selection policies (Collinson, 1987: 32). In the event these policies were not being implemented, or were being subverted.

This evidence begs a number of questions about the likely willingness of some managers to adapt their working practices to meet the demands HRM poses. One of the central weaknesses in much of the literature on HRM is that it takes little account of the possibility that rational self-interest on the part of some managers might impede the adoption of the measures it prescribes. In reality, there are few forms of change that do not constitute a threat to someone, and in this respect HRM is no exception.

This threat takes a number of forms. The first is the problem of managing a more self-reliant workforce of the sort that HRM aims to create. Traditional styles of management, based on authoritarian, non-participatory tenets are unlikely to sit easily alongside demands to communicate with and to involve employees, particularly in circumstances where the management workforce is itself ill equipped to meet the challenge. Bearing in mind the education and training of British managers, it is open to question how genuine would be their welcome for a better-educated, better-trained, more self-reliant and questioning workforce.

British industrial relations history adds to this problem with a system whose heritage of management/workforce relationships has normally centred on the achievement of more or less passive compliance by the workforce to management's instructions, rather than on securing their active commitment to shared goals. It seems not unreasonable to suggest that many managers who have grown up within such a system are unlikely to be entirely happy at the thought of abandoning familiar tried and trusted methods.

At another level, HRM threatens to circumscribe the degree of freedom of action afforded to line managers by demanding a more uniform, systematized and implicitly meritocratic approach to the implementation of company personnel policies. In this respect it is possible to draw some parallels between the prescriptions offered by the proponents of HRM, and the recommendations of the 1968 Royal Commission on Industrial Relations. At first sight these two might appear quite dissimilar, but their juxtaposition is not entirely fanciful. A common link is provided by their calls for greater formalization and regularization of both personnel procedures and the conduct of collective bargaining. The Donovan Commission wanted to see an end to informal bargaining arrangements, and suggested a reform of collective bargaining structures, greater use of formalized written agreements, and the development of corporate industrial relations strategies. HRM, in a similar way, lays stress upon the need for a strategic formulation of HRM strategies at corporate level, and on the value of a thorough sytematization, at all levels of management, of previously informal, loosely linked personnel policies and practices. Paradoxically, HRM is calling for this at a time when British industry is witnessing a greater devolution of decision-making power to line managers, autonomy of smaller units within larger businesses through the creation of profit centres, and new systems of financial control.

Industrial relations research after Donovan identified a number of underlying forces that tend to sustain informality in bargaining relationships and in the exercise of managerial control of industrial relations (see for example Terry, 1977; Armstrong and Goodman, 1979). In much the same way, it is possible to identify similar forces that are likely to militate against the adoption of more formalized personnel practices in many British companies.

As Lee and Piper (1987:7) point out, the prescriptive literature on HRM and personnel tends to assume the actions of 'rational people operating within efficient technical systems'. As we have seen from Collinson's (1988) study of recruitment practices discussed above, this is often not the case. Systems may exist, but they are open to manipulation and distortion by those who operate them. Managers as individuals have a number of goals, only some of which are shared with those of the organization that employs them. These unofficial goals, such as maintaining standing with one's subordinates and avoiding unnecessary conflict, are often realized through the discretion which informality imparts to the manager in the exercise of his or her decision making. Thus the ability to recruit and promote those who do not pose a threat and who conform to one's own stereotypes, and the possession of the organizational leeway to do favours for selected employees, social peers, friends and relatives, are arguably important to many managers. None of this sits very well with the sorts of restraints imposed by HRM's demands for meritocratic objectivity in management decision making as it affects employees.

Conclusion

This last point brings us back to the crucial issue of how genuine much of the interest in HRM really is, and the degree to which this apparent enthusiasm is likely to be translated into action. At present, genuine HRM policies, as defined in this chapter, appear to be confined to a relatively limited group of large companies (Coopers and Lybrand, 1985: 9). They are often ones chiefly competing in international markets, in which it is harder to ignore the deficiencies caused by Britain's traditionally low levels of education and training.

This chapter has argued that training and development are activities central to the reality of anything that can meaningfully be termed human resource management. Indeed, it can be suggested that training effort is one useful litmus test of the reality of the adoption of HRM/HRD policies within British firms. If the training and development of its employees is not afforded high priority, if training is not seen as a vital component in the realization of business plans, then it is hard to accept that such a company has committed itself to HRM.

Unfortunately, as has been outlined above, there are a number of deep-seated factors that appear to militate against significant improvements in the area of training and investment in people. These in turn have implications for the widespread adoption of HRM policies. In view of the importance of many of these barriers to change, it is perhaps surprising that, at least to date, they have not been addressed in detail by much of the literature on HRM. Certainly many of them require further investigation, and it would seem important that they constitute part of any future research agenda.

On the wide issue of the long-term significance of HRM in Britain, it is still too early to reach any final judgement. To date, the number of companies in which it is practised is limited. A number of important potential obstacles to its progress have been identified. There is danger that progress will, to echo the words of the Handy Report, be a case of too little, too late, for too few. If this proves to be the case, the result will not only be to further widen the qualitative disparity between best and worst personnel practice among British employers, but also to heighten the contrast discussed earlier in this chapter between the employment strategies of most British companies and those of their overseas competitors. In a world where international competitive advantage is increasingly likely to turn upon the skills, knowledge and commitment of an enterprise's employees (Cassels, 1985: 439), the economic consequences of such an eventuality are painful to contemplate.

References

Allen, D. (1985) 'Strategic management accounting', *Management Accounting*, March.

Armstrong, P. and Goodman, J. (1979) 'Managerial and supervisory custom and practice', *Industrial Relations Journal*, 10(3).

Ballin, M. (1986) 'How British Steel tempered the job cuts', *Transition*, January.

Beattie, D. (1987) 'Integrating human resource and business plans at ICL', Institute of Personnel Management, National Conference Paper, mimeo.

Benjamin, A. and Benson, N. (1986) 'Why ignore the value of the people?', *Accountancy*, February.

Blackburn, R.M. and Mann, M. (1979) *The Working Class in the Labour Market*. Cambridge: Cambridge University Press.

Bowen, P. (1987) 'High performance management', *Focus on Adult Training*, 12.

Brady, T. (1987) *Education and Training in Lucas Industries*. London: National Economic Development Office.

Brown, G.F. and Read, A.R. (1984) 'Personnel and training policies – some lessons for western companies', *Long Range Planning*, 17(2).

Cassels, J.S. (1985) 'Learning, work and the future', *Royal Society of Arts Journal*, June.

Collinson, D. (1987) 'Who controls selection', *Personnel Management*, May.

Collinson, D. (1988) *Barriers to Fair Selection: A Multi-sector Study of Recruitment Practices*. London: HMSO.

Constable, J. and McCormick, R. (1987) *The Making of British Managers*. London: British Institute of Management.

Coopers and Lybrand (1985) *A Challenge to Complacency: Changing Attitudes to Training*. London: Manpower Services Commission.

Courtney, G. and Hedges, B. (1977) *A Survey of Employers' Recruitment Practices*. London: Social and Community Planning Research.

Daly, A., Hitchens, D.M.W.N. and Wagner, K. (1985) 'Productivity, machinery and skills in a sample of British and German manufacturing plants', *National Institute Economic Review*, February.

Dore, R.P. (1985) 'Financial structures and the long-term view', *Policy Studies*, 6 (1), July.

Fifield, D.M. (1987) 'The implications and expectations of ownership', *Business Graduate Journal*, 17(1), January.

Fox, J. (1988) 'Norsk Hydro's new approach takes root', *Personnel Management*, January.

Handy, C. (1987) *The Making of Managers: a Report on Management Education, Training and Development in the United States, West Germany, France, Japan, and the UK*. London: National Economic Development Office.

Hayes, R.H. and Garvin, D.A. (1983) 'Managing as if tomorrow mattered', *The McKinsey Quarterly*, Spring.

Hendry, C. and Pettigrew, A. (1987) 'Banking on HRM to respond to change', *Personnel Management*, November.

Kaplan, R.S. (1985) 'Yesterday's accounting undermines production', *The McKinsey Quarterly*, Summer.

Leadbeater, C. (1987) 'The YTS: positive effects but improvements needed', *Financial Times*, 18 November.

Lee, R.A. and Piper, J.A. (1987) 'Towards a conceptual framework for analysing managerial promotion processes', Loughborough, Department of Management Studies, Loughborough University of Technology, mimeo.

Mangham, I.L. and Silver, M.S. (1986) *Management Training: Context and Practice*. School of Management, University of Bath, ESRC/DTI Report.

Manpower Services Commission (1985) *Adult Training in Britain*. Sheffield: MSC.

National Economic Development Office/Manpower Services Commission (1984) *Competence and Competition*. London: NEDO.

Parker, P. (1986) 'Can we learn from Japan?', *The Guardian*, 3 March.

Pointing, D. (1986) 'Retail training in West Germany', *MSC Youth Training News*, April.

Prais, S.J. (1985) 'What can we learn from the German system of education and vocational training?, in G.D.N. Worswick (ed.) *Education and Economic Performance*. Aldershot: Gower.

Prais, S.J. and Wagner, K. (1981) 'Some practical aspects of human capital investment: training standards in five occupations in Britain and Germany', *National Institute Economic Review*, November.

Prais, S.J. and Wagner, K. (1988) 'Productivity and management: the training of foremen in Britain and Germany', *National Institute Economic Review*, February.

Richards, M. (1986) 'Crash courses', *Times Higher Educational Supplement*, 5 July.

Rodgers, P. and Tran, M. (1988) 'US feathers ruffled at British invasion', *The Guardian*, 26 April.

Simpson, D. (1986) 'Where hearts and mind are in the front seat', *The Guardian*, 1 August.

Steedman, H. (1987) *Vocational Training in France and Britain: Office Work*, discussion paper no. 14, London: National Institute of Economic and Social Research.

Steedman, H. and Wagner, K. (1987) 'A second look at productivity, machinery and skills in Britain and Germany', *National Institute Economic Review*, November.

Terry, M. (1977) 'The inevitable growth of informality', *British Journal of Industrial Relations*, 15(1), March.

Upton, R. (1987) 'The bottom line: Bejam's ingredients for success', *Personnel Management*, March.

Walker, D.A. (1985) 'Capital markets and industry', *Bank of England Quarterly Bulletin*, December.

Wood, S. (1986) 'Personnel management and recruitment', *Personnel Review*, 15 (2).

19

Multiple pay contingencies: strategic design of compensation

Thomas A. Mahoney

Management literature thrives on subjects of change. Proposals for change in production processes, accounting, organization, leadership, motivation, and compensation are served up daily. Each of these proposals is presented as a solution to a defined problem or concern. There is inevitable suspicion of faddism in management. Jaded employees react numbly as programs of MRP replace programs of JIT, TQC programs replace QC circles, WP&R replaces MBO, and progressive counseling replaces discipline. An observer must question whether the introduction of programs of management practice is merely fad or truly offers promise of improved organizational performance (Doyle, 1989).

One set of topics of change in recent years relates to employment compensation. Proposals for so called non-traditional pay plans abound. Flex-benefits, gainsharing, skill-based pay, golden parachutes, performance shares, two-tier wages, signing bonus, and lump-sum merit awards are among the compensation plans offered up as new and improved methods for pay (O'Dell and McAdams, 1987). Experimentation is occurring with all of these proposed pay plans, with varying degrees of success.

This apparent interest in non-traditional compensation plans poses questions for review:

What are traditional pay plans and how did they achieve acceptance as traditional?
How different are the non-traditional pay plans and what do they offer?
Why the interest in non-traditional plans? How are traditional plans deficient? Will non-traditional plans overcome those deficiencies?

Pay plans, traditional and non-traditional, are reviewed here in light of these questions. It is argued that despite the influence of faddism, interest in a variety of pay plans is warranted as a means of enhancing the complementarity of compensation systems and forms of organization and systems of management. Careful matching of compensation systems and

Reprinted by permission of John Wiley and Sons Inc. from *Human Resource Management* 28(3) 1989: 337–47.

organizational systems, rather than implementation on the basis of fad interest, provides the opportunity to truly reinforce organizational strategy.

Traditional pay plans

There has always been a variety of compensation programs and forms of compensation in American industry. Sales people receive commissions, executives receive stock options, administrators received salaries, production workers are paid hourly wages, and all employees of an organization receive benefits of one sort or another. Yet what seems to be a dominating theme of so-called traditional compensation is what is termed job-based compensation. The primary determinant of differences in pay, certainly within an organization, is the job held by an individual.

The dominating role of job in pay determination can be observed in traditional practices of job evaluation, public policy expressed in the Equal Pay Act and proposals for pay equity and comparable worth, in help-wanted ads which list the rate for the job advertised, and in wage surveys reporting rates paid by different employers for a single job. 'Pay for the job' is a common expression of philosophy, intent, and expectations.

How did job-based compensation emerge as a dominant theme of traditional compensation, what particular purpose did it serve, and why is it viewed as inadequate by proponents of non-traditional pay plans?

Job-based compensation emerged with industrialization, development of the factory system, and mass production. Its development paralleled and is consistent with much of the practice of Scientific Management. Interestingly, the traditional compensation model prior to industrialization was output-based, consistent with custom production of goods by independent contractor craftsmen. That traditional system of pay gave way to job-based compensation with the factory system and mass production. Individual workers in the factory system of production no longer produced an identifiable product; each performed tasks at only one stage in the larger production process.

The concept of job was a unifying concept in the Scientific Management approach to organization and management. Mass production of standardized products permitted the design of stable, long-linked production processes which could be segmented into sequential tasks. Product standardization was achieved through standardization of task performance, and standardized task performance was accomplished by specification of tasks and then grouping tasks into jobs for workers selected, trained, and supervised for those specific tasks. Job, quite naturally, became the basis for all human resource management (Ash et al., 1983). Workforce selection, training, and motivation were all directed toward achieving the standardized task performance specified in job descriptions.

Interestingly, a variant of output-based compensation continued through the early stages of industrialization in the form of piece-rate and incentive compensation for production workers. As it became increasingly difficult to identify and measure job output, however, piece-rate compensation generally was abandoned for job-based hourly pay. Output- and/or performance-based pay tended to be restricted to that work where the individual worker was the major determinant of output (for example, sales, management).

The job-based orientation of Scientific Management, all of HRM and, particularly, compensation had an inevitable influence upon the orientation of the workforce toward work and employment. One such influence was the development and application of a concept of job ownership expressed in the labor movement and collective bargaining. Since pay depended critically upon job, workers came to view job assignment as a right and sought to protect job assignments earned through prior performance of that job. Application of the concept is seen particularly in the elaboration of work rules specifying seniority as the criterion for job assignment and work rules restricting performance to tasks specified in job descriptions. Relatively minor distinctions between tasks were elaborated to justify differentiation between jobs and, naturally, differentiation of wages for jobs.

Job evaluation, however informal and crude, became the dominant method for assigning compensation to jobs. Illustrative of the dominant influence of job evaluation in the determination of pay is the often cited practice of seeking job reclassification as a means of obtaining increases in pay not otherwise possible. Managers as well as office and production workers seek elaboration of job distinctions as the basis for revision of pay.

While job-based compensation has been the traditional basis for pay, other pay contingencies have also been employed in selected situations and as elaboration of job-based systems. Sales positions, for example, continue to be compensated in many instances on the basis of output. Insurance sales, for example, typically are compensated through commission, and the employment relationship resembles that of an independent contractor. Performance-based compensation may also be used as a supplement to job-based pay, as when so-called merit pay is provided. Merit pay is constrained by job pay, however, and the job base dominates. Additionally, other incentive awards such as suggestion awards have been made, again as a supplement to job-based pay.

Job-based pay has become a matter of concern in recent years for a variety of reasons. One concern addresses issues of comparable worth, the determination of comparable pay for jobs of comparable value or worth despite differences in task specifications. It is argued that jobs with different tasks may be worth equal pay and that typical job evaluations often assign lesser worth to tasks found largely in female-dominated jobs.

Another concern relates to the work rules and traditions of job assignment that inevitably develop when job is the primary basis for compensation differentials. The automobile industry, for example, has been characterized as having thousands of differentiated production jobs with different pay rates; associated work rules restrict the performance of a worker to a single job and constrain the flexibility of task assignment. Note, however, that this phenomenon is attributed to the conceptualization of work as job-defined and that job-based pay is merely congruent with that approach to the organization of work. Concepts and practices of work and management organization were the dominant influence and were merely reinforced by job-based pay systems.

Non-traditional pay plans

A number of so-called non-traditional pay plans are proposed by advocates. Many of these plans have been used in industry for some time but have not been as commonly practiced as job-based compensation. They are now being advocated for more extensive application.

Skill-based pay is one such non-traditional pay plan (Lawler and Ledford, 1985; Luthans and Fox, 1989). In concept, skill-based pay assigns differentials of pay based upon differences in skills possessed by the worker. The worker's skills, not the job performed, provide the basis for pay. Forms of skill-based pay have been employed in the past for workers performing variable tasks where specific task-defined job descriptions have been difficult. Craftsmen, for example, have been differentiated in terms of apprentice or learner, journeyman, and master, recognizing differences in skill level; workers at each level perform a variety of tasks appropriate to that level of skill. Similarly, maturity curve compensation has been paid to scientists where pay varies with discipline, degree, and years of experience; a PhD in nuclear physics with five years of experience is presumed to be performing whatever tasks are appropriate to that level of skill. Teachers, also, tend to be paid on the basis of level of education and experience. Finally, management trainees tend to be paid initially on the basis of degree (MBA vs BA) despite similarity of initial job assignment. The defining characteristics of situations where skill-based pay has been employed appear to be variable task performance dependent upon skill level and career paths based upon skill level.

Other forms of non-traditional pay plans being advocated tend to either supplement or modify the traditional job basis for pay. They do not propose replacement of the job basis, as does skill-based pay.

One modification of traditional job-based pay retains the job basis for pay but redefines the concept of job from that of assignment of tasks for individual performance to a broad class of assignments or, in some instances, to team assignments (*Business Week*, 1989). Saturn Corp., for example, recognizes only one classification of production technicians and 3–5 classifications of skilled crafts, in contrast to the thousands of distinct jobs at General Motors. Compensation is job-based, but the many job-based distinctions of the past are replaced with very few. In other instances, members of a production team are assigned the same pay and may perform any of the tasks in the total team assignment. Job is still the primary basis for pay, but the conceptualization and definition of job have been altered significantly.

Another form of non-traditional pay, popular for a few years but now declining, was two-tier wage plans (Ploscowe, 1986). These plans provided that existing workers would continue to receive current rates of job-based pay while newly recruited workers would be paid a lower job-based rate. The job basis for pay differentials was supplemented with a hire date contingency. Two-tier plans effectively reduced job-based rates in the short run for newly recruited workers, were somewhat effective in reducing labor costs, and have since been viewed as dysfunctional in terms of cooperation and morale.

Still other forms of non-traditional pay being advocated retain job-based base pay and propose supplementary pay based upon some other distinction, typically some measure of performance analogous to an output contingency. In general, however, they propose reducing the job-based component of total pay and increasing a supplementary component reflecting another contingency. These proposed plans vary in terms of the performance considered and the size of the performing unit (for example, individual versus group).

One non-traditional plan is the payment of a lump-sum bonus for performance instead of periodic merit increases which are incorporated into base pay. Such a change would more clearly identify performance (as well as job) as a pay contingency and would also make pay and labor costs more variable.

A number of other proposed non-traditional forms alter the measure of performance and the size of the performing unit. Profit sharing and gainsharing are two such examples. Both would be contingent upon performance of some producing unit (plant or company) measured in terms of profit or labor costs. Profit sharing has a long history in the US; there are reports of plans in the 1850s. Nevertheless, profit sharing appears to have been restricted to less than 40 percent of employers (O'Dell and McAdams, 1987) and has not been a dominant form of compensation to date. It appears that profit sharing traditionally was confined to companies with a somewhat paternalistic approach and also has been used predominantly to fund pension plans. More recent installations of profit sharing (as in the automobile industry) were in lieu of change in base wages and were attempts to make labor costs more variable with company performance.

Gainsharing is a related non-traditional plan often viewed as an alternative to profit sharing (McKersie, 1986). Again, while non-traditional, various forms of gainsharing have been used for some time as supplements to base wages. Like profit sharing, gainsharing is contingent

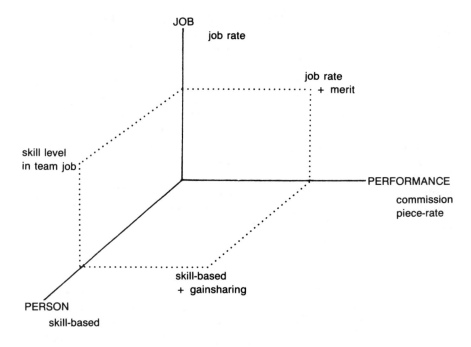

Figure 1   *Dimensions of work-contingent compensation*

upon overall company or plant performance; unlike profit sharing, it provides payments contingent on labor cost savings instead of profit increases. Gainsharing appears to be more appropriate where factors other than cost are significant influences of profit and where innovation and efficiency are sought.

Finally, team performance bonuses have been introduced as alternatives to individual performance bonuses. Typically, these have been related to specific performance targets rather than to overall judgements of performance, as in individual performance appraisals.

All of these non-traditional plans involve revised concepts of work and job and are based on person and/or performance contingencies. Person-based pay includes skill, seniority, education, and/or degree. Performance-based pay includes profit sharing, gainsharing, merit, attendance, and suggestion awards as well as more traditional performance incentives. The different pay plans can be compared in terms of three different contingencies or bases: job, performance, and person (Figure 1). All three bases for compensation have been used in the past and are reflected in the many pay plans discussed today. What seems to have changed over time is the dominant or primary basis for compensation. Reliance on output or performance contingency was replaced by reliance on job contingency, and there is evidence today of shifting emphasis to person and performance contingencies.

Table 1 *Summary illustration of pay–work–organization alignments*

Basis for pay	Examples	Work characteristics	Organizational characteristics
Output/ performance	Piece-rate, commission, gainsharing, suggestion awards	Identifiable and controllable outcomes	Little need for coordination, minimal supervision
Job	Salary, hourly wage	Defined tasks, standardized products	Mass production stable environment and technology, bureaucracy
Person	Skill-based, professional ladder, seniority pay	Variable tasks and outcomes; appropriate skill level	Variable products and technology, flexible organization

Making choices

The attention given to person- and performance-based pay challenges traditional reliance upon job-based pay (Lawler, 1987). Defenders of job-based pay systems respond that the concept of job employed in job evaluation encompasses skill requirements and expected performance outputs as well as task performance and that there is no need to abandon job-based systems (Barrett and Doverspike, 1989). What, if any, are the potential advantages of more clearly differentiating the three different bases for pay rather than merging them in the single concept of job?

In ideal form the three different bases for pay reflect three different concepts and strategies for work and organization, and each strategy is better suited to different situations (Table 1). The three strategic approaches, like the three bases for pay, need not be mutually exclusive in practice; multiple pay plans, each expressing a different contingency, can be combined in an overall compensation program. Maintaining distinction among the three bases, however, permits variation in emphasis among them as appropriate to complement specific strategic orientations, something not as easily accomplished if they are merged in a single concept of job.

The output/performance basis for pay for individuals is most feasible as the employment relationship approaches that of independent contractor. Output/performance objectives can be clearly defined and measured, and their achievement is significantly influenced, if not controlled, by the employee. Output-based pay provides clear direction for performance and closely controls labor costs per unit. There is relatively little need for additional supervision. Associated career paths often involve inter-employer mobility. Work is viewed as the production of outputs, not the performance of tasks, by relatively independent employees. Classic examples of output-based compensation are sales commissions, executive performance shares, garment manufacturing piece-rates, and compensation of auto-mobile body repairs on the basis of standard hours.

Traditional job-based compensation is more feasible in organizations characterized by bureaucracy and traditions of Scientific Management. Standardized production of limited varieties of goods and/or services is accomplished through standardization of task performance. Coordination is accomplished through the sequencing of tasks in jobs. The dominant perception of work is characterized by job tasks. Associated career paths involve job and pay advancement, typically with a single employer. Job-based compensation appears to be most appropriate for organizations employing routine technologies in relatively stable conditions. Classic examples of applications of job-based compensation include mass produc-tion manufacturing, insurance policy issuance and service, administrative activities in financial services, and middle management positions in large organizations.

Person-based compensation appears most commonly for work that is not easily defined in terms of specific and stable tasks, and where skill and knowledge constrain the tasks which can be performed. Elements of person-based pay also include pay and benefits, which vary with seniority. It is associated with occupational career paths of advancing skill and pay, often with a single employer. Classic examples of applications include maturity pay for scientists, teacher career ladder pay, and the seniority-based pay common to much Japanese employment but also observed to a lesser degree in US manufacturing.

The shifting dominance of compensation practice from output-based to job-based and now to application of output-based and person-based compensation has been less a function of fads and more a function of changing strategic orientations toward work and organization. Change in approaches to compensation has served to complement and reinforce change in strategic orientations.

Job-based pay replaced output-based pay as mass production replaced custom production technologies and orientation. Standardized task sequences replaced craft, and job replaced customized product as the focus of work. Mass production technologies and bureaucratic organiza-tions were appropriate for large markets and relatively stable environ-ments. Output- or performance-based pay continued for selected workers (for example, sales), where markets were differentiated and changing and where bureaucratic approaches were less effective. Person-based compen-sation, such as seniority pay, was employed to encourage continued membership where turnover was disruptive. Yet the dominant orientation towards work, organization, and pay was efficient production of standar-dized products.

Conditions appropriate for bureaucratic, mass production approaches are less common today. Increased competition from newly developed economies abroad and also due to deregulation of segments of the US economy has created instability in markets. An increasingly rapid rate of technological and product development has introduced instability. An improved standard of living and changed demographics of the population, and participation in the workforce has contributed to change in product and industrial mix, with a shift from production of goods to production of services. All of these changes have contributed to an overall shift in orientation from product design and delivery to customer satisfaction through increased product variety, improved quality, lower cost, and faster delivery.

Organization and management changes over the same period have sought to increase flexibility, responsiveness, innovation, and cooperation. Matrix organization, project and product teams, QC circles, and related organizational changes were introduced. MBO began to replace traditional job descriptions. Consequently, traditional job-based compensation, which reinforces strategic orientations of mass production and bureaucratic organizations, was less supportive of these changed strategic orientations.

At the same time, there were increasing calls for the linkage between compensation and organizational strategy (Lawler, 1981; Sears, 1984). Output/performance- and person-based pay plans emerged as alternatives to provide better alignment of compensation with organizational practice (Ziskin, 1986). Hundreds of job classifications were compressed into 2–5 classifications to facilitate flexibility of assignment, team compensation and skill-based pay were introduced to complement team-based jobs, and gainsharing was introduced to encourage cooperation, innovation, and overall efficiency.

Looking ahead, it is unlikely that any single pay contingency will replace job-based pay as a dominant form of compensation. Rather, the reintroduction of output/performance- and person-based pay contingencies provides the opportunity for greater customization of pay plans to complement varying situations and strategies (Milkovich, 1988). Recognition of the three different contingencies and their applications provides options less easily recognized when task, skill, and performance are merged in a single job description for job-based pay. It will become increasingly common for a single employee to receive portions of compensation based on all three contingencies, and the portion provided as job-based pay will decline.

Consider an example as illustration. Production tasks will be organized into team assignments. All members of a team will receive the same job base pay. Additionally, members will receive higher rates as they master more of the skills needed in the team. Team bonuses will be provided based on specific performance goals, which will change over time as attention shifts from quality to customer satisfaction or some other concern. A gainsharing formula may be established for an entire plant to encourage innovation and cooperation. And the budget for flexible benefits may be contingent upon tenure in the organization. The use of multiple pay contingencies in this way provides increased flexibility of reinforcement strategies to complement varied circumstances and organizational strategies.

The variety of non-traditional pay plans receiving attention today need not be viewed alarmingly as evidence of managerial faddism. Rather, they offer responses to changes in technology, organization and management practice, and orientation toward work. Variety in organization and management practices has expanded due to increased challenges of competition and rapidity of change, and the variety of pay plans is necessary to complement management practice. The strategic design of compensation plans to fit unique and changing circumstances is aided by recognizing the three different bases for pay, employing multiple pay contingency plans as appropriate. Research and experimentation to determine the circumstances most appropriate for different mixes of compensation contingency plans should be encouraged at this point.

References

Ash, R.A., Levine, E.L. and Sistrunk, F. (1983) 'The role of jobs and job-based methods in personnel and human resources management', in *Research in Personnel and Human Resources Management*, ed. K. Rowland and G. Ferris. Greenwich, CT: JAI Press, 45–84.

Barrett, G.V. and Doverspike, D. (1989) 'Another defense of point-factor job evaluation', *Personnel*, March: 33–6.

Business Week (1989) 'The cultural revolution at A.O. Smith', *Business Week*, 29 May: 66, 68.

Doyle, R.J. (1989) 'Gainsharing is rapidly becoming a fad . . . which could kill a great idea', *Labor Relations Today*, US Department of Labor, May/June.

Lawler, III, E.E. (1981) *Pay and Organization Development*, Reading, MA: Addison-Wesley.

Lawler, III, E.E. (1987) 'What's wrong with point-factor job evaluation?' *Personnel*, January.

Lawler, III, E.E. and Ledford, G.E., Jr. (1985) 'Skill-based pay: a concept that's catching on', *Personnel*, September: 30–7.

Luthans, F. and Fox, M.L. (1989) 'Update on skill-based pay', *Personnel*, 1989: 26–31.

McKersie, R.B. (1986) 'The promise of gain sharing', *ILR Report*, Fall: 7–11.

Milkovich, G.T. (1988) 'A strategic perspective on compensation management', in *Research in Personnel and Human Resources Management*, ed. G. Ferris and K. Rowland. Greenwich, CT: JAI Press, 263–88.

O'Dell, C. and McAdams, J. (1987) 'The revolution in employee rewards', *Management Review*, March: 68–73.

Ploscowe, S.A. (1986) 'Two-tier compensation plans', *ILR Report*, Fall: 23–8.

Sears, D. (1984) 'Make employee pay a strategic issue', *Financial Executive*, October: 40–3.

Ziskin, I.V. (1986) 'Knowledge-based pay: a strategic analysis', *ILR Report*, Fall: 16–21.

Index

Index compiled by Jackie McDermott